Th

Opera
Biographies

Opera
Biographies

Advisory Editor
ANDREW FARKAS

Associate Editor
W.R. MORAN

See last pages of this volume
for complete list of titles

FORTY YEARS OF
OPERA
IN CHICAGO

Edward C. Moore

ARNO PRESS

A New York Times Company

New York / 1977

Editorial Supervision: ANDREA HICKS

———◆———

Reprint Edition 1977 by Arno Press Inc.

Reprinted from a copy in
  The University of Illinois Library

OPERA BIOGRAPHIES
ISBN for complete set: 0-405-09666-6
See last pages of this volume for titles.

Manufactured in the United States of America

———◆———

Library of Congress Cataloging in Publication Data
Moore, Edward Colman, 1877-1935.
    Forty years of opera in Chicago.

    (Opera biographies)
    Reprint of the 1930 ed. published by
H. Liveright, New York.
    1. Opera--Chicago. I. Title.
ML1711.8.C5M7 1977 782.1'09773'11   76-29956
ISBN 0-405-09697-6

Music

FORTY YEARS OF
OPERA IN CHICAGO

Twenty Wacker Drive

The permanent home of the Chicago Civic Opera

FORTY YEARS OF
OPERA
IN CHICAGO

BY Edward C. Moore

1930
HORACE LIVERIGHT · NEW YORK

Manufactured in the United States of America

LIST OF ILLUSTRATIONS

LIST OF ILLUSTRATIONS

FORTY YEARS OF
OPERA
IN CHICAGO

FOREWORD OF THE AUDITORIUM

I

The first performance of opera in the Auditorium, Tuesday, December 10, 1889, "Romeo and Juliet," by Charles Gounod.

CAPULET, a Veronese Noble..Sig. De Vaschetti
JULIET, his Daughter........Adelina Patti
TYBALT, his Nephew........Sig. Perugini
ROMEO, a Montague........Sig. Ravelli
MERCUTIO, Friend of Romeo..Sig. Del Puente
STEPHANO, Page of Romeo...Mme. Fabbri
DUKE OF VERONA..........Sig. Bieletto
FRIAR LAWRENCE...........Sig. Marcassa
GERTRUDE, Juliet's Nurse....Mme. Bauermeister
GREGORIO, Servant to Capulet.Sig. Cernusco

Incidental Dances by Ballet
Conductor ....Sig. Sapio
Stage Director.............William Parry

The final performance by the Civic Opera Company in the Auditorium, Saturday, January 26, 1929, "Romeo and Juliet," by Charles Gounod.

CAPULET, a Veronese Noble..Cesare Formichi
JULIET, his Daughter........Edith Mason
TYBALT, his Nephew........Jose Mojica
ROMEO, a Montague........Charles Hackett
MERCUTIO, Friend of Romeo..Desiré Defrere

3

STEPHANO, Page of Romeo...Irene Pavloska
DUKE OF VERONA..........Antonio Nicolich
FRIAR LAWRENCE..........Edouard Cotreuil
GERTRUDE, Juliet's Nurse....Maria Claessens
GREGORIO, Servant to Capulet.Eugenio Sandrini

Incidental Dances by Ballet
Conductor ....Giorgio Polacco
Stage Director.............Charles Moor

Apparently the two architects of the Auditorium, Louis H. Sullivan and Dankmar Adler, put their energy into building it instead of talking about it afterwards. No comment at all by Adler has been found; in Sullivan's book, "The Autobiography of an Idea," which is also his own autobiography, published just before his death, only this:

"For several years there had been talk to the effect that Chicago needed a grand opera house; but the several schemes advanced were too aristocratic and exclusive to meet with general approval. In 1885 there appeared the man of the hour, Ferdinand W. Peck, who declared himself a citizen, with firm belief in democracy—whatever he meant by that; seemingly he meant the 'peepul.' At any rate, he wished to give birth to a great hall within which the multitude might gather for all sorts of purposes including grand opera; and there were to be a few boxes for the *haut monde*. He had a disturbing fear, however, concerning acoustics, for he understood success in that regard was more or less of a gamble. So he sought out Dankmar Adler and confided.

"The only man living, at the time, who had had the intelligence to discern that the matter of acoustics is not a science but an art—as in fact all science is sterile until it rises to the level of art—was Dankmar Adler, Louis' partner." (Throughout his book Mr. Sullivan constantly refers to himself as Louis.) "His scheme was simplicity itself. With his usual generosity he taught this very simple art to his partner, and together they built a number of successful theatres. Hence Peck, the dreamer for the populace, sought Adler, the man of common sense. Between them they concocted a scheme, a daring experiment, which was this: To install in the old Exposition Building on the lake front, a vast temporary audience room, with a huge, scenic stage, and to give therein a two weeks' season of grand opera, engaging artists of world fame.

"This was done. The effect was thrilling. An audience of 6,200 persons saw and heard; heard, even to the faintest pianissimo. No reverberation, no echo,—the clear untarnished tone of voice and instrument reached all. The inference was obvious: a great permanent hall housed within a monumental structure must follow. This feeling marked the spirit of the Chicago of those days.

"Ferdinand W. Peck, or Ferd Peck as he was genally known—now 'Commodore' at 75—" (Mr. Peck died shortly after Mr. Sullivan's book was published) "took on his slim shoulders the burden of an immense undertaking and 'saw it through.' To him, therefore, all praise due a bold pioneer; an emotionally exalted advocate of that which he, a rich man, believed in his soul to be democracy. The theatre seating 4,250 he called the Auditorium, and the entire structure comprising theatre, hotel, office building, and tower he named the Auditorium Building—nobody knows just why. Anyway it sounded better than 'Grand Opera House.'

"For four long years Dankmar Adler and his partner

labored on this enormous, unprecedented work. Adler was Peck's man. As to Louis he was rather dubious, but gradually came around—conceding a superior æsthetic judgment—which for him was in the nature of a miracle. Besides, Louis was young, only thirty when the task began, his partner forty-two, and Peck about forty. . . ."

Later he says: "The drawings of the Auditorium Building were now well under way. Louis' heart went into this structure. It is old-time now, but its tower holds its head in the air, as a tower should. It was the culmination of Louis' masonry 'period.' "

It was finally finished and opened with lavish ceremonial. There was a dedicatory program on Monday night, December 9, 1889, with acres of speech making, a dedicatory ode, and two songs by "Patti, the divine." The next night the opera season opened with "Romeo and Juliet," and the Auditorium began its career as a home of opera, the initiatory company being under the management of Henry E. Abbey and Maurice Grau. Milward Adams was the house manager.

Just to connect this matter with the rest of the world's doings, what else was happening at the time? The newspaper columns tell us much. Benjamin Harrison was president and Levi P. Morton vice-president of the United States. They had been nominated by the republican national convention in the same hall a year and a half before, the convention being held there because of the size of the enclosure, although the building was nowhere nearly finished. They came on from Washington to be present at the dedication, and were entertained in "true Chicago style," according to the headlines, which means that their hours of sleep were cut to an irreducible minimum. It was undoubtedly not considered part of the entertainment that there were some disquieting rumors in the papers that Grover Cleveland might make something of a showing when the next presidential election came around.

Dom Pedro had just arrived in Lisbon, having been heaved out of his job in Brazil after "forty-nine years of spotless reign," and was proclaiming in excited tones to all within earshot that Brazil was not yet ready for a republican form of government. Jefferson Davis was just dead in New Orleans. Robert Browning was to die that week in London, having lived just long enough to see his final book of poems, "Asolando," come off the press.

In Chicago they were taking subscriptions for the coming world's fair in any sums that contributors could be induced to give, and at that time they had raised nearly $2,500,000. Over in the court house an extremely tired jury was listening to some extremely long-winded final arguments on the Cronin murder case by Attorney W. S. Forrest and his group for the defense and States Attorney Joel Longenecker and his group for the prosecution, a group which included Luther Laflin Mills, W. J. Hynes, and Kickham Scanlan. The jury was to stay out for seventy hours, with rumors of strife and hard language coming from the jury room, and finally return a verdict acquitting John F. Beggs, and giving John P. Kunze a sentence of three years and Daniel Coughlin, Patrick O'Sullivan, and Martin Burke life sentences.

During the first week of opera a group of Sioux chiefs went through Chicago on their way to sign some new treaties at Washington. They did not attend the opera, but were taken to Hooley's Theatre, where they saw a bill of "high class vaudeville," presented, among others, by George Thatcher, "The renowned Irwin Sisters," and "The unique Lottie Collins," and where they witnessed a ballet and heard "Down Went McGinty." Among other entertainments on view at that time, Donnelly and Girard were in "Natural Gas" at the Grand Opera House, "Shenandoah" was at McVicker's, the McCaull Opera Company was singing "Clover" at the Chicago Opera House, Bill Nye and James Whitcomb Riley were about to make a joint appearance at Central Music Hall, Libby Prison was on view where the Coliseum now stands, dime museums were all over the place, the Eden Musee at Wabash and Jackson advertised "Dr. Cronin's Murder With All Its Sensational Features," and at least half a dozen ticket scalpers announced in print that they had choice seats for all performances of opera at prices up to $6—the Auditorium having been scaled at from $1 to $3.50.

Also, and this makes the male reader feel somewhat envious, the best men's suits and overcoats could be bought for $25 or less, the best white shirts for $1.50, and the best shoes for $5.

Tuesday, December 10, was a great day for the newspapers. There were no staff photographers in those days to get out pictures with the magical speed which is the rule now, but there were staff artists with hasty but steady hands to make drawings and have them translated into newspaper cuts. A four-column drawing shows the interior of the Auditorium and its stage, a "Scene at the Congress street entrance" takes a two-column width of space and "A pleasant private box party" two more. Speeches were reported at length, and there are prose pictures of all eminent attendants.

Mayor Cregier opened the floodgates of oratory, to be followed by Ferdinand W. Peck, and he by President Harrison. Then came John S. Runnells, and finally Governor Fifer. But there was also music.

Clarence Eddy played Theodore Dubois' Triumphal Fantasie for organ and orchestra; the dedicatory ode had words by Harriet Monroe and music by Frederick Grant Gleason, both Chicagoans, and was done by the Apollo Musical Club under the baton of William L. Tomlins, with an orchestra made up partly of Chicago players and partly of the operatic orchestra from elsewhere. The Apollo Club also sang "See, the Conquering Hero Comes," "The Heavens are Telling," the Hallelujah chorus, and "America," which last was recognized with special pleasure by President Harrison. Finally came Patti.

All she sang was "Home, Sweet Home," and, since she could not be permitted to stop there, a Swiss song by Eckert, whose trills and ornaments had been on her programs for long years. The musical critic held that she was delightful, simplicity itself, though not devoid of tender feeling, but that two short songs afforded little basis of judgment upon how good she actually was. That was to come in the opera season. He also complained that the operatic orchestra did not apply itself to its choral tasks with the zeal or care that it presumably would do later in opera. However, great credit was due to all. And the next night came "Romeo and Juliet."

One of the most unfortunate facts in the course of delving into musical performances of a former day is that what actually happened must rest upon printed accounts or memories. Think what a well-made phonograph record of Patti in her prime would be as a matter of interest to-day! However, W. J. Henderson dove into his well-stocked memory not long ago in *Musical America* and produced this about her:

"The voice was of the most flute-like character, soft, yet vibrant and far-reaching, voluptuous, yet chaste, 'as if somehow a rose might be a throat' (Sidney Lanier). Her forte was comedy; her Rosina has not been rivaled. Her Semiramide was a glittering maze of vocal beauties. Her Violetta was flawless and unmoving. Her Juliet was to be admired, but not adored. She sang like a lark but not like a tragedienne. She was one of the great singers of all time—as a singer, not as a dramatic force. There has been in my time only one Patti."

The performance at the Auditorium seems to have been just a bit of a disappointment. The waltz song in the first act, one learns, was not remarkable for its brilliancy, Patti evidently saving her voice. Ravelli's voice was "somewhat lacking in true refinement," but had some effective B naturals in it. Del Puente had "scarcely his old resonance of voice," and Perugini "seemed overweighted with his part." Of Patti again, this:

"It is evident that Mme. Patti's voice is not entirely the same that it was formerly, say ten or twelve years ago. The technical facility is still there to a great extent, but it does not possess the same limpid quality, and it is evident that it requires more care in its management than formerly. Even her intonation, which was formerly so faultless, is less pure than it used to be, though the lapses from absolute truth are not so marked as to be offensive. It is a matter of fact, however, that she does sing flat at times. As regards the matter of warmth, which is so essential for the proper interpretation of the music assigned to Juliet, and so imperatively demanded for the delineation of the ardent character of the heroine, Patti never did possess it, so that even were her vocalization absolutely faultless there would still be left much to be desired."

Genuine emotion, however, seems to pervade this paragraph, which preceded the technical musical discussion:

"The doors opened about 7:15 and the procession began at once. People came in shivering and hesitated to leave their wraps in cloak-rooms. It was a magnificent crowd, though, much more magnificent than that of the night before. Every one was in full dress, even those standing up. It was the most brilliant audience probably ever seen in Chicago. Monday night there were many who worked in simply to see the interior. They didn't have dress suits and wouldn't have known how to wear them if they had. These were absent last night; it was an opera audience exclusively."

Forty years later Julius Rosenwald was to tell how, not being able to get a ticket for the opening, he crashed the gate by coming in through the stage entrance, crossing into the front of the house, and losing himself in the crowd.

Patti, incidentally, would be considered well paid even in these days. She used to receive $3,500 a performance, plus ten per cent of the receipts in case they exceeded $5,000. But if she did not quite live up to advance notices and hopes, Francesco Tamagno, who was visiting

America for the first time that year, was acclaimed a "king among tenors." There was delight in print over his more than six feet of well proportioned stature and the magnificent volume of tone with which he poured out B flats and C naturals. "There seemed to be absolutely no difficulty to him to produce those extreme notes, for he gave them as though revelling in their sonority.... In fact it appears as if Tamagno's star was destined to eclipse Patti's."

Patti evidently read the papers and knew how to give out an interview calculated to promote kindly feelings among the best people. The Auditorium was perfect, according to her, Chicago might well be proud of it, the Metropolitan in New York was a beautiful place, but compared to the Auditorium it was like singing in a ballroom, and there was nothing comparable in all Europe. Also, she was sorry that Chicago had not liked "Romeo and Juliet" when it had been appreciated so thoroughly in Paris. The interviewer, however, was not to think that Chicago had not the appreciation and understanding of Paris—it might be a question of taste. She herself would have preferred to open in "Trovatore,"—something that ends with a flourish.

And, "Chicago seems to get everything now. Really, I wonder what is to become of New York."

The season ran for four weeks. One sees notices of Emma Albani in "Faust," Tamagno in "Trovatore," and he and Albani in "Huguenots," he and Nordica in "Aïda," Patti in "Lucia di Lammermoor," "Semiramide," "Martha," and "Sonnambula." Comments thereon grow less numerous as the season goes on, for even with a new Auditorium it was not considered desirable to report every performance every time. However, there are complaints in the society column that opera is extinguishing most other social events, and in the music column that there are too many performances with a single notable to justify them, that notable being inadequately supported by the rest of the cast. This latter has a strangely modern touch.

There was a bit of hard luck at the end. The country was being devastated by what a later generation learned to call the flu, but what was "la grippe" then. On New Year's day the *Tribune* contained this not altogether respectful account of things at the opera:

"Italian opera has the influenza. Sig. Tamagno is ill at the Leland. So is Mme. Guido Valda. So is Mme. Pettigiani, and Mme. Nordica is in bed at the Richelieu. As a result 'Les Huguenots' was on at the Auditorium last evening in place of Verdi's great 'Otello,' and although there was $9,000 in the house, the management was sad.

" 'Only myself and Patti are left,' said Milward Adams, 'and I am not feeling any too well.'

"Sig. Tamagno, the tenor, lay under a mountain of coverlids at his hotel with a red flannel bandage around his neck. He was absolutely indifferent to the wiles of Iago Del Puente. He refused to listen to the story of Desdemona Albani. The friendship of Cassio Perugini weighed not a penny in his mind. He buried his head in his pillow and closed his eyes to the scandal that was the talk of the gay chaps around the Rialto. Sig. Tamagno was sick.

"In the morning Mr. Abbey and Mr. Peck and Mr. Milward Adams called.

" 'We must have a medical examination,' said Mr. Peck. Dr. Ingals was sent for. He made an excursion into Sig. Tamagno's $1,500-a-performance throat. He reported that it was swollen and colored a vulgar red.

" 'He cannot sing to-night,' said Dr. Ingals.

"The party repaired to Mme. Pettigiani's apartment. Mme. Pettigiani looked like a traveler overwhelmed by a snowstorm. Lace and down were piled to the ceiling and only her face was visible.

" 'Mme. Pettigiani cannot sing,' said the doctor.

"The procession moved to Mme. Valda's apartments. Mme. Valda was convalescent in a big, easy chair. Dr. Ingals viewed her larynx.

" 'Mme. Valda is sick,' said the doctor.

"Mme. Nordica was found at the Richelieu. She was also abed. She had a fever. She had a sore throat. She coughed.

" 'It is epidemic,' said the doctor. 'Mme. Nordica cannot sing.'

"With four of its leading artists down, the Auditorium was gloomy. Only Mme. Patti and Milward Adams were in good health. Mr. Adams has not appeared on the stage since he sang 'Silver Threads Among the Gold' at the opening of tne Pecatonica Grand Opera House in 1878, but he cheerily volunteered his services. They were politely but unhesitatingly declined. This left only Mme. Patti. Mme. Patti was sitting in her suite at the Richelieu eating marshmallows, which she says are good for the throat, and toasting her toes over a cannel coal fire.

" 'You are well, are you not?' Mr. Adams asked her.

" 'Perfectly,' said Mme. Patti.

" 'Then you can sing to-night?'

" 'For $4,000.'

"The committee withdrew.

"The Auditorium passed into the dumps. Mr. Abbey thrust his hands deep in his pockets and stalked about angrily. Mr. Peck buried his face in his hands and moaned. Mr. Adams lost his cheerfulness and kicked a man who asked for a pass.

"At this juncture Mme. Albani appeared. Mme. Albani is an American and she is willing. Would she fill the gap? Of course she would. She went on in 'Les Huguenots,' and the $9,000 in the house was satisfied."

But Tamagno recovered enough to sing "Otello" on Thursday, January 2, and it was counted the crowning event of the season. Two more performances and the company was off for Mexico where grippe germs were not.

The first season of opera at the Auditorium played to something over 100,000 persons, and in its twenty-two performances took in $232,952. The biggest audience was the last. Patti closed the season with "The Barber of Seville," the Shadow song from "Dinorah," "Home, Sweet Home," and Arditi's "Kiss" waltz in the lesson scene—another bit that sounds modern—and the audience paid $14,320 to hear it.

All of which was a considerable source of pleasure to Milward Adams. Mr. Adams, it has been noted above, was the house manager of the Auditorium, a position that he held from the beginning until close to the time when the Chicago Grand Opera company was organized.

Though no musician himself, in his business relations he became about as much of an influence in Chicago's musical development during his active career as any other single person in the city.

As a young man he is first discovered in the box office of Central Music Hall, on the south-east corner of State and Randolph streets, for a long time about the only abiding place of concerts and lectures in Chicago. Next he is found as manager of the summer concerts that Theodore Thomas and his orchestra used to give in the Exposition building on the lake front, a structure that vanished a good many years ago. It is true that his name does not appear in the official souvenir program of the "First Chicago Opera Festival" held there April 6 to 18, 1885, but it is quite likely that he had some rather important if quiet share in the proceedings.

This was the operatic season mentioned by Mr. Sullivan for which he and Adler reconstructed part of the building into an opera house, applying thereto their own principles of acoustics. Patti headed the company—one reads, among other amazing statements, that she sang the name part of "Aïda" then—and some of the other artists were Fursch-Madi and Dotti, dramatic sopranos, Scalchi, contralto, Emma Nevada (her first appearance), Nicolini, tenor, De Pasqualis, baritone, Cherubini and De Vaschetti, bassos. There was a "grand festival chorus of 300," a "grand orchestra of 100," and Luigi Arditi, now best known as the composer of the waltz song, "Il Bacio," conducted.

The season was in Italian, though only seven of the fourteen operas were of the Italian school. They were "Semiramide," "Linda di Chamounix," "Lucia di

Lammermoor," "La Somnambula," as it is named in the program, "Aïda," "Il Trovatore," and "I Puritani." The others were "L'Africaine," "Mireille," "Martha," "Der Freischütz," "Faust," and "Lohengrin," with one repetition on the final matinée. But they were all sung in Italian. The purists of opera in its original tongue had not begun campaigning then.

After Mr. Adams moved into the business office of the Auditorium he seems to have become a kindly, if at times drastic, czar over its musical events. Not long ago Lieutenant Commander John Philip Sousa wrote me this about him:

"The first time I met Milward Adams was on the occasion of my first tour with the Marine Band in Chicago. He was then a young man and exceedingly up to date. I remember that it rained very hard on the second day of our concerts, and my manager, fearful of the receipts, said, 'We will not have $1,000 in the house.' Adams said, 'I'll bet a magnum of champagne that it will be double that.' My manager accepted the bet and we had, if I remember right, twenty-three or twenty-four hundred in the house, and when Adams wanted my manager to pay the magnum he hesitated and insisted that a quart was enough to lose. Adams said, 'A quart be hanged. I bet a magnum and if I had lost I would have paid it—you lost and you must pay.' So we had the magnum."

A man of that sort makes warm friends—and equally warm enemies. Mr. Adams had a number of earnest fights in the course of his career, but most of his associates became and remained his friends. He was a good deal of an idealist in music, which is why he became such an important influence in the musical development of the city. At his death, some twenty years after these events, he left his large, interesting, and in many ways unique collection of photographs, souvenirs, and play bills of the celebrities who had appeared under his management to the Newberry Library of Chicago, where it still is.

One notices in some of the newspaper quotations of the period a desire to tease Mr. Adams in print. Newspaper men were a graceless lot in those days, and all you have to do is belong to a newspaper staff now to hear frequently from the old timers that they have not improved. But the teasing sent in Mr. Adams' direction is almost always in kindly mood, which is one way of discovering the esteem in which he was held by his associates and acquaintances.

II

For some time thereafter the Auditorium was used only for concerts. The first was labeled a musical festival for the benefit of the I. N. G. new armory. Dr. Florenz Ziegfeld, the lieutenant-colonel, and for many years the president of the Chicago Musical College, was the musical director. There were bands and soloists, among them Miss Grace E. Jones, soprano; L. A. Phelps, tenor; J. Allen Preisch, bass; August Hyllested, Emil Liebling, and Harrison Wild, pianists; the Schumann Lady Quartet, and the Lotus and Imperial Quartets. The dates were January 19 and 25.

During the week of January 27, Monday and Wednesday evenings and Saturday afternoon, Pablo de

Sarasate, violinist, and Eugen d'Albert, pianist, gave three joint concerts. They were respectively forty-six and twenty-six years old at the time. Assisted by a "grand orchestra" under the direction of Adolph Rosenbecker, d'Albert played for the first, the Chopin E minor concerto and solos by Grieg, Rubinstein, and Strauss-Tausig; for the second, the Liszt E flat concerto and solos by Grieg and Liszt; for the third the Beethoven "Emperor," and solos by Grieg and Liszt. Sarasate's achievements were first, the Mendelssohn concerto and his own "Carmen" fantasy; second, the Beethoven concerto and the Saint-Saëns Rondo Capriccioso; third, the Bruch G minor concerto and his own "Faust" excerpts. D'Albert would seem to have made an enormous hit, but some surprise was expressed over Sarasate, since he did not display the expected degree of Spanish passion, although credited as a very fine violinist.

The Apollo Musical Club, having appeared up to that time at Central Music Hall, moved to the Auditorium for its future concerts, and Mr. Adams announced that in February the J. C. Duff Opera Company would put on a season of Gilbert and Sullivan on a scale of magnificence never before attempted in this country.

It opened with "Pinafore," Digby Bell taking the part of Sir Joseph Porter, Laura Joyce Bell, Little Buttercup, and W. H. Clark, Dick Deadeye, and they said in the papers that the company presented an ensemble difficult to surpass. As a Gilbert and Sullivan work, it was in competition with "The Gondoliers," then on for a run at the Chicago Opera House. In ten days it changed its bill to "The Mikado," and at the same time it was told in the advertisements that the Patti company would come back March 10 for another week of grand opera. This outline showed six performances, Nordica and Tamagno in "L'Africaine," Patti in "Linda," Albani and Tamagno in "Otello," Patti in "Lakmé," Albani and Tamagno in "Huguenots," and, to close, Patti in "Semiramide." Then as now, names of artists were considered quite as important as names of operas in inducing the public to buy tickets. Patti was evidently in a bit worse voice than when she had opened the house. There are remarks about her having to be prompted and that "unfortunately" the prompter's voice could be heard clearly because of the admirable acoustics of the house. There are also comments on large blocks of empty seats. But the "Otello" performance was considered to be of extraordinary merit.

More opera. On April 21 there came a company from the New York Metropolitan to present a season in German and to stay until May 10. Most of the names of the artists are now forgotten, but there was no less a personage than Frau Lilli Lehmann among the sopranos, another, Herr Emil Fischer as one of the bassos, and Mr. Walter Damrosch conducting. Two performances of "Tannhäuser" and one each of "William Tell," "Meistersinger," "The Jewess," and "Lohengrin" filled the first week. Again the opening made the first page, and again opera was treated with only partially complete respect.

"There is a deal of difference," says one account, "between the applause at the German opera and that at the Italian opera. When Patti sings, for instance, the enthusiasm bubbles up in an irresponsible sort of way; people clap and cheer, and very young men cry 'Bravo!'

Lilli Lehmann

Marcella Sembrich

Francesco Tamagno

Victor Maurel

"At the German opera the enthusiasm accumulates in silence; then, of a sudden, it is thrown out in great, solid Teutonic chunks. It is the difference between pelting an artist with roses and presenting him with a house and lot.

"There was plenty of enthusiasm in the Auditorium last night, but it was of a sober and thoughtful sort. And every one looked thoughtful except Herr Possart, who was conscious of wearing a pale lilac-colored coat and waistcoat and brown trousers.

"The house was fairly well filled. The function was much like all first nights. A double line of carriages outside; boys calling 'books of de oprer'; the foyer crowded with young men in the dress that evening makes imperative; the parquet a bouquet of white shoulders and roses and diamonds.

"Then Mr. Walter Damrosch, who looks like a Thuringian noble, raps a tentative rap and starts the orchestra off on the overture. A young woman with fluffy hair and blue ribbons on each shoulder says it is 'wunderbar schön,' and the young man beside her adds that it is "ausgezeichnet.' And so it is—beyond doubt.

" 'Tannhäuser' from the outside may be all right for those who spell art with a big A and have a 'cult' and all that sort of thing. But the only way to study Wagner soulfully is from behind the scenes.

"One stumbles up a pair of stairs to the stage. A score of men in checked blouses are wandering aimlessly about among the chaos of trees and rocks and palaces. A little four-wheeled trolley has been wheeled to the front of the stage and covered with opulent red robes. On this Venus stretches herself gracefully and Tannhäuser covers up her feet. Then he rehearses the embrace he will give her when she will sing sweetly but firmly, 'no, love itself to worship thou beloved shalt move.' It is this remark of hers, by the way, that causes all the trouble. It eats into Tannhaüser's brain like a fifteen-sixteen puzzle and eventually he becomes a 'Wann-sinn'ger.'

"While Venus lies on the trolley and the orchestra plays, twenty coryphees wander about and pirouette and slang each other in choice German. Then a fat man in a green velvet tunic made up with a dust-colored beard, tramps out of the dressing-room, a tin sword dangling at his heels.

" 'Donnerwetter noch e'mal!' he growls. 'Vere de-deffel gomes dis draff out? I haf baid for no draff, undt I dond't vant ihm.'

"While two or three of the stage hands go to look for the imaginary draught, he goes into a corner and sings to himself.

" 'That is Herr Theodor Reichmann,' says an awe-struck chorus girl.

"The bell rings, the curtain goes up; Venus and Tannhäuser begin to row and spoon in an eminently matrimonial fashion.

"The opera begins.

"And after it is all over—the curtain down, the lights out, Mr. Milward Adams' smile folded up and laid away—what shall one say of it?

"As a social function it was an eminent success. The long-haired Wagnerites above-stairs add that it was a religion. The boy who sold 'books of de oprer' on the outside said cynically that the music was of the future, perhaps, but the singers were of the past.

"But no one agreed with him."

The season seems to have been an agreeable one in spite of those who professed to look down upon opera as an entertainment. The best of the singers were willing to work hard in those days. Fischer, for example, sang the first three nights in succession and once or twice more before the week was over. And it did not seem anything out of the ordinary for Lehmann on the second week to have as diverse a program as "A Masked Ball" on Monday, "Fidelio" on Wednesday and "Norma" on Friday. These and "The Flying Dutchman" were the second week's added attractions. Lehmann and Fischer were being spoken of with increasing interest, but there were complaints as to the difficulty of finding adequate tenors. And it seems a bit amusing to find objections being raised to "A Masked Ball" on account of "the somber character of its music." "Don Giovanni" and Cornelius' seldom heard comic opera, "The Barber of Bagdad," were added on the third and final week of the engagement.

Early in June Edouard Strauss and his Vienna orchestra came for four concerts. The chronicler dutifully records that such works as Adam's "If I Were King" and Nicolai's "Merry Wives of Windsor" overtures and others were well played, but he, like the rest of the audience, fell a victim to the entrancing waltzes from the pens of the combined Strauss family. They are still a hit on the occasions when Mr. Stock puts them on the Chicago Symphony programs.

About this time Mr. Adams would seem to have

closed his office in the Auditorium for the summer, for he is found beginning in July at the old Exposition building on the lake front as manager of five weeks of summer concerts by Theodore Thomas and his orchestra.

Thomas had no idea of giving brief programs in these concerts. It was his tenth season in Chicago, and he opened the series with the "Meistersinger" prologue, continued with Schumann's "Rhenish" symphony, and then began to lighten up things with some of the Brahms-Dvořák Hungarian dances, Grieg's "Peer Gynt" suite, Goldmark's "Spring" overture, Philip Scharwenka's "Liebesnacht," one of the Liszt Hungarian rhapsodies, and a group of dance music by Gillet and Strauss, ending with the Berlioz "Rakoczy" march. This was good measure. He was to proceed less at length when he finally got into the Auditorium with his Chicago orchestra.

III

For a considerable time, bookings at the Auditorium were more or less haphazard. The Duff company came back in September for three more weeks of Gilbert and Sullivan; when it had gone Strauss and his orchestra came for five farewell concerts; on October 29 the Auditorium organ was dedicated. Clarence Eddy was the soloist, assisted by Christine Nilsson, contralto, Vittorio Carpi, baritone, Rosenbecker's orchestra, and speeches by Mayor Cregier and Ferdinand Peck. Finally "Babes in the Wood," an English pantomime, came on November 10 and stayed until December 20. After that there are references to MacLennan's Royal Edinburgh Concert Company, lectures on Africa by Henry M. Stanley, benefit performances of various kinds. As previously noted, the Apollo Musical Club was now giving its concerts here, having begun its season with "The Messiah" on December 26. And there was a series of popular Wednesday night organ concerts by Harrison Wild, Louis Falk, and others, each assisted by singers of repute.

On February 17 appeared "The Soudan," an English melodrama with acres of scenery and—they advertised—500 people. If names mean anything now, the cast contained Henry Neville, Louise Balfe, Frank Losee, and the famous boy actor, Master Wallie Eddinger. It stayed four weeks. Then came Theodore Thomas for a week with his "unrivaled New York orchestra, assisted by the great Italian tenor, Sig. Italo Campanini." The last named was the brother, elder by nineteen years, of Cleofonte Campanini, who in later years was to do his part in the making of operatic history in Chicago.

And Thomas was next fall to start the first concerts of Chicago's permanent symphony orchestra. On this visit he had Max Bendix as concertmaster and Victor Herbert as first cellist, and one reads that Campanini's voice is "still possessed of many beautiful tones," which somehow or other does not sound overly enthusiastic.

An interesting advertisement appears for April 17 and 18. It announces the only appearance of the United States Marine Band, John Philip Sousa, conductor, assisted by Miss Marie Decca, soprano. The *Tribune* critic did not so much as mention the name of the conductor in his review, but he discovered that the band as far as accuracy of note and purity of tone were concerned was nearly faultless, and that it was the perfection of band playing, technically considered. Then came Thomas again for seven popular programs, with Marie Jahn, Metropolitan soprano, and Bendix as soloists.

The nearest that the Auditorium got to grand opera that season was during the week of May 3, when the Duff company, having borrowed the services of Miss Decca and Marie Tempest, put on "Carmen," "The Bohemian Girl," and "Mignon." From all accounts, the performances were unexpectedly good.

IV

Friday, October 16, 1891, is an important date in the life of the Auditorium, for then for the first time Theodore Thomas raised his baton over a magnificent organization known then as the Chicago Orchestra, to continue in constant service there almost until the end of his life. After his death it was known for a time as the Theodore Thomas Orchestra, as it was popularly if not technically during his lifetime. Then it became the Chicago Symphony Orchestra, but it is the same organization and one of Chicago's continuing glories.

It was well thought of from the start. After the first Friday afternoon concert,—they called the Friday concerts "public rehearsals" in those days, though there was nothing in the performance to indicate anything except a completely rehearsed program—this comment occurs:

"In this company of eighty-six players Chicago now possesses an orchestral association of which its people may indeed be proud, and the day is only a few months distant when they will be able to say to the similar organizations possessed by older organizations in the East, 'Here is your equal!' The Chicago Orchestra is new, and the only shortcoming possible to find in its work is attributable to that newness. It is a shortcoming which is unavoidable, was expected, and is one for which no one is to be blamed. Eighty-six players, no matter how perfect they may be in the mastery of their art, cannot be brought together and in less than a fortnight give a program containing four great orchestral works without traces of recent organization being revealed. The comparative absence of such roughness was one of the most surprising features of yesterday's rehearsal. Theodore Thomas has long been known for his ability to quickly bring newly-formed orchestras into condition for satisfactory work, but in this instance he has fairly surpassed himself, the results being simply astonishing."

It is not told in this account what the "four great orchestral works" were, except that Rafael Joseffy, the first soloist ever to appear with the orchestra, played the Tschaikowsky concerto, but there are remarks about how the first audience was made up mostly of "music students from the several musical colleges and from the thousand and one professors who in this city teach the young how to play scales and exercises." The absence of professional musicians was noted, also the fact that there were several children in arms in the audience and that one baby furnished an audible obbligato while Joseffy was playing. But of the appearance of the orchestra, this:

"The orchestra players are a fine looking lot of men. There are few eccentric looking geniuses among them such as are generally seen in an orchestra. Seidl's band, for instance, is made up extensively of the men to whom Von Bülow contemptuously refers as 'long-haired musicians.' Mr. Thomas' assistants wore correct afternoon dress—Prince Alberts and the suitable concomitants. Joseffy, however, brought no raiment from New York except an evening suit and a light gray make-up for the street, so he committed the glaring *faux pas* of appearing in a swallow-tail, vest, etc., before 6 o'clock in the afternoon. Mr. Joseffy's toilet was a matter of little importance, however, after he began to play."

Grand opera in Italian and French was now announced. On Monday, November 9, under the direction of Abbey and Grau a company appeared containing these names:

Sopranos—Emma Albani, Maria Pettigiani, Mathilde Bauermeister, Emma Eames, Sofia Ravogli, Ida Klein, Lilli Lehmann, Marie Van Zandt.

Contraltos—Sofia Scalchi, Jane de Vigne, Giulia Ravogli.

Tenors—Fernando Valero, Paul Kalisch, Victor Capoul, Gianini-Grifoni, Roberto Vanni, Rinaldini, Jean de Reszke.

Baritones—Jean Martapoura, Agostino Carbone, Antonio Magini-Coletti, Eduardo Camera.

Bassos—Jules Vinche, Enrico Serbolini, Antonio de Vaschetti, Lodovico Viviani, Edouard de Reszke.

Musical director and conductor—Sig. A. Vianesi.

Assistant conductor—Mr. Louis Saar.

Some of the names have dropped out of memory, but those remaining are enough to indicate that it was the beginning of what Henry T. Finck was later to call the golden age of music.

They gave four performances a week. The first was "Lohengrin," and one is somewhat appalled to learn that it was sung in Italian. Evidently the proponents of opera

ELLISON VAN HOOSE, TENOR
Seasons 1910-11, 1911-12

JOHANNA GADSKI

Photo by Dupont
EDOUARD DE RESZKE

Photo by Dupont
JEAN DE RESZKE

in its original tongue had not at that time attained their final vociferousness. But there is a record tending to show that the Germans in the audience shrugged disgusted shoulders over learning that Edouard de Reszke was discovered as "Enrico l'Uccellatore," or that Brother Jean remarked "Io t'amo" to Elsa. It was the first appearance in America of Eames, Giulia Ravogli and the de Reszkes. The two men got away to a fine start, both being adjudged magnificent artists, but one finds a chance remark to the effect that Eames was "charming, but not a great artist," which shows how history sometimes upsets first verdicts. But perhaps she was nervous on her first night.

The critics liked Gluck's "Orfeo," the second performance, and the public did not, and both opinions were reversed on the third, when Marie Van Zandt made her American début in "Sonnambula."

The second week presented "Romeo and Juliet," in which the de Reszkes kept going up the scale and Eames began to be sincerely liked, following it with "Dinorah" for Van Zandt, and what amounted to an all-star cast of "Huguenots," the first of that variety which were to extend through years of opera giving. Then came "Otello," "Rigoletto," "Faust," and "Martha," "Mignon," "Cavalleria Rusticana" and "Don Giovanni," and on the final week the company celebrated the second anniversary of the Auditorium with a bill made up of the fourth act of "Trovatore," the fourth of "Otello," the second of "The Barber of Seville" and the third of "Carmen."

The next event of interest is that on January 1 and 2, 1892, Paderewski makes his first appearance, coming as soloist with the orchestra and playing the Rubinstein

D minor concerto and the Liszt Hungarian Fantasy. "One leaves the presence of this mighty master of the pianoforte stunned by the sudden discovery of what seems absolute perfection—the unexpected realization of what heretofore had constituted an ideal."

Patti and a small company of singers, also an orchestra of fifty directed by Luigi Arditi, came back in February for four operatic concerts. "She is still Patti, the first vocalist of the world, peerless, suffering by comparison with no one, save the Patti of one, two, three decades ago."

There was no more opera that season.

v

It was nearly two and one-half years before the Auditorium next saw any opera. During 1892 Chicago was getting ready for its Columbian exposition; in 1893 it gave it; after its close about six months were necessary to sweep up the pieces. Also there was a full-sized and adult financial panic on throughout the country at that time.

Instead of opera for 1893, Abbey, Schoeffel and Grau engaged the services of Imre Kiralfy to put on a "stupendous spectacle" called "America," a pageant-like representation of episodes in American history, beginning with the departure of Columbus from Spain and ending, of course, with the Chicago World's Fair. A news note tells that there was a good deal of confusion the first night and that the final curtain did not fall until after one o'clock on the morning of Sunday, April 23. It was later set to run between the hours of eight and eleven. In the cast are found the names, among others, of Louise Beaudet as Progress, and Anna Russell, later better known as Annie Russell, as Bigotry.

The music of the exposition has no particular place here, and anyway it has been recorded at length in other publications. One learns with deep regret, however, that Mr. Thomas, who had been made musical director and had worked out elaborate and far-reaching plans for a six months' musical program, became the subject of so vicious an attack by Chicago business men and Chicago newspapers that he resigned before the fair was half way over. The main point of the attack was that he insisted on using his own judgment as to what was the best piano for his concerts and refused to be coerced into accepting what he thought an inferior grade whether manufactured in Chicago or elsewhere. In fact, one comes to the conclusion that the gibes at Chicago as an artistic center in those days were pretty well justified.

Thomas resigned with no outcry and he never made a public explanation, but he was heartstricken at the results. To the end of his life he used to advise his intimate friends never under any circumstances, no matter what, to permit themselves to be made musical directors of any world's fair.

On March 12, 1894, Abbey and Grau came back to the Auditorium with an opera company from the Metropolitan Opera House of New York for a four weeks' stay. The first week records the first appearance in Chicago of Emma Calvé in the name part of "Carmen," of Sigrid Arnoldson as Cherubino in "The Marriage of Figaro," and of Nellie Melba as Lucia di Lammermoor, in company with such other first magnitude artists as

Eames, Nordica, Scalchi, Bauermeister, Jean Lassalle, another newcomer, Pol Plançon, still another, and the de Reszkes. Luigi Mancinelli was the leading conductor, and the Chicago Orchestra, Mr. Thomas', played.

There can be no particular merit in showing how these artists were liked and how the liking warmed into rapture, but it is undoubtedly true that none of us now alive ever heard such another fine aggregation of star soloists in one organization. They speedily became a tradition, and for once a tradition was justified.

And it continued a year later, March 11, 1895, when almost the same company returned. The principal additions were the return of Tamagno and the entrance of the baritone who was to become famous in "Carmen," "The Barber of Seville," and other works, Giuseppe Campanari, also another famous baritone named Victor Maurel. And a great work, Verdi's "Falstaff," was given for the first time in Chicago.

The opera was a success from the start, as well it might have been. This is the sort of cast it had: Maurel as Falstaff, Eames as Mistress Ford, Zelie de Lussan as Anne, Campanari as Ford, Scalchi as Dame Quickly, Jane de Vigne as Mistress Page, and the other parts distributed among Russitano, Mariani, Vanni, and Rinaldini. And "Don Giovanni" used to be blessed with Nordica, de Lussan, Eames, Edouard de Reszke, and Maurel, and "Les Huguenots" with Nordica, Scalchi, Bauermeister, Melba, Jean de Reszke, Edouard de Reszke, Ancona, and Plançon. Those were the casts that even in those days long afterward cause envious lickings of lips.

On April 15 of the same year came Walter Dam-

NELLIE MELBA

LILLIAN NORDICA

ITALO CAMPANINI

POL PLANCON

rosch, bringing with him another aggregation of notables for a week of Wagner. Among them were Rosa Sucher, Johanna Gadski, Marie Brema, Elsa Kutscherra, Max Alvary, Conrad Behrens, Emil Fischer, and Rudolph Oberhauser. "Tristan and Isolde," "Lohengrin," "Die Walküre," "Siegfried," "Die Götterdämmerung," "Tannhäuser," and "Die Meistersinger" were sung. He returned that fall for two weeks beginning November 18. Gadski, Alvary and Fischer were still in the company, but Katharina Klafsky and Louise Mulder were new sopranos, and Barron Berthald and Wilhelm Gruening new tenors. This time he included more than Wagner, putting on Beethoven's "Fidelio" and Weber's "Freischütz" in the second week. People thought that the last named left an agreeable if not distinguished impression, but the rest of the repertoire was an enormous success, as it had been in the spring.

On March 23, 1896, the Abbey-Grau company was back for two more weeks, the same bewildering crowd of stars as before, presenting conventional operas with great industry. Why go in for novelties when there was such a crowd of first line singers to fill the house with well-known, popular works? And it was always possible to put on an all-star cast of "Les Huguenots," and it was a real all-star cast.

It was some time during this period of the world that Jean de Reszke got into the news columns through an unexpected happening in a performance. Somehow or other an insane man managed to get up on the stage during a performance of "Romeo and Juliet," and began to make threatening remarks and gestures. De Reszke drew his sword and pinned the maniac in a corner, while the rest of the singers on the stage retreated, until the stage hands could get on the spot and remove him. Then the performance went on.

The company was back on February 22, 1897, for four weeks, an unusually long stay, having added four artists to the roster, Salignac, the tenor, Litvinne, soprano, Herman Devries, soon to become a well-known Chicago singer, teacher, and critic, and an American baritone who was making a name for himself in German opera, David Bispham. He opened as Kurwenal in "Tristan and Isolde."

It is a little hard to find operatic comments at this time, for Corbett and Fitzsimmons were training for their fight in Carson, Nevada, and special correspondents were filling the news columns with that subject. But in one place there is a plea against the high prices of the opera company, $1 to $3, the point seeming to be that the public should be allowed to buy standing room and then slip into what seats were unoccupied. It is also learned that Calvé, Creminini and Plançon made a great success in Boïto's "Mefistofele," and that Massenet's "Le Cid," with the de Reszkes, Plançon, and Lassalle was something of a riot. These operas were the two novelties of the season.

Evidently the protests about prices had their effect, for on the final week of the season the house was scaled from seventy-five cents to two dollars.

Another year, or rather thirteen months, and on March 14, 1898, a company was present representing the combined resources of Walter Damrosch and Charles A. Ellis. One finds the names of Melba, Nordica, Gadski, Campanari, Fischer, Bispham, and a repertoire that was

Italian and French on the one side and German on the other.

Maurice Grau went it alone the next season. On November 7, 1898, he brought a company which included Eames, de Lussan, Suzanne Adams (new), Schumann-Heink (new), Sembrich, Bauermeister, Van Dyck, Andreas Dippel (new), Campanari, Plançon, Adolph Mühlmann, and Edouard de Reszke (but not Jean). And still the same old operas were given.

The opening attraction was "Lohengrin," with Eames, Dippel, and Bispham. But—"The great sensation of the evening was made by Mme. Schumann-Heink. Never before in Chicago have we heard a contralto with such splendid vocal gifts combined with such dramatic power."

Ellis also desired a bit of solo management, and on February 13, 1899, he appeared with Melba, Gadski, de Lussan, Kraus, and some others as his principal singers. More important is the fact that he opened his season with "La Bohême," and it was the first time Chicago had heard it. "Be it said at once that 'La Bohême' is an opera of unusual musical interest and value, and that its author proves himself a man not only thoroughly schooled in the technic of his craft, but a musical creator of ability and power."

A little variety from the customary operatic visitants was afforded a month later, for on March 20 the French Opera Company from New Orleans paid a week's visit. Then on November 13 Grau returned with much the same company that he had brought a year before except that Calvé was back and Milka Ternina was making her first appearance. Apparently she was quite a long way from being a success. She was billed for the opening night, but was ill and did not get into the casts until the middle of the third week. There it was found that while there were many impressive features to her impersonation, "vocally she left much to be desired." That fine, crusted old phrase never fails, and you can read almost anything into it that you desire.

VI

The French Opera Company from New Orleans had enjoyed their trip to Chicago so much that on March 12, 1900, they came back, this time for three weeks. These were the good old days when they could play at the Auditorium at a top price of $1.50 and still feel happy over the intake. At that, they had some works that other companies had not cared to present, Reyer's "Salammbô" among them. People thought well of it as a spectacle, but found that the music was not greatly inspired. "Sigurd," by the same composer, was another, and it received just about the same verdict. Meanwhile the Savage company at the Studebaker was doing "Lohengrin," "Tannhäuser," and "The Flying Dutchman," and charging twenty-five cents to $1 a seat. In some respects music-lovers were better off at the beginning of this century, and the cost of attendance was one of them.

For some time the more expensive companies had been passing Chicago by. Christmas eve of 1900 the Auditorium reopened to Henry W. Savage's "Metropolitan English" opera company, and it, too, was a $1.50 show. Running in competition with the same manager's company at the Studebaker though it did, it came for two weeks with a repertoire that included "Aïda," "The Bohemian Girl," "Carmen," "Mignon," "Lohengrin," "Faust," and "Il Trovatore." Some of the singers were Grace Van Studdiford, Zelie de Lussan, Grace Golden, Kate Condon, Phœbe Strakosch, Fanchon Thompson, Lloyd d'Aubigné, Joseph Sheehan, Homer Lind, and Clarence Whitehill.

Newspaper accounts hold that it was an honest company, paying much attention to balance and good ensemble, just as the Castle Square Company had been doing in smaller dimensions. As a matter of fact Colonel Savage did more for the cause of opera in English than any one else, because he did things instead of talking about them, and he kept on presenting opera in English until the public proved that it would have no more of it.

"Esmerelda," by A. Goring-Thomas, was the company's novelty. It was founded upon Victor Hugo's "Nôtre Dame," but at that time people took an extremely moral position on their opera going, as this comment illustrates:

"The book ... is repulsive and unnatural in the extreme—a tale of licentiousness and deep-dyed villainy that would put to blush the most lurid melodrama.... The opera patron must, therefore, need forget the libretto's worthlessness and worse if he would know the enjoyment the music can give. Not that the music is at any time strikingly dramatic or unusually powerful. It is merely melodious, well-made music, showing the hand of a composer whose gifts include refinement, taste, and a creative talent which while undeniably able, did not rise to the greatness of genius."

Mr. Grau held out a forgiving hand for the bad

business his company had done during its last few visits, and came in for a week on April 22, 1901, bringing with him such notables as Melba, Ternina, Fritzi Scheff, Bauermeister, Louise Homer, the de Reszkes—Jean, returning at this time, had been in bad health for some time and had stayed for a couple of seasons in Europe—Plançon, Dippel, Marcel Journet, and Antonio Scotti, and during the week he gave Chicago its first view of "Tosca." Ternina had the name part, and there are stories to the effect that the second act of the opera as done by her and Scotti gave the audience a thrill and started a riot of applause such as was not to be equaled till Titta Ruffo came years afterwards.

March 31, 1902, came the same delectable crew, except Melba and Jean de Reszke, but there were such additions as Sembrich, Gadski, and Schumann-Heink. There was a mishap the first night, for Emilio de Marchi, who was singing Radames in "Aïda," went hoarse part way through the performance, and the audience had to be sent home without hearing the final scene. He was still hoarse on the second night—apparently Grau economized on understudies—and "Tosca" had to be changed to "Tannhäuser." But Calvé came along in "Carmen," and Gadski, Schumann-Heink, Van Dyck, Bispham, Edouard de Reszke did great things in "Lohengrin," and then on Thursday night "The Magic Flute" was given "with the following phenomenal cast": Sembrich, Gadski, Ternina, Homer, Bridewell, Scheff, Dippel, Campanari, Reiss, Mühlmann, Edouard de Reszke. Putting that adjective on that cast does not look like an overstatement. Grau thought so well of it that he raised the prices from

LUIGI MANCINELLI

Photo by Dupont

ANTON VAN ROOY

Photo by Dupont

DAVID BISPHAM

Photo by Dupont

ERNEST VAN DYCK

$3.50 to $5 and charged $2 for standing room, and the box office reported receipts of $15,000.

Another interesting item of this season shows that on April 5, 1902, the first and only performance in Chicago of Paderewski's opera, "Manru," was given. Sembrich, Homer, Scheff, a new tenor named Von Bandrowski, Mühlmann, Blass, and Bispham were in it and Damrosch conducted. The reviews speak of a commonplace and ponderous book, but give high praise to the attractive qualities of the music. However, it was never given again in Chicago.

It was an ambitious if brief season. The second week Grau put on the complete "Ring des Nibelungen," the first time that it had been done in Chicago as a cycle, and it received casting of a high order, too. One finds the names of Ternina, Eames, Scheff, Schumann-Heink, Van Dyck, Blass, Dippel, Reiss, Bispham, and Damrosch conducting. It was a fine week for the Wagnerites.

Saturday and Sunday nights, December 20 and 21, 1902, are dates that will be remembered by a few. Perhaps Pietro Mascagni is one of them, for he appeared at the Auditorium in person to direct his "Cavalleria Rusticana," filling in the extra time with a concert program that had bits of "Iris," the "Hymn to the Sun," and various other excerpts. From all accounts he had come to this country expecting an enormous success, which, however, did not turn out as desired. Later in the season he appeared as conductor in a concert organized for his benefit. At one time and another since then he has been quoted as saying things not entirely enthusiastic about America. This tour may have been one of the causes. At any rate, his singers left him in Chicago after the December dates and sailed back to Italy.

VII

Grau paid his last managerial visit to Chicago in the two weeks beginning Tuesday, April 7, 1903. He opened his season with the double bill of "The Daughter of the Regiment," with Sembrich, Salignac, and Gilibert, followed by "Pagliacci," with Scheff, Alvarez, Scotti, and Reiss. For the rest of the week there were "'Die Walküre," "Die Meistersinger," and "Tristan and Isolde," also "Faust" and "Aïda," and among the important names in addition to those of the opening night were Gadski, Nordica, Schumann-Heink, Homer, Burgstaller, Anthes, Van Rooy, Bispham, and Edouard de Reszke. Mancinelli and Alfred Hertz were the principal conductors.

For the second week they added "Don Giovanni," "A Masked Ball," "Siegfried," a double bill of "Don Pasquale" and "Cavalleria Rusticana," "Le Prophète," "The Magic Flute," and "Götterdämmerung." Running through the reviews, it is seen that all the German performances were considered great, and some of the others were passed as fair. Elsewhere one discovers that on the last afternoon in "The Magic Flute," Fritzi Scheff and Campanari made a great hit in the "Pa-pa-pageno" duet, and that the audience went on applauding even after Mme. Sembrich began to sing.

She halted abruptly and left the stage—and the house. Then Scheff and Campanari gave the demanded encore of their duet. But Sembrich did not reappear, and the closing ensemble was cut.

For the next five years the visits of the Metropolitan company to the Auditorium were to be under the management of Heinrich Conried. The first was of two weeks beginning March 14, 1904. Conried was no such spendthrift as Grau in casting operas, but he gave Chicago audiences their first view of Aino Ackte and Olive Fremstad, and the company that year had Calvé, Ternina, and Plançon as returning joys, and Sembrich, Homer, and Gadski among the holdovers. Felix Mottl and Gustav Hinrichs appeared among the conductors.

And in the next season, one brief week beginning March 20, 1905, he introduced no less a personage than Enrico Caruso the first night and presented "Parsifal" the second.

Caruso appeared as Edgardo in "Lucia di Lammermoor" to the Lucia of Sembrich, and it would seem to be perhaps the second time on record when the famous soprano ever had the show taken away from her. The first has just been told. There are words about Caruso's auburn wig and black mustache, his short stature and stocky build, his air of good nature and bonhomie. But of his voice, this:

"Enrico Caruso sings just as nature prepared him to sing. Art and study may have done something toward fashioning and developing the material given him, but nature 'placed' his voice and he sings accordingly. The voice is of exceptional sympathy and beauty—the loveliest voice heard in this country since Campanini was in his prime. It is a voice similar in pure tenor quality to that of Campanini, and, while possessing all of the lyric charm which made the latter's voice unique in the operatic world, has even more power and intensity in the express-ing of the dramatic." The summary is by W. L. Hubbard.

In "Parsifal," up to that time the private property of Baireuth, the performance began at 5 :10 in the after-noon and the first act ran until 6 :55. Then there was an intermission of two hours for dinner, and the second and third acts ran until about 11 :40. Nordica, Burgstaller, Van Rooy, Blass, Goritz, and Journet were in the cast, and Hertz conducted. They charged $7, an unheard-of price in those days.

Under the circumstances it is a little difficult to get a complete estimate of the performance. The cast was ad-mittedly excellent, but the supposedly semi-sacred char-acter of the work seems to have hampered frank expres-sion of opinion. It was not until later days that people could admit without feeling sacrilegious that Gurnemanz was one of the greatest old bores ever put into a music drama, and this in spite of the fact that elsewhere in the score Wagner put some of his finest music. But even on the first performance there is a bit of complaint over how the flowermaidens kept their eyes too tightly fixed on the conductor's baton. What neither audience nor critics knew was, on the authority of Havelock Ellis, that on the first performance in Germany, Wagner came to the theater in company with a keg of beer, in other words, spiritu-ality allied itself with spirituousness.

Caruso sang "Pagliacci" and "Gioconda," and the company did another "Parsifal," a daytime performance from 11 :30 to 5 :20, and in the evening put on Johann Strauss' "The Bat." There was an operatic combination that was a combination! During the week the company took in something over $80,000, up to that time the largest amount of operatic business for one week in the history of opera in Chicago.

It was in the autumn of 1904 that Theodore Thomas and his orchestra moved out of the Auditorium. Ever since 1891 he had been there, directing superb concerts, fighting a good fight for the world's best music, developing the musical sense of Chicago as he alone could have done it at that time.

Like many other interesting events in the musical life of Chicago, the story of how Orchestra Hall came into being does not belong here. But it was Thomas' supreme dream, and he accomplished it. His life was a climax. He fought on until he reached its top. He saw Orchestra Hall built, he inaugurated its concerts with his great orchestra, and then he laid down his baton forever. His death from pneumonia occurred January 4, 1905, but his orchestra lived on. Since his passing, his place has been magnificently filled by a great musician and great conductor, Frederick Stock. His life, his aims, his ambitions are a whole romance in themselves, and Mr. Stock, with much the same sort of idealistic mind, but a more modern one, has seen to it that Chicago was impelled to step forward in its knowledge and appreciation of fine music. It is what Thomas would have desired. We who know and love Stock as a personality in music realize the wisdom of the Orchestral Association of Chicago in appointing him to his position.

Another week of opera, beginning April 2, 1906, opened with "The Queen of Sheba," sung by Edyth Walker, Marie Rappold, Bella Alten, Heinrich Knote, Van Rooy, Blass, and Mühlmann. It was free from sensational features, but "Faust" the second night was sung by Eames, Caruso, Scotti, and Plançon, and it packed the house. It was then that Caruso became known as a cartoonist, having furnished sketches of Conried, Hertz, Scotti, and himself to go into the newspaper pictures. "Don Pasquale," "Hansel and Gretel," "Lohengrin," "Carmen"—sung by Olive Fremstad and Caruso, and considered spiritless—"Tosca," "Martha," and "Lohengrin" completed the week.

Chicago was destined to have two weeks of opera in 1907, the first by the San Carlo Company beginning February 18, and second by Conried starting April 7. This San Carlo company was not the one that exists at present, although bearing the same name. It was directed by Henry Russell, who in a couple of years was to take the chief post of the Boston Opera Company. In its names we find Nordica, Alice Nielsen, a recent graduate from the operettas of Victor Herbert, Fely Dereyne, Florencio Constantino, a young Spanish tenor who became greatly liked, Riccardo Martin, a young American tenor later with the Metropolitan and Chicago forces, Campanari, the Spanish basso, Andres de Segurola, and a number of others now almost entirely out of sight. Prices ran as high as $2.50 for the best seat.

The performances were good, but with more personal successes for individual members than distinctive steps forward in the art of giving opera. But when Conried's company got here it presented Chicago with its first view of Geraldine Farrar in "Madame Butterfly," and there was a new Italian baritone, Riccardo Stracciari, who was to have a number of appearances at the Auditorium, these in addition to Fremstad and Eames and

Photo by Mishkin

LOUISE HOMER AS DELILAH

Photo by Moffett

ERNESTINE SCHUMANN-HEINK

Schumann-Heink, and Caruso and Scotti and Plançon and the other notables.

"Miss Farrar clearly is an artist who thinks, and the number of such is so small that an addition to the ranks is subject for sincere rejoicing. Her Butterfly last evening proved a veritable dramatic portrayal. Thought and intelligent care had been expended on its every part, and a characterization beautifully rounded and consistent, logical and clean cut was the result."

January 20, 1908, the San Carlo returned, this time for three weeks. The company was much as before except that the names of Mmes. Olitzka and Claessens are added to the contraltos, Jane Noria to the sopranos, and Victor Maurel to the baritones. Again there were personal successes.

And Conried did another week from April 20, the most interesting item of which was Mascagni's "Iris" which not even the efforts of Eames and Scotti were able to save from derision.

VIII

In George L. Upton's "Musical Memories" he gives a summary of operatic matters in the Auditorium up to this point. As a matter of interesting reference, his table is included here.

Opening Date	Company	Season
Dec. 10, 1889	Abbey, Schoeffel, and Grau	4 weeks
March 10, 1890	Abbey, Schoeffel, and Grau	1 week
April 21, 1890	Metropolitans German	3 weeks
Nov. 9, 1891	Abbey, Schoeffel, and Grau	5 weeks
March 12, 1894	Abbey, Schoeffel, and Grau	4 weeks

Opening Date	Company	Season
March 11, 1895	Abbey, Schoeffel, and Grau	3 weeks
April 15, 1895	Damrosch	1 week
Nov. 18, 1895	Damrosch	2 weeks
March 23, 1896	Abbey, Schoeffel, and Grau	2 weeks
Feb. 22, 1897	Abbey, Schoeffel, and Grau	4 weeks
March 14, 1898	Damrosch and Ellis	2 weeks
Nov. 7, 1898	Maurice Grau	3 weeks
Feb. 13, 1899	Ellis Opera	2 weeks
March 20, 1899	New Orleans French Opera	1 week
Nov. 13, 1899	Maurice Grau	3 weeks
March 12, 1900	New Orleans French Opera	3 weeks
Dec. 24, 1900	Savage Metropolitan English	2 weeks
April 22, 1901	Maurice Grau	1 week
March 31, 1902	Maurice Grau	2 weeks
Dec. 20-21, 1902	Mascagni	2 performances
April 7, 1903	Maurice Grau	2 weeks
March 14, 1904	Conried	2 weeks
March 20, 1905	Conried	1 week
April 2, 1906	Conried	1 week
Feb. 18, 1907	San Carlo	1 week
April 7, 1907	Conried	1 week
Jan. 20, 1908	San Carlo	3 weeks
April 20, 1908	Conried	1 week

This was the end of Mr. Upton's compilation. During its course he counted up 278 performances of seventy-nine different operas, grand and light. For the saving of space and time the dates of first performances and the number of times each was performed may be omitted, but the operas themselves were these:

"Romeo and Juliet," "William Tell," "Faust," "Il Trovatore," "Lucia di Lammermoor," "Aïda," "Semiramide," "Martha," "Huguenots," "Traviata," "Sonnambula," "Otello," "Barber of Seville," "Pinafore," "Mikado," "Pirates of Penzance," "L'Africaine," "Lin-

da," "Lakmé," "Salammbô," "Tannhäuser," "Meister-
singer," "La Juive," "Lohengrin," "Masked Ball," "Fly-
ing Dutchman," "Fidelio," "Queen of Sheba," "Norma,"
"Barber of Bagdad," "La Poupée," "Don Giovanni,"
"Walküre," "Iolanthe," "Trial by Jury," "Patience,"
"Carmen," "Bohemian Girl," "Orpheus," "Dinorah,"
"Rigoletto," "Mignon," "Cavalleria Rusticana," "Phile-
mon and Baucis," "The Basoche," "Marriage of Figaro,"
"Hamlet" (fourth act), "Pagliacci," "Werther," "Fal-
staff," "Tristan and Isolde," "Siegfried," "Freischütz,"
"Götterdämmerung," "La Navarraise," "Mefistofele,"
"Le Cid," "La Bohème," "La Favorita," "Sigurd,"
"Manon," "Esmerelda," "Tosca," "Magic Flute,"
"Manru," "Rheingold," "Daughter of the Regiment,"
"Don Pasquale," "The Prophet," "The Elixir of Love,"
"The Gondoliers," "Parsifal," "La Gioconda," "Fleder-
maus," "Hansel and Gretel," "Madame Butterfly,"
"Robin Hood," "Serenade," "Iris."

Which of these do you think was the most popular,
as shown by the number of performances? You are right,
it was "Il Trovatore," which was given thirty-eight times
in that period. It was followed closely by "Carmen,"
with thirty-seven. The light opera, "Pinafore," comes
next with thirty-two, "Lohengrin" and "Cavalleria Rusticana" tie with twenty-seven, "Huguenots" has twenty-
two, and there is another tie with twenty each for "Aïda"
and "Robin Hood."

There was a good deal of theatrical but non-operatic
activity during the greater part of the 1908-09 season.
Among the names appearing in the advertisements were
"50 Miles from Broadway," the policemen's benefit show
of that season, Richard Carle, Andrew Mack, Gertrude

Hoffmann, Victor Moore, "The Newlyweds," the Zieg-
feld Follies, the Burns-Johnson fight pictures, and "The
Shepherd King." Finally on April 12, 1909, F. Wight
Neumann took over the house for two weeks for the
Metropolitan Opera Company under his own local man-
agment. This time the Metropolitan manager was Giulio
Gatti-Casazza, just entering upon his long New York
career.

High among the announcements were those of the
first Chicago appearances of "the eminent Italian conductor, Arturo Toscanini," and of "the Bohemian soprano, Emmy Destinn, who probably claims first in public curiosity." They both appeared on the opening night
in "Aïda." The orchestra was considered ideal. Mme.
Destinn, although "an unfortunately chosen makeup
robbed her of the personal beauty which is said to be
hers," with black braids of hair that "marred her facial
charm and made her figure seem misshapen," made a
great hit by the beauty of her singing. Homer was the
Amneris, and the public had a chance to get acquainted
with Giovanni Zenatello as Radames, Pasquale Amato as
Amonasro, and Adamo Didur as Ramfis. "Die Meistersinger" came up on the second night with Karl Joern as
Walther and Gadski as Eva, both destined to appear together on the same stage in Wagnerian opera—though
not in the Chicago company—exactly twenty years later,
and both still going strong. In the same edition of the
newspapers appears a report that Caruso was in danger
of losing his voice, and a statement from Mary Garden
that the story of her quarrel with Oscar Hammerstein
was entirely unfounded. And Geraldine Farrar repaid to
Mrs. Bertram Webb of Salem, Mass., the last install-

Photo by Dupont

ARTURO TOSCANINI

Photo by Moffett

GIORGIO POLACCO

ment on a loan of $34,000 advanced to her over a period
of ten years for her musical education. Mme. Destinn
closed her own engagement here by appearing in the first
Chicago performance of Smetana's "The Bartered
Bride." And on Sunday the audience paid $18,000 to
hear "Parsifal." Fremstad, Anthes, Amato, Allen
Hinckley, Otto Goritz, Herbert Witherspoon, Homer
and Mühlmann were some of the cast, and Hertz conducted.

Turn now to January and April, 1910, the last dates
with which this foreword is concerned. On January 10th
the newly organized Boston Opera Company, Henry
Russell, director, paid a two weeks' visit to the Auditorium, and as it turned out, the only time it ever came
to Chicago. Here were Nielsen, Maria Gay, and Constantino, and here also were two greatly talented Rus-
sians, Lydia Lipkowska and Georges Baklanoff, both
newcomers.

Lipkowska made her first appearance in "Lakmé,"
which had not been heard since Patti did it twenty years
before. She was a ravishing singer with considerable
knowledge of how to act, and consequently she was a
great success. But the talked-about individual that night
was Thamara de Swirsky, as she called herself then, who
did a series of solo dances after the opera. The audience
was pretty well what they used to call agog, because she
was the first of the epidermic school of dancers that had
appeared here. And she was abundantly so.

The visitors from Boston sang well, acquitted themselves in a seemly manner in all respects, and went on
their way with the good wishes of all. Then on April 4
came the Metropolitan to stay four weeks and never

again to appear in Chicago. It was a lavish, not to say riotous display that they gave, the most liberal outpouring of vocal resources in their history before or since. The reasons became evident later.

Here were a few of the leading artists of that season: Destinn, Nielsen, Alda, Gadski, Farrar, Hidalgo, Gluck, Alten, Fremstad, Homer, Maubourg, Sparkes, Caruso, Martin, Bonci, Slezak, Amato, Scotti, Campanari, Segurola, Pini-Corsi, Gilly, Didur, Soomer, Blass, Mühlmann, Jadlowker, Clement, Whitehill, Joern, Goritz, Hinckley, Reiss, with Toscanini and Hertz leading the corps of conductors. Even with the marvelous old-timers of the nineties all gone, it was an extravagant crew to get together in one company.

There are still memories of Slezak in "Otello" and "Aïda," of the glorious "Meistersinger" that Toscanini conducted, of Hertz's "Parsifal," of many other good things too numerous to mention. In fact that four weeks averaged grand opera with a pronounced accent on the grand.

Of course such an organization could not expect to make money. The list of singers shows how ruinous it must have been. But a wonderful time was enjoyed by all who attended.

It completed the first or preliminary half of what Mr. Peck had tried to make the Auditorium mean. Now was to come a time when it was even more closely identified with Chicago and its interests. Wherefore one now turns to a new chapter and begins a new phase of musical life in Chicago.

Enrico Caruso

Photo by Matzene

Leo Slezak

CHAPTER I

In 1910 Chicago developed operatic growing pains. For sixty years previous, beginning in 1850, opera in Chicago had consisted merely of such visits to the city as traveling companies chose to give. The Metropolitan, as has been seen, used to come to the Auditorium in the spring for two weeks, three weeks, four weeks, what it was thought the city could stand as an operatic orgy.

That was all. It was not enough in the minds of certain Chicagoans. Chicago had had its own symphony orchestra for nearly two decades. Founded by Theodore Thomas and continued after his death, January 4, 1905, by Frederick Stock, it had taken rank in the minds of those who knew as one of the noteworthy orchestral organizations of the country and of the world. Besides, Boston, in addition to having its own great orchestra, had begun operations with its own opera company. Wherefore, said the same certain Chicagoans, it is time for Chicago to show some operatic activity: let us then go out and make a few artistic gestures of our own.

A set of fortuitous circumstances aided them. A terrific battle for the operatic control of New York had been going on for three or four seasons. Oscar Hammerstein, he of the silk hat, the spade beard, and the cigar making machinery, had built the Manhattan Opera House and organized the Manhattan Opera Company, with the avowed intention of putting the Metropolitan out of business, and the Metropolitan was equally avowed in its intention of not being put out of business.

The giants fought tooth and nail; they raised a furious uproar in the columns of the newspapers; they spent money as the press agents say money is being spent in Hollywood to-day. Hammerstein organized a brilliant company which gave New York its only real view of French opera up to that time, and Italian opera almost as glamorous. The Metropolitan concentrated on Italian and German opera, engaging every singer of note that could be engaged.

Mary Garden made her first operatic appearances in America with Hammerstein. John McCormack was a member of the Manhattan, so were Maurice Renaud and Hector Dufranne and Gustave Huberdeau; the Metropolitan had Caruso and Slezak and Gadski and Scotti, to name only a few offhand of the forces of either. Hammerstein brought Cleofonte Campanini to this country to be his chief conductor; the Metropolitan took delight in Arturo Toscanini.

It was a wonderful row while it lasted and a time of deep and abiding joy for all beholders. Probably never in the history of the world had there been such a chance to observe so many fine operatic performances so lavishly cast or so brilliantly performed. Competition was the life of operatic trade just then; it was also the cause of galloping tuberculosis in operatic bank accounts.

The last time that the Metropolitan company visited Chicago, which was in the month of April, 1910, its Italian and German wings were actually two companies. This is not in the least an exaggeration. There were two sets of principals, two choruses, two complete orchestras, two sets of conductors, Toscanini at the head of one, Alfred Hertz leading the other. In effect there were even two general directors, though these bore different titles, Giulio Gatti-Casazza and Andreas Dippel.

It is true that Toscanini used to conduct some German operas in addition to his Italian list, as he has done with marvelous effect ever since, glory to his eloquent baton! His dealings with "Die Meistersinger" have never been forgotten in Chicago even after all these years. It is also true that Slezak would be an ideal Walther in the same "Meistersinger" and then raise the roof with his Radames in "Aïda," a few nights later, and that Gadski, primarily a Wagnerian soprano, had a list of splendid Italian rôles in her repertoire. But in practice if not in theory, the Metropolitan was a double company.

Such a fight could have only one result. The war chest of the Metropolitan was deeper than Hammerstein's, and finally the brilliant Oscar had to succumb. The Manhattan Opera Company went out of existence at the end of the season of 1910. Among Hammerstein's articles of capitulation was a signed agreement to keep out of operatic activities in New York for a period of ten years. The Manhattan forces were without financial or artistic leadership, and the Metropolitan had about twice as many people as it needed. It was Chicago's chance.

Probably if Hammerstein's money had not run out, he would have been fighting yet. Though he never included Chicago in his scheme of operations, and though his passing was the biggest single item in the formation of the Chicago Opera Company, I, for one, always regretted his passing, if for no other reason than that he was the most picturesque figure in the operatic history of our times. He had' the imaginative soul of the creative artist, he dearly loved a fight, and he was the only one of his time or since whose tongue was warranted to be quicker than Mary Garden's. A former New York reporter once told me that when he and a few of his fellows were out on their day's rounds and unable to turn up anything interesting in the way of news, they made a constant practice of dropping in at the Manhattan to call on Hammerstein. They generally came away with something worth printing, and it was frequently worth printing on the front page. It was he who used to say, "Praise me if you can; roast me if you must; at any rate mention me." If he did not invent the theory, he believed in it and acted upon it. Publicity was frankly his life's blood.

One year Miss Garden got into a row with him, walked out and sailed for Europe before the season was over, giving out an interview at the dock saying that she was leaving because Hammerstein had treated her worse than a chorus girl. The reporters, with praiseworthy curiosity, marched straight up to the Manhattan Opera House to find out what Hammerstein had in the way of a comeback. He had one. This was it. Oscar took a puff of his cigar, grinned, pushed back his silk hat, and said:

"Miss Garden has no right to say that I treated her worse than a chorus girl. I never treated her worse than a chorus girl or even like a chorus girl. Miss Garden owes me $5,000 at this moment, and no chorus girl that ever lived was ever able to do that to me."

With his passing, the decks were clear for the organization of a new company, and a committee of prominent Chicagoans and New Yorkers put themselves to the task of the formation of the Chicago Grand Opera Company. The Chicagoans were there because they wanted the company. The New Yorkers joined them because they were desirous of sitting on Hammerstein's operatic grave and seeing for themselves that he staged no resurrection.

For he was dangerous at any time, likely to make a flank movement at the precise moment in which he was supposed to be most thoroughly licked. Having built opera houses in Philadelphia and London in addition to the Manhattan, he was in a fair way to develop the habit, and he nearly gave the crowd heart disease by threatening to build one in Chicago.

Whether he really had such an idea, or whether it was just one of his highly complex jokes, will never be known, but he came to Chicago, accompanied by two associates, Max Rabinoff and Ben. H. Atwell, and, trailed by a group of reporters, he drove around the city all day, pausing here and there to inspect possible building sites. He even went over to the lake front to survey a huge heap of stone, the remains of a building just torn down, measuring blocks and jotting down figures in a note book. As a bit of pantomime calculated to produce jumpy nerves in unfriendly beholders, it was an act that never has been surpassed, but nothing more came of it.

The first board of directors of the company was a long one. It included the names of Frederick W. Bode, Richard T. Crane, Jr., Charles G. Dawes, Robert Goelet, George J. Gould, Frank Gray Griswold, Frederick T. Haskell, Charles L. Hutchinson, Otto H. Kahn, Philip M. Lydig, Clarence Mackay, Harold F. McCormick, John J. Mitchell, Ira Nelson Morris, LaVerne W. Noyes, Max Pam, Julius Rosenwald, John C. Shaffer,

John G. Shedd, Charles A. Stevens, Harry Payne Whitney, and H. Rogers Winthrop.

Out of these was formed an executive committee with Mr. Mackay as chairman, Mr. Shaffer vice-chairman, and Messrs. Kahn, Dawes, Rosenwald, Shedd, Whitney, and Winthrop as other members. The officers of the new company read thus: Harold F. McCormick, president; Charles G. Dawes and Otto Kahn, vice-presidents; Charles L. Hutchinson, treasurer, and Philip M. Lydig, secretary. Andreas Dippel was released from the Metropolitan to become general manager, Cleofonte Campanini was appointed general musical director, and Bernhard Ulrich business manager.

The roster of the company makes interesting reading after a lapse of years. Maestro Campanini, being general musical director, was also first conductor. The other conductors were Attilio Parelli, Ettore Perosio, and Marcel Charlier. The stage director was Fernand Almanz. The stage manager was Joseph C. Engel, who had served through the Hammerstein régime and was one of the few persons able to claim continuous membership in the Chicago company from its foundation to his death on July 2, 1928. One of his assistants was Carlo Muzio, whose fame is mostly vicarious, since he was the father of Claudia Muzio, too young at that time to have begun the career that has made her name known to the opera goers of three continents.

The other assistant stage manager was Sam Katzman, the chorus master was Pietro Nepoti, the ballet master Luigi Albertieri. The Chicago company, you see, started in fully equipped, even to its ballet, and with a première danseuse named Esther Zanini.

The list of principal singers was rather startingly long for a new company. It would seem almost over-lavish in these days, though it had the addition of several famous guest-artists. For the Chicago company started its operations by being able to invite guests of high degree to take part in its performances. Like a good many other good things, the system fell into disuse as years went on, registering among the many things that might make opera seasons more stimulating but that are not being done.

At any rate, here is Chicago's 1910 roster of artists:

Sopranos—Marie Cavan, Suzanne Dumesnil, Minnie Egener, Geraldine Farrar (guest from the Metropolitan Opera), Johanna Gadski (guest from the Metropolitan Opera), Mary Garden, Lillian Grenville, Jeanne Korolewicz, Marie La Salle-Rabinoff (guest), Lydia Lipkowska (guest from the Boston Opera), Nellie Melba (guest), Carmen Melis, Jane Osborn-Hannah, Mabel Riegelman, Serafina Scalfaro, Marguerita Sylva, Carolina White, Alice Zeppilli.

Mezzo-sopranos and contraltos—Clotilde Bressler-Gianoli, Tina di Angelo, Eleanora de Cisneros, Giuseppina Giaconia, Rosa Olitzka (guest), Ferrari Pattini, Marian Walker.

Tenors—Amadeo Bassi, Enrico Caruso (guest from the Metropolitan Opera), Florencio Constantino (guest from the Boston Opera), Charles Dalmores, Jean Delparte, Francesco Daddi, Mario Guardabassi, John McCormack, Emilio Venturini, Edmond Warnery, Nicola Zerola, Dante Zucchi.

Baritones—Wilhelm Beck, Alfredo Costa, Armand Crabbé, Desiré Defrere, Hector Dufranne, Nicola Fossetta, Maurice Renaud (guest from the Boston Opera), Mario Sammarco, Antonio Scotti (guest from the Metropolitan Opera).

Bassos—Nazzareno de Angelis, Vittorio Arimondi, Berardo Berardi, Gustave Huberdeau, Pompilio Malatesta, Constantin Nicolay, Michele Sampieri.

With the exception of the guests, these, as has already been indicated, were mostly from the Hammerstein company, with a few accretions from the Metropolitan and other sources. The scenery, costumes, musical scores, and various other physical odds and ends going toward an operatic season, had been bought in a mass—and at panic prices—after the collapse of the Manhattan company. After years of fighting on one front and months of planning on another, everything was now ready.

And so on the evening of Thursday, November 3, 1910, the curtain of the Auditorium went up, and Chicago stepped out with its own opera company.

Those who came discovered that the interior of the house had been considerably rebuilt. As a result of that frightful calamity, the fire in the Iroquois theater several years before, a new set of building and fire regulations for other theaters had gone into effect. One item forced upon the Auditorium was the building of a fireproof wall through the middle of the second floor promenade. In order to overcome this effect, a line of boxes, afterwards to become two lines, had been built across the rear of the main floor, thus converting the box tier into a veritable horseshoe. In later years and in another opera house, the boxes were to be at the rear only, but at the birth of Chicago's first opera company the boxes extended along both back and sides.

Margaret Matzenauer

John McCormick

Photo by Strauss Peyton

Everythings had been freshened and redecorated. Everything was in festal array; every one was in festal mood. Lights went down; spirits went up; Chicago met its opera company.

CHAPTER II

AÏDA

Opera in four acts by Giuseppe Verdi. Presented by the Chicago Grand Opera Company at the Auditorium, Chicago, Nov. 3, 1910. The cast arranged as follows:

THE KING .... Berardo Berardi
AMNERIS .... Eleanora de Cisneros
AÏDA .... Jeanne Korolewicz
RADAMES .... Amadeo Bassi
RAMFIS .... Nazzareno de Angelis
AMONASRO .... Mario Sammarco
MESSENGER .... Dante Zucchi
PRIESTESS .... Mabel Riegelman

Incidental dances by Esther Zanini and Corps de Ballet

General Musical Director...Cleofonte Campanini

Talk about the event of the season! Never was there such an event or such a season. Chicago took its opera, and took it hard. The newspapers fairly turned over their whole editions to the opening: the critics evolved adjectives by the thousand, special writers searched their souls for descriptions of the glory of the occasion, pictures of the artists were printed all over the place, and society editors wrote descriptions of costumes by the running foot. It was a grand and uplifting time, and no one with the least charity in his heart grudged any of the participants the good time that they had.

As memory goes back nearly a score of years, it was a pretty good performance at that. "Aïda" is the best festival opera ever written, and recollections are still vivid of the way Campanini used to lift the roof with soloists, chorus, orchestra, and stage band in the triumph scene. This one was a real triumph, and the applause that went up at its end made any services of a claque entirely unnecessary. Of course no American opera company ever had a claque—officially: any opera manager will tell you that. But this was a time when it was absent in reality.

The curtain was raised and raised again, and the singers bowed until every one lost count of the calls. Campanini was greeted with approving shouts, but speech-making in English was never in his line. He merely waved his arms in the directions of the vocal and instrumental participants. The single speech of the evening was made by Andreas Dippel, and he dove into the recesses of an opera hat to find his notes.

It was polite, tactful and brief, concluding, "I am not alone in speaking for myself, but in the name of our general musical director, Cleofonte Campanini, and on behalf of our artists and staff, in stating to you who are present and to those who in the future may lend their support to the Chicago Grand Opera Company that we all promise our most sincere and earnest efforts to make its success as great as possible." Then every one in the audience settled back to take an admiring look around and answer the questions of reporters, for every one with the least degree of artistic or social prominence was interviewed that night.

"It's splendid—I never saw the opulence of the East better staged than right here," said Arthur Meeker. "Not one feature is lacking. The artists are splendid, the costumes and scenery brilliant and magnificent," said Philip M. Lydig. "There is no question of the entire success of the Chicago Grand Opera Company, especially from an artistic standpoint," said Max Pam. Some of the reporters, for want of anything better to do, interviewed as many artists as they could get hold of, though in this case the interviewees were even more unanimous than all the rest. One might imagine in their remarks a not wholly unworthy desire to retain recently acquired jobs.

And just about this time the newspapers began to talk about the desirability of having opera in English, a durable and undying topic, shared by every one except those whose function it is to buy tickets and make opera in English commercially possible.

In the foreword this account has already gone back to the opening of the Auditorium. That in many ways was even more picturesque. One reads in ancient newspaper files of how on December 9, 1889, "the orator of the evening in eloquent language sized up the Parthenon, the Pyramids, and the Acropolis with the Auditorium and found them shy." Some of the remarks on that historic occasion really deserved to be made permanent, as when Governor Fifer stated that "we have passed in half a century from the warwhoop of the savage to the ravishing strains of a Patti." Or when Mayor Cregier delivered himself of this:

"Permit the eye, that masterpiece of nature's work, to survey the outlines of this grand structure, and we shall see everywhere in trained symmetry and art the children of that noble and ancient science—Geometry!"

Chicago undoubtedly considered itself a bit too sophisticated by 1910 to permit any one to get away with
such empyrean-assaulting oratory as clogged the air at
the dedication of the Auditorium. But the dedication of
the opera company was sufficient of an event for it to
seem desirable for a little time to allow the dust to settle.
Not much time was allowed, however. The Auditorium
was dark on the next—Friday—night, but on Saturday
afternoon a new page of operatic history went onto the
presses.

PELLÉAS ET MÉLISANDE

Lyric drama in five acts by Claude Debussy. Presented for the first time in Chicago by the Chicago
Grand Opera Company at the Auditorium, Nov.
5, 1910. The cast is as follows:

PELLÉAS .... Edmond Warnery
GOLAUD .... Hector Dufranne
KING ARKEL .... Gustave Huberdeau
LITTLE YNIOLD .... Suzanne Dumesnil
A PHYSICIAN .... Armand Crabbé
MÉLISANDE .... Mary Garden
GENEVIEVE .... Clotilde Bressler-Gianoli

General Musical Director.Cleofonte Campanini

Yes, the first time in Chicago of the Debussy music-
drama, the first, since the times, years before, when she
had sung in church and, perhaps, student concerts, of
Mary Garden. Here was a direct provocation for more
columns of newspaper space. But if "Aïda" had been a
festival, not to say a three-ring circus splurge of opera,

"Pelléas et Mélisande" was something to exhaust all their wisdom upon.

And didn't we treat it seriously in those days? We wrote thousands of words explaining just what it was that Debussy meant and how he got that way; we, at least some of us, spelled his name with a capital B, thus, De Bussy. There was even a noble effort to consider the score as "fourth-dimension music" until some one came to the conclusion that none of the auditors had been provided with fourth-dimension ears, and we would have to consider it with the ears that nature had provided us. Then we gradually got acquainted with it, and discovered, perhaps with some amazement that, unfamiliar idiom as it was at that time, it was a persuasively fascinating, elusive three hours of music, phantoms in blue darkness, entirely lacking in anything to be carried away from the theater in the way of theme or tune, but entirely enjoyable, and not in the least unsolvable.

It is true that "Pelléas et Mélisande," revived every once in a while through the history of the company, never became a best-seller of operatic wares, but Mary Garden promptly did, and began the process that Saturday afternoon.

Ever since then there have been two camps in all opera seasons, those for whom Miss Garden can do no wrong, and those who are never satisfied with anything she does. Between the two, the person who tries to be reasonable and analytical, to estimate her position in her various rôles, gets simply nowhere. He might as well retire and keep his thoughts to himself.

It can be admitted that she never scorned the artful aid of newspaper publicity. For years a Garden interview has been a newspaper feature. She always managed to say the right thing at the right time to get it printed. An old newspaper man once said that if Miss Garden's taste had led her to newspaper work instead of opera, she would have been the most famous newspaper woman the world had ever known, because she had an unfailing eye for a vivid feature.

So, browsing among the newspaper clippings of the first weeks of the opera season one discovers that Miss Garden had brought something new in a Paris skirt to Chicago; that somewhere in the offing was a Turkish pasha to whom she was engaged—he was never heard of after the first season—; that she thought Chicago was "rotten" and the suffragettes worse; that she disapproved of cigarettes; that she left a theatrical performance— Fritzi Scheff in "The Mikado"—rather than comply with an usher's request to take off the broad-brimmed, plumed Chinese pagoda of a hat which was the mode at that time, and that she stated in print—with a picture of herself and the offending hat appended—"Take off my hat? Why, the idea! I would not take off my hat for the King of England unless I just felt like it." Considering the quite large amount of competition she had at that time, it was going quite a bit for a few weeks.

But she was booked for some famous operas that first season, and she gave some superb performances. There was "Pelléas et Mélisande," there was "Louise," there was "Thaïs," most of all, there was "Salome." By the side of the Garden accomplishments the other events of that season seem almost inconsiderable, though they were not. Carolina White began on the course that led to her rapid rise and more rapid decline; John McCormack was then an opera singer, only indicating at occasional Sunday concerts the manner with songs that afterwards made him the best known and best loved concert singer of two hemispheres; Melba visited the company as a guest-artist, so did Farrar, and so, for the first and last time, did Caruso. Incidentally, one reads in one review, "The public seems to have lost interest in Puccini's opera, 'Tosca.'" Remember, if you please, that this was written eighteen years ago, and remember also what Garden, Raisa, Muzio, and several others, to go no further than the ranks of the Chicago Opera, have done in it since then. One grows humble about pronouncing judgments when one goes over back files of the newspapers.

LOUISE

Musical romance in four acts by Gustave Charpentier. Presented for the first time in Chicago at the Auditorium, Nov. 9, 1910.

THE FATHER .... Hector Dufranne
THE MOTHER .... Clotilde Bressler-Gianoli
LOUISE .... Mary Garden
JULIEN .... Charles Dalmores

and about forty more, with Campanini conducting

It was the second novelty of the season, and it put French opera and Miss Garden into considerably more popularity. "Pelléas et Mélisande" had been puzzling, but "Louise" was fascinating. Miss Garden left off being a wraith and became an uncommonly human sort of a being.

"Louise," the opera, was a stroke of genius, anyway.

For once in his life Charpentier was touched with flame when he conceived the idea of putting the voice of a city into music. In fact whenever any one strolls around Paris as a sightseer, he is more likely to think of "Louise" than anything else, certainly more than of "Andrea Chenier," of "Manon," or the other operas that make Paris their background.

In fact cities have definite voices. There is a place up on the hill of Naples, close to the old museum, where you can stand late in the afternoon and hear the sound of all Naples, voices, songs, the chatter of children, dogs barking in the distance, an occasional obbligato of a tram wheel squeaking on a curve. Next to attending a good performance of "Louise," it is one of the most fascinating experiences of the world. No composer has ever got around to working out a similar idea for an American city, though the voice and philosophy of an American city is quite as definite as that of a European one. Of course, an important part of the "Louise" plot hinges on the purely legal question of the parents' permission as a preliminary to marriage, a matter not looming quite so large in these United States, so a different sort of plot would have to be devised in case Chicago or New York or New Orleans were chosen as a subject. At the same time, the atmosphere of "Louise" is considerably more important than its plot, and the musical treatment of the voice of a city is a fascinating idea.

When they first began to give "Louise" in Chicago, they had the rag pickers and artists and old clothes man and street peddlers that play so large a part in that great scene in the second act, but they also included a scene almost as good, the dressmaking atelier. When the piece was revived some years later, this scene was omitted, and no amount of pleading has ever been able to cause its subsequent inclusion. It was a great mistake, because the scene was a beautiful one, and its excision was a deforming surgical operation.

However, these were early times when people were willing to give a great piece in all its greatness, and Miss Garden, Mr. Dalmores, and most particularly Mr. Campanini were important people in Chicago by virtue of the performance. Chicago began to want to revive its former title of the Garden City and transform it into the Mary Garden City. Whereupon Miss Garden took to herself another full page of publicity in one of the Sunday newspapers in which her most important pronouncement seemed to be that the worst thing about the American girl is her voice, and the worst thing for her voice is chewing gum. She also told how she was going to learn the principal part for Puccini's coming novelty, "The Girl of the Golden West," but this she did not do, as will be told later.

CHAPTER III

Having bemused Chicago with the misty wistfulness of "Pelléas et Mélisande" and set it cheering with the romantic realism of "Louise," it next became the showman's duty of Mr. Campanini, Miss Garden, and some of their associates of the opera company to afford a bit of a shock, and this is what they proceeded to do. Here is the event that touched off the fireworks heard for weeks pretty well around the United States, with a few repercussions from Europe.

SALOME

Musical drama in one act. Book by Oscar Wilde. Music by Richard Strauss. Presented by the Chicago Grand Opera Company in the Auditorium, Chicago, Nov. 25, 1910. The cast:

SALOME	Mary Garden
HERODIAS	Eleanora de Cisneros
HEROD	Charles Dalmores
JOKANAAN	Hector Dufranne
NARRABOTH	Edmond Warnery
PAGE OF HERODIAS	Giuseppina Giaconia
FIRST JEW	Jean Delparte
SECOND JEW	Emilio Venturini
THIRD JEW	Francesco Daddi
FOURTH JEW	Dante Zucchi
FIFTH JEW	Berardo Berardi
FIRST NAZARENE	Gustave Huberdeau

SECOND NAZARENE ....Desiré Defrere
FIRST SOLDIER ....Armand Crabbé
SECOND SOLDIER ....Constantin Nicolay
A CAPPADOCIAN ....Nicola Fossetta
A SLAVE ....Suzanne Dumesnil

General Musical Director...Cleofonte Campanini

And what a row there was! Here was a topic of conversation good for weeks to come. All that had been said
for, against, and about the Chicago Opera was stolid,
tongue-tied silence compared to what arose over "Salome" and its ways. The critics wrote about it by the running foot—they did over everything operatic in those
days—newspaper space has become a scarcer commodity
since—and most of them found themselves in the predica-
ment of trying to carry water on two shoulders.

Miss Garden had not only made an enormous hit
with her previous rôles, but had established a warm and
entirely sincere admiration for herself as a many sided
artist. In one case it had even gone to this comment:
"That she should have consented to introduce herself to
Chicago in the rôle of Mélisande is in itself a convincing
testimonial to the refinement, the pure beauty, of her
artistic ideals."

So here they were, committed to the future of the
Chicago Opera as a public institution, as was eminently
proper, convinced in any event because the Chicago Opera
was accomplishing notable things, liking and admiring
Miss Garden, and yet confronting her in a piece that
really shocked most of them, if for no other reason than
its sheer physical, half-insane realism. I wonder if any
one remembers one of the lesser shivers of the piece in

the scene where the executioner descends into the cistern to cut off Jokanaan's head. In that passage Strauss decreed that the double bass players in the orchestra should press their strings close up to the bridge and saw away with their bows, producing a sound strangely like that of a knife slithering off from a bone. That was merely a minor incident in a piece that had plenty of greater ones.

So the next day the papers were full of double-barreled remarks about its being great art but—, a magnificent performance but—, it was horrifying but—, with many variants and a few disquisitions on the true nature of art and morals. Curiously enough, the best account of Miss Garden's performance was written not only by a musical but a dramatic critic, Percy Hammond of the *Tribune*, who also was present at the first performance. Or perhaps it was not curious at all, since he had not committed himself beforehand. At any rate, this is what he wrote:

Miss Garden as a Dramatic Artist

"It is said by those proficient in the criticism of both arts that it is Miss Garden's genius as an actress rather than as a singer which constitutes her the feminine colossus who doth bestride our operatic world. Be that as it may, there can be no doubt that her impersonations of Maeterlinck's shadowy Mélisande and Wilde's monstrous Salome indicate the possession of an amazingly comprehensive power to act.

"Of course as the 'curieuse et sensuelle' lady of Wilde's creation with its brutal, voluptuous, sensational perversions and abnormalities the opportunity for effective unrestraint is limitless. The sheer sensationalism of temperament unleashed is enough to make the Salome performance easily the more notable popularly.

"But it is as the elusive Mélisande that Miss Garden's instinct, intuition, or genius is most impressively denoted. There she is, to the eye at least, the fragile marionette of Maeterlinck's idea—a will-less creature, moving through a drear dream, expressing absolutely the Fleming's sense of the mystery and pathos of man's 'little life in the midst of the immensities'—the puppet of nature and destiny. Even those who regard 'Pelléas et Mélisande' as a morbid and stygian pollution of the drama may see in Miss Garden's acting this difficult detachment—peculiarily difficult for a young woman so splendidly flesh and blood.

"Wilde dreamt his Salome to be like Titian's painting. 'Her lips disclose the boundless cruelty of her heart,' he wrote; 'her splendor is an abyss, her desire an ocean; the pearls on her breast die of love; the bloom of her maidenhood pales the opals and fires the rubies, while even the sapphires on her fevered skin lose the purity of their luster.'

"Like Huysmans, he imagined her 'strewn with jewels, all ringing and tinkling in her hair, and her ankles, her wrists, her throat, inclosing her hips, and with their myriad glitter heightening the unchastity of her unchaste amber flesh.'

"With this authoritative prospectus Miss Garden seems privileged to indulge in much burning detail, and so she does. The velvet seductiveness in her wooing of Jokanaan; the pantomime of her scorpion fury as a 'woman scorned'; the venomous, insistent cruelty of the reiteration 'Give me the head of Jokanaan,' are incredibly real. At the cistern the impatient rage of the cry, 'Well, I tell thee there are not dead men enough!' freezes with its dire import. She is a fabulous she-thing playing with love and death—loathsome, mysterious, poisonous, slaking her slimy passion in the blood of her victim.

"A large order for a timid artiste, but timorousness is not among Miss Garden's characteristics. From the moment she beholds the 'ivory prophet,' gazing on him with hot and hungry stare, on through the passion maddened scenes to the hideous finish, where, huddled over the head, she dies, Miss Garden makes no polite concessions. She is Salome according to the Wilde formulary— a monstrous oracle of bestiality. Even when Dalmores indulges in his realistic frenzies of drunken hysteria as Herod, and Salome stretches like a sphynx, silent and immobile upon a couch, it is still Salome who rivets the eye and mind. But it is simply a florid, excessive, unhampered *tour de force,* lawless and inhuman. Any extravagance almost harmonizes with the scarlet picture. As an exhibition it outshines Miss Garden's Mélisande, but as acting there is no comparison."

But no account of what Miss Garden did in "Salome" can so much as faintly mirror what "Salome" did to Chicago. The first thing any one knew, we were all mixed up in a rather comic tempest over its morality. Some one had written a protest in advance of the performance to Arthur Burrage Farwell, president of the Chicago Law and Order League; he had forwarded the protest to the then chief of police, Leroy T. Steward, and Col. Steward attended the first performance. His comments on it upset the kettle. As quoted in the newspapers, they were:

"It was disgusting. Miss Garden wallowed around like a cat in a bed of catnip. There was no art in her dance that I could see. If the same show were produced on Halsted street the people would call it cheap, but over at the Auditorium they say it's art. Black art, if art at all. I would not call it immoral. I would say it is disgusting."

For once, Miss Garden was reduced to speechlessness. The reference to a cat and a bed of catnip was a little too much for her, and who can blame her? A few days later she announced that Mr. Steward and she did not speak the same language nor think the same thoughts—happily. She added: "I always bow down to the ignorant and try to make them understand, but I ignore the illiterate."

After all, this did not seem to be in Miss Garden's most pointed style, but the rest of Chicago and a good part of the middle west took it up and plunged into the fray, whether they had attended and formed opinions or not. Chicago theaters were having a periodic cleansing at that time anyway. A play called "The Nigger" at McVicker's Theater fell under the ban for handling an unpleasant subject in an unpleasant way, and a minor vaudeville performer was notified to blue-pencil some of his lines. So "Salome" fell into the same sort of trouble.

A second performance was given a few nights later, wherein the ticket scalpers cleaned up quite a harvest, and a third was announced. By this time, however, the storm was rising high. Scores of people had been interviewed and had expressed themselves for or against, an evangelist took a couple of shots at it during a revival meeting, and even Pat Crowe, the central figure in the

MARY GARDEN AS FIORA IN "THE LOVE OF THREE KINGS"

Cudahy kidnapping case of a few years before, and at that time a mission speaker himself, had his say.

Mr. Farwell announced: "Mary Garden as Salome is a great degenerator of public morals.

"Performances like that of 'Salome' should be classed as vicious and suppressed along with houses in the red light district.

"I wish Miss Garden would come to see me; I should like to reform her.

"I am a normal man, but I would not trust myself to see a performance of 'Salome.'

"Arthur Burrage Farwell,
"President Chicago Law and Order League."

Miss Garden responded: "Any one whose morals could have been corrupted by seeing 'Salome' must already have degenerated.

"Performances of 'Salome' should be inspiring to the right-minded and objection to them shows ignorance and narrow-mindedness.

"I should like to meet Mr. Farwell to see what he is like, but I do not think he could do me any good.

"Mr. Farwell evidently hasn't much strength of character if he would not trust himself to see 'Salome.'

"Mary Garden,
"Portrayer of Salome in Grand Opera."

Then it was suggested that Miss Garden "tone down" her Dance of the Seven Veils, which she strenuously refused to do. Finally the directors ordered the third performance withdrawn, and "Salome" went into the silence, to be heard no more until Miss Garden became general manager of the company. Mr. Dippel stated that owing to objections, the management thought it best to withdraw the piece. Miss Garden renewed her protest, and said that Chief Steward had a "low mind." Col. Steward announced that the piece was "vulgar and repulsive, not fit for a respectable public to witness." Mr. Dalmores was "shocked" at the withdrawal. Mme. de Cisneros said that the chief of police had made Chicago a place of ridicule of the civilized world. At last Oscar Hammerstein in a telegraphed interview from New York said:

"If they'd put some flannel petticoats and things on Miss Garden, that might help tone things, too. Mary really ought to be petticoated, I think, considering Chicago's climate. You know, when she worked for me, she had a deadly fear when singing 'Salome' of getting cold feet."

In the meantime Milwaukee and St. Louis were feeling their own vibrations. The Chicago company had been invited to go to both places and present the work. There were religious objections, aldermanic obstacles, and continued invitations on the part of the citizenry. Finally the company went, presented the opera—and was never invited to repeat it.

But it was a wonderful and joyous row while it lasted.

CHAPTER IV

"Salome" was finally removed, the official statement being to the effect that it was not because of prejudice nor of crusade, but because there had been a falling off in the demand for seats. This was as diplomatic a way out as any. Of course there have been other operas for which no particular public demand was manifested which were not taken off on that account, though a failure to buy tickets always and rightly weighs heavily with operatic managements, no matter what the artistic element may believe.

The best advertised performance of the season was thus out of the way, but several other items showed themselves well above the surface. Geraldine Farrar came on from the Metropolitan to do Cho-Cho-San in "Madame Butterfly," likewise Antonio Scotti to do Sharpless, both to the high delight of the beholders. She was a heavenly artist in the part in those days. Mr. Scotti is still performing the part of the consul, and doing it just about as well as he did then. He used to set the pace for the whole Sharpless tribe, also the Scarpia of "Tosca," until Georges Baklanoff came along and fixed his own standard.

Johanna Gadski, another guest, came to do Aïda in the opera of the same name, a performance mainly notable at this distance because Nicola Zerola, the tenor of the performance, donned mustache and goatee in plausible imitation of Chief Steward as part of his makeup for the part of Radames.

Baklanoff, by the way, had been anticipated as one of the guests from Boston. He had been one of the most interesting members of the Boston Opera Company when it made its first and last visit to the Auditorium the January before. But about this time he got into a row with Henry Russell, the manager of the company, and was discharged. According to newspaper accounts, the best evidence available at this time, he had been cast for Iago in "Otello" for the Boston performances, but about this time Mario Sammarco did a little guesting from Chicago to Boston, and was promptly billed for the part. Baklanoff went on strike as regards his own rôle in "La Habanera," and Russell wired to Dippel that Baklanoff had been discharged "owing to outrageous breach of discipline."

He was therefore an absentee, but Lydia Lipkowska and Florencio Constantino came on from the Boston company to appear together in "Lucia di Lammermoor." Miss Lipkowska was a coloratura soprano of much skill, and, like many another Russian singer, had some definite ideas about how to inject acting values into even the most venerable operas. Mr. Constantino, since deceased, was a good bit of a tenor personality in his time, immensely proud of his own muscular development, and rejoicing in his ability to sing many kinds of parts, dramatic or lyric. He used to do them well, too.

Nellie Melba paused in Chicago long enough to sing Mimi in "La Bohême" with a purity and certainty that sounded miraculous. Her contribution to the press agentry literature of the year was a story to the effect that she bore with her some $500,000 in jewels in a handbag, and that the chief detective of the Congress Hotel nearly developed a nervous breakdown before she was safely on her way again. The newspapers used to print such things.

Miss Garden came to bat again with the first performance in Chicago of Massenet's "Thaïs." The critics found that the "Meditation" was an instance of high musical inspiration and wagged wise heads over the fact that thrills were strangely lacking in Miss Garden's performance. However, it promptly became one of her best sellers, operatically considered, and remained so for a period of years even up to now. Meanwhile there began to be word of the coming novelty, "The Girl of the Golden West." This was one of the most interesting experiments ever tried by the Chicago Opera Company in all its history, mainly as demonstrating that with the best intentions in the world the manufacturers of grand opera are sometimes quite unable to foretell public taste.

For several years Puccini had been casting about for the right kind of a libretto, knowing well that the Puccini vogue was dependent partially upon the unfailing Puccini flow of suave, juicy, singable melody, but also upon the selection of an unfailingly popular drama as libretto. Witness, for instance, "La Bohême," "Madame Butterfly," and "Tosca." He had read and rejected a number of plays. Finally in "The Girl" he and his advisers thought they had hit on the right answer.

Here was a play that had gone under the hands of David Belasco to a big American hit, with a reasonably romantic story and packed full of supposedly accurate, at any rate theatrically effective, western color. Where-

fore Puccini set himself to composing a score, and as
soon as it was off the presses all plans were made for an
almost simultaneous opening in New York and Chicago.
Puccini himself came to New York to oversee the rehearsals; Tito Ricordi, head of the Milan music publishing firm, came to function similarly in Chicago. Weeks
of rehearsals went on, mostly behind closed doors.

Miss Garden had been mentioned as the Girl and
had declined the part, alleging her unfamiliarity with
the Italian language, and meanwhile, with a grouch still
smoldering over the fate of "Salome," had told how she
would never sing in Chicago again, but would go to
Paris and then to Russia—but she didn't. The New York
Evening World quoted her as saying: "Don't forget that
I love America and Americans. They made me what I
am, and while I have criticized Chicago, I have not
criticized all Chicago people, and Chicago is not all of
America by a damned sight." Then she made up for
it by telling a Chicago reporter that Carolina White
was the finest possible selection for the Girl, that she
was a singer of remarkably fine voice and a woman of
unusual beauty, that as the Girl she would be a perfect
success and that the rôle would carry her to fame at a
bound. At that, it came near to working out just about
that way.

Meanwhile the plot was being printed here, leading
musical themes there, Mr. Ricordi was announcing to a
waiting world that Miss White was a wonder, Miss
White was responding in terms of what a later slang
would have translated into "so is your most recent novelty," explaining that it was truly American, full of the

breath of life, and a relief from old style conventions. Finally it came to performance.

THE GIRL OF THE GOLDEN WEST

Libretto by G. Zangarini and C. Civinini on play by David Belasco; music by Giacomo Puccini. Produced at the Auditorium, Dec. 27, 1910, by the Chicago Grand Opera Company with this cast:

MINNIE	Carolina White
DICK JOHNSON	Amadeo Bassi
JACK RANCE	Maurice Renaud
NICK	Francesco Daddi
ASHBY	Nazzareno de Angelis
SONORA, Miner	Hector Dufranne
TRIN, Miner	Edmond Warnery
SID, Miner	Nicola Fossetta
BELLO, Miner	Michele Sampieri
HARRY, Miner	Dante Zucchi
JOE, Miner	Emilio Venturini
HAPPY, Miner	Berardo Berardi
LARKENS, Miner	Pompilio Malatesta
BILLY	Gustave Huberdeau
WOWKLE	Clotilde Bressler-Gianoli
JAKE WALACE	Armand Crabbé
JOSÉ CASTRO	Constantin Nicolay
THE PONY EXPRESS RIDER	Desiré Defrere

Once again pages of reviews and general jubilations, but unfortunately just a trifle artificial. For somehow or other "La Fanciulla del Ouest" did not deliver all that was expected of it. It is easy to look back now and see that continuous dialogue was too much of a handicap for Puccini's golden melody, and that this was its greatest fault. But the play did not translate operatically. One hears that it was popular for a long time in Italy, where it was regarded as a faithful transcript of early American life, but in America the opera patrons began to laugh at it, and worse, stay away from it. They were amused at the operatic miners who wore pistols on the wrong side of their belts. They derided the idea of a bartender pouring out drinks for his customers and being permitted to escape with his life. They rejoiced at the "Allo" and "Eep, eep, urra," with which the piece was plentifully punctuated, and when it came to the beautiful and stately Miss White pulling four aces out from her garter in the poker game with the sheriff, their emotions were too deep for tears.

In other words, illusion came off second best, and while grand opera is one's notion of no place to expect illusion, at the same time one might have been let down a bit more easily. The famous poker game, by the way, was being burlesqued about that time by the Weber and Fields company of experts as a game of checkers played with lumps of coal for the black pieces and soda crackers for the whites, and Minnie used to win the game by diverting the sheriff's attention and then eating the crackers.

Of all the participants, Mr. Renaud and Miss White came out by far the best. Once more it seems advisable to quote from Mr. Hammond's account of the performance rather than from the musical critics.

"Mr. Renaud's impersonation of the sheriff," he said, "is an accurate transcript of that of Mr. Keenan, the creator of the rôle, showing the sinister exterior and the burning passions underneath most vividly. He is less austere and his dress less effective than the original, but for grand opera he is a marvel of realism, save when intercepted by a song.

"Miss White is pictorially more than enough as the Girl, and, besides, she projects the crude, honest nature of the character if she does not altogether realize it. She seems to lack the personal spark which turns interest into fascination, the magnetism which transforms faults into virtues. But she sings, which is more than Miss Blanche Bates did, and one may not expect everything, even from a prima donna. Mr. Bassi's road agent is ingénue, a tenor bandit who would be more at ease in purple tights and a plumed hat. Some way or other a top note does not sound well when emanating from a supposedly desperate person in leather pants and a flannel shirt. And in the last act they do a most cruel thing to him. They tie his hands and ask him to sing."

One pauses here for a reflection on the refining influence of opera as shown in an item from the St. Louis *Globe-Democrat*. During these ten weeks the company used to make trips on off nights to Milwaukee and St. Louis, and under the date of Jan. 4, 1911, the *Globe-Democrat* proudly points this out: "During the two nights of grand opera, police and detectives have not made a single arrest, nor has there been an arrest for violating the traffic law."

The season was nearly at an end. It gave a final flash when Caruso came from New York to give two performances, one as Canio in "Pagliacci," the other as Dick Johnson in "The Girl." Both were worthy of the occasion. Caruso always was the Canio of Canios, and as the Italo-American bandit he had had the personal instruction of Belasco for the New York production of the Puccini piece. It was rather astonishing to see the difference he made in it. No one had ever accused Caruso of being an actor in any way comparable with his golden voice. It was as a singer that he had melted hearts. But Belasco had taught him how to walk through the part with some degree of credibility, to touch some of the high spots if not all of the subtleties, above all, to avoid as many as possible of the operatic absurdities. Wherefore, although Renaud had left the company and gone back to Boston, leaving the Sheriff's part to Sammarco, who by the way was only a brief interval behind him in ability, the Caruso performance of "The Girl of the Golden West" stands out in memory as being considerably better than the first one.

Unfortunately it was the last time that Caruso ever appeared at the Auditorium. At the close of the season in Chicago, the company moved on to Philadelphia, where for a period of weeks it was to be known as the Philadelphia-Chicago Grand Opera Company, and where incidentally it got unmercifully roasted. The trip east was broken by a pause at Cleveland, where Caruso sang another "Pagliacci." But there or on his way back to New York he caught a violent cold which removed him from active operatic circulation for some little time. From that time on an edict admitting of no change went forth from the Metropolitan forbidding Caruso to do any further gadding to other opera companies. It was not till toward the end of his life that he came again, and this time only in song recitals, immensely profitable to him, apparently equally pleasing to his audiences, but at the same time not opera.

During this first season of Chicago's own grand

opera, its patrons had witnessed sixty-three regular performances, one gala performance, eight orchestral concerts on Sundays with Campanini conducting and one Sunday song recital. Twenty-one different operas were presented. "Thaïs" was given six times; "Aïda," "The Girl of the Golden West" and "I Pagliacci" five times; "La Tosca," "Rigoletto," "Pelléas et Mélisande," "Louise," "Cavalleria Rusticana" and "The Tales of Hoffmann" four times; "La Bohême," "Carmen," "Faust," "Madame Butterfly" and "Il Trovatore" three times; "La Traviata" and "Salome" twice and "Lucia di Lammermoor," "Masked Ball," "Otello" and "Les Huguenots" once. Two special ballet performances also were given.

During the Philadelphia season, the company gave ten Friday night performances in Baltimore and ten Tuesday night performances and one special Saturday performance in New York City. Two performances were given in Milwaukee during the Chicago season and St. Louis had the company for five performances, three evenings and two matinées.

CHAPTER V

Ten weeks is hardly enough of a season for which to organize a company of such dimensions as the Chicago Opera, but ten weeks was all that in the consideration of the promoters Chicago could absorb. More time and other communities became necessary, which was why Philadelphia was picked out. There were some interesting bits of history during the few seasons that Philadelphia was included as an integral part of the company's operations, but it seems desirable to confine this account chiefly to what was done at the Auditorium with only passing mention of what went on elsewhere.

At the end of the 1910-11 season there are indications in the newspapers that Philadelphia was maintaining an attitude of considerable indifference to the opera company, even though its own name was appended to the company's title, and that it was likewise displaying some unwillingness to assuming its share of the financial burden. These difficulties were gradually straightened out, it was finally settled that for the second year Philadelphia's season was to be split, a few weeks before and a few weeks after the ten weeks in Chicago, and meanwhile Chicago began to prepare for its own second season.

With all the good will in the world, there was some glamour about the first season of the company that was difficult to preserve on a permanent basis. Possibly this was sensed in operatic quarters, for one begins to note increased activity among the press agents, official and private. Arguments began to creep into print as to why hitherto unknown singers from small middle west communities should not be received with the same acclaim as artists with established reputations in Europe and America.

This was a fairly harmless occupation, performing the several functions of filling space in the newspapers, keeping the name of the Chicago company before the public, and pleasing the ones whose future performances were to be so greeted—perhaps. More interesting is the fact that the shops and department stores began to display operatic consciousness. Women's opera, party, or theater costumes began to be advertised, also imported wraps, theater bonnets, and the like, and one slightly naïve advertisement explained how many men utilize a "Full Dress Suit," capitals and all, only on rare occasions, wherefore this particular establishment was prepared to furnish in large black type men's full dress suits of high quality for $35, and in considerably smaller type other dress suits. at prices upward to $100.

Finally on Nov. 22, 1911, the Auditorium curtains pulled aside for the first performance of the second season. It was Saint-Saëns' "Samson and Delilah." The cast:

DELILAH ....Jeanne Gerville-Reache
SAMSON ....Charles Dalmores
THE HIGH PRIEST......Hector Dufranne
ABIMELECH ....Armand Crabbé
AN OLD HEBREW.......Gustave Huberdeau
A PHILISTINE MESSEN-
    GER ....Emilio Venturini

FIRST PHILISTINE ......Joseph Demortier
SECOND PHILISTINE .....Desiré Defrere
PREMIÈRE DANSEUSE
    ETOILE ....Rosina Galli

General Musical Director.Cleofonte Campanini

Here were two newcomers, Mme. Gerville-Reache, since deceased, but a beautiful contralto in her day, and Signorina Galli, who began to give point and brilliancy to the ballet section of the company. Miss Galli remained with the company two years and then went to the Metropolitan in New York, being greeted on her arrival there by an enraptured but unenlightened reporter who filled a full column with her "first impressions of America," probably considered good journalism in New York at that time. She has been there ever since, an excellent dancer trained to the most exacting perfection in the school of the Italian ballet.

But superb contralto, brilliant danseuse, well trained company, and Campanini at the baton were not enough to save the performance. It probably holds a record for being the dullest opening night in the history of the company. This was the first time that "Samson and Delilah" had been put on in operatic form in Chicago. Up to that time it had been sung only as an oratorio, and hopes were freely expressed that after that night it would go back permanently to the oratorio organizations. It did not, however.

At the best it is slow moving, dignified, and quite lacking in the alert sparkle that one expects in an opening performance. The lavish spectacle and ballet of the third act came so late that the eagerness of the audience had been blunted on long, beautiful, but unexciting and motionless musical numbers, and even so fine a singer as Mme. Gerville-Reache could not smother a feeling that occasionally, just once in awhile, a few notes from a brilliant soprano voice would by its contrast brighten things up considerably. The greatest bit of joy in the proceedings was contained in the libretto, which gravely informed the world that in the first scene of the third act "Samson is discovered working like a horse."

But Mme. Gerville-Reache had a rather more exciting time the next night. Miss Garden had been announced to appear in the name part of "Carmen," her first appearance in the part here. About that time, however, she got into a private altercation with an ulcerated tooth, and woke up that morning with a face swollen much too asymmetrically for scenic illusion. Wherefore Mme. Gerville-Reache was besought to step into the breach, and did so, tired from the night before, in borrowed costumes, but saving the day, or night, and thereby making her record two opening nights instead of one.

About this time, too, the first effort to promote a scalpers' scandal took place. Bernhard Ulrich was supposed to have "confessed," according to one of the papers, that he sold some 1,650 tickets at a price of $8,250 to certain hotel lobby theater agents, and all the papers made gestures of striking nobility over the affair. Upon investigation it came out that while the number had been in the neighborhood of 1,650 and the price as stated, they were divided into groups of thirty-one for each of the fifty-two nights, at full box office prices and under terms which forbade the return of unsold tickets. This struck the general public as being about zero in confessions, and the "scandal" promptly collapsed of its own absurdity.

This out of the way, there was a chance to consider some of the new members of the company. Mme. Gerville-Reache's double service had given her enough prominence for a good many people to learn how to spell her name and a few to pronounce it. Before the season it had been printed variously as Garville-Reache, Gerville-Raeche, and Gorville-Roache, and the variants of pronunciation had been even more extraordinary. Then came Maggie Teyte.

She was a mite of a soprano about twenty years old, with a voice about four times as large as she was. Her press notices said that she was Irish, but she talked with a pronounced cockney twang. However, she could sing. Her first appearance was as Cherubino in Mozart's "Marriage of Figaro," with Miss White as the countess, Alice Zeppilli as Susanna, Louise Berat as Marcellina, Gustave Huberdeau as Figaro, Mario Sammarco as the count, and, as ever, Campanini at the baton. The elements were a little racially diverse for a well blended performance, but it made a good bit of a success, with special honors to the tiny Cherubino.

And then came Luisa Tetrazzini. Sister-in-law of Campanini—Mme. Campanini as Eva Tetrazzini was a famous soprano in her own right before she retired— she came and laid every one low. With the most disdainful ease she made the art of coloratura to glow as it has never glowed since. Physical illusion was not in her line at all; she was the size of three or four Maggie Teytes. But what a voice!

Even after all these years one can recall the warm

Photo by Dupont

Luisa Tetrazzini

Photo by Foley

Emma Eames

Photo by Dupont

Emil Fischer

Photo by Dupont

Geraldine Farrar

reediness of its qualities, the joyous certainty with which it swooped into all the cascades and fireworks of coloratura display, the piercing intensity which somehow or other never became shrill. She was the complete embodiment of the ideals of a former generation which demanded perfect singing and little else in opera, and there can be little doubt that if she had lasted, her coloratura would have been an earnest competitor to Miss Garden's singing-acting.

She sang five rôles in two weeks, "Lucia di Lammermoor," "Traviata," "Rigoletto," "The Barber of Seville," and "Lakmé," with an extra "Lucia" for good luck, and went on her way, leaving the coloratura schedule for the rest of the season to be finished by Jenny Dufau, an arrangement that came near ending before it started.

For Miss Dufau was not much bigger than Miss Teyte, and she had come to Chicago under a contract whereby the opera company was to provide her costumes, or most of them. Being economical in small matters, the company undertook to reconstruct some of the Tetrazzini costumes, with results that at times verged on the tragic.

The first night that she was to appear as Lakmé, the curtain was held for a considerable time. A representative from the front office going back to investigate found Miss Dufau in tears. They were wrapping the Tetrazzini girdle twice around her waist instead of once, and even then it was falling off over her hips. After spending much time and using dozens of safety pins, the performance finally got started, but it was noticed that

for some time Miss Dufau was measurably and pardon-
ably preoccupied.

Massenet's "Cendrillon" was one of the novelties
of that season, a dainty, highly artificial, and more highly
effective setting of the Cinderella story. It was well liked
for some time, with Miss Teyte as Cendrillon, Miss
Garden as the prince, Miss Dufau as the fairy, and some
amusing comedy scenes by Louise Berat, Hector Dufranne, and Francesco Daddi.

It was uncommonly pleasant while it lasted, though
they never quite learned the trick back stage of handling
the lights in the transformation scenes. Finally it went
out of the repertoire, to the regret of a good many
patrons, the scenery was broken up or redistributed, and
in recent years the first act scene of "Traviata" has been
the ex-ballroom scene presided over by the prince in
"Cendrillon." But to this day there is in the Fine Arts
Building a large painting of Miss Teyte at the ball.

Miss Garden appeared in other new rôles about this
time, among them another boy's part, Jean, in Massenet's
"Le Jongleur de Nôtre Dame," and as Carmen in the
Bizet opera of the same name. Massenet never did anything as lovely as the score of "Le Jongleur," and Miss
Garden's performance of the ragamuffin young juggler
was as wistful and plaintive and moving as the music.
Unfortunately the public never regarded this performance with as much favor as it did some of her more
spectacular rôles, so it was not given as often as it deserved. Her Carmen, however, became a permanency of
the repertoire.

"Le Jongleur de Nôtre Dame" is a short opera,
and in order to fill out the evening it used to be coupled

with the first Wolf-Ferrari opera to be played in Chicago, "The Secret of Suzanne." This was a merry, tuneful little farce, involving nothing more serious than the efforts of a bride to keep her cigarette habit from the knowledge of her husband, Miss White and Mr. Sammarco being the married pair, and Mr. Daddi the butler of unfailingly comic pantomime. It seems an uncommonly harmless piece, but it, too, had its effect on the social order of the day.

Miss Lucy Page Gaston, founder and president of the Anti-Cigarette League of America, came to the Auditorium to find out what it was all about, and apparently found out plenty. After the third cigarette of the piece, she arose and stepped—forever, she said—out of the defiled atmosphere of the Auditorium. The *Tribune* quoted her:

" 'Horrible!' she exlcaimed, when she had recovered speech. 'Perfectly horrible. One after another! I saw her with my own eyes.' No one disputing the fact, Miss Gaston continued more calmly:

" 'It is enough to turn one forever against grand opera. An artful embellishment of a pernicious vice which should receive the stamp'—Miss Gaston stamped—'of disapproval from every true American woman. Miss White in this attitude is a menace to the entire community. The only possible excuse is that Miss White indulges in the habit only on the stage!'

"Miss Gaston was assured that such was not the case.

" 'Well, then,' she said, 'that settles it. The box-holders and patrons of the Chicago Grand Opera Company ought to stay away from the theatre until this vicious and immoral play is discontinued.' "

But Miss White said that she could not see any harm in the opera or the practice, and the *Tribune* followed its news story with an editorial advising in mocking language the creation of an opera wherein the lady's indiscretions should center around a samovar. Meanwhile operatic babies arrived to the wives of two officials, Mrs. Bernhard Ulrich, in whose case the stork flew sixty miles an hour and overtook her on a New York train, and Mrs. Alfred Szendrei, the wife of one of the conductors. Miss Garden announced that she was much too busy to think of getting married, so with one consideration and another the operatic cigarette crusade made only a brief appearance in the news columns of the newspapers. Likewise there were some other important operatic performances to be considered.

CHAPTER VI

NATOMA (*In English*)

Grand opera in three acts by Victor Herbert. Presented by the Chicago Grand Opera Company at the Auditorium, Chicago, Dec. 13, 1911.

THE CAST

NATOMA .... Mary Garden
BARBARA .... Carolina White
LIEUT. PAUL MERRILL...... George Hamlin
DON FRANCISCO .... Henri Scott
JUAN BAUTISTA ALVARADO... Mario Sammarco
FATHER PERALTA .... Hector Dufranne
PICO .... Armand Crabbé
KAGAMA .... Constantin Nicolay
JOSÉ CASTRO .... Frank Preisch
CHIQUITA .... Rosina Galli
A VOICE .... Minnie Egener
SERGEANT .... Desiré Defrere

General Musical Director.... Cleofonte Campanini

The oldest inhabitant would have had trouble in remembering any more stirring scene than took place on this occasion. Here at last was American opera, so we hoped, the first flowering of what was to grow into a mighty lyric garden. Of course it was American opera. Joseph Redding, the librettist; Victor Herbert, the composer, if Irish by birth, had been an adopted American

95

for years before, had become and continued to be a power in the light opera field; the story was American, telling about early days in Santa Barbara, even if that was a period and locale of American life that few of us knew anything about. And was there not an American naval lieutenant as the leading tenor character, and cowboys— Spanish brand—and Indians, one of them, the halfbreed, Castro, heap bad medicine? Why not get out and cheer?

We all did. Records and memories tell how every one connected with the matter was called and called again before the curtain, how Miss Garden made a ringer with a wreath of laurel over the head of Mr. Herbert, how she tried to make another on Mr. Campanini which he lithely evaded, how she tossed a rose into the prompter's box, and how the audience, taking a great liking to the Herbert melodies, asked for and received repetitions of no less than four musical numbers. For those were the old, inartistic days, when the fact of an enthusiastic audience demanding an encore was considered sufficient reason to give it one. Since then ideals of art have been changed. It is now believed that the atmosphere of an opera like, let us say, "Il Trovatore," is so tenuous and evanescent as to be completely ruined by permitting a number to be repeated. No orders, however, have ever been issued against permitting an artist to step out of his part down to the footlights and bow and show his teeth as long as a single pair of palms continues to come into patting contact, that is, not until Mr. Vladimir Rosing conceived the idea that some operas might have a continuous dramatic action and should be presented by the American Opera Company with that idea in mind.

"Natoma" had been staged the year before in Philadelphia, with John McCormack in the part done by George Hamlin here, but by this time he was beginning to step out into his concert career, and Mr. Hamlin, who had been a concert artist of renown in Chicago and elsewhere, commenced his operatic career. Both were good arguments on the possibility of making the English language an understandable and beautiful singing language, for both knew about all that there was to know about singing English. For the practical usability of English was one of the important considerations in "Natoma." The only previous attempt that the company had made was a translated version of "Hansel and Gretel," and as an argument for the use of the vernacular it was distinctly not a success in spite of Miss Teyte's immortal spoken line, "O see those little children dear; I wonder where they all came from."

As a matter of fact "Natoma" was older than the date of its first performance. Herbert had written it several years before at the invitation of Hammerstein, when that impresario was still a power in New York. He told me once that he had had an entirely different cast in mind at the time of its composition, that if, for instance, he had known in advance that Miss Garden was to have had the leading part, he would have constructed her music in quite another manner.

However, here it was, and there it went. The enthusiasm of the first night's audience was shared by other audiences, and in Chicago and on the road it received at one time and another no less than thirty performances. Mr. Herbert himself conducted the thirtieth and last at the Auditorium. By that time Alice Zeppilli had succeeded to Miss Garden's part in the work.

There would seem to be a certain resemblance between the careers of Herbert in America and Arthur Sullivan in England. Both were enormously talented in the art of writing music for light operas, both were ambitious to write grand operas, and both were disappointed at the final results. In Herbert's case, both in "Natoma" and in a later attempt, the trouble lay largely with the libretto. The story of "Natoma" was melodramatic in tone and scrappy in treatment, and only slightly related to American life. The lyrics were nothing much to fire the imagination of a less fluent composer than Herbert, but he was able to spurt melody at the slightest excuse. We used to think that if he were put to it, he could compose a perfectly singable tune to any given column in the telephone directory. At any rate, one of the best songs in "Natoma," Alvarado's serenade, was a sprightly and lilting setting of this:

> Oh, my lady love; oh, my lady love,
> Leave me not in the dusk to repine,
> Oh, my lady love; oh, my lady love,
> Bid me to sing to thy beauty divine.

A couple of illustrative though minor side lights on operatic life were discovered by the newspapers. A certain married woman, whose name at this point is of no importance, was discovered to be working in the chorus under the name of "Miss Brooks." She told all the reporters within hearing distance that she was tired of being "more or less of a bird in more or less of a gilded cage." Then she enlarged upon the theme.

"I am ambitious," she said. "I have something to live for. I am no longer a 'loyal wife' (Oh, how I hate that word), or a model housekeeper (that phrase drives me crazy), or—a stunning dresser.

"I am ambitious and self-centered. I am ambitious and have developed a sublime faith in my genius. Pretty soon I shall acquire temperament. Then I'll get a job as a prima donna. I can sing—listen."

It seems rather too bad to be forced to record the fact that after so many perpendicular pronouns and such a candid statement of the prima donna's credo, "Miss Brooks" was never heard of again.

One also began to discover what grand opera cost in those days. More was learned about it a couple of years later, but local managers of the present may look with envy upon a receipt dated Milwaukee, Dec. 8, 1911.

Received from Mrs. Clara Bowen Shepherd Sixty-eight Hundred Dollars ($6800.00) being the Guarantee for the Performance of Samson and Delilah given at the above Theatre and Date by the Chicago Grand Opera Company.

MAX I. HIRSCH.

The next attempt to capture public attention through the medium of novelty was "Quo Vadis." This, also, had been shown to Philadelphia the season before, and, if any one is now interested, the date of the first performance at the Auditorium was Dec. 19, 1911.

"Quo Vadis" had been made into an opera libretto by Henri Cain out of Sienkiewicz's novel of the same name, a best seller in its day, and set to music by Jean Nougues. Does anybody remember the performance? Recollections are somewhat vague. There had been every intention of constructing a spectacle that would put "Aïda" into the permanent shade. It was to contain the burning of Rome by Nero; a gladiatorial combat; Ursus was to strangle Croton and throw his body into the Tiber which was to receive him with a splash of real water; other signs of real genius like these. It needed a cast of ten principals, fifteen lesser principals, and all the chorus and ballet and supernumeraries that could be crowded on to the Auditorium stage.

But one remembers chiefly some greatly noisy and greatly unimportant music that ran for hours and hours and hours—one of the newspapers records that the final curtain fell at 12:10 in the morning—and a conflagration scene at which you might possibly have warmed your hands, but which certainly did not look convincing enough for the destruction of the first city of the world. These, and the scene where Nero ordered Chilo's tongue to be torn out. It consisted of a gentle huddle on the stage, nowhere nearly as active as any first down in any football game, following which Mr. Dufranne as Chilo turned around and faced the audience with a smear of red paint dripping down the length of his whiskers.

Looking back over the by-products of the season, one's eyes are gladdened by the first defiance of the claque—it was by Jane Osborn-Hannah—and the first official denial by the company that there was a claque, or if such a malign influence should have imposed upon managerial innocence, that it would be promptly driven out of town. This became a serial that endured for years.

Mrs. Osborn-Hannah appeared as Sieglinde in "Die Walküre" that season. It was a good cast, containing the names of Mr. Dalmores as Siegmund, Clarence Whitehill as Wotan, Mme. Ernestine Schumann-Heink in a guest appearance as Fricka, Minnie Saltzmann-Stevens as Brünnhilde, and Dr. Szendrei conducting. Concerning Mrs. Saltzmann-Stevens, the press agents had worked overtime. It was the Cinderella theme in real life, from a clerk in a Bloomington, Illinois, shop, through a refusal to be accepted as pupil by Jean de Reszke, to a leading part in the Chicago Opera, including—though this has always been a bit hard to believe—the possession of a vocal compass of four octaves. In spite of all this flurry of publicity, she succeeded rather well.

By now the decks were being cleared for the final novelty of the season, Ermanno Wolf-Ferrari's "The Jewels of the Madonna." Here Chicago was to have a real American première. It had been given a performance in Berlin, whereupon the composer caught the first boat to be present at the Chicago event, Jan. 12, 1912. He was present only as a spectator, but during his stay Chicagoans gave him dinners and suppers and made speeches at him in German and Italian until he was glad to escape with his life. Just before he left he conducted the Apollo Musical Club in the first performance of his cantata, "The New Life," which displayed a side of his talent not covered by either "The Jewels of the Madonna" or "The Secret of Suzanne."

"The Jewels" promptly made itself a permanent item in the repertoire. Its Italian folk tunes at once became popular, so did the composer's own personal melodies. It had color and action and speed, the first act with its vendors of macaroni, toy balloons, water, fruit, and flowers, its monks and peasants and camorristi and vagabonds, its second act with an ending so startling that Percy Hammond was moved to say that it added discomfort to blasphemy, its third act back to the noise and confusion and speed of the camorristi's tavern.

One hears that Italian audiences are accustomed to regard "The Jewels" somewhat scornfully, looking at it about as American audiences look at "The Girl of the Golden West," as something much too impossible to be taken seriously. If this is true, it evens up the score, for "The Jewels" went as strong in America as "The Girl" did in Italy. Audiences and critics alike outdid themselves in saying nice things about it. Learned essays were written on its music and its drama. I remember reading a pronouncement somewhere that it was "a slice of life," and this, one would think, was going some for any opera. At any rate Miss White made the hit of her life as Maliella, and Mr. Sammarco the hit of his as Rafaele, with scarcely less enthusiasm for Mr. Bassi's Gennaro, Mme. Berat's Carmela, and the thirty or forty lesser characters who put their picturesque bits into the action.

This was the last notable achievement of the season. On to Philadelphia again, with side trips to Baltimore, New York, and the like. Then a summer's rest, and the whole thing to do over again. Such is opera.

CHAPTER VII

We hardly realized it at the time, but the beginning of the 1912-13 season was a period of peace after protracted battle. Manager Dippel over a year before had come to the conclusion that too much was being charged by the publishing house that controlled the American rights of certain Italian operas, coupled with the fact that when he contracted for the use of certain operas which he wanted, he was obliged as part of the engagement to take over certain other unpopular ones that he did not want.

It is a system practiced in many branches of music, notably by concert managers lucky enough to have the services of an artist who scores as a box office attraction. A city wanting this box office attraction is obliged to take other artists unable to draw enough to pay the local expenses. In opera or concert, such a course of procedure is both expensive and exasperating, and it is one of the reasons why some managers just now are rubbing dazed eyes and wondering publicly what is the matter with the concert business.

So Mr. Dippel, in 1911, with the full approval of his board of directors took a short way out. He went on a single-handed but potent buyer's strike. If you will look back over the summary of the season just closed, you will see no mention of the Puccini operas, nor of "Aïda," nor of quite a few others currently supposed to have important places in every well regulated operatic season.

A buyer's strike when it means loss of both money and prestige usually has only one result. It was destined to be Dippel's stormiest year as will be told in its place, but this time he would seem to have dictated the terms of peace. At any rate the 1912-13 season began with the first performance in Chicago of the first opera in which Giacomo Puccini made himself talked about, in other words, "Manon Lescaut." It had this cast:

MANON LESCAUT .... Carolina White
LESCAUT .... Mario Sammarco
CHEVALIER DES GRIEUX... Giovanni Zenatello
GERONTE .... Vittorio Trevisan
EDMONDO .... Emilio Venturini
LANDLORD .... Frank Preisch
A MUSICIAN .... Ruby Heyl
BALLET MASTER .... Edmond Warnery
A LAMPLIGHTER .... Emilio Venturini
SERGEANT .... Nicola Fossetta
CAPTAIN .... Constantin Nicolay

General Musical Director... Cleofonte Campanini
Stage Director .... Fernand Almanz

In a good many ways "Manon Lescaut" has always been my favorite of the Puccini operas. It is by no means as fully developed as the later "La Bohême," "Madame Butterfly," or "Tosca," but listening to its pages closely, you hear the germ of all of them. In fact one might almost say that for the rest of his melodious career the principal part of his employment was to write amplifications and variants of "Manon Lescaut."

It was a good performance, but promptly put upon the shelf. Miss White added another part to her list of triumphs. Mr. Zenatello, though in a state of pristine innocence regarding acting or impersonation or anything else except singing, was the owner of a superb voice that threw out its high B flats and C's as though they were nothing at all. Down in a comparatively unimportant part was Vittorio Trevisan, a new member of the company, and not then known for the unbelievably amusing comic bass characters that later made him famous.

All this, however, was promptly overshadowed by the approach of an artist whose advance publicity made even Miss Garden look to her laurels. This was the "greatest of all baritones," Titta Ruffo. An unbridled imagination had worked for months preparing his advent. Ruffo, if you will believe what got into the papers, had come out of the ranks of the iron workers of Rome, had been turned down by his singing teacher for incompetence—how many dozens of singers like to have their patrons believe this—was the recipient of the largest fee on record ($2,000 a performance was admitted) and spent all his spare time between working ornamental iron candlesticks and reading Shakespeare. The last touch was a bit unfortunate, for Ruffo in the course of his Chicago season appeared in Ambroise Thomas' version of "Hamlet."

But what a sensation he was when he first appeared! Apparently he had been born with a highly efficient knowledge of the stage as applied to several Italian rôles, and his voice made his hearers weep tears of pure joy. Then and thereafter its most effective range was its upper octave, but that octave was almost enough to eclipse memories of Tetrazzini the season before. It had a B flat in it, and it could hold its own against any orchestral din that Campanini chose to invoke. In later years when

constant pounding had blunted the brilliancy of the great
trumpet tones, the case was different, but these were the
early and golden days.

So "Rigoletto" with Ruffo in it was suddenly converted from just another Italian opera into a shuddering
masterpiece of tragedy. Then there was that curious muti-
lation of Shakespeare's masterpiece which Thomas chose
to consider an opera, having cut out about half its plot
and all its psychology, and Ruffo in spite of a greatly
uneven performance as the prince of Denmark triumphed
again. Finally, and most sensational, the Tonio of
"Pagliacci."

No one else has ever done Tonio the same way.
Ruffo's Tonio was mournful, tragic, imbecilic, trembling
on the verge of epilepsy, a condition portrayed with
almost the accuracy of a clinic. But it was a whirlwind
of passion, and as far as the audience was concerned, it
was a riot. They said that ushers gathered up split white
gloves by the basketful after the performance was over.

Does any one now remember an opera called "The
Cricket on the Hearth"? It was given that season, Carl
Goldmark's music set to a version of the Dickens story,
with Miss Teyte in the leading part and the men's characters taken by Mr. Dufranne, Mr. Scott, and finally
Mr. Hamlin wearing one of the most extraordinary sets
of whiskers that ever diversified the human countenance.
It was sung in English, too. At one time and another
the Chicago Opera Company in its various phases has
given its audiences plenty of chance to pass on the subject of opera in English, and if the entire repertoire is
not now being sung in the native tongue, it is undoubtedly
because those who approve it have made a practice of

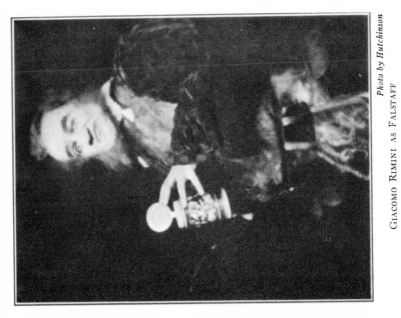

Photo by Hutchinson

GIACOMO RIMINI AS FALSTAFF

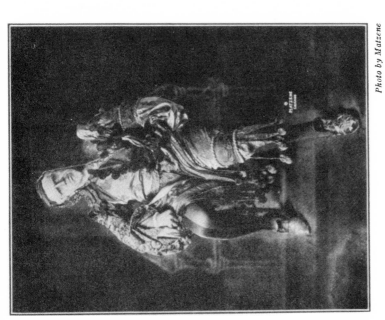

Photo by Matzene

TITTA RUFFO AS RIGOLETTO

buying fewer tickets than the letters they write on the subject. At any rate "The Cricket" was a pretty little work, though not of long life.

Meanwhile Miss Garden was pausing in Boston to play "Tosca" with Vanni-Marcoux in the opera company of that city, and, as usual, she was getting into the news columns. This time it was something to the effect that Mayor John F. Fitzgerald had threatened to revoke the license of the Boston Opera house unless the second act was toned down. When Miss Garden finally got to Chicago she denied it all, saying that Mayor Fitzgerald was a most pleasant person and that she had had a delightful interview with him, then adding that she was going to insist that Vanni-Marcoux come on to Chicago and play Scarpia to her Tosca. But that plan fell by the wayside, and she finally appeared with Sammarco, singing her part in French while the rest of the opera was in Italian. But as regards the Boston episode, "Some one," said an editorial in the *Tribune*, "is always running Miss Mary through a printing press, and she never seems to provoke the attention."

Massenet's "Hérodiade" came on about this time, a feeble piece, though Miss White, Mme. de Cisneros, and Mr. Dalmores were personally successful. Also Lillian Nordica came on the scene to sing Isolde to the Tristan of Mr. Dalmores and the Brangæne of Mme. Schumann-Heink, a performance which used to take her a full act and a half to warm up, but which from then on she sang like a soprano angel. Also Julia Claussen came over from Sweden and gave a great performance of Ortrud in "Lohengrin," and, a few nights later, a greater one as Brünnhilde in "Die Walküre." Add to these various events the further one that "Cendrillon" was revived, this time with Helen Stanley instead of Miss Garden in the travesty rôle, and wearing the costume of Prince Charming with such a manner as to incite one persistent but nonprofessional patron to the remark that nothing of the sort had been seen on the stage since Frankie Bailey was sixteen years old. Frankie Bailey, it may be added, used to be a chorus girl in the old Weber and Fields shows, of countrywide fame for her shapeliness.

About the middle of December, 1912, appears the news item that the company, 300 strong, would go to New York after the Chicago season, and that it would then entrain for a tour to the Pacific coast, to Dallas, Texas, then to Los Angeles, from there to San Diego and three weeks in San Francisco, and home by way of Portland, Seattle, Salt Lake, Denver, Kansas City, St. Louis, Omaha, and Minneapolis.

This tour subsequently became famous for several reasons. First, it was a big undertaking successfully carried through; second, that by virtue of guaranties previously underwritten, it paid its financial way; finally, that it was the time of a permanent breach between Campanini and Tetrazzini.

It was with Tetrazzini as one of the stars that the tour had been arranged, for she had some years before made her American début in San Francisco, and she was famous up and down the Pacific coast. It has been already noted herein that she and Mme. Campanini were sisters, but neither family nor artistic relationships nor the sum of the two kept her from an occasional clash with her brother-in-law. This was the final one.

The two had a row over some details of a performance one night during an intermission, and from all
accounts it became personal in tone, ending with a reported opinion from the madame that she was the star
and the artist and the box office attraction and that he
was merely the conductor. Campanini would seem to
have considered that he came off second best in the inter-
change, but he bided his time in vengeful patience. Finally
his chance came in Los Angeles, and he took it.

She was singing Gilda in "Rigoletto" and he was
conducting. She had reached "Caro nome," and had sky-
rocketed into the cadenza with which she ended the aria
when somehow or other she lost her place and her pitch,
ending on a note which was high enough but many degrees away from the true one. Campanini's quick ear
caught the mistake.

Now a kindhearted conductor, even Campanini, if
he had not had the previous row in his mind, would have
allowed her note to die away, and while applause was
raging, brought the orchestra in gently and softly, and
probably no one in the audience would have detected the
mistake. Instead, he sensed a devastating revenge. He
took a firm grip of the baton, signaled the orchestra, and
produced a crashing chord that jarred the roof and
showed every one in the opera house the discordant,
spine-chilling distance that she had removed herself from
the correct pitch.

This is what "merely a conductor" can do when
unamiable. The two never appeared in the same performance again, never spoke again, in fact Mme. Tetrazzini never sang in Chicago again until after Cam-

panini's death. And when she came to get out her autobiography, she made no mention of ever having sung
in Chicago, and of Campanini only the dry fact that he
had married her sister.

CHAPTER VIII

This, however, is a bit in advance of the chronology of the season. There were some novelties to be done, and some brewing temperamental rows at home. Of the first, there was "Noël," a brief and depressing piece from the pen of Baron Frederick d'Erlanger of France.

It had about as much advance publicity as any other novelty, including the item that Mrs. Minnie Saltzmann-Stevens, who took the principal part, had gone shopping for an eighty-nine cent nightgown so that she might die with full dramatic accuracy in the charity ward of a hospital during the last act. But when it came out on the night of Jan. 8, 1912, it was discovered to be a candy lyric tragedy of some poor but generally honest beings of southern France, a sort of Gallic "East Lynne." One newspaper made the none too enthusiastic comment that it was probably the best music ever written by a baron, and the others hardly reached even that pitch of excitement, so "Noël" speedily went into the lasting silence.

It was a better time for the news columns than the critical corner, so Miss White told the world that she was going on strike. She said that she had been overworked and underpaid, adding that Mr. Dippel was a slave driver and with a habit of discriminating against American singers in favor of the foreign importations. Once again this was, in the newspaper language, front page stuff.

As a matter of fact for several weeks Miss White had been worked rather hard. Pending the arrival of Miss Garden from Boston, she was the most available leading soprano on the roster, and she was able to point out a record of four major performances in five days as one of her causes for complaint. But Mr. Dippel seldom allowed any member of his company to catch him napping on a contest of wits, and this was his dictated response:

"I give you an excerpt from her contract and the dates on which she has sung. You will observe that the letter of the contract has been observed, and if she didn't wish to keep it, she shouldn't have signed it. The prima donnas do not work too much; they eat too much. It is terrible the way they have been entertained by society here in Chicago. Too many dinners and too many late hours. I eat too much—we all eat too much—but I don't complain."

This, too, was devastating. It startled an editorial writer on the *Tribune* into this:

"Heroic Mr. Dippel. Bring on the boar's head and the roast apples, the roast side of beef and the suckling pig, the pheasant, grouse, and mallard, ortolans and reed birds, Missouri turkey and Virginia pig, anchovies and pickled herring, puddings and mince pie; bring even buckwheat cakes and scrapple, johnny cake and maple syrup, little pig sausage and fried mush—Mr. Dippel may flinch, but he will not complain.

"This, however, is bound to give our culture a gross reputation, and we are so recently divorced from the flesh and wedded to the spirit that the breath of calumny may yet destroy us."

So the newspapers leaped upon the item with great

joy, setting out at length one of Miss White's daily
menus, and giving further space to the continuing reproof
valiant on one side and the countercheck quarrelsome on
the other. Finally some sort of a truce was declared, Miss
White went so far on her strike as to stay out of one
scheduled "Aïda" performance—and to give a dinner
party on that night. Then she went on a concert tour.
"Sold to the minors," the headlines had it, but it was
really a previously planned contract arrangement.

One of the most interesting items of the year took
place on the afternoon of Jan. 4. It was a performance
in concert form of the first opera ever written, Claudio
Monteverde's "Orfeo," with Mr. Sammarco as Orpheus
and Miss Stanley as Eurydice. Being done without scenery
or action, there was no chance to estimate its visual
values, but musically it was a jewel, of old-fashioned cut
but still fine quality. It proved among other things that
opera composition may have gained something of deft-
ness in 300 years, but certainly little in actual musical
beauty. The nobility of Mr. Sammarco's singing is still a
memory after sixteen years.

But it was a contest between art and the box office.
The public was—and is—far more interested in the personalities of singers than the operatic score itself, no
matter how fine, and the Auditorium was only about a
third filled that day. So Mr. Campanini's aspirations toward the unusual in art suffered a setback, and the piece
was put away, never to be given again. Too bad, for as a
work of art it was worth many performances.

Other episodes, rather minor in character from this
distance, took place. Mr. Sammarco's feelings were se-
verely wounded about his "Tosca" Scarpia, first because

Miss Garden wanted to have Vanni-Marcoux instead of him in the part, second because of some of the things said about him when he finally did it ("His personality is ill suited to the part; even his legs are good-natured," was one), and he expressed himself in print vigorously on both counts. The chorus went on strike because of an extra performance wherein Adeline Genée, a delightful dancer in her time, was to have half the bill. At last "Conchita" began to draw near.

This opera was another partial failure at the time, though there is no particular reason why it should be now. It was composed by Riccardo Zandonai, just then being talked about as one of the new and advanced Italian composers, and its principal part was taken by Tarquinia Tarquini, who came to Chicago to do that part and no other, and who since has become Signora Zandonai and retired from the stage.

Musically it was then a bit startling, just a trifle in advance of its period, but I, for one, believe that both it and the old "Orfeo" would have a good chance if given now. "Conchita" was a story of Spain, considered a trifle daring in theme, though it was most circumspect in performance, surrounded by music not in the least like that of "Carmen" but with some entrancing scenes in it, and with one episode which may have been sound psychology but seemed a trifle comic at the time.

It was a scene where Conchita's lover, with patience lost over her whims and tantrums, falls upon her and gives her a thorough and well deserved beating. Whereupon, exhausted and blissful, she sinks into his arms, murmuring—the translation is approximate—"Did you then love me so much that you treat me this way?"

The season was weaving its way to an end. It finally finished, the company went on its long tour and came back, with every one exhausted but elated, bearing the insignia of both artistic and financial success. And then, without notice, more fireworks, and all of them centering around Andreas Dippel. For suddenly, unexpectedly, after many fights but by far the best of the three seasons of the Chicago Opera, Dippel resigned.

In its time a number of mysteries have attached themselves to the Chicago Opera, but this has always been one of the greatest and the least subject to logical explanation. For that matter, no explanation was ever made. Nothing appeared in the newspapers or in any other place of record; all that was known was that one Saturday afternoon there was a directors' meeting, and when it was ended there was the fact of Dippel's resignation and Campanini's appointment to the position of general director of the company. When Dippel got outside the committee room, he is reported to have said, "My God, I spoke too soon." True or not, it would have been characteristic of him.

It could not have been that Dippel did not know his opera, for he had been in it all his life as artist and director. Neither could it have been that he was at all lacking in the art of the operatic showman, in other words the salesman of operatic wares, for during his three years he had displayed an uncommon acumen in estimating the public taste and in catering to it in a wise and efficient manner.

It is true that the weakness of his régime had applied to mechanical matters of the stage, particularly to lightings, but this applied to much of Campanini's reign also.

If during the first few years of the Chicago Opera there was ever a time when a change of lighting was made on its proper cue, neither memory nor record reveals the fact. It was very nearly a perfect score of errors. They were continually apologetic about it, but they never improved. Not until considerably later did the company ever get within shouting distance of what the ordinary dramatic stage considers the merely primary in effects.

At any rate, Dippel was out, Campanini was in, Bernhard Ulrich was business manager, and the 1913-14 prospectus tells of the following as officers and committees:

President—Harold F. McCormick; vice-presidents, Charles G. Dawes and Otto H. Kahn; treasurer—Charles L. Hutchinson; executive committee—John C. Shaffer, vice-chairman, R. T. Crane, Charles G. Dawes, Harold F. McCormick, La Verne W. Noyes, Max Pam, John G. Shedd; board of directors—Frederick Bode, H. M. Byllesby, R. T. Crane, Charles G. Dawes, Frederick T. Haskell, Charles L. Hutchinson, Otto H. Kahn, Harold F. McCormick, John J. Mitchell, Ira N. Morris, La Verne W. Noyes, Max Pam, George F. Porter, Julius Rosenwald, John C. Shaffer, John G. Shedd, Charles A. Stevens, F. D. Stout.

It will be noticed that with the exception of Mr. Kahn, the New Yorkers and Philadelphians had dropped out in great numbers from the board as it had existed when the company was first organized three years before.

CHAPTER IX

Cleofonte Campanini's consulship, which extended from the summer of 1913 until his death, was a time of deep and abiding joy for all beholders, if not for all his operatic exploits, which at that were notable, at least for his personality. He was nearly as picturesque a character as his old chief, Hammerstein, and by that token, the Chicago Opera entered into a new phase.

The nineteen years' younger brother of Italo Campanini, who was the greatly famed dramatic tenor of the eighties, he was by family relationship, tradition, and routine of life a man of the theater. The stage was his life, it was in his blood, he breathed its air as the rest of us breathe a breeze from the woods. It showed in everything that he said, everything that he was, from the dye that used to run out of his mustache down the corners of his mouth, after a hot session of conducting, to his theatrical, not to say spectacular funeral exercises on the stage of the Auditorium.

First of all he was a fine musician, one of the foremost operatic conductors of his time. Otherwise all the glamour and scenic effect with which he loved to surround himself would never have gotten him to the conductor's stand in the foremost opera houses of the world, nor permitted him to stay there if accident had put him there. People used to say that no one was ever slower to learn a score than he. A new score used to mean months of unremitting, grinding labor before he got it well into his head. They still tell stories at the Auditorium of his twenty-seven full rehearsals of "The Jewels of the Madonna," orchestra, cast, and chorus, and I remember how he worked with the orchestra on "Salome," strings alone, woodwinds alone, brasses alone, then in combinations, afterward the full orchestra, and finally orchestra and singers. In these days of union prices for rehearsals, his preparatory dealings would cause a constant succession of heart failures in the auditing department of any opera company, but his theory was that to be ready is to be right.

When he finally pronounced himself and his company ready, one could be prepared for something quite out of the ordinary. Some of the performances he gave have never been equaled for their power, their imagination, their color and finish. In spite of the fact that in all his years in this country he preferred to talk Italian— his French was highly imperfect, his English worse, and he had no German at all—he was ever the internationalist in music. He loved and admired the works of his own land, naturally, but he loved and admired Wagner quite as much, and he was the American pioneer in works of the French school, in works by Massenet and Debussy and a list of others that had never crossed the ocean. In his concerts he used to direct Debussy's "La Mer," and he trained his orchestra into playing the Ride of the Valkyries in "Die Walküre" with only such direction as he gave it with a glance of the eye. His exhumation of Monteverde's "Orfeo" has already been mentioned, but it is not generally known that up to the time of his last illness he was planning a gradual but increasing importa-

CLEOFONTE CAMPANINI

tion of a list of Russian works. The Chicago Opera presented "Boris Godunoff" and "Sniegurotchka" after his death, but these merely followed his plans, and he had several others under consideration.

In such matters he was a great man; in a good many others he was an interesting, sometimes amusing, always rather fascinating character. He was superstitious no end; the sight of a man afflicted with a humpback was enough to change his day's program, and he recognized, or thought he did, more cases of the evil eye than have been known since the middle ages. Desiré Defrere, one of the very few in continuous service with the Chicago Opera since its inception, tells how one night he called upon Campanini in his hotel to discuss some operatic matters, and unthinkingly tossed his hat upon the bed. Campanini promptly took the hat, opened the window, and threw it into the street nine floors below, not at all as a matter of etiquette, but to avert bad luck. He promised to replace it with a new hat, and he made good on his promise, but as Mr. Defrere ruefully commented: "The hat he threw out of the window cost ten dollars; the one he gave me cost four."

One of his most pronounced idiosyncrasies was a belief in the efficacy of old nails picked up from the street or elsewhere, and it was no unusual thing for him to have a quarter or a half pound of such junk metal in the pocket of his coat. One day some person with a malicious heart and a knowledge of his weakness strewed a line of old nails through the tunnel leading from the Congress Hotel to the Auditorium, and down the hall leading to the offices of the opera company. Campanini was extra rheu-

matic that day, and it must have cost him many pangs to
secure them all, but he did not miss one.

As it happened, when he finally eased himself into
his chair and began opening his mail, the first letter told
of a member of the company who had been ill but was
recovered and ready to come back. The second announced
that another singer with whom he had been figuring was
ready to sign a contract on his terms. The third had news
that negotiations for a new opera were proceeding in a
most satisfactory manner. All these in one mail. You may
imagine how far an argument about superstitions would
get with Campanini after that. He was more confirmed
than ever.

He was a warm friend and a hot enemy, and when
anything happened to make him suspicious, he was quite
certain to be an enemy. One of the vivid memories during
his régime is the running warfare that three of us
carried on with him through one winter. He hated to
make announcements until he was absolutely certain he
could go through with them, having once in an indiscreet
moment told of a pending all-star performance of "Don
Giovanni" that for one reason and another had collapsed
into nearly an all-eclipse performance.

Nevertheless he liked to talk over his plans with
those he thought he could trust, though in this list he did
not include the newspaper crowd, since on that and similar occasions they had been disrespectful to him in print.
Frederick Donaghey, James Whittaker, and I, all music
critics at that time, discovered that at a certain hour of
the evening Campanini and one of his Italian friends were
sure to appear at the Auditorium bar. (Those were the
days when there was a bar.) He was temperate in matters

of alcohol, but he would order a glass of mineral water and sip it, meanwhile discussing operatic things with his friend.

In a few minutes he would leave and we would depart for our newspapers. Whittaker understood more Italian than we others, so before separating he would give us a summary of the conversation, the next day three Chicago newspapers would contain news of Campanini's plans, and Campanini's blood pressure would take another leap upward.

He moved heaven and earth that season trying to discover the leak. He would seem to have threatened his whole office force with death by slow torture, and it is certain that one day he called in state on the bosses of our papers, demanding, like Salome before Herod, our journalistic heads on a charger. None of the three heads were granted him, but he continued to hate us with a hatred that should have turned our food into poison if it did not. However, next season, with equal formality and more diplomacy, he forgave us fully, and some time later Donaghey was taken into his full favor. Whittaker left for the war before his particular hatchet could be buried, and I do not imagine that the two ever came to terms. But up to the day of his death Campanini never discovered that he himself and only he was responsible for the leak.

Once upon a time I chanced to be chatting with Leopold Kramer, a fine violinist who had come from the concertmaster's chair in the Chicago Symphony Orchestra to take the same position with the orchestra. He said, "I like to play with Mr. Campanini. We all feel that he is like a rock on the stand, that no matter what happens he will never lose his head or his composure." It was some seasons after that conversation that one night a maniac tried to set off a bomb in the Auditorium, a Galli-Curci night while Campanini was conducting. But that event must wait for its turn.

CHAPTER X

So in 1913 Campanini took charge and things began to hum. Just by way of getting started, of stretching his newly fledged managerial wings, the company staged and sang thirty different operas in the first six weeks of the season. This was a record that probably was never equaled before or since, and it left the singers, the audiences, and the critics gasping for breath.

Just before the company went into its mass production a news item interesting in many ways was made public. On Oct. 30, 1913, the *Tribune* announced that all of the company's stock that remained in the hands of eastern shareholders had been purchased by President Harold F. McCormick, thereby giving not only control but complete ownership of the company to the Chicago group. The item quotes an unnamed director as saying:

"Under the old arrangement we were entirely dependent for our eastern season upon the guarantee of one Philadelphian, E. T. Stotesbury, which was all that prevented a regular deficit. He will now make arrangements with the Boston company to make flying visits to Philadelphia.

"We always made money in the once-a-week appearances in New York, but we as regularly lost it in Washington and Philadelphia. The eastern engagements did not pay.

"On the other hand our western tour showed a book

profit last year. This was wiped out by the too small reservation we made for scenery and costumes, but that will not happen again, for we will manage our own tour instead of leasing it. We will have a longer western tour and we will make more money."

One can imagine the sardonic smile with which subsequent directorates have read that last sentence. In fact the smiles of the same directorate grew more than a little lopsided no later than the next spring, learning, as they did, that there is considerably more to a western tour than merely decreeing it.

But on Monday, Nov. 24, the Campanini season opened with "Tosca," Mary Garden in the name part, and this time with her heart's desire of the season before, Vanni-Marcoux as Scarpia. Bassi was the Cavaradossi, and the discovery was also made on that night that if you want to have an altogether exceptional performance of "Tosca" it is essential to cast Vittorio Trevisan as the sacristan.

The rest of the first week had performances in this order:

Tuesday—"La Gioconda," with Carolina White, Julia Claussen, Ruby Heyl, Aristodemo Giorgini, Titta Ruffo, and Henri Scott.

Wednesday—"Don Quichotte," first time in Chicago, with Miss Garden, Vanni-Marcoux, and Hector Dufranne.

Thursday afternoon at popular prices—"Madame Butterfly," with Alice Zeppilli, Margaret Keyes, Bassi, and Francesco Federici.

Thursday night—"Die Walküre," with Jane Osborn-Hannah, Margaret Keyes, Julia Claussen, Charles

Dalmores, Henri Scott, and Clarence Whitehill. The
afternoon performance was unexpectedly comic; the evening unexpectedly fine.

The house was dark on Friday night, but on Saturday afternoon there was an announcement of historic
value. The opera was "Aïda," and in the cast were no
less débutantes than Rosa Raisa as Aïda and Cyrena Van
Gordon as Amneris, some of the others in the cast being
Bassi, Scott, Giovanni Polese, and Gustave Huberdeau.
In the evening came the thirtieth and final performance
of "Natoma," as told a little time previously, with the
composer, Victor Herbert, conducting. Alice Zeppilli had
the name part, and Mrs. Osborn-Hannah, George Hamlin, Mr. Scott, and Mr. Dufranne were others in the
cast.

It was a week to give people something to think
about. The "Tosca" passed as just a good performance,
Miss Garden singing in French to the Italian of the rest
of the cast, Mr. Vanni-Marcoux working his sinister plots
to the entire satisfaction of the audience, if not with quite
the horrifying shock that had been confidently expected
from the telegraphic reports.

But "Don Quichotte" sent people away with a sense
of high satisfaction. It is one of Massenet's later operas
and by no means his best musically, though a few seasons
later we were to hear in "Cleopatra" how sad an operatic
score can be when its composer's invention has been completely worked out, but Vanni-Marcoux and Dufranne
made a startling, vivid, memorable bit of fantasy out of
its acting values, and Miss Garden surprised every one
with her entire competence in the performance of some
reasonably entertaining coloratura display music. Prop-

erly cast, the piece would make an interesting revival now.

From the point of view of the present day, the most important event of the week was the Saturday afternoon performance, since Miss Raisa and Miss Van Gordon were destined to become notable figures in the Chicago Opera. At this time they were both very young. Miss Raisa's chief asset in the performance, since her youthful good looks were greatly obscured by her dark makeup, was a voice the like of whose power had never been heard on that stage.

Campanini was spoken to about her and her voice. His reply in effect was: "I know she is young now and not fully developed artistically, but mark my word, one of these days she will be known all over the world as one of the greatest dramatic sopranos." And Miss Raisa was once quoted as saying: "Oh, you think I sing loud here? You ought to hear me in South America, where they really like loud singing."

This "Aïda" performance had one incident unplanned and unexpected. The Nile scene was drawing near to its close, and Campanini, baton in hand, was just swinging into Radames' phrase, "I am dishonored," when suddenly two Ethiopian gentlemen from South State street who had taken part in the triumph scene, derby hats tip-tilted over left ears, were observed casually walking up the bed of the Nile and through its "water." They had mistaken the way out from the stage. Radames, Aïda, and two hundred Egyptian soldiers helped chase them off the stage, and they say that Campanini's remarks established a new record for fervency. Meanwhile the audience laughed as no grand opera audience is ever supposed to laugh.

Then came Ruffo again as Rigoletto, another success; a greatly daring repetition of "The Girl of the Golden West," which by this time was very far from being a success; another "Samson and Delilah," which by this time was better liked than when it was first played two years before; and finally a novelty for Ruffo. This was "Cristoforo Colombo," a supposedly historical opera by Baron Albert Franchetti, in which Ruffo appeared as Columbus, Miss Raisa as Queen Isabella of Aragon, and a lot of others in a lot of other rôles which just now do not matter in the least.

Although up to that time unheard in America, it was by no means a new work, since Baron Franchetti—the nobility went in heavily for composition in those days—had written it for the four hundred years' celebration in Genoa, Italy, in 1892. Disclosed in Chicago, it was discovered to have two acts of well-made, theatrically accurate music without any trace of transfiguring inspiration. As to its plot, Eric De Lamarter wrote this in the *Inter Ocean:*

"It is not an opera according to our pet formulas. It is lacking in any emotional appeal. It is strenuously celibate as to passion. It is carefully guarded from anything approaching dramatic action. It is a series of animated pictures, which are little more than pages from a diary Columbus did not write.

"The first act showed how the mob jeered the explorer, then admired him, then hated him again, and finally went away from the convent courtyard crushed by the doubt as to whether Columbus ought to be stoned or his protector respected. Then the queen prays fifteen minutes in the top soprano register and hands him her jeweled crown.

"The second act passes on shipboard. Sailors run hither and thither. One makes a wonderful effort at seamanship and throws the jib-sheets overboard. Another discovers the compass two decks below the helmsman's aerie and is surprised to find it disagreeing with the course. There is fear in the ship's crew, which would have filled a whole armada of Pintas with loveliness in breeches —and subsequently there is attempted mutiny. Columbus quiets all these outbursts, even to the compass.

"Then comes a truly inspiring scene in the sighting of land. The discoverer is overcome with emotion, the numerous crew strains at the leash of decorum in expressing their joy, the dawn throws a rich red light upon the bridge deck and, in a grandiloquent outburst from the orchestra, the curtain comes down. It is a most effective scene.

"Lastly, the hero is found at the catafalque of his dead queen, and, in grief at his misfortunes, dies at the bier."

So "Cristoforo Colombo" did not last long.

It is possible that the demise of some of these works was hastened by the stage management, especially the lighting department, which continued to be a cause of joy or sorrow depending upon the amount of irreverence in the mind of the beholder. I find a comment written at this time about the change of illumination in the first act of "La Bohême," always a tricky time for the electrician, to the effect that light is stated by the physicists to travel at the rate of a good many thousand miles to the second but that in the land of grand opera, particularly in the land of the Chicago grand opera, it travels about as fast as a lame man can walk. The same report tells that in the second act the choristers part of the time had to use their mouths to sing through; in the intervals they used them for confidential communications at top voice which were audible as far as the sixth row from the back of the main floor.

The novelties continued. Arnold Winternitz on December 9 conducted a piece by Wilhelm Kienzl called "Le Ranz des Vaches," in which his wife, Marta Dorda, took the principal soprano part. In spite of its title it had little to do with cows, but with the Swiss guard during the French revolution and a proscribed Swiss song whose name is the name of the opera. The slaughter by guillotine of the most high-minded members of the cast was paralleled later in Giordano's possibly more effective "Andrea Chenier," otherwise there might be an occasional performance of "Le Ranz des Vaches" these days, for it had a lot of charming music in it, with much use of Swiss folk tunes and French court dances and bergerettes.

Alice Zeppilli did an energetic job of double service by singing Gilda in "Rigoletto" with Ruffo in Italian on Saturday afternoon and Marguerite in "Faust" in English the same evening. For among Campanini's other activities, he had ordered a complete set of Saturday night English performances at popular, or half prices. The English series was greeted with the calm demeanor and lack of interest which the advocates of opera in English have always insisted would be transformed into educational stimulus and rapt enthusiasm were all operas given in English. One of the most puzzling features of all the puzzling business of presenting opera is that anything so logically impeccable as opera in English should be so economically discouraging when it is tried. But the season went on with undiminished fervor.

"The Barber of Seville," in which Ruffo was immense as Figaro, opened the week. Then came the début of Lucien Muratore in "Faust," as handsome a person as ever had been a tenor matinée idol gifted with a glorious voice, trained in the traditions of French acting. Lina Cavalieri, who had been announced to appear with him as Marguerite, did not do so, resigning her place to Miss Zeppilli. In fact she did not appear at all, although also announced in the name part of "Fedora" on the Saturday afternoon of the same week. Wherefore "Faust" was sung again on Saturday, and Muratore's two performances in it brought him enough acclaim for twenty artists. The excuse made for Cavalieri's non-appearance was rheumatism, but years later, after their separation, she told the press a different story. She said that Muratore was jealous and would not let her sing then or any other time.

Ruffo came to the front again in the name part of Mozart's "Don Giovanni," a rôle which he should gently but firmly have been argued out of ever singing at all. For the Mozart opera contained few high notes for him to trumpet forth and his audience to get hysterical over, and it was about as far from his manner dramatically as vocally. Vittorio Trevisan, however, was bully as Masetto. Wherefore it was now time for another novelty.

It was "Zingari," by Ruggiero Leoncavallo, and Leoncavallo himself came on to conduct its first two and only two performances in Chicago. In advance it looked like a time for jubilation. "Pagliacci," by the same composer, had always and has always ranked as an operatic best seller—it was paired with "Zingari" that night, and, as usual, Ruffo as Tonio—and all the admirers of "Pagliacci" bought tickets for "Zingari," prepared to welcome another work hoped to be of the same order.

Curiously enough, however, and with the best intentions in the word, Leoncavallo never scored conclusively except with the one opera. The music of "Zingari" was melodious, uncomplex, warm, dramatic, everything that a score should be, but it was never given again. Perhaps the story had something to do with it, for in the work the injured tenor lured the erring soprano and baritone into a barn, locked them in, and set fire to the building. The thought of broiled prima donna and toasted baritone was a little too much for a public inured though it might have been to many sorts and varieties of unusual operatic deaths.

But the audience that night made a festival of it anyway. To an accompaniment of blistering palms, no curtain fell without recalling composer and singers before it at least ten times and sometimes more. Leoncavallo scarcely had time to change into dry clothing, for he fairly steamed with perspiratory energy while at the baton. At one time and another, however, he found time to bestow public kisses upon Miss White, who was in "Zingari," upon Ruffo, and finally upon the stage director of the company, Fernand Almanz. The last was the most impressive of all. The sight of two tightly waistcoated but well rounded façades rolling up on each other so that two pairs of leonine mustaches might meet in osculation was a spectacle seldom to be equaled and never to be forgotten.

CHAPTER XI

Mary Garden returned at this point to open in "Le Jongleur de Nôtre Dame," again making it one of the most elusive, deft and rarely lovely performances in her long gallery of portraits. Then she and Ruffo combined forces in a performance of "Thaïs." Some one had hinted beforehand that relations between the two artists were not entirely cordial, that Ruffo had told some of his friends that the star part of this performance was going to be Athanael, and that Miss Garden had been told of the remark. In any event, it developed into a highly diverting artistic battle between the two.

It was a tactical error on Ruffo's part for two reasons: one that here was another part written too low for his effective register, another that he was confronting an extremely adroit and resourceful artist who considered that the star part of the opera was Thaïs herself. Ruffo had all the first scene and half the second in which to register himself. He did his best, but then Miss Garden appeared, letting out a few extra convolutions in her pantomime and personality, and the rest of the opera was a complete rout for the baritone. He had enough. Never again was the Italian evangelist to busy himself with the wiles of the French-Scotch-American charmer.

Muratore appeared with Mme. Claussen in "Carmen" and was acclaimed the finest of all the Don Josés, Mme.

Claussen's section of the performance also receiving high praise for its remarkable singing, if not for its histrionic witcheries. Also Frieda Hempel came on for two performances in "Traviata" and "Lucia di Lammermoor," and was praised in both. Meanwhile rehearsals were going on for the first performance by this company of Wagner's "Parsifal." Artists were feverishly active, and, since the performance was scheduled to begin at 4:30 o'clock in the afternoon, Chicago men were wondering whether they should wear afternoon garb, evening dress, or business suits, or whether under the circumstances it might not be better to stay away altogether. The performance finally came to pass on Sunday, Jan. 11. The cast:

AMFORTAS ....Clarence Whitehill
TITUREL ....Henri Scott
GURNEMANZ ....Allen Hinckley
PARSIFAL ....Charles Dalmores
KLINGSOR ....Hector Dufranne
KUNDRY ....Minnie Saltzmann-Stevens
A VOICE ....Ruby Heyl
FIRST KNIGHT ....Desiré Defrere
SECOND KNIGHT ....Constantin Nicolay
FIRST ESQUIRE ....Beatrice Wheeler
SECOND ESQUIRE ......Ruby Heyl
THIRD ESQUIRE ....Ralph Errolle
FOURTH ESQUIRE ......Stanislaus Grundgand

Klingsor's flower maidens
Group I—
Amy Evans, Minnie Egener, Helen Warrum
Group II—
Mabel Riegelman, Alice Zeppilli, Marta Dorda

Conductor ....Cleofonte Campanini

This was an uncommonly good cast, Mr. Whitehill doing a particularly fine performance, but it was scarcely a German cast, though most of the leading principals had received their training for it in Germany. Some of the lesser principals had never sung in German before, however, and the strange language annoyed them intensely. Mr. Nicolay, an able linguist in several tongues, was one of these. In a pained tone he once said to me:

"My friend, I wake up in the middle of the night, I think of those German words, and I assure you I break into a transpiration."

The success of the performance was marked though badly handicapped. For Mr. Hinckley had suddenly developed a violent cold, and, though starting each act in fair voice, he became huskier and huskier, almost to the point of complete inaudibility before the fall of the curtain. And "Parsifal" uncut, too.

But Mr. Whitehill, Mr. Dalmores, Mr. Dufranne, and Mrs. Saltzmann-Stevens were splendid, and Mr. Campanini was fine beyond all telling. He convinced the most pronounced of all the Baireuthians that he knew his Wagner, not only its merits, but its conventions as well.

Florence Macbeth was one of the season's débutantes, and every one liked her. She had had the misfortune of being overadvertised; some misguided individual got the statement into print that she was a second Patti, which would have been an absurd thing to say if a second Patti had actually come. But Miss Macbeth was young and talented, and in "The Barber of Seville" and the aged "La Sonnambula," as sleepy as its name, she made a definite success for herself.

Frances Alda did a Mimi in "La Bohême," not altogether well, and then Miss Garden and Mr. Muratore came together for the first time in Massenet's "Manon." This time the tactical error was hers. For nearly four years a steady battle among opera goers had been raging about the relative tensities of her singing and acting, the theory in favor of her singing being, as nearly as can be learned from reading contemporary articles on the subject, that anything which the world at large considered a bad tone was merely the world's ignorance, that in reality such a tone should be considered an interpretation of the most profound dramatic import. However, the most unbridled of her defenders were forced to admit that as far as "Manon" was concerned, Mr. Muratore had a delightful evening.

Melba restored the balance of "La Bohême" by coming and singing Mimi as only Melba could at that time; Campanini gave his fourth annual dinner to the directors of the opera company and the musical critics— these were solemn but noble affairs;—it was permitted to be made public that operatic activities were costing $50,000 a week—the cost has raised since then;—and the last novelty of the season went on.

On Wednesday night, Jan. 28, Chicago got its first view of "Monna Vanna," and it registered as an event. Miss Garden appeared as Vanna, Muratore as Prinzivalle, Vanni-Marcoux as Guido, and Gustave Huberdeau as Marco. This, ladies and gentlemen, was a cast! It would be hard to find weaker music than Henri Fevrier wrote for this piece, but Maeterlinck had been inspired to write a great play and a great operatic libretto, all in the same motion. Whatever Miss Garden had lost in her ill-advised "Manon" venture, she regained and more in

"Monna Vanna," for the work is so constructed that the soprano and tenor can never compete but must always coöperate. It was a piece that touched Miss Garden's brilliant imagination, Mr. Muratore's as well, and for a number of years they used to appear together in it with striking success. One may add also, that Joseph Urban had constructed three stage settings nearly as imaginative and as fine as the performance.

"Parsifal" was repeated, this time with Mr. Hinckley restored to voice, and on the final Friday evening of the season a "grand gala" performance was given according to the custom of all operatic seasons. This ceremony has always been one of the most amusing features of the whole business of opera giving. For some reason, perhaps justified by receipts, it has always been considered that an evening made up of disjointed and separate acts of opera must always exert a tremendous lure on the minds of ticket buyers. Perhaps it is the bargain idea, the possibility of hearing many stars though ever so briefly in one evening. At that, it frequently happens that some of the most noted stars find it possible not to appear on a gala evening.

However, here was the gala bill of Jan. 30, 1914:

1. Act II of "Samson and Delilah," with Julia Claussen, Charles Dalmores, and Hector Dufranne; conductor, Marcel Charlier.

2. Act III of "Aïda," with Carolina White, Beatrice Wheeler, Amadeo Bassi, Giovanni Polese, and Henri Scott; conductor, Ettore Perosio.

3. Mad scene from "Lucia di Lammermoor," Florence Macbeth; conductor, Attilio Parelli; followed by the

"Tannhäuser" overture, conducted by Cleofonte Campanini.

4. Act II of "Tosca," with Mary Garden, Amadeo Bassi, and Giovanni Polese; conductor, Cleofonte Campanini.

5. Act III of "La Bohême," with Rosa Raisa, Mabel Riegelman, Aristodemo Giorgini and Francesco Federici; conductor, Giuseppe Sturani.

6. Ballet divertissement by Rosina Galli, première danseuse étoile, and corps de ballet.

This ought to have been enough for any one, and was, especially as a few were favored with a spectacle not granted to the audience at large. The few who happened to be back stage that night—yes, that was another difference between old times and new, one was occasionally permitted behind the scenes during a performance—saw Miss Galli in a shower of enraged tears because at first she had been billed in the fourth position and then transferred because Miss Garden wanted the place.

Stormy as she was, there was a limit to her display of temperament, and it consisted of her sitting before the mirror and carefully mopping the tears out of the corners of her eyes with a bit of absorbent cotton so as not to streak her makeup, meanwhile telling what she thought of Miss Garden, Campanini, and most of the members of the Chicago Opera in voluble and exceedingly pointed Italian. This contest between volcanic rage and personal caution afforded one of the most interesting psychological spectacles that the Chicago Opera ever produced.

A final performance of "Martha," a note from Campanini to the newspapers thanking one and all for their kind attention and promising better things for his next season, and the company departed on its western tour.

To the unconcealed horror of the directorate, instead of a profit of $68,000 as on the previous season, there was a net loss of something like $250,000, and the company came back in what can only be described as ostentatious silence. The directors saw the world through a haze of blue for months afterwards, but held a meeting in May wherein Campanini and Business Manager Ulrich were formally absolved from blame for the deficit.

In a further effort at recovery they began to make plans for the next season—

And then came more fireworks.

CHAPTER XII

The war broke out in 1914, and the directors promptly tossed their operatic project overboard. In fact, promptly is hardly the word to describe the case. They acted with a speed so bewildering as almost to require a mathematical symbol to fit the case.

At one time and another I have heard their action named as unsporting, especially as the Metropolitan Opera Company carried on in New York, the Chicago Symphony Orchestra in Chicago, and for that matter, the Chicago Opera itself when the United States later took a hand in the conflict. But while it is impossible to think of them as being in any way audacious in conduct, complete justice needs the qualification that they had just suffered what then was considered a heavy loss, and in addition, the summer of 1914 was no time to formulate clear ideas on any subject.

So they found themselves with an opera company and many contractual obligations on their hands, and no season or any other chance of income. There was only one thing left to do and they did it. With equal speed they threw the Chicago Grand Opera Company into bankruptcy, and that was the end of Chicago's first operatic organization.

Many of the company's debts were in the form of contracts with the singers for the season which was not to take place. The company, as a corporation, denied all such claims, basing its stand on the clause in all contracts reading thus:

"Furthermore, the company has the right to abrogate the contract in case of fire or destruction of the theatre, in case of war, of epidemic, or of the closing of the theatre by the authorities."

It became a nice point, as lawyers say, whether the war restriction should be construed to mean that the United States was at war or not. But what was of more interest to the public was that during the bankruptcy proceedings most of these contracts became public information. Up to that time what the singers earned had been only a matter of gossip, the company taking the possibly not unjustified point of view that it was none of the public's business what was paid.

So it came out in the newspapers that Mary Garden was being paid $1,600 a performance with a minimum guarantee of fifty performances a year, totaling $80,000; that Maria Kousnezoff, who was not to come until later, was to have $1,500 a performance; Mme. Ernestine Schumann-Heink and Lucien Muratore $1,200 each a performance; Titta Ruffo $2,000 a performance and Alice Zeppilli half that sum; and Maria Barrientos, who was under contract but never came to the company, $1,500 a performance.

From another and less official, but seemingly accurate list compiled by the *Musical Courier* for the seasons before, it was learned that Dippel had been paid $22,500 a year, Campanini $30,000 a year, and Ulrich $10,000 a year. Of the singers during that period—the list was long and unnecessary to reproduce fully here—it appeared that Olive Fremstad had sung four performances at

$1,000 each; that Johanna Gadski had come on the peculiar looking basis of singing four performances at $1,000 each and then of adding two performances gratis; Minnie Saltzmann-Stevens, ten performances at $250 each, later raised to fifteen performances for $6,000; Jane Osborn-Hannah, twenty performances at $350 each; Helen Stanley, five months, $5,000; Tetrazzini, $2,000 a performance, the first season eight of them and the second, which included the tour, twenty-eight; Maggie Teyte, $300 a performance, later raised to $400; Amadeo Bassi, $800 a performance for forty-five of them; Charles Dalmores, the same rate for fifty; George Hamlin $200 each, later raised to $300; and John McCormack, ten weeks at $1,200 a week.

There were some ten pages of singers in the bankruptcy petition, all with claims not recognized by the company, but all with a year's income to be wiped out. It is not the only time in history that there has existed a certain feeling of cynicism toward singers by managements and vice versa. Perhaps it is a compensation for the idealizing adoration exhibited toward them by the public.

About $350,000 more of debts were scheduled by the company, the largest single item being a promissory note for $260,000 held by Harold F. McCormick, which would seem to have had an intimate bearing on the operations of the company during the 1913-14 season. The announced assets were $9,000 in cash, $25,000 worth of scenery and costumes that cost $400,000, and outstanding accounts to the amount of about $25,000, in other words, less than $60,000 as against some $700,000 of claims.

So that was that. Chicago's opera that season consisted of a visit from the Century Opera Company, an English singing organization which had been appearing at the Century Theatre in New York under the direction of the brothers, Milton and Sargent Aborn.

It came in November and stayed eight weeks, incidentally going into the permanent silence at the end of that time, a fact that I have never heard mentioned by the opera-in-English enthusiasts. Nothing has ever been the matter with the enthusiasm of this group. The only trouble is that either from lack of numbers or lack of desire they do not buy enough tickets.

The Century Opera Company was neither in numbers nor in brilliancy comparable to the defunct Chicago company or the continuing Metropolitan, but it was an entirely respectable organization claiming about 220 members in its various departments, and with such artists as Orville Harrold, Morgan Kingston, Louis Ewell, Helen Stanley, Kathleen Howard, and Louis Kreidler among its leading artists. Otto H. Kahn was one of its principal stockholders, and the chairman of its board of directors. In its repertoire were such works as "Lohengrin," "Traviata," "The Jewels of the Madonna," "Faust," "Madame Butterfly," "Carmen," and "La Bohême," to name only a few, and for some entirely inexplicable reason, "William Tell." That moribund work was given during the Chicago season, the first time, so they said, in twenty years. This was often enough. The overture rightly continues to be put on orchestral programs, but little of the rest belongs anywhere outside of a museum of antiquities.

One of the company's achievements was the celebration on Dec. 14, 1914, of the twenty-fifth anniversary of

the opening of the Auditorium. As on the opening performance, the opera was "Romeo and Juliet," Miss Ewell
singing the part of Juliet which had been done by Patti
a quarter century before. It is remembered as a rather
able performance, though with an ending not contemplated by Gounod and probably never done by Patti.
Miss Ewell in Juliet's death throes fell off the bier and
rolled down the steps, continuing her roll until she had
gone beyond the curtain line. There she lay, but when
the curtain began to fall, with a commendable desire not
to be cut off altogether from her friends and associates
in Verona, she rolled back again until she was within the
margin of safety. A more dependable corpse never died.

Chicago's own opera, however, was destined to revive. On March 17, 1915, a statement signed by President
Harold F. McCormick and issued by Vice-President
Charles G. Dawes, told that on the following season there
would be opera again, and that a guarantee of $110,000
a year for two years had been secured. Campanini was
again to be the general director and Ulrich the business
manager. A list of the guarantors followed. It included
the names of Robert Allerton, J. Ogden Armour, the
Blackstone Hotel, E. B. Butler, Carson, Pirie, Scott &
Co., the Congress Hotel, R. T. Crane, Charles G. Dawes,
Marshall Field & Co., F. T. Haskell, Charles L. Hutch-
inson, Samuel Insull, L. B. Kuppenheimer, W. V. Kelley,
A. J. Lichtstern, W. A. Lydon, Harold F. McCormick,
John J. Mitchell, Max Pam, George F. Porter, Julius
Rosenwald, Martin A. Ryerson, John G. Shedd, Charles
A. Stevens & Bros., Frank D. Stout, and Edward F.
Swift.

Thus began for a period of seven years the second

phase of Chicago's opera. For when the two years' guarantee period had expired, a similar one of five years was put together. On'Dec. 15, 1916, Mr. Dawes made an entr'-acte speech to the operatic audience explaining the fact, and naming as the new guarantors J. Ogden Armour, Count Giulio Bolognesi, R. T. Crane, Charles G. Dawes, Charles L. Hutchinson, Samuel Insull, N. M. Kaufman, L. B. Kuppenheimer, A. J. Lichtstern, Cyrus H. McCormick, Mrs. Edith Rockefeller McCormick, Harold F. McCormick, John J. Mitchell, Max Pam, Julius Rosenwald, Martin A. Ryerson, John G. Shedd, Mrs. H. H. Spaulding, Frank D. Stout, and Edward F. Swift.

A new company was incorporated under the legal name of the Chicago Opera Association, and as soon as passage could be arranged through the troublous lines of war, Campanini went abroad to see what could be done about assembling a new roster of artists and repertoire of operas.

CHAPTER XIII

The going in 1915-16, the first season of the new Chicago Opera Association, was not altogether easy. War and a year's intermission had had their effects in scattering operatic forces. Miss Garden elected to stay in Paris; Miss Raisa was in other parts of the world in pursuit of operatic fame; Ruffo did not come back, nor did Sammarco. As a matter of fact the new company had not been organized until the spring of that year and Campanini's hands had been tied up to that time. When he was finally permitted to begin assembling his company, a good many artists that he would have liked to secure were engaged elsewhere, and he was obliged to get along with what he could find. Under the circumstances he made a remarkable showing, bringing back a company-that was weak in certain spots, to be sure, but with many figures to keep interest alive.

On Monday night, November 15, the curtain went up once again, to open the new season with "La Gioconda." In the cast were Emmy Destinn, Frances Ingram, Eleanora de Cisneros, Amadeo Bassi, Mario Ancona, and Vittorio Arimondi, Campanini conducting. Then came "Louise," with two newcoming women, Louise Edvina in the name part and Jeanne Mauborg as the mother, Dalmores as Julien, and Dufranne as the father, with Marcel Charlier conducting.

On Wednesday night came "Tristan and Isolde," with

Francis Maclennan and Olive Fremstad in the name parts, Julia Claussen as Brangæne, Clarence Whitehill as Kurvenal, James Goddard as King Mark, and Graham Marr as Melot, Egon Pollak conducting.

As has been said, Campanini was an internationalist in music and saw no reason for taking operatic sides between warring nations. Sometime later people began to see a sinister and deep laid plot against the peace and well-being of the American republic in Wagner's music. The feeling grew so strong that in time Campanini, much against his will, had to yield to it, but that season and the next he decreed plenty of Wagner, the work just mentioned, the four sections of the Nibelungen Ring, "Parsifal," and others. The great disservice to the Wagnerian cause was to give the operas in their uncut versions, and, for American audiences, this manner in time grew to be a great bore. Three hours of opera in America was ever better than five. In Germany the case is different. There, somehow, one soon gets into a leisurely way of doing things, operatically and otherwise, but in America there is always the feeling that it ought to be made snappy—and briefer than Wagner planned.

Campanini from the beginning had done much in the Wagnerian cause, engaging the best singers available, sometimes conducting personally but in any event always having a good conductor. Dr. Szendrei had been excellent and had made a fine impression until one day in an undiplomatic moment he had given out an interview announcing himself as a bearer of Wagnerian light into Chicago dark places. It was just another case of a foreigner talking of things that he knew nothing about, but its complacently condescending tone stirred operatic

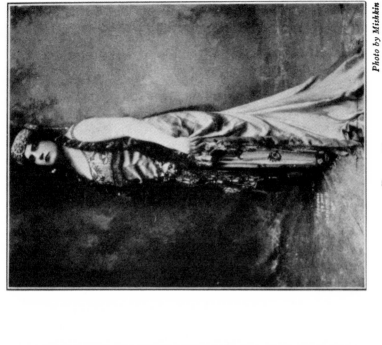

OLIVE FREMSTADT

Photo by Mishkin

EMMY DESTINN

*Photo by Mishkin*

patrons to wrath, and Szendrei was not reëngaged. Winternitz had been another good conductor, the war intervening to keep him away. Pollak was the best of all. Loomis Taylor was engaged as stage manager for the German series, the first one ever able to make the scenery behave and keep the lights from stuttering. Pollak was a first rate leader, and the cast shows what kind of singers Campanini engaged for him to lead. When "Siegfried" was reached there was a new sensation in the person of Florence Easton (Maclennan), as Brünnhilde. She sang only once that season, but she became the most talked about person of the company. Her performance was a revelation of beautiful voice and perfectly placed tone. And the "Tannhäuser" rendition on Thanksgiving night assumed a fame not entirely warranted by the performance because the program gravely announced that the first scene of the first act was laid in "The Interior of Venus."

The first week continued with Massenet's "Werther," sung by Muratore, Conchita Supervia, Dufranne and Nicolay, and conducted by another new director, Rodolfo Ferrari. "La Bohème" brought Melba back to sing with Bassi, Irene Pavloska, Marcel Journet, and Ancona, and the week closed with "Monna Vanna," with Marguerite Beriza, Muratore, and Alfred Maguenat, Campanini conducting.

This last was the occasion of one of the many press agent stories that have attached to the company. An earnest press agent called up the city editor of an afternoon newspaper to say that Muratore was singing with his former wife, Beriza, while his then wife, Lina Cavalieri, was sitting in a box, and, in the opinion of the city editor, wasn't that a good story?

The city editor in a tired voice answered, "Yes, that's always a good story. Send it over." For the same set of persons had been associated in the same manner in Boston the season before, and that city editor had been city editor of a Boston paper at that time and had printed the story.

One notices a tendency in the newspapers about this time to use less congratulatory gush about the opera company and more earnest and sometimes pointed criticisms. In reality they were treating the company more seriously, opening up more possibilities than they had ever done before. An editorial in the *Journal* has this:

"At a recent performance of 'The Valkyrie,' thirteen of the fourteen principal performers were Americans, and the other was a Swede. To give this opera in German, therefore, required all the singers to use an alien tongue and one familiar to only a small part of the audience. It demanded a special effort on the part of every singer to keep the listeners from understanding the text! Could absurdity go farther?"

And about this time there was something queer by Saint-Saëns called "Dejanire" in which Muratore was called on to act a neurotic looking Hercules. It had the musical qualities of clarity, logic and symmetry, and not the slightest trace of effectiveness for the theater. Percy Hammond dropped in to see part of it and fell afoul of its dramatic characteristics thus in the *Tribune*:

"Through a barbarian in a leopard's skin at the opera, I found the way to happiness at Wednesday night's performance of 'Dejanire.' Arriving at the beginning of the last act, I resolved myself into a state of mind —as one who, liking burlesque, should say, 'Here is a burlesque of opera, done most seriously, as burlesque should be done, with all its vices slightly exaggerated.' Mr. Muratore's singing of the nuptial hymn was so showy and effective that I was at first disappointed; but at once the burlesque began. It was just as Weber and Fields would have done it in the old days. The funny postures, the funny, awkward ballet, the meek, round-shouldered supers in armor, and the chorus in a comic frieze surrounding it all were the quintessence of travesty. Mr. Muratore climbed upon a strange structure resembling a Fenimore Cooper log cabin and steam pipes began to hiss and spout on all sides of him. He was supposed to be upon a pyre, and the steam represented smoke and flame. You theatergoers will not believe that they had a transformation scene at the end, showing the hero in heaven, surrounded by seraphim! But they did. It was like a large German Christmas card, except that it was funny."

Memories of this season include the appearance of Vernon Stiles as Parsifal. Starting in what looked as though it would be an adequate performance, more than adequate as far as Whitehill, Hinckley, and Fremstad were concerned, he had not much more than got into the first act when he took a long breath and burst his belt. For the rest of the long act he was concerned, not to say anxious, about his costume, and he did not take a curtain call at the end, for all of which it is easy to pardon him.

He attempted apologetic explanations to Stage Manager Loomis, who dismissed him with the remark, "Oh, that's all right, Stiles. I didn't notice anything out of the way. I thought it was just another of those Baireuth gestures."

Several visitors from the Metropolitan became visible and audible ,during that period. Albert Reiss came on to do his brilliant Mime in "Siegfried"; Margaret Matzenauer or Margarete as she called herself then, appeared for the Brünnhilde of "Die Götterdämmerung," and was magnificent therein; Geraldine Farrar came for a whole succession of rôles (non-Wagnerian), Carmen, Cho-Cho-San, and Marguerite among them, a wise and tonic personality who could not help being noticed just by being on the stage, though unfortunately with her voice not up to what it had been a few seasons before.

Edvina sang a good many of the Garden rôles, plus Maliella in "The Jewels of the Madonna," without, however, effectually effacing memories of Miss Garden or Miss White. The last named artist, by the way, was at that time making a tour of the greater vaudeville circuits. It occurred to Mme. Edvina and her private advisers that a little newspaper publicity might not come amiss, and at the proper time some of the papers announced that she was in possession of an operatic parrot capable of singing some of her finest arias and under her instruction for the rest. But there the matter rested, with no publicized continuation to the tale.

What happened became known only privately and some time afterward. It appeared that a musical parrot had been discovered in a Chicago park who was able to pipe a few notes approximating a tune if heard with a liberal imagination. This was the bird which was to have been borrowed, sent to Mme. Edvina's apartments, and exhibited before a group of wondering reporters—not music critics.

But there was a slip between the bird cage and the

newspaper item. Some one, probably an employe, mistook the bird, and instead brought down one of similar appearance but of long residence in the Panama Canal Zone, where it had learned to curse volubly in three languages. Everything had been carefully staged for the exhibition, but the bird's first manifestation was a burst of profanity that abashed even the reporters. The press agent took to his heels, and the story was completely ruined. No explanation was possible.

There was Conchita Supervia from Spain who did a nice, girlish, little Carmen, a rather pleasant Charlotte in "Werther," and as good a Mignon as was ever heard on the Auditorium stage. She might have done more, but she was ill a good part of the season. There was Carmen Melis, singing all sorts of parts and ending with Zaza, a performance to be forgotten with great enthusiasm. Then came Campanini's most advertised find of the season, Maria Kousnezoff.

They liked her greatly as Juliet to Muratore's Romeo. Muratore, by the way, had been going in great shape the whole season. He was at the top of his form and was singing magnificently, though James Whittaker complained bitterly of the way he used to come to the footlights at the end of "Salut, demeure" in "Faust," and assume what Whittaker called the tenor spread as an invitation to applause. Mme. Kousnezoff was a Russian who had lived some time in Spain, acquiring while there a Spanish husband and considerable training in dancing. As she sang the waltz song in the first act of "Romeo and Juliet," she waltzed about the stage without pause. The incident should be recorded, if for no other reason than that no other soprano before or since ever had that much breath control. Another incident in the same performance showed her control of her wits. In the last act, as she was leaning over Muratore-Romeo, complaining that he had used up all the poison in the vial, he startled her by saying "Mon dieu, Maria, I haven't a dagger on me." Her answer was, "Sing," for he had fallen behind the orchestra. Then she turned her back on the audience, grasped an imaginary dagger, perforated herself with both hands and died an utterly painless death. And not a person in the audience knew it.

She was graceful and rather good looking, she had a pleasant and well trained voice, she was alert in all matters of costuming and stage devices, but she made one serious mistake. She consented to appear in the name part of Massenet's "Cleopatra," its first showing in Chicago.

With all its diaphanous costumes and epidermic display, its impressive scenery, its long cast, it was one of Massenet's latest works, and written after his sense of tune had in great part deserted him. Sometime it may be an interesting experiment to compile a list of the world's worst opera scores, in which case "Cleopatra" will undoubtedly take a prominent place. Neither Mme. Kousnezoff then nor Miss Garden later was ever able to make anything out of it except just another evening at the Auditorium. But she serenely appeared in a piquant, seductive, and rather exhilarating performance of "Thaïs," and every one was happy again.

The season grew late. As a gesture to American composers, Campanini put on Simon Buchalter's "A Lover's Knot," which had one consecutive performance in that and all following seasons. George Hamlin sang the tenor part in it, also in "Tosca," with which it was coupled, and in the latter work made the acquaintance of Mme. Melis for the first time when she walked upon the stage in the first act.

The final exploit of the season was what permanently wrecked Campanini's belief in lavish advance notices. It was "Don Giovanni." At the beginning of the season it had been billed as the operatic treat of the year, to be sung by Antonio Scotti, John McCormack, Emmy Destinn, Alice Nielsen, and Helen Stanley. It was announced for January 3, then postponed to January 19. When it finally came to performance, Mr. McCormack and Miss Stanley were present, but of the others, Frances Rose substituted for Mme. Destinn, Myrna Sharlow for Miss Nielsen, and Ancona for Scotti, and even then Miss Rose had a bad cold.

At that it might have been much worse. McCormack, whom the dramatic critics were beginning to compare favorably with Chauncey Olcott as a singer of Irish songs, demonstrated what the musical critics had been saying about him for some time, that he was a Mozart singer beyond compare. Miss Sharlow in the soubrette part of Zerlina made a notable hit. Trevisan's Masetto was highly praised, and Marcel Journet got by with Leporello. But those who had seen Scotti in the name part grew joyous and irreverent over Ancona.

He had been a fairly competent though never first class baritone, and at this time he was getting old, playing the part of the Don as a stout, elderly person who was forever getting into difficulties because he lacked the wit to keep out of them. One of his exploits was in the first act duel scene. When he drew his sword, it flew to pieces and the fragments spread all over the stage, so the Commendatore (James Goddard) died from a thrust of Ancona's forefinger.

Two attendants of the performance were heard discussing what they called the Ancona incident, referring to the Italian ship of the same name that had suffered the fortunes of war. One held that he should be interned for the duration of hostilities, the other that he should be sunk. And it was by no means understating the case to say that Campanini was wrathful.

There was no tour that year. Campanini had intended taking the French wing of the company to New York, but the plan fell through. The company therefore dispersed, but later that season the Auditorium was visited by one of the loveliest organizations that ever visited Chicago. It was Serge Diaghileff's Ballet Russe. For several years Anna Pavlowa had been delighting audiences with the beautiful perfection of her classic art, but here was ballet brought down to modern times as dance, as music, and as spectacle. Will any one who was present ever forget the breathtaking loveliness disclosed by the rise of the curtain upon "L'Oiseau de Feu," with "Scheherazade," "Carnaval," "Petrouchka," and the rest of the long list to come?

Opera in America never so much as got started on developing ballet to the great art that it became in Russia. Unfortunately it never had leaders with the imagination to see its possibilities. The visit of the Diaghileff organization was a big event. Financially it was a failure—but so was the opera.

And so, on to another season.

CHAPTER XIV

This was the season that Chicago made a discovery of its own, without previous incitement by press agentry. It was called Galli-Curci.

Science has carefully erased the word magic except as a figure of speech from the modern vocabulary, but there is one bit of magic that it has never attempted to explain. That one is the process by which a musician suddenly gets into the air and overnight becomes a national, perhaps an international figure.

Galli-Curci's is a case in point. Here was a young woman whom no one in Chicago had ever heard or heard of. Later it was learned that she had had a reasonably long and trying apprenticeship, that she had toured, trouped is perhaps the more accurate word, in Italy, Central America, and points adjacent, that she had camped on the doormat of the Metropolitan and been refused admission, had sung a week in a movie theater under an assumed name and been denied a continuing engagement, that Campanini had finally offered her two appearances with the promise that they would be all unless she did something to justify keeping her longer. In default, in despair of anything better, the publicity herald had told of her having a title—which happened to be true—and one of the newspapers had printed a picture of "Marquise Amelita Gallie-Curci," attributing the title to the wrong country and getting the name wrong, which was something of a record even for caption writers.

In other words, we who went to the Auditorium that Saturday afternoon, Nov. 18, 1916, were in an entirely calm, unhopeful mood, expecting to hear just another performance of "Rigoletto." For one scene and ten or fifteen minutes of the next, that was all it was, just another performance. Then things began to happen.

Suddenly a figure appeared from the door into the garden on the left side of the stage, an oval, medieval face with a large nose and an ivory pallor, a gracious, winsome manner, a throat out of which poured the most entrancing tones the generation had ever heard. The audience promptly rose up, shouted, screamed, stamped, stood on its figurative head, and otherwise demeaned itself as no staid, sophisticated Saturday afternoon audience ever acted before or since. Galli-Curci was made, not only for Chicago but for the United States, and Campanini hastened back to her dressing room to sign her up for other appearances, any number of appearances, as many as she could sing for the rest of that season and all seasons to come.

This is the magic that happens occasionally in music, and, when it happens, compensates for a lot of boredom. You cannot explain it. It just happens. Some of the best trained, best equipped, most intelligent musicians never find it, in fact most of them never do. The technique of musicianship has little or nothing to do with it.Galli-Curci herself, as we began to discover later, was no niggling marvel of technical precision. She frequently had trouble with her trill, and she sometimes sagged under her intended pitch. Never in her life was she within even

Photo by Hartsook

LUCIEN MURATORE AS FAUST

Photo by Lumiere

AMELITA GALLI-CURCI AS VIOLETTA IN "LA TRAVIATA"

bowing distance of Tetrazzini's carefree, bewildering vocal gestures.

But she had that delicately lovely, that cream velvet, that entrancing quality in her voice, and public and critics alike fell down and worshiped. From that afternoon on, the whole American public has apparently tried to shove the greater part of its opera- and concert-going budget into the window of her box office. Yes, there were others in the performance that day, Giacomo Rimini as Rigoletto, Juan Nadal making his Chicago début as the Duke, Vittorio Arimondi as Sparafucile, Giuseppe Sturani conducting, but for all the credit they got in the public prints, they might as well have stayed at home.

Galli-Curci's popularity survived some of the most extraordinary press stories ever put out about a singer. One of the most unbridled in imagination told how she had learned to sing by sitting on a fence and listening to the caroling of the birds. Musicians snorted speechlessly at that one, but after all, musicians make only a small proportion of another and successful musician's following.

One came in time to recognize her husband about the Auditorium, the Marchese Curci, a pale, slender, gentle-mannered, soft-spoken person almost completely hidden behind a large mass of black whiskers in intensive cultivation. Their romance, it seemed, had been that of the first act of "Tosca." He had been painting a picture in a Roman church, she had chanced to visit the church on that day, they had met, had formed a mutual attraction, and had married. By the time she came to Chicago, his art labors consisted almost entirely of designing operatic and concert costumes for her, in which he was greatly successful. They were the best she ever had, with a color and line that accentuated and gave atmosphere to the medieval charm of her personal appearance.

Galli-Curci's discovery was not the first performance of the season, though if Campanini could have foreseen what was going to happen, it without doubt would have been. Rosa Raisa was back after a long absence, this time to become one of the company's most dependable and famed permanencies. With her were Giulio Crimi, tenor, and Giacomo Rimini, baritone, whom she afterwards married. The three opened the season with "Aïda," and two nights later appeared in "Andrea Chenier." The second night's performance was "Hérodiade," Elizabeth Amsden and Maria Claessens making Chicago débuts, Dalmores, Dufranne, and Marcel Journet also in the cast.

Thursday night was "Le Prophète," an antiquity by Meyerbeer that has never seemed worth reviving, though Dalmores sang Jean and Mme. Claussen Fides. On Friday night Geraldine Farrar and Muratore appeared in "Carmen"; the Galli-Curci conflagration in "Rigoletto" on Saturday afternoon has been mentioned; the Saturday night "pop" was "Hansel and Gretel," with Dora de Phillippe, Irene Pavloska—she spelled it Pawloska then—and Rosa Olitzka, followed by a pretty but unimportant piece composed and conducted by Victor Herbert called "Madeleine."

Another series of Sunday Wagner performances began, with Pollak continuing as conductor. In "Das Rheingold" the cast was Clarence Whitehill as Wotan, Hector Dufranne as Donner, Warren Proctor as Froh, Francis Maclennan as Loge, William Beck (ex-Wilhelm;

it was war time) as Alberich, Octave Dua as Mime (he learned the rôle here and in "Siegfried" under protest for its difficulty and made the success of his life), James Goddard and Vittorio Arimondi as the two giants, Julia Claussen as Fricka, Marcia Van Dresser as Freia, Cyrena Van Gordon as Erda, and Myrna Sharlow, Irene Pavloska and Miss Van Gordon as the Rhine maidens.

A new note in journalism appeared in the *Examiner*. Instead of interviewing the notables of business and society about the opening night, the busy reporter called on members of the company. So Muratore said it was magnificent for about two hundred words, Florence Easton said that it was glorious and better than Europe could do for about the same length, and Campanini said that his heart had been warmed and that he had almost felt as though he were in Naples instead of Chicago.

Alfred Maguenat arrived a few days later with the news that his steamship, the *Chicago,* had been swept by fire off the Azores, and that the score, orchestrations, costume and scenic designs, in fact the whole paper plan of Raoul Gunsbourg's "Venise," up to that time in his care, had been destroyed. Apparently no other complete copy existed, so one opera was out, but in view of the same composer's "Le Vieil Aigle," as done later, there began to be opinions that something might be said in favor of war.

Galli-Curci tipped the house over again in "Lucia," confirming her "Rigoletto" success so definitely that she forthwith went into her long series of coloratura heroines. Florence Easton started on some non-Wagnerian parts; her first, Nedda in "Pagliacci" stood up firmly by the side of Muratore's Canio, which gives some idea of how good she was. Coupled with "Pagliacci" according to abiding custom 'was "Cavalleria Rusticana," and Raisa did her first glorious Santuzza.

More German opera. Pollak brought out the wistful and lovely "Königskinder," by Humperdinck, with Farrar as the goose-girl and Maclennan as the king's son, and a first rate cast, not forgetting the pigeons, two of which flew out into the body of the house the first night and stayed there, and the dozen and a half geese that fluttered and squawked and preened themselves with anserine disregard of everybody and everything. They were features of every performance until the end of the season, when Miss Farrar had them slaughtered and given to the stage hands. Poor things, when so many humans go into opera and are permitted to escape with their lives!

Showing what operatic impresarios have to face at certain times, the male chorus, forty-three strong, went on strike just before "Die Götterdämmerung" was ready to ring up on Sunday afternoon, December 10. The *Tribune,* greatly moved by the occurrence, reported it operatically thus:

ACT ONE

Bare stage of Auditorium theater, curtain down. Scenery for "Götterdämmerung" pushed back. Maestro Campanini, in center of stage, facing four chorus men in civilian attire. Forty other chorus men in civilian attire, grumbling in group, up center.

CAMPANINI:
    What means this rest?
    Why aren't you dressed?

QUARTET:
>As a committee we come to you (Come to you)
>To tell you what we're about to do (About to do).
>We want more mon-on-nee, we want more mon-on-nee,
>We won't work on Sun-un-dee
>Without more mon-on-nee.

CAMPANINI:
>Why won't you sing this day?
>Why won't you work, I say?
>Your answer give me, pray.
>What's the matter with your pay?

COMMITTEE:
>It's not enough, our life is tough,
>We cannot make ends meet.
>We get twenty-four, we're asking more,
>Or we refuse to tweet.

CAMPANINI (*excitedly*):
>I'm slipping you twenty-four bucks per week;
>I couldn't do more for my dad.
>Excuse my emotion, I can hardly speak,
>You make me almighty sad.

COMMITTEE (*turning to grumbling group*):
>We are given to understand
>He refuses our just demand.
>The curtain on art is rung.
>Gotter-der-dammerung.

ACT Two

Auditorium theater alley, stage door back center.

STAGE MANAGER (*flinging open the stage door*):
>Rouse, you lazy louts; get thee gone from off our stage.
>A curse on your artistic hides, you fairly make me rage.

STRIKERS (*in unison*):
> We are striking, for a living wage;
> We are martyrs starving for the sake of art.
> Our connections with the opera we now disengage.
> We are asking recognition on the labor mart.

STAGE MANAGER:
> Silence, stop your clamor, on your noise please put a curb.
> Cease this clatter, end this rabble, lest the singers you disturb.
> The audience is sleeping and your lament must desist.
> They're not wise for a minute—why, you are not even missed.

STRIKING CHORUS (*spying approach of cops in distance*):
> Here come the cops, to chase us wops,
> Now whaddye think of that?
> We'll get fulla hops and break up th' props,
> And show 'em just where they're at.

THE POLICE (*enter left, strikers exit on right*):
> At last here's a cinch for to make a pinch.
> It's only in grand operee—
> In real life we flinch, when we meet in a clinch,
> But this is a regular spree.
> So we're ready to club the very first dub
> Who opens his mouth to shout.
> If he stars a hubbub he'll get trun in de tub,
> In the house that is steel and is stout.

Back on the stage "Götterdämmerung" is in progress. Octave Dua, Belgian tenor, who last spring had some difficulty with a young woman in a nickel show, rises to the occasion and breaks the strike. In the place of the chorus he sings as follows:

> The horrible things of a celluloid show
> Were vastly beyond belief.
> But I'll be a strike breaker and sing yo-ho,
> And give Campanini relief.

(CURTAIN)

To be strictly accurate, Dua was joined by Desiré Defrere, an assistant stage manager named Sam Katzman, and Constantin Nicolay in breaking the strike. A quartet sang the Gibichung music instead of over forty. But in essence, in spirit, if not in detail, the above account is true. Maclennan, Whitehill, and Hinckley were in the cast, Matzenauer was borrowed from the Metropolitan to sing Brünnhilde, and Easton appeared as Gutrune. The strike broke a day or two later. When the strikers found that Campanini was giving "Manon" by cutting some of the chorus parts and letting the women sing the rest, and that "Rigoletto" went on with the choral ministrations of Katzman, Rocco Franzini, Emilio Venturini, and Vittorio Trevisan, they grew discouraged, and came back just in time to get into "Aïda."

Mary Garden cabled that she was on her way back from Paris.

CHAPTER XV

Fremstad came on to sing in "Parsifal"; her Kundry was a little chipped and worn by advancing years, but still an Old Master. Rimini and Raisa appeared for the first time in Chicago in "Falstaff," Rimini as Sir John, Raisa as Mrs. Page, parts that they have done at intervals since to the growing delight of their audiences and to growing enthusiasm for one of the three great comic operas of the world. By a coincidence, Sir Herbert Tree was playing in "The Merry Wives of Windsor" in a Chicago theater at the time, just as in the 1927-28 season were Otis Skinner and Mrs. Fiske. Then and thereafter, the Verdi opera was a better show than the Shakespeare play. Sage critics have at one time and another remarked that only an Anglo-Saxon can understand Shakespeare well enough to act him, but Mr. Rimini was unctuous, comic, and, in spite of singing in Italian instead of speaking in English, more credible than Mr. Skinner, and Miss Raisa was a visual and auditory delight.

Farrar sang Elisabeth in "Tannhäuser" delightfully and a Carmen not so well and departed. Mary Garden appeared, announcing that she had lost nineteen pounds and that Campanini had told her she had "the memory of a fly" with some Italian intensives added because she had left her Mélisande costumes behind her in Paris and he wanted, or said he wanted, to revive the Debussy opera. So she appeared as Thaïs, making it a

New Year's eve celebration. Later she appeared in "Le Jongleur" and "Carmen," and finally in "Griselidis," a Massenet opera that for some reason was never repeated, a charming Provençal legend with a devil played by Maguenat in peagreen tights and bat wings, Miss Garden in a feminine and unfeline part, and some of Massenet's pretty music. It was not particularly well cast, with the exception of these two, and the public did not take to it.

Galli-Curci had added Juliet to her list of rôles, singing it with Muratore as Romeo, and the Auditorium was crowded every time they appeared. In the midst of an uncommonly busy season she had to jump in one Saturday afternoon for a "Traviata" because Louise Edvina, announced for the name part of "Louise," was ill. For the most vivid account of the event, the liberty is taken of quoting from Ring Lardner as he wrote it for the *Tribune.*

"Riverside, Jan. 2.——

"Friend Harvey:

"Well Harvey I fell so hard a year ago for Miss Edvina in Armour's D. T. Re that when I seen in Fred Donaghue's write ups that she was going to play Louise I starved for a week and bought a couple of tickets. The show was to come off Saturday P. M. but when we got down there they was a sign up saying Miss Edvina had a hang nail or something and a hyphen named Miss Galli-Curci was going to hit for her and of course they had to have her play some other piece on acct. of her name not being Louise like Miss Edvina's, but Amelia or something. But they have not got no opera named Amelia so they asked Miss Galli etc. what she could sing and she says La Traviata and that means Lost One in the Wop league. We was kind of disappointed but the management treated us fine, giving us programs of Louise so as we could pretend like that was the opera they were pulling off.

"I suppose they was a hole lot of people that was like myself and not habituals at the opera and wanted to know who the leading men was but did not have no Traviata program and was afraid to ask their neighbors. Well Harvey that is where brains comes in. Before the show was ½ over I had 2 of the boys spotted from their pictures that was printed in the back part of the program. The guy that was stuck on Miss Galli was named Creamy and his father was Mr. Beck. I could of found out who played the Dr. too if he had not of made up his face with an old mop.

"Well Harvey the plot of the piece runs something like as follows: Of course the leading lady don't sew for a living or it would not be opera. So there having a party at Violet's house, Violet being Miss Galli's name on the stage. And Creamy, whose name is Alfred on the stage, comes to the party and sings tenor solos. So he asks Violet will she pass up wine women and song for a spell and go out in the country with him and spear hazel nuts. And she says: 'You know me, Alfred.'

"So in the next act there down on the farm and Violet is paying the bills and Alfred finds out that she sold her Ohio Cities Gas to raise money for him to live on, so that makes him feel like a rummy and he beats it for Paris to raise money to pay her back and he is going to sell out his business which is a dairy and that is why they call him Creamy. But while he is in Paris his old man comes to see Violet and asks her will she please leave his boy alone because his daughter is engaged to one of the basses that sings Sunday afternoon only and the bass won't go through and marry her if her brother is mixed up with a girl that can't sing German opera. So Violet agrees to pass up Alfred who is costing her a bbl. of money any way, and she goes back to Paris and mates up with a guy named Barron and there having a party up in Flora's room when Alfred busts in and calls her every Italian name he can think of for quitting him. You see he thought she just plain quit him and did not know nothing about she making a sacrifice, third to first.

"Well, Alfred and Mr. Barron play a few hands of double dummy to give Mr. Beck a chance to clear his throat and then he comes in to the party and balls Alfred for balling Violet, and Mr. Barron and Alfred are matched to go twenty rounds at New Orleans to a decision.

"Of course by this time Violet knows she is going to die because the last act is coming and she done the same thing in Romeo and Juliet. So she thinks she would rather do it in her own room and she goes home. But being kind of new in grand opera, she don't know that your always supposed to carry a pt. of poison on your hip, so she has got to think of some other way. She finally solves it by taking a good look at the Dr. Mean times Alfred and young Barron have put on a fake fight and got chased out of New Orleans and Alfred and his old man comes to see Violet die. Alfred has been tipped off by his old man about the sacrifice bunt and he is sorry he said all them nasty things. So while she is dying he stands around and pats the top of his bean to express grief, or maybe its to keep the pores open so his head tones can get out.

"Well, Harvey, we catched the 5.43 and come home and had dinner and by midnight I was 12 up on Miss Galli because she only Lost One and I lost thirteen and in a thirty cent limit game at that.

"Resp.

"R."

On the night of Jan. 5, 1917, Campanini presented the first Chicago performance of "Francesca da Rimini," music by Riccardo Zandonai, who had composed the previously performed "Conchita," book adapted by Tito Ricordi from the play of the same name by Gabriele d'Annunzio. The cast:

FRANCESCA	Rosa Raisa
SAMARITANA	Myrna Sharlow
OSTASIO	Constantin Nicolay
GIOVANNI	Giacomo Rimini
PAOLO	Giulio Crimi
MALATESTINO	Emilio Venturini
BIANCOFIORE	Cora Libberton
GARSENDA	Alma Peterson
ALTACHIARA	Myrtle Moses
DONELLA	Dora de Phillippe
LA SCHIAVA	Virginia Shaffer
SER TOLDO BERARDENGO	Octave Dua
IL GIULIARE	Vittorio Trevisan
IL BALESTRIERE	Desiré Defrere
Conductor	Giuseppe Sturani

Here was an opera that might have succeeded if a little more wisdom had been used in its construction.

D'Annunzio had drawn one of the great stories of the middle ages out of his magic inkpot, Zandonai, a thorough-going man of the theater, had given it a score that was frequently effective and sometimes struck through with the flash of sincerity. After a dozen years there is still a vivid recollection of the charm of the first act, the home of Francesca, and later on in the piece there was a love scene as fine and fiery and passionate as any love scene ever ought to be. The trouble was that there were other things.

Ricordi's adaptation would seem to have consisted principally in cutting down the d'Annunzio play from about 4,000 lines to something like 1,200. He should have cut more, for he included a battle scene as the point of interest of the second act.

Such a battle scene as it was! Any battle scene is hard enough to stage with any degree of illusion, but this passed all bounds. Campanini, a better man of the theater than any of them, distrusted it in advance and begged to have the opera given with this scene omitted, but the Casa Ricordi was insistent, not to say hard-headed, and refused permission to make any cuts whatever.

Here was a scene in which realism was to be worked out to the last detail and no faith given to the audience's faculty of imagination. Dead and wounded were all over the place, there were spears, swords, arrows, catapults, and melted lead poured from the battlements. And when a couple of arrows wafted themselves up to the blue sky, stuck there, and remained sticking until the end of the act, and when a few large catapult balls sailed over the wall and down upon the struggling throng, hitting chorus men on the head and bouncing gently to the stage without appreciable damage to anybody or anything, the audience shouted with glee. It completely ruined "Francesca da Rimini," though the work had too many fine things in it to deserve ruining. Two more performances were given to see if the audiences would keep on laughing. They did.

CHAPTER XVI

By all odds the most exciting incident of the 1917-18 season belonged to Galli-Curci and Campanini, with some assistance from Dua and Rimini. It occurred on the first Friday night of the season, November 16, and had to do with what had every appearance of being an explosive bomb.

"Dinorah" was getting its first performance as a Galli-Curci vehicle. She had made her first act appearance, had left the stage, and Dua and Rimini were in the midst of their dialogue duet following. Suddenly a stench filled the Auditorium, a hiss as of a shooting flame, an excited ejaculation or two, and before any one knew it the orchestra had suddenly struck into "The Star Spangled Banner," the audience was standing, and Galli-Curci had run back to the footlights and was leading the anthem with every high note in her ravishing throat. She did not know the words, but she did not need to.

There really was a bomb, though it turned out to be a dud. What had happened was that some maniac had through hook or crook procured a seat near the tunnel entrance of the right hand center aisle, deposited his burden under the seat and then gone away. When it began to fizz and emit odors, a fireman with plenty of nerve, Battalion Chief M. J. Corrigan, later the Fire Marshal of Chicago, dashed in, stripped off his coat, wrapped the bomb in it, and ran out to the street, dropping coat and bomb into the gutter. There it lay and sputtered until it went out. He lost a coat, but he averted a panic. In other words, he lived up to his job.

It was war time, remember, and people's nerves were keyed up. There could easily have been a panic, even though, as it turned out, there was no danger from the bomb itself. A cry, a rush for the exits, and a calamity might have been precipitated. But the Chicago public that night treated itself to a display of great good sense and coolness. One member of the audience is reported to have leaped the orchestra rail and crouched down behind a violoncello, which would have been about as effective a protection as a mosquito netting had there been a real explosion. The others remained in their places, controlling themselves and each other with calm demeanor. After a moment or so, another fireman appeared on the stage before the footlights, assuring the audience that there was no danger, and the performance went on to the end. During one of the intermissions, the ushers passed out special editions of the two morning papers, each with a well-written column story of the event, and the patrons, reading within an hour what they had actually seen, laughed and congratulated each other that nothing serious had happened.

Campanini told a reporter about it the next day. "There ees nothing to tell, young man. Last night? Well, I heard a noise behind me and smelled a smell and I thought 'the devil.' I thought, 'Ah, it has come, the thing I have always waited for, the sound of panic.' You know heem? An 'Ah,' held for five beats. For thirty-five years I have been a director, always with the musicians. But never have I heard this 'Ah' held for five beats coming from behind. And then the smell of smoke. 'It ees come,' I say to myself. 'Now I can do my bit. The orchestra mus' play the mos' grand and beautiful music, whatever ees come.'

"This I know for thirty-five year. So, I command heem to play. And he play. Every one of them. Without a mistake. In time. Excellent. He play 'The Star Spangled Banner' and I call to Galli-Curci, 'Sing, madame.' And she sing. In time. A whole octave high. Then the lights go up and I think maybe the people are flying away and terrible things are happening. But we play until I sneak a look in back of me, and, ah, the devil! The people are standing close by their seats all safe, and I want to seeng myself.

"Pardon, I have work. Goo' by."

Another man with plenty of courage to be called upon just when it was needed. But it was more of a shock than Campanini himself or any one around him realized at the time. One can almost believe that his death dated from that moment. He was no longer young, he had lived intensely upon his nerves all his life, and his heart was not what it had been. He went on living and directing, it is true, but he missed several assignments at the baton during the next couple of weeks, and as the seasons went on he displayed less and less of the brisk vitality that had always marked him. In due time came the end. But in this time of crisis, he was distinctly there.

The bomb was later picked up out of the gutter and carefully disemboweled by some powder and bomb experts and Chief of Police Schuettler and some of his assistants. It was a piece of gaspipe containing two ounces of smokeless powder, a load of buckshot, fifteen or twenty .22 caliber cartridges, and some sawdust and blotting paper. It must also have had a fuse and some odorous substance that burned in the Auditorium, but it was plainly a novice's job, and in all probability the powder, had it been touched off, would not have been powerful enough to crack the pipe.

The person who made it and left it in the Auditorium was in course of time picked up, but, being war time, his name was never made public. He was, however, quietly put away on the war-time charge of having explosive material in his possession. They found enough to justify the charge in the place where he had been living, and that would seem to have been the end of him.

Ever since that time something has happened in all operatic performances which very few people know about. A squad of quietly dressed operatives are on hand, distributed about to see that nothing of the sort happens again, and you and I and all of us are quite without our knowledge subjected to careful scrutiny before we take our seats. They are not necessarily looking for infernal machines all the time. Pickpockets and other anti-social persons have been known to get into operatic crowds with the idea of plying their trade.

Turning back from this Friday night to Monday night, November 12, we discover that the season was opened with the first performance in America of Pietro Mascagni's "Isabeau." This was the cast.

ISABEAU	Rosa Raisa
ERMYNGARDE	Myrna Sharlow
ERMYNTRUDE	Jeska Swartz
GIGLIETTA	Carolina Lazzari

Folco ....Giulio Crimi
Re Raimondo ....Giacomo Rimini
Messer Cornelius ....Constantin Nicolay
Il Cavalier Faidet.........Alfred Maguenat
L'Araldo Maggiore ....Desiré Defrere
Un Vegliardo ....Vittorio Trevisan

Conductor ....Cleofonte Campanini

"Isabeau" was a long ways from being Campanini's most accurate guess on what would be a popular opera, though it had the Lady Godiva legend as a story and a long history of litigation and bad language to give it a start. As far back as 1910 the firm of Liebler in New York, otherwise George Tyler, had conceived the idea that a Mascagni opera for the use of Bessie Abott would bear artistic and financial fruit.

A contract was thereupon made with Mascagni, who summoned his librettist, Illica, and "Ysobel," so it was first termed, was decided upon. Illica journeyed to Coventry, England, to investigate the Godiva story, and Mascagni in Italy began to turn the story into sound.

Months went on and the opera was not delivered. By 1911 Mr. Tyler announced that he had already invested upwards of $100,000 in a work that he had not received, that he had discovered that when questionings were likely to prove embarrassing, Mascagni was in the habit of taking his unfinished manuscript under his arm and going off to the mountains leaving no address behind, and that this was likely to continue indefinitely. Moreover, the composer decided that he did not care to come to America and conduct the piece, as he had promised.

So lawyers wearing pleased expressions jumped in on both sides, Mme. Mascagni made some unkind, not to say acidulated remarks about Miss Abott's voice, Miss Abott made a tour of the United States in "Robin Hood" as a substitute opera, and "Ysobel" or "Isabeau" went to Buenos Aires for a performance. In course of time Campanini secured its rights for this country.

Apparently he had a lively belief in it. At least he gave it a mounting that threw into the shade all the "Aïdas" and "Giocondas" and other stage shows of past seasons, he rehearsed it thoroughly, and he performed it with processions and crowds, motley, glitter, color and light. All the bravery of a thoroughly festive occasion was there, and a sensational scene besides.

As I have said, it was founded on the Lady Godiva story, and the press agent had whispered softly but industriously that the audience would have a chance to get the same view as fell to Peeping Tom of Coventry, but without his penalty of subsequent blindness. At the appointed time Miss Raisa threw aside her mantle and revealed herself in silk fleshings and a wig that covered her about as completely as the cloak itself, strode off the stage, and was seen again astride a horse as it plodded past the windows at the rear of the stage. In a subsequent season Anna Fitziu in the same part wore an even longer and thicker wig.

All of which was enough to make the audience slightly self-conscious, but not enough to save the opera. For if the history of the Chicago Opera has taught anything, it is that the way to operatic salvation lies through good tunes and the other adjuncts of good music, and here was where "Isabeau" was markedly and distressingly missing. It had noise, it had stage knowledge, it had plenty of other assisting virtues, but Mascagni would seem to have practically exhausted his supply of tunes with his first work, "Cavalleria Rusticana." At least, he never came within recognizable distance of their fruitiness again.

It frequently happens that when an operatic director is disappointed in the success of a new work, he falls back on the personalities of his company in works that are better known and approved. Campanini was lucky or far-seeing enough to have some personalities to fall back upon. He had Raisa as dramatic soprano, Galli-Curci as coloratura, Muratore as tenor, and he had imported Genevieve Vix from Paris to sing the Garden parts, while Garden stayed there. Likewise he had secured the promise of Marthe Chenal for what would seem to have been the same purpose, but she failed to keep her assignment. As it was, it looked like the right kind of a group upon which to place reliance, though it caused Campanini some trouble before the end of the season. But at the start everything looked fairly rosy.

So on the second night of the season one reads of a tremendous triumph by Galli-Curci in "Lucia di Lammermoor." It was always a best seller when she sang it. She was just then beginning her second season as a first magnitude star, and her delight in her position and her affectionate gratitude to the public for putting her into it were apparent in every phrase she sang. Later it became an old story to her but just then she was in a condition of exuberance that carried her past technical flaws and everything else that stood in the way of her being a mechanically perfect singer. There was a quality in her voice that won the heart, and Galli-Curci was the most famous singer in America.

Another personality appeared at this time, Georges Baklanoff, who had walked out of the Boston Opera Company after a row with Henry Russell and then had won the injunction proceedings by which Russell tried to restrain him from singing elsewhere. He made his first appearance with the Chicago company in "Faust," and it was a notable cast, Baklanoff as the unclean, ophidian specter of a Mephistopheles, indifferent as might be to the low notes of the score but an unforgettable picture; Muratore, the Faust to challenge the memory of Jean de Reszke; and Melba, again a guest artist, as Marguerite, arriving after a series of accidents that would have sent a younger soprano to a sanitarium for the rest of the season.

She had, it appeared, been with the company on its autumn tour about the country. Down in Fort Worth, Texas, she had got in the way of some falling scenery, been completely knocked out and badly bruised, later she had been in an automobile collision, and on the way to Chicago the rear car of the train in which she was riding had detached itself and come to rest out in the middle of the prairies, leaving its passengers in the none too comfortable position of not knowing whether they would be knocked fore or aft in case another train should happen to come along. Such were the joys of travel during a war administration. But the only effect these various items had on Melba was to make her sing a little more faultlessly than before.

Anna Fitziu, having changed her name of Fitzhugh in Italy so that the Italians could pronounce it, made her début as Tosca on November 19, and thereby headed the procession of sopranos who have since moved from

GEORGES BALANOFF AS THE FATHER IN "LOUISE"

VANNI-MARCOUX AS THE FATHER IN "LOUISE"

musical comedy to grand opera. Baklanoff appeared as Scarpia for the first time in Chicago, and from that time all Scarpias were measured by the degree that they fell short of his impersonation. It was one of the best things in all the Chicago opera. A few days later Riccardo Stracciari appeared to sing the name part of "Rigoletto," and thereby managed to balance the cast, for the Gilda was Galli-Curci. Finally came Vix, with Manon as her first vehicle, and a publicity sideline consisting of a Russian prince in the offing whom she was supposedly going to marry.

Without quite becoming a sensation then or ever, she made good, singing in the small, edgy, expressive voice which had become the Parisian fashion, acting adroitly and cleverly, in all respects becoming a first rate foil to Muratore, who was immense as the young des Grieux. Later she appeared as Jean in "Le Jongleur de Nôtre Dame" and the name part of "Louise," but in these she was up against the memory of too strong competition, for, as Frank Tinney used to say, Miss Garden had fixed those parts so that no one else could ever do them. But about that time Miss Raisa made her first appearance as Maliella in "The Jewels of the Madonna," and the opera-going public lifted up its voice and rejoiced. Then and therafter she became the first Maliella of the world.

About this time there was another effort toward American opera, a world première at that. It deserves a new chapter.

CHAPTER XVII

AZORA

(*Daughter of Montezuma*)

Romantic opera in three acts; text by David Stevens; music by Henry Hadley. World première at the Auditorium, Dec. 26, 1917.

THE CAST

AZORA .... Anna Fitziu
PAPANTZIN ....Cyrena Van Gordon
XALCA .... Forrest Lamont
RAMATZIN ....Arthur Middleton
CANEK ....Frank Preisch
MONTEZUMA ....James Goddard
PIQUI-CHAQUI ....B. Mann
CORTEZ ....George Wilkins
A SLAVE GIRL ....Clara Shaw

Incidental Dances by Annetta Pelucchi and Corps de Ballet
Conductor-composer ....Henry Hadley

As may be inferred here and there in these pages, if American opera never arrived at the dignity of founding its own new school, it was not the fault of Campanini. He gave it every possible chance, and never a better one than in the Stevens-Hadley opus. Here was a sort of junior American "Aïda," with a call for lavish staging, processionals, ballets, colorful costuming, big musical numbers. Campanini gave it a cast of Americans, most of whom knew the complete art of singing, and decreed that all the resources of the organization should be turned loose on its mounting. Also, when Mr. Hadley used to conduct his own music, he carried it along with irresistible swing and spirit, and he had put some mighty good music into this score.

Yet "Azora" was not a success. It would be easy to revive some of the post-mortems of the period, to tell how the libretto was no good, or if the piece had been put on in another manner it would have got across. Once, some years later, these ears heard a statement in a speech that the opera had been given "a disgraceful cast," which registers the highest so far among the unintentionally comic remarks evolved by those who think they are doing a good turn to opera in English.

In fact the apologists made a high score of wrong reasons. The true one came out in Campanini's private office, and never got into the newspapers.

"Azora" had its première, with a crowded house, hectic applause, encores, curtain calls, silver wreaths, and all the ceremonials of a first performance. It was given again about a week later. Then Hadley called upon Campanini, saying that he wished to discuss the question of putting on "Azora" in the forthcoming New York season. Campanini was unenthusiastic, not to say cold. He answered that he did not believe that there was enough public interest in the piece to justify him in going to the expense of moving it to New York.

Greatly surprised, Hadley argued that in two performances there had been two full houses. Campanini admitted the full houses, but stated that there were times when the Chicago Opera Association unfortunately found it advisable to issue passes in order to fill up large gaps in the theater seats. "How many people do you think bought main floor seats for your second performance?" he wanted to know.

Hadley opined that there might have been five hundred. "Too many, much too many," said Campanini. "Try again." This time the figure was put at possibly three hundred, and again Campanini shook his head. Hadley kept revising his estimate downward and Campanini's smile kept growing more sardonic. Finally he sent for the box office statement, which had the official figures.

Outside of the regular season subscribers for this night, exactly five persons had bought seats on the main floor.

No more pointed or merciless comment was ever made upon the cause of American opera. Then and now there has always been an infinite amount of conversation on the subject. Shrieks of neglected composers pierce the ear drums; lavish lectures are spoken and articles written holding that artistic and patriotic considerations demand support of the native article. But when it comes to paying out money for tickets to support the native article, there is a sudden shift of activity.

As it turned out, a campaign was started by some of Mr. Hadley's friends in New York, and enough tickets were subscribed so that Campanini after all included "Azora" in the New York season. But since then it has been in that graveyard of frustrated hopes, the warehouse. Too bad, for it deserved a better fate. Plenty of worse music has got by, and there is no need of discussing the dramatic values of the libretto, for the dramatic absurdities of some successful operas are beyond telling. But the exotic flower of grand opera has its own special problems in America, and one of these is general apathy.

Another American opera had a tryout shortly after the new year. Arthur Nevin, at that time in charge of the army music at Camp Grant, came up in khaki uniform and conducted his "A Daughter of the Forest," a one-act piece sung by Frances Peralta, Mr. Lamont, and Mr. Goddard to a libretto by Randolph Hartley. Here the story dealt not with American Indians but with the American Civil War, but in spite of that, "A Daughter of the Forest" was not the opening number in an American school of operatic composition.

"Isabeau," too, went into the silence; Galli-Curci and Muratore sang "Lakmé," an unwise choice on his part, since the music lay uncomfortably high for his voice; Miss Garden came back from Paris for the final three weeks in Chicago, to do "Carmen," "Monna Vanna," "Pelléas et Mélisande," and some of the others in her list.

About this time there was a bit of trouble from an unexpected source. Galli-Curci was so much the popular idol of Chicago that throughout this season she was not far from being the operatic life-saver. But Campanini, realizing her box office value, billed her over and over again until she was fairly worn out. With her weariness she grew panicky over the coming New York season. "If I go there and cannot sing well," she explained, "all the critics will say, 'Dio mio, what a nose!' and there will be nothing else to say." Finally she announced that she would not go at all.

Ring Lardner had been moved at one time and another to make joyous and puckish comment on operatic doings, as witness what he gravely stated to be the translation of the sentence pronounced upon Isabeau:

> He speaks in an awed way:
>   "This noon, right down Broadway,
> With none of your clo'es on,
>   No shoes and no hose on,
> And us looking at you,
>   You stubborn young brat, you
> Shall ride on a palfrey.
>   The show shall be all free."

Whereupon when the Galli-Curci strike made the front pages, he wrote:

"They's been only the 1 big story and that was the brawl between Campanini, the orchestra leader over to the Auditorium, and Amelia Galli-Curci, that sings the air.

"It seems like Cleo had dated her up to sing some songs in Boston and N. Y. when she got through here and all of a sudden she says she was too tired. So he says:

> " 'But my Galli! You promised!'

> " 'But I tell you I'm tired out,'

"she says. So he says:

> " 'A few more shows won't hurci,
>   Amelia Galli-Curci.'

"And she says,

> " 'You tell that stuff to Swini,
>   Conductor Campanini.'

"And that give her the last word, but she wasn't satisfied. So she began telling how little she got for singing."

He would seem to have told the essential if not the literal truth, but like other tempests, this one blew over with the assistance of a few mutual concessions. Campanini gave her a two weeks' layoff with instructions to do nothing but rest, she agreed to come to New York, and the matter of salary was dropped by both.

In the meantime Vix appeared in the name part of Massenet's "Sapho," a depressing event then, and scarcely better when Miss Garden revived it a decade later. Another new opera was put on at almost the final performance of the season, "Le Sauteriot," by Silvio Lazzari, which, also, for excellent reasons, was not played in subsequent seasons. Finally the company packed up and went to the Lexington theater in New York, built by Oscar Hammerstein but never used by him for opera.

The season opened with "Monna Vanna," with Garden, Muratore, and Baklanoff, with a record of thirty curtain calls. After her rest, Galli-Curci rejoined the company and made an equal hit. Garden appeared in most of her repertoire, Melba sang a performance or two, "Isabeau" and "Azora" and "The Jewels of the Madonna" were presented, and the New York critics were unwontedly and unexpectedly kind to the Chicago singers. In fact the musical critic of one of the Boston papers was moved to wrath about New York's "discovery" of Galli-Curci when by this time she was pretty well known all over the country, speaking scornfully about the way New Yorkers were "capering about the parish pump."

Three weeks was the stay in New York. Then came two weeks in Boston, where the critics were also kind, but not so unexpectedly. The tour was no financial triumph, and Campanini had no expectation of making it so, but it was an artistic one.

So ended another season.

CHAPTER XVIII

Probably the most important item in the 1918-19 season was the first appearance with the company of Giorgio Polacco, later destined to become musical director of the present Civic Opera. At that time, however, his official title was merely conductor, and his engagement for a season only.

Campanini's health had begun to worry him. He had been warned by his physicians that the task of rehearsing and conducting operas according to his custom in the past was putting too much of a strain on his heart, and that while he could be permitted to make occasional appearances in the pit, he must no longer consider it as a steady thing.

He therefore sent for Mr. Polacco in New York one day and had a long discussion with him, pointing out the condition of his health, the fact that he was obliged to relinquish part of his labors, the further fact that another conductor, Gino Marinuzzi, had already been engaged for the following, the 1919-20, season, but that principally during the season under discussion, a place existed in Chicago for the talents, industry, and disciplinary methods of Polacco.

For Polacco, a kindly, gentle and sympathetic soul when away from the stand, was noted far and wide for his flaming light as a conductor and his complete lack of patience with all singers who flagged in their efforts on the stage. Like other members of the operatic profession, he for years had wandered up and down the face of the earth. A native of Venice, his first opportunity to conduct had come when he was only eighteen years old. He had gone to London to play in an operatic orchestra directed by Luigi Arditi, having charge of such bits as the bells and the organ in "Cavalleria Rusticana" and similar matters. One day there was a call to conduct one of the Gluck operas, and Polacco, who had learned the work thoroughly in his conservatory studies, responded. From that day on he would seem to have been marked as a man of the baton.

His career carried him into nearly every major opera house on three continents. He was the first to conduct "Louise" after its world première in Paris—he conducted it in Rome—the first to introduce "Boris Godunoff" to South America. In London, Barcelona, and several other theaters he was the immediate successor of Arturo Toscanini. He was in San Francisco when Tetrazzini sang there, her first appearance in the United States, and he had been associated with Toscanini at the New York Metropolitan, remaining there for five or six years after the departure of that extraordinary genius.

For the moment he was at a loose end, but it did not take him long to make up his mind. At the end of their conversation he and Campanini shook hands in agreement, and he was a member of the Chicago Opera. He has been heard to say that he was too precipitate that night, for no later than the next day an offer came for him to take the baton of the Boston Symphony Orchestra, a post then vacant following the departure to Germany of Dr. Karl Muck at the urgent invitation of the United States government.

Mr. Polacco says that Campanini derided him joyously for so much as thinking of taking the Boston position. He himself thought of it as a place of ideal peace among the great works of music, but Campanini assured him that he would be bored to death in less than a week, and that his place in the world was down in the orchestra pit to strike terror to the souls of lazy operatic singers. This was the undoubted truth, for Polacco was ever a man of the theater.

So he came to Chicago, and if any of the artists thought that conditions were going to be relaxed because Campanini's hand was less firmly on the tiller, they were speedily disillusioned. For Polacco knew his job. He was a sincere and cultured musician with high ideals of performance, he went to the theater with every detail worked out in his mind, and he had a ready, not to say pointed manner when things went wrong of calling the attention of the offenders.

Usually one reproof was enough. I shall never forget the amazed look on the face of Rosa Raisa one night in a "Tosca" performance. For just a moment during the "Vissi d'Arte" aria her attention had lapsed in the matter of holding a long note. Polacco sustained the chord in the orchestra as long as he dared, until the violin bows were drawn out to their uttermost tips. Then he and the orchestra moved on, leaving Raisa in a manner of speaking between sky and earth and with little knowledge of how to get back.

It was an unexpectedly comic performance any way, for Raisa herself had a score to pay off that night, and she paid it. The Mario of the performance was Alessandro Dolci, a tenor of superb voice, but a man whose habits on the stage made him intensely disliked by his associates. Raisa had suffered with him until, as far as she was concerned, patience was no longer a virtue. Her chance came in the final scene.

Then, as you will remember, Mario has been shot by the firing squad and lies stretched out on the terrace. Tosca with a cry of despair flings herself across his body, but Raisa managed to fling herself in such a way that two vigorous elbows bored into what can be best described as his equatorial line. With a grunt that could have been heard out in the lobby, Dolci's feet went up in the air and he deflated like a burst football. Even that was not enough for Raisa, for in getting up to run over to the parapet before jumping over it, she, quite by accident, of course, stepped on his palm with the sharp heel of her shoe. The audience burst into a shout of laughter, and Polacco nearly had a fit because his line of vision was cut off by the top of the stage and he could not see what was happening further back. In some opera performances a great deal goes on that never gets into the official reports.

But Polacco had begun developing his Chicago reputation long before this. He conducted the first performance of the season, "La Traviata," with Galli-Curci, Guido Ciccolini (début) and Riccardo Stracciari, and also the second night, "Madame Butterfly," with Tamaki Miura, Irene Pavloska, Forrest Lamont, and Auguste Bouilliez (début), and was talked about quite as much as any of the singers.

The first night was far more of a gala night than most of the performances officially so labeled. The war had come to its end a week before, and it was quite fitting that the Chicago Opera should make formal comment. So during the intermission after the first act a procession of conductors marched into the pit, Campanini leading, and followed by Marcel Charlier, Polacco, Louis Hassel-mans, another newcomer of that year, and Giuseppe Sturani. The curtains were drawn, discovering the chorus in a massed group.

Then entered Mr. Bouilliez dressed as a Belgian soldier, carrying the Belgian flag, to sing La Brabançonne, Charlier conducting. Polacco took the stick and Stracciari sang the Garibaldi hymn. Muratore in his Rouget de Lisle clothes sang the Marseillaise to Hasselmans' conducting, and Polacco took the stick again when little Miura toddled out in kimono for the hymn of her faraway Japan, a song which it is safe to say that no one but she was up on, either words or music. Cyrena Van Gordon, looking like every war poster of Britannia ever drawn, followed with "God Save the King." Finally Galli-Curci, escorted by the ballet, appeared on the stage, Campanini mounted the stand, and every one let go all the combined enthusiasm in "The Star Spangled Banner."

During the rest of the evening Polacco wrought with the faded "Traviata" score in a way almost to convince some of the unbelievers that there was some vital music in it after all. Of course Galli-Curci was a delight, and she had a good cast around her. The next night Polacco did even more with "Madame Butterfly," because there he had some newer and juicier music with which to deal. Miura, the little mite of a Japanese who used to appear as "Madam Butterfry," as she called it, gave naturally the most complete physical illusion of any one who ever did the part. Curiously, however, the picture, expert as it was, played havoc with the spiritual qualities of the part. Miura always delighted the eye, but seldom wrung the heart.

"Isabeau" was put on again, Anna Fitziu and Forrest Lamont taking the leading parts, Raisa started them talking again about her Aïda, and some strangers began to make débuts. Yvonne Gall, from Paris, was one of these. She started as Thaïs, a performance made possible because Miss Garden had shortly before parted with her appendix in France and was unable to be in Chicago in time for the opening.

Seeing Miss Gall's Thaïs again at Ravinia in the summer of 1928, one learned that in ten years she had changed her mind about the proper costume for a semi-tropical vamp. In her 1918 version, every one was convinced that she wore Jaeger flannels for the part, and the further the piece advanced the higher grew her neckline. A few nights later she appeared as Juliet, upsetting the customary Galli-Curci-Muratore combination, and made a notable hit. Her voice was and is a thing of beauty, and then she excelled in the classical rôles. Galli-Curci, on her part, went on as Mimi in "La Bohème" with John McCormack, who returned to make one of his infrequent operatic appearances—he had promised one a year before and had been snowed in before he could get to Chicago—and proved what some of us had been believing, that while the high notes and the flute obbligatos of coloratura singing were what were making her popular and prosperous, she could, had she chosen, made of herself a notable lyric soprano.

John O'Sullivan was another newcomer. In spite of

his name, which truly indicated his birthplace, he classified
as a French singer, for he had lived in France for years,
chattered the language like a native, and sang only French
parts. He was introduced in "William Tell," why, no
one was ever able to say, except that no one else could
sing the tenor part and O'Sullivan could. It is a vile part
for most singers, abounding in B's, B flats, and C's almost
without number, and O'Sullivan, after he conquered his
first nervousness trumpeted them out so easily as to make
a personal hit of his own. It was a tiresome opera however, no better than when the Century Opera Company
had given it, and it soon retired into the discard.

Does any one remember the pigeon story of that
season? Marcel Journet was singing bass parts with the
company at that time, and doing rather well by them,
but he got the most publicity over something he would
rather have had passed by in silence. One day he reported
to his hotel that the drain pipe leading from his bathroom
was stopped up. A plumber investigated, and reported in
his turn that the pipe had been stuffed full of feathers.
A low-minded and suspicious reporter straightway
evolved, and what is worse, printed his theory that Journet had been snaring pigeons on his window sill, killing
them and cooking them in his room. It was a front page
story, and merrily, not to say maliciously, spun.

You have perhaps been present when an indignantly
voluble singer was voicing a series of protests. Journet
was one of the most indignant and most voluble in my
experience, though I had not written the story. His explanation to me, if I remember its main thread, was to
the effect that he had made much money in his life, was
feeling quite at ease in financial matters, and was fully

able, if he desired to eat pigeons, to go out and buy them.

Polacco was greatly desirous of extending his operatic achievements, with Raisa, in spite of her "Tosca" misadventure, as the leading soprano. He was particularly anxious to put on the early Italian "Norma" and the late Italian "Loreley," and started her and other singers on their rehearsals. But midway in the season Raisa in her turn was forced to go to the hospital and get a divorce from her own appendix. "Norma," therefore had to be canceled, but Miss Fitziu learned the "Loreley" part at short notice and sang it twice. In a later season Claudia Muzio also sang it, but it is hard to believe that the opera will ever be a permanent feature in the repertoire.

Miss Garden finally got back from France and hastened to appear in the first performance on any stage of Henri Fevrier's "Gismonda," a setting of the elderly Sardou play of the same name, composed about ten years after the "Monna Vanna" setting. Critical effort the next day showed a marked straining to make the piece a success, but it could not be done. There was eyefilling scenery, there was Miss Garden, both eyefilling and stagewise, Campanini conducted with all his craft, the composer was present, in his box all the time the performance was going on, and before the curtain most of the time when it was not, there were wreaths and handshakes and kisses and all the customary ritual of a first performance. But after the first performance the public would have little of it.

Another first performance—at least for America—fell to the lot of Conductor Hasselmans, and was not given until the final Saturday afternoon of the season.

It was "Le Chemineau," by Xavier Leroux, the setting
of a play by Jean Richepin which in a translated version
called "The Harvester" used to be acted by Otis Skinner
some twenty years ago in America and as "Ragged
Robin" by Sir Herbert Tree in London.

"Le Chemineau" has always been a source of great
annoyance to the Chicago Opera management and to Mr.
Eckstein in Ravinia. In spite of the box office statements,
they know that it is a piece of high and fine art, but the box
office statement is generally unfavorable. Every once in
awhile their optimism is too much for their fears. They
take it out, dust it off, and hope for the best. Then they
learn that the public stays away in large numbers, and they
put it back again. But as it used to be sung and acted by
Miss Gall, Mr. Maguenat, and Mr. Baklanoff, it was
one of the most affecting pieces of the repertoire, a poignant tragedy of poor peasants whose feelings were just
as near the surface as though they had been better
dressed.

There was another "Loreley," another "Gismonda,"
a "Carmen" with Miss Garden, a "Cleopatra," also
with her—she seemed determined that year not to do the
things in which she was most fondly remembered—a
"Faust" with O'Sullivan and Gall, various other odds and
ends, and the company went on tour again, another visit
to New York, then doubling back by degrees to Pittsburgh and to Detroit, its first visit there. A few weeks
before departure Campanini put on "Crispino e la
Comare," and Galli-Curci and Trevisan made a delectable
entertainment of it. For some unknown reason it has not
been done much in this country. It is an elderly piece with
no tune in it that you would ever care to remember, but

audiences loved it the few times they had the chance to hear it.

Here and there on this visit to New York one begins to notice a change in the critical attitude. There had been lavish praise the season before; even now they liked the novelties which the Metropolitan Company had not given them; but occasionally a warning finger was being lifted. In later seasons the finger was to become converted to a clenched fist. Just now they were contented with beginning to point out that the Metropolitan had a cerain "dignity" which was lacking in the Chicago organization, and that the Chicago performances were conventional "except in a few spots." Just what this last means any one is at liberty to figure out at leisure. In any event it no doubt relieved the soul of the writer.

CHAPTER XIX

The 1919-20 season was a sad one for the Chicago Opera. Right in the midst of it, in all the turmoil and confusion and incessant rehearsals and performances of an operatic season, Campanini died.

He had come back to Chicago in the fall, a little frailer than before, complaining of a hard cold that he had taken on the way, not up to the physical strain of a few years ago, but still at his desk during the day and in his box for a few of the first performances of the season. Then one night he was missing from his accustomed place, and it was told that he preferred to stay in his room and rest. It should have been enough to warn the world that all was very far from being well, for nothing less than complete physical disability would have kept him out of the opera house when a performance was going on.

Never a night during all his years of service that he and Mme. Campanini were not at the theater, she always in her box, he on the stand if he was conducting or with her if he was not, vanishing out to dash behind the scenes three or four times in the course of the performance with a suggestion about a detail of costume, a pose, a stage picture, what not. They say that he used to make a personal inspection of all costumes before every new performance whether he was the conductor or not; he had been known to call for a pair of scissors five minutes be-

fore the rise of the curtain and trim down a set of stage
whiskers to suit his ideas of what was scenically fitting.

Mme. Campanini was as wise and as interested in
stage affairs as he. As Eva Tetrazzini, sister of the more
famous coloratura, Luisa, she had been well known in
operatic performances of her time, leaving the stage permanently, however, when she married him. For the rest
of his career her operatic endeavors were vicarious, working through the efforts of others, but she knew the stage
thoroughly and he always respected her advice.

So when neither appeared at the Auditorium, it
should have been a sign that matters were seriously
wrong. A few days later he was moved out of his rooms
at the Congress Hotel to St. Luke's Hospital, and on
the morning of December 19, 1919, he, the real Cleofonte
Campanini, moved away from the hospital and the world
for good.

The physician's bulletin said that it was weak heart
and pneumonia. It was really forty years' hard work in
the theater. For him there was perhaps only one sorrow-
ful feature about it. He died in a Chicago winter when
he had always wanted to live in the Italian sunshine.

For Campanini's Latin temperament manifested itself both in a love of art and a love of light and gayety.
A joke was dear to his heart, and if it happened to be a
practical joke, so much the better. He used to tell with
tears of laughter running down his cheeks of the trick he
once played on his friendly enemy, Gatti-Casazza, the
general director of the Metropolitan Opera Company.

It happened that during the second year of the war,
Campanini, as a non-combatant, was permitted to unravel
the miles of red tape necessary in such cases and penetrate

behind the German lines in search of undiscovered operatic talent. Armed with all official credentials, he went into Switzerland, and crossed Lake Constance by steamer to the German side. Somewhere on the trip he met Gatti-Casazza, who had been doing some unraveling on his own behalf, and was on a similar errand.

Arrived upon German soil, the passengers were herded into an intelligence bureau, where the officer in charge took them, two by two, into a booth to be undressed and searched. Campanini and Gatti-Casazza went together, and Campanini's ordeal was brief. In a moment, he said, he was climbing back into his clothes and laughing at the spectacle of his fellow impresario, shivering without them.

"The officer was a dull fellow," he said. "I went close to him and whispered. 'And what about information written in invisible ink on the skin?' And what does the German do with my friend Gatti but send for a nice green lemon and rub him until he looked like a magnificent, ripe tomato."

There is no report that Gatti ever hated him for the trick or for the story. No one ever hated him, even in the midst of the fiercest battles that he used to wage. His singers worshiped him at all times. They remembered his sharp discipline as director, but they also remembered his many acts of kindly, warm-hearted generosity when rehearsals and performances were over.

His funeral was like his life, of the theater. His coffin, escorted by the directorate of the Opera Company, was moved to the Auditorium stage, where on Sunday afternoon, December 21, a musical service was held to his memory.

At three o'clock the curtains were noiselessly drawn. There in the center of the stage, heaped high with flowers, with the brilliantly illuminated Transformation Scene of "Parsifal" above and about it, lay the casket containing the body of Cleofonte Campanini. At either end was a burning wax candle. His baton and one of his opera scores rested on his conductor's stand. The house was thronged.

The orchestra, concealed from view behind the stage, broke the silence with the Prelude to Saint-Saëns' "The Deluge," with Charlier conducting. Alessandro Bonci's voice floated out in the "Ingemisco" from Verdi's Requiem Mass, De Angelis conducting. Hasselmans added a prelude by Fauré, then the new conductor of the season, Gino Marinuzzi, took charge, and Rosa Raisa's voice rang out in the "Inflammatus" from Rossini's "Stabat Mater."

This number was peculiarly appropriate and peculiarly touching, for almost exactly a year before Campanini himself had conducted the "Stabat Mater" one Sunday night at a concert in the Auditorium, and Miss Raisa had been fairly ablaze as she sang the excerpt. At its end, and while the audience was doing its collective best to raise the roof with applause, Campanini stepped off the stand, kissed Raisa on both cheeks, then stepped back and repeated the number.

The last movement from Tschaikowsky's "Pathétique" Symphony, and the musical service was over, but for three hours thereafter Chicagoans filed past the coffin of the departed maestro. Funeral services next day at Holy Name Cathedral were conducted by Very Reverend John Cavanaugh, former president of the University of Nôtre Dame. The body was placed in a vault

VITTORIO TREVISAN AS AND IN "DON PASQUALE"

at Calvary cemetery until the next spring, when it was carried back to Campanini's home in Parma, Italy.

There it is now, and there, too, is an ornately sculptured stone memorial to his honor, for which, though she declines to talk about it, Miss Raisa is largely responsible. For among the other deeds in his busy life, Campanini discovered Raisa when she was very young and very poor, driven out from Poland into Italy. Having found her, he and Mme. Campanini gave her advice, instruction, material aid, and the encouragement to take the place in opera which she afterwards occupied. And Raisa is not the person to forget.

So passed a brave and fascinating figure from the world of opera.

CHAPTER XX

The first rule of the theater is that the show must go on. Campanini had planned and outlined a heavy season, with more effort and disregard of expense than ever before in the attempt to find another "Jewels of the Madonna," or some novelty of the sort which could become a permanent item in the repertoire. During his disability and after his death, his lieutenants carried on according to his plans. Before the season was over, there began to be a certain amount of comment that the master's hand was missing, but that sort of comment, sometimes justified, sometimes not, is inevitable. The excuse was the greater this time, because several of the experiments turned out unsuccessfully.

The first was "La Nave," a dramatic poem by Gabriele d'Annunzio, cut down into libretto length by Tito Ricordi, and set to music by Italo Montemezzi. It opened the season on November 18, 1919, and Montemezzi himself came on to conduct the performance. The cast:

Marco Gratico	Alessandro Dolci
Sergio Gratico	Giacomo Rimini
Orso Faledro	Vittorio Arimondi
Basiliola	Rosa Raisa
Il Maestro dell'Acque Orio Dodo	William Rogerson
Una Voce	Emma Noe
Il Piloto Lucio Polo	Constantin Nicolay

IL TAGLIAPIETRA GAURO.....Arthur Boardman
IL MULINARO BENNO........Lodovico Oliviero
IL TIMONIERE SIMON
   D'ARMARIO ....Vittorio Trevisan,

and ten or twelve more who do not matter at this time.

Here was another case of trying to pick personal successes out of an opera which was not in the least a success itself. For "La Nave" was not another "L'Amore dei Tre Re." It was another allegory, this time based on an episode in the history of early Venice. Hope springs eternal in the general operatic breast that allegory is the true answer for an operatic libretto, just as strongly as in the American operatic breast that Indian themes are the true answer for an American opera. The chances are strongly against both. "L'Amore dei Tre Re" succeeded for two reasons, one, that the plot is so poignant that its symbolism is forgotten, the other, that its music was composed in white hot passion.

"La Nave" failed in both cases. The allegory went to the place where all dead plays go when they become opera librettos, and the music dawdled in the composer's brain where it should have run like swift blood. An enormously massive—and heavy—equipment of scenery had been designed by the American husband-and-wife firm of Norman-Bel Geddes, and if you wanted to hear an eloquent not to say pointed opinion of how operatic scenery should not be made, you should have talked to the back-stage force about that time.

From the front, it merely looked heavy and not much more. One still remembers a special ineptitude about it. In a prologue and three acts, four scenes in all, no one was ever able to make an entrance from the rear center, all being forced to dodge around pillars, altars, what not. Another case was where Miss Raisa was called upon in the dramatic action to draw a bow and arrows and shoot down some prisoners confined in a pit. The pit was so built that Miss Raisa had to shoot left-handed, holding her bow about on a level with her eyebrows, with the result that the arrows would hardly have disturbed a Venetian mosquito, much less a Venetian prisoner.

Miss Raisa, with a voice in her soul and a soul in her voice, as one of the critics remarked at the time, took the greater share of the applause by putting more heat into the performance than Montemezzi had put into the score. But single handed the task was too much for even her great ability, and "La Nave" soon passed into the forgotten. I am told that the stage force raised a special and quite non-operatic chorus of joy on its own behalf when it was ordered to break up the scenery.

Miss Garden made another effort to galvanize the moribund "Cleopatra" into something resembling life; Miura was still doing "Madame Butterfly," Bonci, most expert and best known of lyric tenors—Tito Schipa was just about to begin his American career—was on to sing in "A Masked Ball" and incidentally to do certain things in it that no one has ever equaled. Then some new singers began to attract attention. Carlo Galeffi was one. Edward Johnson was another. Mr. Schipa was a third.

Before the season opened, Campanini told me that Galeffi was "a young Titta Ruffo," and he came near being just that, though without the preliminary blare of publicity that helped to make Ruffo the sensation that he had been. He started in "A Masked Ball" and "Rigoletto," time-honored baritonal tests, disclosing a glorious voice and marked stage sense, and when the Puccini "Trittico" was finally made public, a striking ability for works a bit outside of the operatic conventions.

His American career was brief, due principally, it was said, to his undue belief in his own monetary value. Perhaps Campanini, had he lived, could have browbeaten him into accepting a fee somewhere near his true value, for Campanini had a good deal of talent in that direction. In that case Galeffi would probably have become a leading figure in America.

Mr. Johnson had paused temporarily in operetta on the way to his operatic prominence. As far back as 1907 it was discovered that he, already well known in concert and oratorio, was the only singer in America capable of putting through the tenor music in Oscar Strauss' "The Waltz Dream." So he went into the piece and made so good that he would have been in position to name his own pay for future commitments in operetta.

Instead, he quit the piece at the end of its New York run, took his earnings to Italy and invested them in operatic study, with the result that he became a celebrity there. He originated the tenor rôles in both "L'Amore dei Tre Re"—he is still the best Avito in the world—and "La Nave," and out of thirty performances of "Die Meistersinger" at La Scala, "I Maestri Cantori," as they call it there, he sang the part of Walther twenty-seven times. From his first appearance in Chicago, Loris in "Fedora," he was one of the company's most admirable artists, and the Chicago Opera never suffered a greater loss than when, on its next reorganization, through no fault of his or the company's, he was taken by the Metropolitan in New York.

Mr. Schipa was unknown when he came to Chicago, but his charm of voice and personality did not permit him to remain so for long. He came here from South America where he had been on a tour, attended by a train of South Americans who learned less English during their stay here than almost any group on record. One there was who on the first of the year greeted his acquaintances with "Happy New York." Another complained that he nearly starved in the United States because for three weeks the only article of food he knew how to order in a restaurant was "ham y eggs," and he grew tired of that three times a day.

Mr. Johnson and Dorothy Jardon made their first appearance in "Fedora," Umberto Giordano's somewhat antiquated drama of the same name. But the piece contains one lovely melody, "Amor ti vieta," and here Mr. Johnson began his subsequently many times repeated practice of "stopping the show." It was a marvel of free throated, passionate, but always controlled singing. More interest, however, attached to the arrival of Gino Marinuzzi.

This conductor arrived in Chicago a few days after the beginning of the season from South America, bringing with him the scores of Puccini's three one-act operas, "Il Tabarro," "Suor Angelica," and "Gianni Schicchi," to be done together as a single entertainment and known as the "Trittico." It would seem that less than five minutes after his arrival in Chicago he was in the midst of the first rehearsal. Such a whirlwind of nervous energy has seldom been seen. He was all over the place at once, explaining the stories, playing a theme on the piano, placing the participants on the stage, showing them how to act, and always infusing them with his own enthusiasm. He talked Italian to them when he came, but inside of three weeks he was talking idiomatic and plainly pronounced English. It was the speediest job of learning a language that I ever had occasion to observe. Where he found the time to do it no one can tell, for Campanini's disability threw the brunt of the season on his shoulders, and his English studies had to be taken up at odd hours. Evidently he had a photographic memory that worked with a high speed shutter, for among his other achievements, he conducted everything from memory.

One of his most astonishing feats happened later during a performance of "Lohengrin." Scenes and acts are sometimes interchangeable in operatic practice, and Marinuzzi must have thought that the first scene of the opera's third act, involving a complete change of scenery on the stage, would take a full intermission. At any rate, he left the orchestra pit and went to his room just off the stage.

But suddenly and without signal the lights were lowered, trumpets began to blow on the stage, the new scene was on, and no conductor in sight. The concertmaster of the orchestra jumped to the stand, took the baton and tried to get the orchestra going, the orchestra meanwhile not understanding a new set of signals and rapidly slipping into a nose dive. Just a second before the crash, the door flung open and a white faced Marinuzzi leaped into the pit. I am sure that he made the last fifty feet in not more than three steps, calling signals to the orchestra as he went, grasping the baton as he landed on the stand. "F sharp" in one direction, "A natural" in another, "Section 513" in a third, and before the audience realized that there had been any danger of going wrong, the performance was on an even keel and running smoothly again. And'this, too, without a score.

The "Trittico" when it was staged scored two-thirds of a success. "Il Tabarro," with Miss Jardon, Mr. Johnson, and Mr. Galeffi, was a stirring melodrama with music which, if not the most potent Puccini, was at least in the skilled Puccini manner. "Suor Angelica," with lovely etherealized bits throughout it, did not quite register. It was long and slow moving; even the manifest talents of Miss Raisa could not pull it up. I have always believed that its leisurely course with nothing but women's voices on the stage created a physical effect of monotony because of its lack of contrast.

But "Gianni Schicchi" turned out to be a roaring farce. Who but the Italians could ever have evolved something side-splittingly funny out of a tale about a corpse and the family quarreling over a will? And who will ever forget the old Florentine as acted by Virgilio Lazzari as he limped over and blew out the great candles when he learned he had been left out of the will, or the terrific row between Mr. Galeffi and Maria Claessens of the marriage of their (stage) children, Mr. Johnson and Evelyn Herbert, or the Rabelaisian touch given to the orchestra at the entrance of the doctor, Vittorio Trevisan?

Puccini may or may not have had the idea of composing a huge symphony in terms of opera, stopping, however, with the scherzo movement. At any rate, when the publishers finally consented to allow the operas to be played separately instead of insisting on the three together, it was the scherzo, "Gianni Schicchi," which survived, and which has been played various seasons ever since to the constantly increasing joy of its hearers. It has become one of the durable items in the Chicago Opera's repertoire. At that, "Il Tabarro" is about due for a revival. Properly cast, it would be almost sure to succeed.

Miss Raisa got her chance, a year deferred, to sing the name part of "Norma," a noble performance on her part of an opera so long discarded that it was a novelty to all but the oldest of us. A season or two, and it went into the silence again, a silence enduring almost ten years.

Another attempt at finding the great American opera was made with "Rip Van Winkle," which Catskill legend was given book by Percy MacKaye and music by Reginald de Koven. It loomed into sight, it had its strenuous rehearsals, it came into first and second and third performances, and it passed into oblivion.

Once again the elect stroked their chins and declaimed by all the gods of music and drama that it was a good opera, meanwhile going furiously into efforts to explain why so few others of the public thought as they did. The most ingenious argument discovered was to the effect that (1), no Americans knew how to sing their own language; (2), even if they did, American audiences had debased their ears so long by listening to tunes in an unknown tongue that they did not know how to recognize their own language when they heard it. This was actually and seriously argued out at length in the columns of a Chicago newspaper. It shows what those who believe in the English language but also believe in putting it on a sane basis have to contend with in order to save the cause from those who say that they are its friends.

No one thought to say that many of Mr. MacKaye's words were buried so deep in Mr. de Koven's orchestration that the most skilled singers in the world could hardly have exhumed them. And no one thought to say that Mr. de Koven, considerably older than when he wrote "Robin Hood" and various other of his operetta masterpieces, had come to the conclusion that the main difference between opera and operetta was that in opera no tunes should ever be finished, but should be broken off short and welded on to scraps of other tunes. After all, the music of an opera is of some importance.

Georges Baklanoff was the Rip of the performance, and the one who got most of the applause. It was a strenuous season for him, because in its midst he was arrested on a federal warrant and threatened with deportation on a charge of immorality. After a considerable series of hearings before the commissioner, the charges were considered not sustained and were dismissed, but it upset his rehearsal time considerablv not to say his equanimity.

About this time, too, the claque question bobbed up again. Official denials went out that there was such a thing, but artists began to tell how they were being approached with a demand for from $50 a performance up, how some admitted yielding, others refused, still others actually asked for the service.

The claque leader was identified as an assistant stage manager. He has been out of the company a good while, but while he was there he seemed to have the matter pretty well organized. Extra tickets in those days were through one source and another generally available—some of the leading artists had an item of extra tickets in their con-

ROSA RAISA AS NORMA

tracts—and strong armed and hard palmed applauders were stationed around in various parts of the audience, usually in the balconies, to start the applause at the right time and keep it up when it showed signs of dying out. Those who refused to pay the fee were given strong hints that their performance would not go so well. Nothing so crude as a hiss was employed, but the psychological effect of the threat had its importance at a time when nerves were tense during a performance, and sometimes applause was started at the wrong time during a solo, with the result of ruining its climax.

I have never been able to believe that any of this had a final effect on the artistic status or value of a member of the Chicago Opera, but it was an annoyance, and in later seasons the management of the company succeeded in pretty well wiping it out.

It was in this season, too, that the company began to go in for ballet for its own sake and not merely as an entertaining incident in an operatic performance. A long campaign had put ballet into the public mind. The lovely Anna Pavlowa and her group of experts had been making more or less regular visits to Chicago ever since 1910; Serge de Diaghileff's Ballet Russe, with all the light and color and fascination of the modern school, had also come to the Auditorium for an engagement. The latter was far too expensive an undertaking to be a financial success, or for that matter to break even, but it had left unforgettable memories of what a fine and vivid spectacle the art of the dance could be.

Meanwhile Serge Oukrainsky and Andreas Pavley had detached themselves from the Pavlowa company, had settled in Chicago and had sought and found an engagement as ballet masters and principal dancers with the opera company. Likewise, Adolph Bolm, a notable artist, a brilliant choreographer, and a leading member of the Diaghileff organization, had decided to settle in America and was pursuing his profession in New York.

Wherefore Oukrainsky and Pavley put on "Boudour," a work with a plot worked out by themselves to music by the Chicago composer, Felix Borowski. The Norman-Bel Geddes firm gave it scenery and costumes, extravagant, brilliantly colored orientalism, with feathered head dresses yards long and trains that required the services of a dozen or more bearers. Mr. Borowski himself conducted it several times in Chicago and later in New York, and it became one of the successful incidents of the season.

At about the same time Mr. Bolm came to Chicago to put on "The Birthday of the Infanta." Here John Alden Carpenter had taken as a basis a pantomime presentment of Oscar Wilde's like named play, had written a score, and Robert Edmond Jones had designed the scenery and costumes. Mr. Bolm staged and rehearsed it, taking the part of the dwarf, and Ruth Page was presented in her first full length ballet part, the pretty little Infanta.

Artistically and structurally it was a big thing, one by which to have warm memories of Campanini, for though he did not live to see it, he had decreed it. If he had continued on earth, probably several more of the same sort would have issued, for "The Birthday of the Infanta" was something to delight his artistic soul. In any event it remains as one of the finest achievements of the Chicago Opera. Since his time the company has turned an unresponsive ear to similar undertakings on the ground of their expense, but this time it was put across.

Once again the company packed up and went to New York and Boston. People began to talk about Campanini's successor. Morris Gest was mentioned for the post. So was Mary Garden. What finally happened was still in the future.

CHAPTER XXI

Whatever may be said about the actual achievements of the season of 1920-21, they certainly happened speedily. The newspaper files will tell you how speedily. Let us therefore call on apt quotation's artful aid. In some cases it will be necessary to read between the lines as carefully as the reporters wrote in that unsatisfactory location.

From the Chicago *Tribune,* Monday, December 20: "The performance of Leoncavallo's opera, 'Zaza,' which was to be featured to-morrow night by the operatic début of Mme. Ganna Walska, the 'world's most wealthy prima donna,' has been indefinitely postponed. That announcement was made yesterday by Herbert M. Johnson of the Chicago Opera Company.

"Simultaneously with the above announcement it became known that Mme. Walska checked out Saturday from her luxurious quarters in the Blackstone Hotel. She left no forwarding address. Friends said she had returned to her husband's home in New York City.

"Various explanations were vouchsafed, among them being that of Mme. Walska herself which she gave to friends:

" 'There is a great deal of trouble, and I am tired.'

"Efforts to communicate with the singer at her husband's home last night were futile.

"It was explained last night by Director Johnson

that 'Zaza' was postponed because of the overwhelming amount of work before the artists during the holidays.

" 'We simply found that "Zaza" was not ready, that we could not get it ready, and so we postponed the performance,' he said.

" 'We will no doubt try to give "Zaza" in Chicago this season, and if we do, Mme. Walska will certainly have an opportunity to play the rôle if she desires; but we're tremendously busy now. Too busy.' "

"And while Mme. Walska is in New York preparing to get still further away from Chicago by hibernating in Paris, there continues to be a strange babel of many tongues behind the scenes at the Auditorium."

The buzz of comment on this had hardly begun to wear down when on Jan. 7, 1921, the *Tribune* published the following:

"Gino Marinuzzi, operatic conductor and composer, who took the position of artistic director of the Chicago Opera Company following the death of Cleofonte Campanini last winter, has resigned. Beginning to-day, Sig. Marinuzzi will take his old position as one of the conductors.

"Sig. Marinuzzi gave an explanation of his action during the last intermission of 'Lohengrin' at the Auditorium last night to a *Tribune* reporter. He said that the artistic temperaments of the company's stars had turned him into a victim of insomnia, and in order to save his health he was forced to resign as director of the operas.

"Sig. Marinuzzi exhibited all traces of a man physically tired as he told his story. His face looked drawn and deep lines imbedded his brow.

" 'I could not stand the wrangling of the stars any longer, so I resigned as artistic director,' said Sig. Marinuzzi. 'Now I am just a conductor. I will not assign any more rôles and when the stars have objections they cannot complain to me. They will have to speak to Mr. Johnson.

" 'They have given me nothing but sleepless nights. Their voices have been in my ears twenty-four hours a day. Each one with a grievance, each one objecting to a rôle I have assigned to some one else.

" 'First there is a tenor who approaches me with venom in his eyes. He has just heard that I have assigned another tenor to a certain rôle. He wanted that rôle himself.

" 'Then comes a soprano. She is angry because she has not been given a certain rôle. Ah, they bring their troubles to me. Then I go home. I try to sleep. I cannot . . . I get up and pace the floor until five o'clock in the morning. In a few hours there are rehearsals. I get no rest. I cannot listen to their talk any longer.'

"Sig. Marinuzzi is scheduled to conduct four operas next week and is also preparing for the production of 'Salome' the following week.

"Cable dispatches announcing the arrival of Mme. Walska, Polish prima donna, and wife of Alexander Smith Cochrane, one of New York City's richest men, in Europe were received in Chicago last night. Mme. Walska is quoted as blaming Mary Garden for her withdrawal from the Chicago Opera Company."

And Miss Garden, called from her sleep to speak over the telephone about the last paragraph, answered,

ADOLPH BOLM

Photo by Daguerre

MME. TAMAKI MIURA

Photo by Moffett

"The rumor is an absurdity and I have nothing whatsoever to say about anything whatsoever."

Whereupon, on Friday, January 14, the *Tribune* printed a front-page story with an eight-column streamer head, "Mary Garden Opera Head." The article was some three columns long, but the gist of it was in a quoted statement from the executive committee of the opera company, signed by Gen. Charles G. Dawes and sent to the newspapers by Harold F. McCormick. As an important document in the operatic history of Chicago, it deserves reproduction in full. Here it is:

"Miss Mary Garden has been elected general director of the Chicago Opera Association.

"This election took place at a meeting held to-day of the executive committee, with members of the board of directors, and can now be announced. The election and the new administration will be effective at once.

"Miss Garden assumes the responsibilities involved in the position offered on the basis of accepting no compensation as general director for this season or the coming one, and she will only receive, as heretofore, cachets from regular performances as an artist of the company. She will continue, therefore, in the dual rôle of general director and artist, just as Maestro Campanini continued to conduct operas while he was general director.

"This particular program applies directly only to the remainder of this season and next season, which will terminate the present régime, or the duration of the present five-year guaranty.

"Last spring, pending further consideration and final determination of a successor to Maestro Campanini as general director, the position of executive director was created and Herbert Johnson was asked to fill it; and the position of artistic manager was created and Gino Marinuzzi was asked to fill it. Mr. Johnson has resigned as executive director and his resignation has been accepted. Mr. Marinuzzi has resigned as artistic manager and his resignation has been accepted. These two positions have now been abolished. Mr. Marinuzzi continues as conductor.

"Miss Mary Garden, as general director, will have, therefore, general charge and direction under the executive committee of the affairs of the Chicago Opera Association, both artistic and executive.

"Announcement shortly will be made of appointment of a business manager and others who may be desired to perform the respective duties assigned them and to assist Miss Garden in the work. Otherwise the management and staff remain the same as heretofore.

"Under this development Miss Garden undertakes to lead and guide the destinies of the Chicago Opera Association during this and the coming season, and will contribute the same spirit and magnetic leadership which were so pronounced in Cleofonte Campanini, and will continue for Chicago the work which for ten years he incessantly and with devotion and consecration built up to the point which placed the Chicago Opera Association as second to no opera organization in the world. For this prospect of service for our civic enterprise the community is greatly indebted to Miss Garden.

"The directors are glad to feel that, in announcing this new procedure, the public and the patrons of opera and the artists, staff and members of the association will acclaim Miss Garden and give her their hearty support in the work to come, and she, in turn, can be counted upon to present opera in Chicago and elsewhere throughout the country in a manner worthy of such support from those who have the interest of the organization at heart.

"The members of the board are contented in the firm belief that the permanency of grand opera for Chicago is more assured than ever before, and that therefore we face the future under splendid auspices."

This statement came out, as noted previously, through the agency of Mr. McCormick and above the signature of Gen. Dawes. The other directors at the historic meeting were John G. Shedd, Charles L. Hutchinson, Samuel Insull, Stanley Field, and R. T. Crane, Jr.

Congratulations by the thousands from all corners of the earth poured in on Miss Garden. She received them calmly. The day after her apointment she was due to sing in "Monna Vanna," so she remained in retirement, seeing no one, after the custom of opera singers with heavy performances in front of them. When she got around to being interviewed she was highly discreet in her utterances, saying a little about her hope of putting Italian, French and German opera on an equal footing, of producing English operas if she could find some good ones to produce, about her objection to any form of translated opera—and no one dared mention her own "Tosca" performances—and little else.

On January 22 George M. Spangler was appointed business manager, coming over after a series of years as convention manager of the Chicago Association of Commerce. There had been talk of the appointment of Charles L. Wagner, manager at that time of John McCormack, Galli-Curci, and other notables in the music world, in fact he came from New York to Chicago at just about that time. But nothing came of the gossip. Mr. Spangler took charge with a rush and made himself famous with his first interview. Enlarging on his theory that he must "sell the idea" that opera must be popularized, especially with the men, he said:

"If the men don't want to wear their 'soup and fish,' why, they don't have to. It's their support, not their dress suits, we want. Even if they wear overalls, they're welcome."

Miss Garden sent for Jacques Coini to be stage director. He had been stage director for Hammerstein in the old Manhattan days when she was a member of the company. And when the Chicago organization moved on for its annual session in New York, she cabled to Giorgio Polacco in Italy to return and take charge of musical affairs. Mr. Polacco sailed on the first available boat, and has been with the company ever since.

Looking over the records of the season, there is little which at this time seems as interesting as what got into the news as distinguished from the musical columns. Proceedings got under way November 17 with Marinuzzi's own opera, "Jacquerie," a work concerning itself with the fleshly droit du seigneur of the middle ages and a subsequent peasants' revolt. Edward Johnson, Yvonne Gall, and Carlo Galeffi sang the principal parts. It had the customary first night's applause, but whatever chance of permanent success it had was lost because it was not given again for three weeks, by which time it slumped a little in performance and its public interest had begun to evaporate.

Baklanoff, returning to take up his engagement with

the company, was held at Ellis Island for a few days while the authorities debated whether or not they should deport him on charges of immorality, based on the trouble that he got into the season before. He was able to prove that he was not guilty of the charges made against him and was allowed to proceed, to the great disgust of the organizations opposing his entry, who announced that he had escaped on a "technicality." But it was no technicality. It was an actual case of being charged with a definite offense of which he was able to clear himself.

It had a curious effect on his audiences. He made his first appearance as Scarpia in "Tosca," on Saturday afternoon, November 20, and his entrance was the signal for a riot of applause. It seemed as though he stood with head bowed for fully five minutes while the patrons applauded and refused to let the performance go on. Such a demonstration never happened on a Saturday afternoon before or since. Baklanoff was then as ever a bit of a philosopher. His only comment was, "Yesterday is forever yesterday."

Joseph Hislop, a Scotch tenor, was a new member of the company that season. He got into print through his complaint that only French and Italian artists were permitted to engage upon a performance without molestation tending to impair its artistic worth. It is a statement sometimes heard from singers who fail to arrive, and seldom from those who do not fail. The most vivid recollection of Mr. Hislop during that season was his non-comformist ways with the rôle of Romeo, when, during the marriage scene, he did not remove his hat.

Another tenor, American this time, made a lasting impression. One day Rosa Raisa surprised me by saying,

"We are going to do 'Otello.' " Knowing that no tenor in the company was capable of lasting through a single act of that trying work, I said, "Who will sing the name part?"

"A stranger, an American," Miss Raisa answered. "He has been singing in Italy under the name of Carlo Marziale. I think his name in English is Marshall. I have just been rehearsing with him and the maestro in my room. Of course I do not know how he will sound in a theater, but I assure you, in a room I have never heard the equal of his voice."

In due time "Otello" was put on with Charles Marshall as Otello, Miss Raisa as Desdemona, Titta Ruffo as Iago. Miss Raisa was quite right. Mr. Marshall began to be famous for the part that night. Vocally, physically, and temperamentally he was made for it. He had done it in Italy, as she said, but finding engagements few, he had settled down to become an unnoticed teacher in Philadelphia. Then his chance came, and he took it. Incidentally I was greeted with cold looks around the Auditorium for days afterward, because he was intended to be a surprise to the Chicago public. Miss Raisa, not knowing about the publicity plans, had told me the news, and I had printed it, thereby ruining a perfectly good campaign of press agentry.

Ruffo, desirous of getting a star part for himself, also appeared in Leoncavallo's last opera, "Edipo Re." It was a fairly faithful though somewhat shortened version of the Sophocles drama, but Leoncavallo never wrote but one score that lived, and "Edipo Re" was not it.

"Aphrodite," by Erlanger, was put on as a New Year's opera with Miss Garden and Mr. Johnson in the

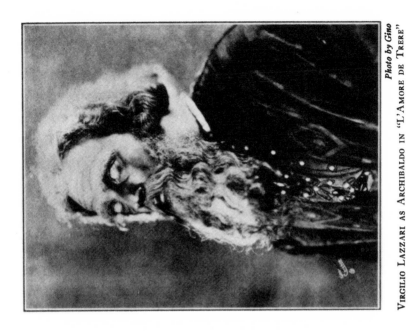

Virgilio Lazzari as Archibaldo in "L'Amore de Trere"

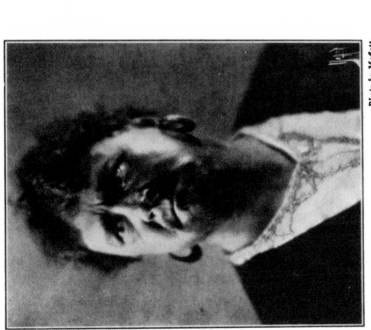

Charles Marshall in "Othello"

leading parts. It was a work characterized by extreme economy, not to say niggardliness in good music, and extreme extravagance in epidermic display by both singers and ballet. It died hastily.

Galli-Curci, having first obtained a divorce from her first husband, whom she charged with great liberality in the spending of her earnings, coupled with physical cruelty toward her personally, married her accompanist, Homer Samuels, in Minneapolis, January 15, and was one of the first to send a congratulatory telegram to Miss Garden over her new position. Miss Garden herself before her election had approved prohibition and the good looks of the Chicago police, had quarreled with Conductor Henri Morin and had made up with him, all of which was duly inscribed in print.

So the decks were cleared for the Garden consulship.

CHAPTER XXII

Mary Garden's year as general director was the last year of the Chicago Opera Association. For though with the exception of the 1914 season opera in Chicago has been continuous since 1910, the company has operated under three different names as three different corporations. Wherefore Miss Garden's operation was to be the final and climactic season of the second company and simultaneously the organization of the third, the Chicago Civic Opera Company.

Financial matters of the Chicago Opera Association had steadily been growing less satisfactory. Four years before Campanini and his associates had brought together a group of guarantors who put their names on the dotted line for a period of five years and amounts that added up to $110,000 a year. He himself had made a faithful effort to operate the company within such limit, but he was now dead, and since the war costs had been mounting in every direction to a harrowing extent.

Rather than let the company cease operations for want of money, Mr. and Mrs. Harold F. McCormick of Chicago had with great generosity assumed the burden of paying its obligations, or such of them as remained after the guarantors had paid their stipulated sums. Plenty remained. More remained every year, until at the time Miss Garden took charge one sees a statement to the effect that the deficit for the year had run up to

$350,000. One of the first quotations attributed to her
was to the effect that this amount must be cut down. With
what success it was cut down is now to be told.

Possibly a light on her operations may be afforded
by a comparison of the rosters of 1920-21, the season
before she took the management, and 1921-22, her year
of direction. They are taken from the company's records.

1920-21

Sopranos—Olga Carrara (new), Elsa Diemer
(new), Dorothy Francis (new), Yvonne Gall, Amelita
Galli-Curci, Mary Garden, Marcelle Goudard (new),
Florence Macbeth, Margery Maxwell, Rosa Raisa,
Rosina Storchio (new), Ganna Walska (new).

Mezzo-sopranos and contraltos—Gabriella Besanzoni (new), Philine Falco (new), Rose Lutiger Gannon
(new), Carmen Pascova (new), Cyrena Van Gordon.
In addition there was Maria Claessens, who had not been
reëngaged, but was sent for in haste after the season
started and it was found how seriously she was needed.

Tenors—Alessandro Bonci, Joseph Hislop (new),
Edward Johnson, Forrest Lamont, Charles Marshall
(new), Riccardo Martin (new), Jose Mojica, Lucien
Muratore, Lodovico Oliviero, Albert Paillard (new),
Tito Schipa.

Baritones—Georges Baklanoff, Sallustio Civai
(new), Desiré Defrere, Hector Dufranne, Carlo Galeffi,
Giacomo Rimini, Titta Ruffo.

Bassos—Edouard Cotreuil, Teofilo Dentale (new),
Virgilio Lazzari, Constantin Nicolay, Vittorio Trevisan.

Conductors—Gino Marinuzzi, Pietro Cimini, Henri Morin, Gabriel Santini, Alexander Smallens.

Count the names and compare them with the following list.

1921-22

Sopranos—Lina Cavalieri (début), Jeanne Dusseau (début), Claire Dux (début), Amelita Galli-Curci, Mary Garden, Maria Ivogun (début), Nina Koshetz (début), Alice d'Hermanoy, Lydia Lipkowska (début), Florence Macbeth, Mary McCormic (début), Edith Mason (début), Margery Maxwell, Marguerite Namara, Graziella Pareto (début), Rosa Raisa.

Mezzo-sopranos and contraltos—Maria Claessens, Marguerite D'Alvarez, Philine Falco, Frances Paperte, Irene Pavloska, Eleanor Reynolds (début), Jeanne Schneider (début), Cyrena Van Gordon.

Tenors—Octave Dua, Edward Johnson, Forrest Lamont, Charles Marshall, Riccardo Martin, Jose Mojica, Lucien Muratore, Lodovico Oliviero, Tino Pattiera (début), Theodore Ritch (début), Antonio Rocca (début), Tito Schipa, Richard Schubert (début).

Baritones—Georges Baklanoff, Vicente Ballester (début), William Beck, Desiré Defrere, Hector Dufranne, Alfred Maguenat, Giacomo Rimini, Joseph Schwarz (début), Jerome Uhl (début).

Bassos—Sallustio Civai, Edouard Cotreuil, Edward Lankow (début), Virgilio Lazzari, Constantin Nicolay, James Wolf (début), Paul Payan (début), Vittorio Trevisan.

Principal conductor—Giorgio Polacco.

Conductors—Pietro Cimini, Angelo Ferrari, Gabriel Grovlez, Alexander Smallens.

And more were taken on at intervals during the season. A few did not appear at all, Ganna Walska in the first list, as has already been told, Lina Cavalieri and Lydia Lipkowska in the second. But at that there is considerable difference in size in rosters. In fact when the season was footed up, it was found that many of the singers were entitled under their contracts to fees that they had never been given chances to earn. In other words, the company had contracted to give more appearances than could possibly be given in the length of the season. More will be told of this later.

Looking back at the situation after it had settled down, it would seem that Miss Garden made her greatest mistake in the form of the agreement by which she was to take over the company. It was announced at that time that she would donate her services as general director, taking cachets only for her appearances on the stage as artist.

This was a magnificent gesture, but wholly impracticable. It is a full sized job to be the general director of a major opera company, another to be a popular and busy artist, the two together are more than one person ought to be expected to sustain. Campanini had been both general director and conductor, but he died before his time. And even he could put in more time as director than any singer-director, because on the days that singers appear, they make it a point to remain in seclusion and quiet until it is time to go to the theater. So if Miss Garden, artist, were announced to appear three times in one week, and there were several of those occasions, Miss

Garden, director, would be absent from her desk for those three days. At such times it is not impossible to imagine that questions might come up demanding prompt decision, with no one at hand to decide them. From a practical standpoint, it would undoubtedly have been better if Miss Garden had taken a salary as director and donated her appearances as artist.

But she made a gallant, if heart-breaking effort to function in the two capacities. In the spring of 1921, having returned from the company's tour to the Pacific coast, she gave permission to the company's singers to appear at Ravinia during the summer season if they desired, something that Campanini had always frowned upon, she signed up part of the list of artists just quoted, and departed for Europe to sign up the rest, pausing in New York to dictate her autobiography for a newspaper syndicate, a history which in its later chapters included her editorial opinions on love, marriage, jazz music, and the eighteenth amendment to the federal constitution.

Meanwhile an earnest, lively and finally successful movement was started to assure the permanence of opera in Chicago. A Chicago operatic committee was organized to make a drive for five hundred guarantors, each to agree to subscribe for a period of five years whatever percentage of $1,000 a year should be necessary to pay the company's annual deficit. It was later found advisable to modify the plan both as to number of guarantors and size of guaranty, but the goal was $500,000 a year for five years, and that goal was in due time reached.

The general chairman of the citizens' committee was Robert E. Kenyon, the vice-chairman, Elmer T. Stevens, and Mrs. Jacob Baur was made chairman of the women's section.

On the executive committee were William Rufus Abbott, William B. Austin, George W. Dixon, Evan Evans, Marquette A. Healy, Samuel Insull, Dr. Harry Pratt Judson, L. B. Kuppenheimer, Henry C. Lytton, Clayton Mark, Arthur Belleville McCoid, John J. Mitchell, Dr. Frederick B. Moorehead, Charles F. W. Nichols, Samuel C. Osborn, Augustus S. Peabody, Charles S. Peterson, Julius Rosenwald, F. L. Ryder, Joseph T. Ryerson, John C. Shaffer, John G. Shedd, Andrew R. Sherriff, H. C. Sherman, Redmond D. Stephens, Edward E. Swadener, and Frederick W. Upham.

The general committee consisted of Dr. Frank Billings, Thomas M. Boyd, Arthur Dunham, Livingston Fairbank, Samuel Felton, Albert Fink, August Gatzert, C. H. Hammond, Harry W. Jarrow, George Harvey Jones, Thomas D. Knight, A. J. Korr, A. F. Kramer, Alexander Legge, Sidney Lowenstein, George H. Lounsbury, George Lytton, Robert H. McCormick, Marvin B. Pool, Otto Schulz, Frank E. Scott, Boetius H. Sullivan, and Charles G. Willson.

Even before the season started, there was word of a delay. Lina Cavalieri was announced for the name part of the second night's "Tosca," but the week before she was bulletined as "too ill to appear," and that "her local début was postponed." The postponement became permanent. The name of Cavalieri was corrected to read Raisa, and the opera bill was unchanged.

Just after Miss Garden's appointment as director, the lamented B. L. T., the famous conductor of "A

Line o'Type or Two" in the *Tribune* wrote a poem on
the subject for the Line. He called it:

TO MARY GARDEN—WITH A POSTSCRIPT

So wonderful your art, if you preferred
  Drayma to opry, you'd be all the mustard;
For you (ecstatic pressmen have averred)
  Have Sarah Bernhardt larruped to a custard.

So marvelous your voice, too, if you cared
  With turns and trills and tra-la-las to dazzle,
You'd have (enraptured critics have declared)
  All other singers beaten to a frazzle.

So eloquent your legs, were it your whim
  To caper nimbly in a classic measure,
Terpsichore (entranced reviewers hymn)
  Would swoon upon her lyre for very pleasure.

If there be aught you cannot do, 'twould seem
  The world has yet that something to discover.
One has to hand it to you. You're a scream,
  And 'tis a joy to watch you put it over.

POSTSCRIPTUM

If there be any test you can't survive,
  The present test will mean your crucifying;
But I am laying odds of eight to five
  That you'll come through with all your colors flying.

CHAPTER XXIII

Samson and Delilah (in French), libretto by Ferdinand Lemaire, score by Camille Saint-Saëns, at the Auditorium, Monday, Nov. 15, 1921. The cast:

SAMSON ....Lucien Muratore
DELILAH ....Marguerite D'Alvarez
THE HIGH PRIEST OF
    DAGON ....Hector Dufranne
ABIMELECH, Satrap of Gaza.Desiré Defrere
AN OLD HEBREW ....Paul Payan (début)
A PHILISTINE MESSENGER.Octave Dua
FIRST PHILISTINE........Lodovico Oliviero
SECOND PHILISTINE......Jerome Uhl (début)

Conductor ....Giorgio Polacco
Stage Director...........Jacques Coini

"Chicago is at last sophisticated," hymned one of the enraptured reviewers in print next day. As much of Chicago as could crowd into the Auditorium had a chance to prove its sophistication, for Mme. D'Alvarez on her first entrance, standing at the top of the steps of the temple, slipped and fell all the way to the bottom. In fact she slid into the middle of the stage. It was one of the most striking instances of the self-discipline of artists on record, for while the audience gasped, thinking she might have cracked her spine, she, with practically a continuation of the same motion, rolled to her feet and came up with the note between her teeth and on pitch.

She finished the opera with no delay and no complaint, though she was rather lame the next day. But the next time she appeared in this work she took the precaution to apply rosin to her sandals until you could have heard their squeak to the back of the house.

It was a bit of shrewd showmanship, one of Miss Garden's best, that she did not appear under her own direction the opening night. Nor did she on the second, for then Raisa appeared with Tino Pattiera, a new tenor, and Baklanoff in "Tosca." Even on the third night she chose to watch the performance from her box next the stage on the right hand side. Then it was that Edith Mason in "Madame Butterfly" began the lovely singing that ever since has made her one of the glories of the Chicago Opera.

Finally on Thursday night, the fourth of the season, Miss Garden appeared in the name part of "Monna Vanna," to the Prinzivalle of Muratore and the Guido of Baklanoff. Just to fix the opening date, the Monday before, Chicago's opening date, had been the Metropolitan's opening date as well, and in New York Galli-Curci had begun the season in "La Traviata," with Gigli and De Luca as her associates. It was the first time in fifteen years that Caruso had not opened the New York season, but that famous tenor had come to the end of his earthly career early in the previous August.

There was another way of fixing the date, for the next day, Friday, Nov. 18, Business Manager George M. Spangler resigned, and to make it more annoying, no one was ever able to find out exactly why. Here was the account as printed in the *Evening Post,* and typical of all the rest:

MARGUERITE D'ALVAREZ AS DALILA IN "SAMSON ET DALILA"

" 'I will say nothing,' Mr. Spangler said. 'If anything must be said, Mr. McCormick will say it.'

" 'The move was for the best interests of the opera,' Mr. McCormick said when reached. 'I can say nothing further.'

"Spearman Lewis, publicity director of the organization, said that his lips were sealed.

" 'I can tell you nothing,' he added, 'except what the formal announcement contains.'

"Miss Mary Garden, director general of the company, could not be reached."

That is the handicapped way we used to try to collect news. The *Tribune,* however, added this:

"There was a report that Mr. Spangler's retirement was due to the known differences between Harold McCormick and Mrs. McCormick—contentions that involved policies with respect to the opera. This rumor was to the effect that Spangler represented the views of Mrs. McCormick. On the other hand there was a story that Mrs. McCormick objected to the 'salesmanship' method of Spangler and that her husband, in deference to her views, called for Spangler's resignation.

"A friend of Spangler's declared that 'he was between the devil and the deep blue sea trying to carry out orders for two masters.' "

Clark A. Shaw, who had been the company's tour manager for six years and has been in the same position ever since, was appointed business manager to finish the season. One of the problems of the new régime was to obtain 248 more signatures to the guaranty list. Spangler had already signed 252.

To add to the general publicity situation, Luigi

Curci, first husband of the singer, now composed the story of his life and hers at great length and with pictures, carrying it up to the time of their divorce. Not that it got him anything except what he and presumably the actual, or "ghost" writer of the biography were paid by the newspapers using it.

What with one thing and another, the season was so busy that looking back at it now seems like looking into an active kaleidoscope. There were operas new and operas old. Wagner in German came back for the first time since the war. There had been a gesture in that direction the year before with "Lohengrin" in English, but this time Miss Garden decreed "Tannhäuser" in German. Raisa, who had been the English Elsa, was now the German Elisabeth, though neither language was native to her. She was a glorious wave of emotion and music as she swept into "Dich theure Halle," and she held it to the end. The Tannhäuser was an importation, Richard Schubert, rated, at least the publicity department insisted that he was rated, as Germany's foremost tenor. But his singing was nothing more sustained than a melodic dot-and-dash system, and he was not a wave of any kind.

Claire Dux, another ideally lovely singer, was brought to the United States in this season, but it now seems evident that no one in the opera company knew what a charming artist she was. At least no one took the trouble to present her under the best auspices. She proved afterwards that she was a beautiful Elsa in "Lohengrin" and a Mozart singer beyond compare, wherefore they introduced her to her first Chicago audience as Mimi in "La Bohême."

This is a fair sample of the way many great opportunities were tossed away that year. Not that Miss Dux was not a good Mimi. She was. The point is that in a company steadily growing more and more Italianate, there were always many good Mimis. On the other hand there were other things in which Miss Dux was supreme. It was nothing less than folly to make her compete with the others when she might have been on a distinct pinnacle of her own without competition. In course of time she found it anyway.

About this time some alarming reports began to issue from the company about the possibility of not raising the guaranty fund. This was probably a tactical move intended to jar Chicagoans into a realization of what would happen if the opera had to go. It was accompanied by the promise of a budget and economy in all departments. The public was given another chance to come in.

Galli-Curci returned to New York to take up her ten performances, and Miss Garden busied herself with a revival of "Salome." She was to have sung it on Dec. 18, and Richard Strauss, its composer, was to have been present, but overwork and Chicago climate intervened, and Miss Garden retired to her north side apartment to fight off a threatened attack of pneumonia. She was successful, and the performance took place after a ten days' delay. Then came "Love for Three Oranges."

This was without doubt an opera ahead of its time. Serge Prokofieff had been in the country for several years, composing, playing, conducting his somewhat advanced music. If he had not succeeded in making it entirely popular, he had made himself well known, so much so that Campanini had commissioned him to write an opera. "The Love for Three Oranges" was the result.

Both libretto and music were his. He founded his book on a story by the eighteenth century Carlo Gozzi. Being Russian himself, he wrote it in Russian, and Miss Garden forthwith proved her faith in the value of opera in its original tongue by having it given in French.

He had announced that it would be a satire in a reasonably savage manner, but it turned out to be fantastic burlesque, and while satire is sometimes hard enough to project across the footlights, burlesque is much worse. At any rate, it left many of our best people dazed and wondering.

The scenery and costumes had been built at Campanini's orders by Boris Anisfeld, and their presence was one reason why the opera was given. It was no end brilliant as a spectacle and no end technically difficult to stage and sing. The chorus in the corners, grouped as tragedians, comedians, lyricists, empty heads, and absurdities, made running comments on the action. The action, inspired imbecility, sublimated clowning, benighted awkwardness, was quite as amusing as Prokofieff meant it to be. But the music was enigmatic for the public of that day, a public that felt that without tunes, what was the use of opera?

Repeated, given over and over again, until some acquaintance had been made with the score, just as "Pelléas and Mélisande" had to be repeated, it might finally have made its way. But "Quel désastre!" as sung by Defrere at the end of one of the most amusing scenes of all, was echoed in the hearts of later and more fearful managements. Worst of all, the scenery had been built in so fragile construction that it soon began to fall apart, and what was left was deliberately knocked to pieces. So "The Three Oranges" passed, probably for good and all as far as Chicago is concerned, though it was later given in Germany with considerable success.

Maria Ivogun came for one performance and went. Beatrice Kottlar appeared to sing Isolde to Schubert's Tristan, and seldom has there been a less convincing case made out for the music of Wagner, though Conductor Polacco wrought wonders with the orchestra. Mr. and Mrs. McCormick, who had kept the opera alive for three or four years, were divorced, and Miss Garden announced a new find, Ulysses Lappas, tenor. He sang the part of the virtuous bandit in a revival of "The Girl of the Golden West," and Miss Garden emphatically announced his tenorial and dramatic virtues, though the audience manifested a preference for Miss Raisa's Minnie.

And Galli-Curci swore that she would never desert Chicago. Then Muratore said he was going to resign.

It can safely be estimated that toward the end of a highly intensive and none too smoothly running season, a good many members of the company began to get on each other's nerves. The newspapers began to bristle with accounts of back stage rows, although most of these are subject to deep discounts. Any one who has ever attended an operatic rehearsal will be sure to hear sharp remarks handed about, and in a foreign language they are likely to sound terrifying, but generally there is no malice about them. But when Muratore resigned, he apparently meant it.

He was not entirely tactful in the way he did it.

He said it was "impossible to come back here under the management of Mary Garden."

Miss Garden did not stop to call a stenographer for a reply. She sat down and wrote this: "Foreign dictation is a thing of the past. We are to have a little American dictation for a while and see how that will work out. It is a great pity to see an artist of the value of Monsieur Muratore so badly counseled. Mary Garden."

That, for the time being, was that, with the "directa," as Miss Garden insisted on calling herself, accredited as winner. The company moved on to New York. Muratore sang one performance, "Carmen," with Miss Garden, by the way, and promptly achieved a permanent separation from his appendix at the hands and knives of Dr. C. F. A. Locke and Dr. Aspinwall Judd at the Audobon hospital. He recovered just before the end of the New York season in time to sing one performance of "Monna Vanna," again with Miss Garden, and a few times on tour, but that was his final year in America.

A short spring tour, and all that was left was to pick up the pieces. That there were more pieces than usual was indicated in a speech made by Samuel Insull before the Friends of Opera, an organization of leading Chicago women busied with the sale of boxes and the continuing activity of getting signatures for the guaranty fund. Mr. Insull was reported by the *American* as saying:

"No contract will be signed by any general director or business manager or any other individual from this day on. Every contract in future must bear the signature of the chairman of the finance committee and one member of the board of directors. We will spend *our own* money."

But just how many the pieces were and how serious their breakage became known only later in the spring, when it was noised about that the losses of the season had not been $350,000, as in the year before. They were $1,100,000.

Money had been spent, and, one might say, lavishly. If this was the most exciting season of the Chicago Opera, it was also the most expensive. For several weeks Mr. Shaw's chief employment as business manager was to plead with, cajole, and browbeat various of the artists into accepting less than the face values of their contracts, since in a good many cases there had been no chance for the company to give them the number of performances to which they were entitled. He was successful in saving between $200,000 and $300,000 out of the wreck, but plenty was left.

It was a grand year, financially speaking, for some of the artists. Baklanoff was reported to have been given a contract for forty appearances at $1,000 each, plus his income tax. He was kept reasonably busy during the season, but there were plenty who were not.

Muratore's fee has already been mentioned. But years before Campanini had delivered judgment on Muratore thus: "Muratore is expensif arteest because he no draw. De people all say, 'Yes, Muratore, magneeficent arteest.' But when Muratore sing, dey all stay home—sit at table and mak' de dinner."

Maria Ivogun was brought from Europe and she sang once. Lappas came from Monte Carlo and sang twice. Claire Dux appeared three times. Vicente Ballester, Spanish baritone, sang twice, once as a relief to Joseph Schwarz, who declared himself ill in the middle of a performance. Marguerite D'Alvarez sang twice and went away with a check for six more performances which she did not sing. Marguerite Namara sang once; Nina Koshetz, Charles Marshall, and Edward Lankow twice each.

Riccardo Martin was on a salary of $1,000 a week, and appeared in three performances. Edward Johnson, one of the finest artists ever in the employ of the company, was confined to his few appearances in "Madame Butterfly." Forrest Lamont was up three times. Johanna Gadski was reported to have been paid $7,500 to cancel her contract with the company, and at that when it got to New York, she brought suit for $500,000, alleging defamation. Florence Macbeth and Lydia Lipkowska were not heard at all, and Graziella Pareto appeared once in New York.

"In any week of the season," said one of the regular patrons, "the lobby company far outnumbered the singing company."

There were also some costly productions. "Love for Three Oranges" was credited with having cost $100,000. It was given twice in Chicago and once in New York.

But Harold F. McCormick and Mrs. Edith Rockefeller McCormick made good on their pledges. They paid off all debts and turned over all of the physical properties of the Chicago Opera Association free of charge to the new company, henceforth to be known as the Chicago Civic Opera Company.

At a meeting held Jan. 11, 1922, the new company was organized. It had these as officers: Samuel Insull, president; Gen. Charles G. Dawes and Richard T. Crane,

Jr., vice-presidents; Charles L. Hutchinson, treasurer; Stanley Field, secretary.

The permanent finance committee, from then on to be in control of financial management and policy, consisted of Mr. Insull, chairman; Mr. Field, vice-chairman, and John J. Mitchell, John G. Shedd, and L. B. Kuppenheimer.

The board of trustees was made up of the officials already mentioned and also Cyrus H. McCormick, Harold F. McCormick, Mrs. Edith Rockefeller McCormick, Ernest R. Graham, Robert Allerton, Joseph R. Noel, Frank D. Stout, Martin A. Ryerson, Edward F. Swift, Edward E. Gore, Robert E. Kenyon, Max Pam, and S. A. Kauffman. It was announced that the first business of the organization would be to raise the second half of the guaranty fund of $500,000, but that as before, it was really up to Chicago.

And when the company got back from its western tour, Miss Garden resigned as "directa," and Mr. Insull stated that in his opinion she had acted "in a very gentlemanly manner."

CHAPTER XXIV

While opera in the city of Chicago was making its way through years of ups and downs, another opera company not far away was developing itself into prominence through a series of summer seasons. This was the company at Ravinia Park, situated in the southern part of Highland Park, twenty-five miles north of the Chicago loop and close to the shore of Lake Michigan. Ravinia deserves more than passing mention, not only because its accomplishments were and are definite and fine, but because the same accomplishments are so widely different from what was originally planned.

Early in the present century an electric traction line was built connecting Chicago and Milwaukee, and paralleling the already existing Milwaukee division of the Chicago and Northwestern Railway. Presumably for purposes of real estate development, the electric line took over forty acres of land in the Ravinia section of Highland Park, constructed an amusement park there, and named it Ravinia Park. Except that it was better and more artisically built than the vast majority of similar enterprises, going in for architecture on the semi-bungalow, semi-country club order, it was like other amusement parks, with café, band stand, theater, a large grand stand facing a lawn of baseball dimensions, merry-go-rounds, wheels, and what not. Musically it looked little higher than an occasional, casual band concert.

But real estate development has its perils, as the Chicago and Milwaukee line discovered. Long before the lake shore north of Chicago was built up to a sufficient extent to make such an enterprise profitable or even feasible, the line got into financial difficulties and was forced to separate itself from all activities other than transportation. Among other extraneous matters thus split off was Ravinia Park, which was taken over by a group of Chicago and north shore residents. Converting the enterprise into a corporation, they elected Louis Eckstein its president and began to cast about for summer entertainment.

For a quite considerable time, concerts, in the afternoons and evenings, were the only musical activities. Frederick Stock and the Chicago Symphony Orchestra used to go there for part of the summer season; Walter Damrosch would bring his New York Symphony Orchestra for another part; occasionally the Minneapolis Symphony Orchestra would pay a visit, or one and another of the concert bands of that period would fill in a few weeks.

In due course, other forms of entertainment began to be sought. The dance was popular for some time. Joan Sawyer and her partner, pioneers in exhibition ballroom dancing, were there one summer; Rosina Galli and Bonfiglio another; Ruth St. Denis and Ted Shawn—I am not attempting to cite these in chronological order—a third. Meanwhile Mr. Eckstein had rebuilt the band stand, making it the back wall of a stage extending west, and had constructed a large pavilion of wood, open on three sides, in front of it.

One summer Ben Greet and his company of dewsteppers came to Ravinia to play Shakespeare in the open air. A raised terrace, sodded and edged with shrubbery at the left of the pavilion was the stage, and the audience sat under the stars facing it. The season opened with "A Midsummer Night's Dream," and the orchestra, conducted by Chevalier N. B. Emanuel, an excellent musician, since dead, was placed between the terrace and the pavilion to play Mendelssohn's incidental music.

Unfortunately the weather turned bitterly cold that night, as Chicago's weather sometimes does in early summer. The only one who looked entirely happy during the performance was George Vivian, in the part of Puck, and he was called upon to turn handsprings a good part of his time on the stage. If you looked around to the field behind the stage, you could have seen a bevy of fairies doing foot races up and down in the moonlight in an effort to keep warm. Meanwhile we in the audience, with no chance at such diversions, turned up our coat collars and tried to forget our numbing fingers and toes. At that, it was an entertaining performance, and, matters of temperature apart, one of the most enjoyable of that play I ever witnessed.

Finally Mr. Eckstein's attention began to be directed toward opera. It was experimental and tentative at first. There was no intention of barging into the picture with a fully organized company and more than a chance of an enormous loss. Mr. Eckstein has always had considerable respect for public demand as an indicator for public entertainment, and while he has never run Ravinia at a profit—on the contrary, his balance sheet has always shown something far removed from a profit—at the same time he could see no reason for making too rash a gesture in the beginning.

So at first only a few singers were engaged, and they did no more than to present a single act of opera on certain evenings of the week. The public showed every sign of approving the move, and the next season there were more singers and more acts. Before long there were full evenings of opera, and concert programs began to lessen and operatic evenings to increase.

Almost before we in Chicago realized it, so modest and unostentatious had been the beginnings, Ravinia had burst into full and astonishing operatic florescence. Almost without knowing it, a major opera company had developed under our eyes. The little stage which was once the front of a band stand was being peopled with the foremost artists of the world; performances began to take on as their normal course an intensity and beauty such as you would find only occasionally in the foremost opera houses of the world. Suddenly Chicago began to be talked about in America and Europe not only for its winter opera at the Auditorium but for its summer opera at Ravinia.

This is not in the least an exaggeration. Mr. Eckstein makes a practice of engaging the most famous artists in the most lavish manner. More than that, he has frequently taken brilliant singers when they were not well known and added to their repertoires until they became very well known indeed. Claudia Muzio was a highly applauded figure at Ravinia before she was considered more than just one of the sopranos at the Metropolitan, before she had ever been heard in South America, and long before she was engaged at Chicago. Edith Mason's

ideally lovely voice rang from the Ravinia stage for seasons before the·Chicago Company took her. Antonio
Scotti came there for two seasons and appeared, among
other pieces, in "L'Oracolo," the only times that lurid
work was ever done in the neighborhood of Chicago.
"Boris Godunoff" was heard at Ravinia before it was
heard in Chicago. "La Vida Breve," with the bewitching
Lucrezia Bori in its principal rôle, was a signal success at
Ravinia, and has never been heard in Chicago. No later
than the summer of 1928, Mr. Eckstein presented
Leroux's comic opera, "Marouf," which they refer to in
Paris as "the last smile of French music before the war."
What is more, he made of it the success that it is in Paris
and not the failure that it was at the Metropolitan.

It is submitted that a company containing, as the
1928 company did, the names of Elisabeth Rethberg,
Yvonne Gall, Florence Easton, Florence Macbeth, Julia
Claussen, Ina Bourskaya, Edward Johnson, Giovanni
Martinelli, Tito Schipa, Mario Chamlee, Armand Tokat-
yan, Giuseppe Danise, Mario Basiola, Desiré Defrere,
Léon Rothier, Virgilio Lazzari, Louis D'Angelo and
Vittorio Trevisan, not to mention a considerable number
of those who appeared in less important capacities, has
gone a marked distance beneath the surface of opera
giving. Such names are to be treated by no means casually. In addition to all this richness of artists, Miss Bori
had been engaged and announced, but at a late date ill
health forced her to cancel her appearances and go to a
sanitarium in Italy for the summer.

The chorus, forty in number, are selected from the
best choristers of both the Chicago and Metropolitan
companies. The orchestra, about fifty, has from the be-

ginning been taken from the Chicago Symphony Orchestra, always including the first desk men, and it is rated as fine an operatic orchestra in the summer as it is a symphonic organization in the winter. For a number of seasons Gennaro Papi and Louis Hasselmans have divided the task of operatic conducting, and more recently Eric De Lamarter has taken over the concert programs, in all cases with the highest credit to themselves and the organization.

In speaking in as high terms of the Ravinia performances as has been done here, a slight definition is necessary. There are some limitations of time and space. Of time, because a comfortable section of the Ravinia patronage is brought there and taken home by steam and electric trains, and these, though specials, necessarily run on schedules. Wherefore it is necessary to time the performances, ending them, as closely as may be, at eleven o'clock at night. Some of the longer operas must therefore be cut. "Carmen" must submit itself to the surgery of becoming a three-act version, "Lohengrin" of two. It is curious to find, however, how many works are capable of being given complete, or at the most with very trifling excisions, if other delays are corrected. Some time when you find you are being held to untoward hours in a performance of winter opera, try timing the intermissions, and you will be more than likely to find that they are responsible for a good part of the length.

As to space, Ravinia has not gone in for grandiose dimensions. The stage is of medium size, the pavilion, all on one plane, seats about 1,800 patrons. Highly complex and elaborate stage spectacles are not practicable there, and are not attempted, though with skilled stage management and lighting, some astonishingly attractive stage pictures are composed every year.

In other respects, however, Ravinia's moderate dimensions become a positive advantage. There are many operas which gain by being performed at close range and which lose much of their charm in the vast distances of huge opera houses. In fact this applies to nearly everything except specially designed spectacles. The old comedies, "The Barber of Seville," "Fra Diavolo," "Don Pasquale," "The Elixir of Love," gain much by intimacy, so do the Puccini works with the possible exception of "Turandot," so do a good many others. For one thing, many of them were planned and written for auditoriums not of the greatest size, and their inflation for the larger houses does away with some of their magnetism. One can be certain that there are two reasons for the success of "Marouf" at Ravinia over its failure at the Metropolitan. One was its greatly superior cast—Mario Chamlee and Yvonne Gall were unbelievably amusing and attractive. The other was that the performance could be given at close range.

In one of his visits to Ravinia Otto H. Kahn once made a speech to the audience in the course of which he declared that if Ravinia were plucked up from where it is and set down somewhere in central Europe, people would make pilgrimages from all over the civilized world to visit it. As a matter of fact, they come near to doing that now. The greater part of the patronage is naturally from Chicago and the north shore, brought there by steam, electricity, automobile, and on foot. But many come from great distances. If you examine the license tags on the cars parked in the fields during the course of a season, you will find representatives of every state in the union and several of the Canadian provinces. Tourists from everywhere, native and foreign, make a visit there, and having made one, make others.

It is the least formal of any operatic center, which is one of the reasons for its abiding charm. On popular nights there may be as many patrons outside the pavilion as in it. The entire structure being of wood, impossible in a city because of fire ordinances, but entirely practicable in the country, gives the musical tone a suave, mellow and astonishingly carrying quality. I, myself, have heard the sound of the orchestra and the singers' voices, when conditions were favorable, at a distance more than a mile from the stage.

It has the potent achievements of fine art; it has the informal, comfortable atmosphere of a country club; it competes with no other operatic institution on earth. This has been Louis Eckstein's contribution to the musical art of America. How great a contribution it is, people are just beginning to realize.

CHAPTER XXV

Chicago was now, beginning with the 1922-23 season, to witness the beginning of an operatic phase which, looking back at it seven years later, can only with difficulty be described by another word than romance. It was the romance of business, certainly, but business has its imaginative dreams, its flashes of foresight, and it has a most satisfying habit of making its dreams come true. The dream of Mr. Insull and his associates in this case was to put the opera company on what seems to have worked out as an unshakably permanent basis, to move it into a magnificent new home of its own, and to provide it with funds for operation which should last through many generations to come. How this dream became a living reality is now to be told in somewhat more detail than can be compressed into a paragraph.

It did not come in a moment nor in a season. In fact, in the beginning it looked like a task to daunt any but the most incurable of optimists. Just consider for a moment what the new Chicago Civic Opera company was confronting. Ever since 1910 the opera had been running along more or less as merely an expensive amusement, more or less at haphazard as far as permanent existence was concerned. It had culminated in the magnificent, smashing ruin of the season before.

Worse, there was a fairly widespread public opinion that opera could hardly be anything more than an expensive amusement running at haphazard. In a few words, the job of the new organization was to pick up the pieces of the old company and then convince the public that they would stay picked up and in place. Any one who believes that this is not a job of large dimensions is welcome to stay in his illusions and cherish them.

At any rate, here was a goal, and the new company began to move toward it. Possibly the progress was not altogether steady. Some steps were taken that had to be retraced; some experiments were tried and then discarded. But the end of each season began to mark an advance over the season before. In the end there was something for the world to pause and marvel over.

The company was therefore reorganized into its third corporate manifestation, the Chicago Civic Opera company, and its proponents quietly but firmly announced that hereafter opera would be run on a businesslike basis. This in itself was something of a shock to those who had been in the habit of observing opera from the outside. Hammerstein in the height of his glory used to proclaim loudly that opera was not a business but a disease. Here was a group of Chicago business men, entirely in the habit of keeping their heads in moments of emotional stress, who were proposing to run it like any other big undertaking, not for profit and not for aggrandizement, but solely with the idea of putting it on its own feet and thereby doing something for Chicago. And the only comment that need be made upon this revolutionary idea is that it worked.

The first task was to complete the guaranty fund, and this was accomplished with signal success. A high pressure, intensive drive was put on, directed and operated by men who know how to run such campaigns, and by summer it was officially told that the complete fund of $500,000 a year for a period of five years had been signed. In fact the figures added to $525,000, since the directors figured that in a period of five years a certain number of guarantors would probably die, move away from Chicago, become insolvent, or in various other ways turn into difficult collections, and that a margin over and above the exact amount would be desirable.

In order to reach the goal, it became necessary to modify the original plan of the guaranty. Instead of lining up 500 or 525 individuals, each with a set liability of $1,000, lesser sums were accepted, and consequently the number of guarantors increased. Some signed for $500, some for $100, some for smaller amounts. Consequently the number of guarantors last reported in the season of 1928 ran to over 3,000.

With nothing but a business organization perfected, the next step was to form the artistic organization. Here business foresight decreed that there must never again be such losses as had occurred on the season just closed. In order to prevent them, orders went out that a budget as complete as studied foresight could make it was to be put together, and that it was to be adhered to. Among other things, this meant that fewer artists were to be engaged, and that the day of fantastic salaries was past.

What is a high fee for an artist and what is a low one is always a matter of debate. Like a good many other questions of costs and rewards, including the question of opera in its own tongue versus the translated article, it is regulated to a great extent by public demand. The artist whom the public wants to hear is always the

CLAUDIA MUZIO

one to draw the high fee. A saying was attributed to Gatti-Casazza some years ago, still a good basis for discussion, that the best of the artists, considered purely as operatic singers, should not command more than $500 a performance, that whatever they actually commanded in excess of that sum should be estimated in terms of drawing power, that is, of the box office. On that basis, he added, Caruso was his cheapest artist, cheap no matter how much he demanded, for every time that Caruso was announced, the house was sold out to complete capacity.

On that basis, too, Miss Garden has always been one of the Chicago company's cheap artists, for her popularity began with her first performance in 1910 and has continued practically without break to the present day. So, too, was Tetrazzini cheap in the old days, so was Ruffo when he first came to this country, so was Galli-Curci during her period with the Chicago opera. But Muratore, as Campanini had proclaimed, was "expensif," and there were many others who were "expensif" in the same way.

So Mr. Polacco, musical director, and Mr. Shaw, business manager—hereafter there was to be no general director—applied themselves to the task of assembling an artistic personnel for the Civic Opera out of the ruins of the dismantled Chicago Opera Association. In a good many cases the task was merely the formal one of lining the artists up to put down their names on a new contract. But some objected strenuously to accepting a salary cut and refused to return, some were not wanted under any circumstances, and still others stayed away for other reasons.

To balance matters, Claudia Muzio, soprano, was signed by the Chicago company away from the Metropolitan. This was a brisk maneuver, for she signed her contract in the stateroom of her European steamship less than half an hour before sailing time. Some other notable artists were engaged about the same period, among them Richard Hageman and Ettore Panizza, conductors, and Adolph Bolm, ballet master and leading dancer.

Louise Homer, greatly popular American contralto, was engaged for a few special performances, Ina Bourskaya became a regular member of the company, and it was announced that Feodor Chaliapin, not so long before freed from the restrictions and poverty of artistic life under the Soviet régime, would appear in "Mefistofele."

Just before the Civic Opera Company started its season it received notice from the Treasury Department in Washington that it need no longer charge the customary 10 per cent war tax on its tickets. It was the first organization in the country to be thus exempted, the basis of the ruling being that the company was educational and not for profit. There were plenty of Chicagoans willing to agree with the latter part of the statement.

CHAPTER XXVI

"Aïda," in four acts and seven scenes; libretto by Antonio Ghislanzoni, music by Giuseppe Verdi; presented at the Auditorium, Nov. 13, 1922. The cast:

THE KING OF EGYPT..Edouard Cotreuil
AMNERIS, his daughter.Ina Bourskaya (début)
RADAMES, captain of
   the guard ....Charles Marshall
AIDA, an Ethiopian
   slave ....Rosa Raisa
RAMFIS, high priest....Virgilio Lazzari
AMONASRO, king of
   Ethiopa ....Cesare Formichi (début)
PRIESTESS ....Melvena Passmore (début)

Incidental dances by Anna Ludmila, Konstantin Kobeleff, Amata Grassi, Franklin Crawford, Jean D'Evelyn, and corps de ballet.

Conductor ....Giorgio Polacco
Stage Director........Emile Merle-Forest
Ballet Master........Adolph Bolm

Just as twelve years before Chicago's resident company had begun operations with a performance of "Aïda," so did the new Civic Opera Company. In fact there those who say that no opera season anywhere in the United States should ever begin with anything but "Aïda." It is a great opening bill, to be sure, calling for

255

fine voices, full of noble music, scenic effects, processionals, ballet, pomp and circumstance generally. Curiously, opera companies in general seem to feel that it
is something of a reproach to inaugurate their seasons
with it. But on at least two specially notable occasions,
the Chicago company did.

And as twelve years before Mary Garden had sung
in the second performance of the season, so she did here.
This time, however, instead of appearing as Mélisande,
she took the title part of "Carmen," to the Don José
of Riccardo Martin, and the Escamillo of Georges
Baklanoff, with Richard Hageman making his début in
the pit as associate musical director of the company.

There were some unusual features about the opening of this season, among them the fact that the whole
first week went with signal success. It is by no means
uncommon for a season to begin with a brilliant first
night and then go into a nose-dive, for a night or two
later, but this one kept up the brilliancy. For on the
third night Edith Mason as Mimi and Irene Pavloska as
Musetta lifted "La Bohême" to altogether unusual
heights, and Ettore Panizza showed his own marked gifts
as a conductor.

Then came "Sniegurotchka," otherwise known as
"Snow Maiden," by Rimsky-Korsakoff. It had been in
the repertoire of the touring Russian company, with
Bourskaya as Lehl, a part that she took in this performance. But the Chicago production was something quite
different. Nicolas Roerich had made a complete set of
unconventional and gorgeous scenery and costumes, Bolm
and Ludmila led the ballet, Hageman conducted.

"Sniegurotchka" became the striking success of the

season, artistically and financially, a position that it never came within miles of hitting again in seasons to come, though after painstaking revivals, and even a revival in English. I have always believed that Mr. Hageman had a good deal to do with its success this season, for he carried along the performance with a pace and color that no other conductor ever equaled. Mason, Pavloska, Minghetti, Baklanoff, and a host of lesser principals were in the cast.

Then on Saturday afternoon Miss Garden appeared as Fiora in "L'Amore dei Tre Re," with Crimi, Baklanoff, and Lazzari as the men, and on Saturday night Raisa, Claessens, Lamont and Rimini ended the week with "The Jewels of the Madonna." It was truly a brilliant week, and the only word of dispraise spoken in my presence was for Crimi's Avito in "L'Amore dei Tre Re."

"God gave him his legs," said an irreverent feminine onlooker, "but who gave him that petticoat?" And a man who witnessed the impassioned love scene of the second act between Crimi and Miss Garden pronounced after due thought his opinion that the piece ought to be renamed "She Who Gets Bit."

This season was the first to see an attempt to broadcast the opera. There was a great deal that was not known about the theory and practice of broadcasting in those days, in fact, notable improvements have been occurring at an average rate of about one a week ever since. But they made their first efforts then, thereby starting the still unsettled discussion on how music is going to be affected by the radio, whether people will pay money for tickets when they can hear music by switching it on at their own homes, whether it is going to be worth while for any one outside of the chosen radio few to go in for a career of music, and so on. People are still asking the same questions and waiting for the answers. One of the answers, which up to date is still true, is that a notable musician can generally make a good living and a mediocre one generally has a hard time, and this was true before ever an antenna was raised.

Mme. Louise Homer came to the company as guest-artist and started the house cheering with what she did as Azucena in "Il Trovatore." The same opera took on another unexpected bit of interest in another part because the stage manager got his cues crossed and Conductor Polacco had to play one introduction three times before Giacomo Rimini heard it and got to the stage. Mme. Bourskaya made another hit in the name part of "Carmen," but as this was classified at that time as one of the "Garden rôles," she for a none too unobvious reason was not encouraged to sing it often. The "Tiger of France," Georges Clemenceau, the aged war premier of France, visiting Chicago, also visited the opera, a performance of "Sniegurotchka" on November 29, and the curtains were drawn after one act while the chorus lined up and Edouard Cotreuil sang the "Marseillaise" and Cyrena Van Gordon "The Star-Spangled Banner." It was a coincidence of time that just about this date the management began to complain about attendance at German opera.

For under the new system of opera giving, it was found that an extremely sensitive operatic nerve ran into and through the box office. Works that did not draw were speedily packed away. "Parsifal," even with the brilliant performance of Joseph Schwarz as Amfortas, drew two poor houses and went into the discard. "Die Walküre" also disappeared in the same manner, and "Tannhäuser" was taken off the list for the year.

I shall not attempt here to defend the box office as the sole arbiter of what shall be given in an operatic season. I can see without difficulty that under such circumstances the repertoire would never grow—it grows far too slowly as it is—and that there are certain occasions when it is the duty of an opera company to step out into an artistic adventure. But this season, with the memories of the previous season's appalling losses still fresh in memory, the Civic Opera Company was stepping cautiously, not to say fearfully.

Claudia Muzio made her début December 7 in the name part of "Aïda," and scored the first of the long line of hits that attended her performances in the Auditorium. "The Girl of the Golden West" was revived with Raisa as the Girl and Rimini as the sheriff, and drew more money than "Parsifal" had done a few days before.

Then came Feodor Ivanovitch Chaliapin, to transform a bit of stage management. It was in Boïto's "Mefistofele." Having come on for a rehearsal of the opera, he pronounced himself dissatisfied with it, took it all apart and put it together again.

Will those who saw the performance ever forget it, not alone Chaliapin himself, but those surrounding him? Who, for instance, can forget the Brocken scene, where, after some instruction by the star, the customarily placid chorus was suddenly converted into a whirling, shrieking, frenzied crew of minor devils on a diabolical spree? And over them all sat the giant himself, half nude, gloating, flaming, dominating his followers, deriding the world, blazing out in his voice of golden trombone, sweeping back the stageful with a wave of the arm. It was one of the most magnificent scenes in all the history of the Chicago Opera. It was also a pitiless exposure of how artificial, how conventional grand opera can be at its worst.

This was by all odds the climax of the season. As a matter of fact not a great deal was left to report about it. Miss Muzio added "Il Trovatore," "Pagliacci," and "Tosca" to the "Aïda" with which she had begun. Mme. Galli-Curci, who about that time was thirsting for the acclaim of lyric as well as coloratura parts, sang "La Bohême," "Madame Butterfly," and the "Manon" of the Massenet version, but they did not remain permanently in her repertoire. The most memorable episode of "Manon" is that Conductor Hageman, finding himself in possession of some frightfully imperfect orchestral parts and no conductor's score at all, called an orchestral rehearsal with a piano score in front of him and corrected the whole set by ear, mistake by mistake, as it was played. It took him practically all of one day, but at the end of the time the opera company had a set of correct and playable parts. If you do not think that this was something to do, try it some day for yourself.

Oh, yes, and Miss Garden, still continuing to be a faithful reader of the newspapers and an estimator of their news values, announced and got it printed that Emile Coué, he of the "Every day, in every way" formula, visiting this country at that time, had cured her of bronchial pneumonia, buzzing in the head, little colds, irritability, and depression. And the company again tried to make friends with American opera with the one-act

Joseph Schwartz as Count di Luna in "Il Trovatore"

Photo by Daguerre

Feodor Chaliapin as Mefistofele

piece, "Snow Bird," by Theodore Stearns. Mary Mc-
Cormic and Charles Marshall sang in it. And Ganna
Walska, newly married to Harold F. McCormick, arrived in New York and began announcing that she would
appear in opera, the first and even now unconfirmed announcement having to do with the Russian Opera Company.

The Civic Opera Company's "gala" evening was
given a new slant from the fact that the company guarantors were the guests of honor. The bill consisted of the
first act of "Pagliacci," the third act of "Aïda," the
second act of "L'Amore dei Tre Re," the fourth act of
"Mefistofele"—without Chaliapin—and the second half
of the third act of "Die Walküre." At the end of the
"Tre Re" scene Mr. Insull stepped before the footlights
and announced that the famous French tenor, Fernand
Ansseau, had been engaged for the next season, and that
the guarantors, large and small, would kindly be prepared
to come through with 70 per cent of their guaranties.

A bit of arithmetic produced the information that
the call on the guarantors would be $350,000. Final
figures on the season's losses came to $290,000, as com-
pared to the $1,100,000 of the season before. With this
in their ears, the guarantors went home and the company
packed up and went to Boston instead of New York as
the first item on its post-Chicago season, a practice which
it has maintained ever since.

CHAPTER XXVII

At one time and another a good deal has been said about operatic performances that failed to succeed, new productions put on with great and lavish preparation which the public refused to admit into its list of favorites.

This has been in no mood of Nero fiddling over the conflagration of Rome. Disasters are not pleasant to contemplate at any time. What has been chiefly in mind here was to demonstrate by example instead of precept what an extremely difficult matter it is to assemble a workable and standard operatic repertoire, to point out what an opera company must undergo by the method of trial and error before it feels safe in confronting its public with an efficient list of works. This promptly became one of the Civic Opera Company's problems.

Some years ago a strange book made its appearance, so out of the ordinary that it has become one of the rarities in the book market. It is John Towers' "Dictionary of Operas."

John Towers, it would seem, had the instincts of a collector. Instead of collecting porcelains or early American bottles or postage stamps, however, he devoted eighteen years of his life to collecting the names of operas. There is no way to account for this labor of love, except that it was a manifestation of the collector's instinct. Certainly a less commercial enterprise could hardly be imagined.

At any rate he got it published in the year 1910 and, I am informed, died a few years later. Quite a number of operas have been written since that time, and some of them have managed to become widely and favorably known. But Mr. Towers managed to accumulate the almost incredible total of 34,000 names.

It is a curious book to run through. Both operas and operettas are included—the line is sometimes hard to draw—but this list has the qualification of being works that have been actually performed on the public stage, not merely written and put away.

This does not mean that there were 34,000 composers by a considerable degree. Without making an exact count, it would be safe to estimate about 7,000 since Monteverde produced "Orfeo" and Peri about the same time announced "Eurydice." There is apparently something about composing an opera that leads to the composing of other operas. Some astonishing figures come out of Mr. Towers' book, figures that cause one to wonder whether some of these old composers ever did anything else but write operas.

It is the merest commonplace to find men like A. C. Adam with 45 operas to his credit, T. Albinoni with 52, F. A. Barbieri with 77, and A. Caldara with 82. Think of figures like these: J. A. Hasse, 94; B. Galuppi, he to whom Browning once addressed a poem, 109; N. Piccinni, 145; G. Paisiello, 123; A. Draghi and P. Guglielmi, 149 each; Wenzel Mueller, 166. The British islands have had their share in the total. Michael Kelly wrote 56, Charles Dibdin, 91, and Sir Henry R. Bishop, 102. In spite of such industry, it is entirely probable that all these operas are dead beyond hope of resurrection.

Some stories were evidently great favorites with composers and audiences in former days. We of this era know "The Barber of Seville" in Rossini's music and "Faust" in Gounod's. But "The Barber" has had fourteen other settings, and "Faust" twenty-five. The story of Romeo and Juliet under one name or another has been set over twenty times, of Cleopatra twenty-six, of Francesca da Rimini twenty-three, and Arthur Honegger had fourteen predecessors before he wrote "Judith" for Miss Garden's use.

But even these were not the great favorites. One finds references to a "Demetrio" with thirty-nine settings, to a "Demofoonte" with forty-three, to an "Alessandro nelle Indie" with sixty-four. Did you ever hear any of them? Nor did I.

"The bearings of this observation," remarked Captain Bunsby, "lies in the application on it." Since the first performance at the Auditorium in 1910, the Chicago company has presented something in the neighborhood of 125 or 130 different operas. Of these, some forty or fifty can be classified as belonging to the standard repertoire. The annual repertoire consists of between thirty and forty. If you are fond of arithmetic, you can figure from 34,000 down to these figures and see what the mathematical chances of a new opera are for permanent success. It is not every day or every year that a "Jewels of the Madonna" or "Rosenkavalier" is discovered.

Mr. Insull once remarked that the three most popular operas in the Chicago repertoire were "Aïda, "La Traviata," and "Il Trovatore." This statement was based upon attendance during the history of the company, and the figures are unassailable. They are cited here because in spite of the fact that they are always given in their original tongue, Italian, they have a curious bearing on the greatly vexed subject of opera in English, at least on the subject of having an understandable libretto.

For "Aïda," finest of the festival operas, is all pageantry and pompous processional, ballet, resounding chorus, brilliant solos, for at least the first half of its length. Not until the Nile scene, the third of the opera's four acts, does the drama of the piece really begin. Up to that time one's attention is taken up with gorgeous music and equally gorgeous stage pictures. The dialogue makes not the slightest difference. It might be given in Chinese and still be as good an opera.

"La Traviata" presents a dramatic story so plainly that it is perfectly obvious. Again the language makes no difference, but this time it is because every one can tell what is going on. "Il Trovatore" has a story so complex and full of details that a translation into English would not be able to clarify it. No one understands what is going on—a slightly irritated commentator once expressed doubt whether Verdi understood it when he made the setting—and no one cares. The full blooded, vital, Verdi melodies save it.

As to opera in English, it has always been up to the public. From the beginning, the Chicago Opera Company has always given opera in English every chance in the world. Time after time an English performance, native or translated, has been offered, to be withdrawn because the public indicated that opera in English was not to its taste. "Natoma" survived thirty performances and came the nearest to being a success. But even now the management of the company has not lost interest in the subject.

This trial and error method and its successes and failures makes a fascinating subject to look back upon, though at times it must have been extremely discouraging to those who had the welfare of the company most at heart. Sometimes, as in the case of "Conchita," the score would seem to have been a few years in advance of public taste, a meritorious work that needed to let the world catch up with it. Sometimes a single bad act, as in "Francesca da Rimini" left an unfavorable impression. Sometimes a single artist became so identified with a single work that it was successful only when that artist appeared in it. Miss Garden in "Thaïs," and Galli-Curci in "Lucia di Lammermoor" are cases in point. No one but Miss Garden was ever able to make much of a success out of "Thaïs," and Galli-Curci always drew the greatest houses of her Chicago career in "Lucia."

Her Chicago career ended, by the way, in the 1923-24 season. Seemingly through bad judgment, she permitted herself to become the leading figure in a dispute with the management over whether she should open in "Dinorah" or "Lakmé." After the dust had settled, it became apparent that she was in the wrong, having agreed to "Lakmé" long enough in advance for the repertoire to be fixed, and then having changed her mind. But she made an issue out of it, took it to the newspapers, and declaimed that as far as the Civic Opera Company was concerned, she was through at the end of that season. The Civic Opera Company agreed with her.

There were several other changes in the lineup about

this time. Conductor Hageman had left the season before; Adolph Bolm and Chaliapin were to disappear
shortly thereafter; Mr. Johnson returned to the business
department of the company under the title of assistant to
the president. As such he was able to relieve Mr. Shaw of
his duties and labors as business manager and allow him to
concentrate on his former function as tour manager.
Soon Mr. Johnson was to become business manager
technically as well as actually, a position that he has
held ever since.

CHAPTER XXVIII

The season of 1922-23 began with "Boris Godunoff," Chaliapin in the name part. It proved, as has been proved more conclusively since, that only Chaliapin should appear in it. With him, it is a magnificent, thrilling, stirring epic; without him, it is just another opera, more interesting than many of them, it is true, but still, just another opera. It is expressly intended for an artist of his inches and spiritual ponderosity, and when he appears in it, it is transfigured.

It was about this time that Chaliapin, desirous of seeing the operations of a large metropolitan newspaper, called at the *Tribune* office one night and asked to be shown through the plant, inquiring, among others, for me. I was out at the time, but when I returned, the message taker, whom Frederick Donaghey in the *Line o' Type* used to refer to as Kartoffeln Karon, told me that "a big Swede named Charley Appel" had been asking for me. Reproved for having mixed up his facts in inaccurate and unjournalistic fashion, he answered, "Well, what if he is a Russian? All foreigners is Swedes except when they're Germans."

In his autobiography, "Pages From My Life," Chaliapin speaks of this incident. He says:

"My manager took me to visit a certain Chicago newspaper office. The representative of the paper, who greeted us in shirt sleeves and trousers, appeared very much embarrassed.

" 'Pleased to meet you,' he stammered. 'Didn't you come from Czecho-Slovakia? What do you do, and how did you happen to come here?'

"My manager appeared most upset, probably because he had informed me that this celebrated paper very much wished to make my acquaintance.

" 'Pardon me,' I answered. "I am not from Czecho-Slovakia, but from Russia! And,' I think I continued in a soprano voice, 'I sing.'

" 'Oh!' was the reply. 'In which operas?'

"To save the situation my manager hurriedly stated that M. Chaliapin was very much interested in American newspapers, whereupon the gentleman, becoming exceedingly amiable, showed us through the building and revealed several secrets of the art of printing."

He refers to another event in his Chicago engagement, one in which the newspapers printed an account of a supposed row that he had had during a rehearsal. His own explanation is that he was explaining to another member of the cast (Jose Mojica) what should take place in the scene between him and Shouisky in "Boris Godunoff," and explaining the dramatic action with loud language and gestures. From this it was concluded that he was having trouble, and the report was spread wide.

Because of these and a few similar occurrences, he says that he is obliged to conclude that Chicago newspapers have a special psychology. He also promises to discuss his Chicago engagement more at length in another book that he hopes to write sometime.

A gesture was extended to the Chicago Symphony Orchestra by asking Frederick Stock to rehearse and conduct a performance of "Siegfried." Mr. Stock is without doubt one of the finest Wagnerian conductors who ever stepped into the Auditorium pit. Among his other achievements, he cut a full hour out of the ordinary running time of the piece in such an expert fashion that not the slightest dramatic or harmonic break could be discovered anywhere, and he conducted the performance with the same masterly expression that make his Wagnerian performances high spots of the symphony season.

But more than a master conductor was needed to save "Siegfried." From a popular standpoint it is the least interesting of the four works that make up the "Ring des Nibelungen." One reason is that not until the final scene, a short one, does the appearance of Brünnhilde make a break in the constant succession of men's voices, for the remarks of the concealed bird in the forest scene are too brief to make a contrast.

Another performance, and "Siegfried" went into the discard.

Curious changes occurred all through this season. "Sniegurotchka" was revived, but Mme. Bourskaya as Lehl and Conductor Hageman had departed, and with them the fervor that they put into the performance. It was astonishing to be there and note the difference, for the opera suddenly became respectable and dull, and the audience stayed away in great numbers.

On the other hand, Charles Hackett joined the company, and his début performance of "Romeo and Juliet" with Edith Mason became a bit of new life. Here were two stars, and there were two more when Rosa Raisa and Charles Marshall went on in "La Juive," sung in Italian. The latter's serviceable tunes, plentifully dealt out to every member of the cast, promptly became greatly

CYNARA VAN GORDON AS DELILAH IN "SAMSON AND DELILAH"

CHARLES HACKETT AS ROMEO IN "ROMEO AND JULIET"

popular. As much could not be said, however, for the Crimi-Raisa, afterwards Marshall-Raisa, performance of "L'Africaine," another French work also sung in Italian. It never quite clicked with the public, in spite of a large assortment of tunes of the same general order.

Adolph Bolm was doing no end of fine work that season. For the ballet music of "L'Africaine," a triumph of uninspired mediocrity, he transcribed an actual dance of India, wherein he appeared in a devil-mask as the spirit of evil whose onslaughts were repelled by the priestess of the temple, assumed by Anna Ludmila. In "Lakmé," he told another story of the orient, the Hindu equivalent of the Greek myth, the musical contest between Apollo and Marsyas, transferred to terms of the dance. In "Aïda" he vitalized a collection of Egyptian frescoes; in "Samson and Delilah" the dance in the temple became a whirling, throbbing bacchanale.

Never before, except a few years previous when Bolm had come on to stage and appear in John Alden Carpenter's ballet, "The Birthday of the Infanta," had the Chicago Opera been given such fine, sincere, superb art in its ballet department. Never since has it come within miles of touching that level. But this was Bolm's final year with the company. Meanwhile the department behind the curtain whose duty it was to decorate the stage used to fill up the furnishings of the second act of "La Juive" with large busts in placid disregard of the rule against graven images in orthodox Jewish homes. They learned better afterwards, but it took years before they were convinced.

Claudia Muzio scored highly with Fernand Ansseau and Baklanoff in "Monna Vanna," and with Giulio Crimi

and Cesare Formichi in "La Forza del Destino," two
works in which performances far outran musical values.
Galli-Curci sang through her final engagement to what
was even for her unexampled applause—by the way,
Schipa was ill at the beginning, and the tenor part of
"Lakmé," over which the row arose, was sung by Ralph
Errolle.

Cyrena Van Gordon was awarded a verdict of
$15,000 for personal injuries received two years before,
when an automobile in which she was riding was struck
by a street car.

An item published about this time shows that the
working force of the opera company comprised an average of 500 persons. There were fifty-two principals, a
chorus of eighty, an orchestra of seventy, a ballet of
thirty-five. On the producing staff there were twenty-one
electricians, twenty wardrobe workers, four armorers,
eight carpenters, and twenty men handling properties.
Ten artists made new scenes and refurbished the old, two
stage crews, of seven by day and eleven by night, with
ten extras, erected them for the operas. Day and night
crews in the storehouse accounted for thirty-two. Eight
conductors and assistants prepared and directed the musical parts of the performances after the scenery had been
moved from the storehouse and set up on the stage. The
house employees numbered one hundred, seventy-five being ushers, door men, carriage men and maids, ten check-
room men, and fifteen janitors of day and night service.
Eighteen were employed by the administrative staff,
mostly clerk and stenographic help.

Miss Garden returned at Christmas time to do
"Louise" as she alone could do it, with Ansseau, Bak-

lanoff, and Maria Claessens to round out a notable quartet. Then came another saddening episode, Claire Dux in "Königskinder."

An exquisite artist in an exquisite opera, but once again one person was required to carry almost all the burden. For while some in the long cast knew their parts, others were unfamiliar with the opera and even with German, there was a tenor who sang into the wings instead of to the audience, and everywhere there was evidence of restraint and discomfort. Even at the final rehearsal Miss Dux had been seen instructing some of the cast in such primary bits of "business" as where to stand on the stage. They did not know and there was no one to tell them. So a beautiful opera failed of its effect and an extraordinary artist was not given full chance to prove how good she was. The best are helped by proper support and hampered by its lack, and the best know it. Joseph Schwarz, arriving in Chicago on the heels of this performance, delivered himself of a few operatic maxims, none ever truer.

"Opera can be judged only by the success or failure of its ensemble," he said. "To achieve success in opera individually, you must become one of the ensemble. Together, everything is possible. Alone, nothing."

Mr. Shaw completed his plans for the spring tour of the company, and as its itinerary is a fair sample in space and time of what has become the normal, annual course of events, it can be itemized here. From Chicago the company was booked in Boston for two weeks. Then, becoming in every sense of the word a touring organization, it visited Cleveland, Pittsburgh, Detroit, Cincinnati, Chattanooga, Tulsa, Houston, Dallas, Los Angeles,

San Francisco, Portland, Seattle, Salt Lake City, Denver, Wichita, and closed in Kansas City, a jaunt of some 10,000 miles.

In spite of operatic optimists who preach the doctrine of opera for opera's sake, the cities of the tour insist upon having stars. In Boston, where the company is in the habit of staying two weeks and giving sixteen performances, sixteen different operas are presented, but the road tour proper means presentation of a few works for a few notables. In this case "Boris" and "Mefistofele" were carried for the use of Chaliapin, Edith Mason appearing with him in the second, "La Juive" for Raisa and Marshall, and "Cleopatra" for Garden.

The expense of such a tour runs into impressive amounts of money. When all costs are added together, they are not far from $1,000,000 a year. At the same time, the risk to the company is almost nothing, in fact it generally pays its own way. This is because every road engagement is guaranteed. Months before the arrival of the company a group of residents in each city is formed into a committee of underwriters, each making himself liable for a certain sum, the total $15,000 or so for each performance. It has been found by experience that a large committee liable for small individual amounts is better, because the larger the group, the more individuals interested in making the engagement a success, and the more general effort to make it a success. Frequently, one may say generally, public interest is stirred up to the extent that the intake renders it unnecessary to make a demand upon the underwriters. Sometimes they even make a profit, which is generally put into the bank as a nest egg for the next season's engagement.

When there is a loss, the underwriters are called upon for a percentage of their guaranties sufficient to clear the account. What happens then depends a good deal upon the varying phenomena of human nature. It is by no means incredible that a man who has suffered a loss for such a reason one year should decline to run the risk again, but there have been plenty of cases where losses were met cheerfully with a request for another chance. Sometimes the guarantors grow indignant over the public spirit of their communities, and insist upon being given the opportunity to stir it up.

In any case the company brings back newspaper clippings to be measured not by the yard, but almost by the rod and furlong. And so from coast to coast Chicago is advertised every year not only as a commercial center but as the home of one of the leading opera companies.

It is interesting to discover what can be learned about costs from a good accountant. One of the virtues of the Civic Opera Company has always been that while it seldom makes public exact figures, it does enough for those with a taste for arithmetic to make some estimates of their own. More than that, it clarifies many ideas.

Opera admittedly always runs at a deficit. One of the most popular conceptions is that this is caused by the fees paid to famous artists. The man on the street hears of fees—cachets is the operatic slang for the word —of $1,500 to $3,500 a performance, and comes to the conclusion that if some way could be devised to abolish them, opera would pay its own way.

But this conception is a misconception. For one thing, if famous artists did not appear, neither would audiences. For another, it is not true. The Civic Opera

Company sent out figures about the previous season, its first, showing that if all fees paid to all principals had been abolished, there would have been a deficit anyway.

It told how for every dollar taken in, $1.547 had been spent. That, taken in connection with the call of of $350,000 upon Chicago guarantors, indicates that the cost of the Chicago season had been in the neighborhood of $1,200,000. Then it began to itemize its expenses in decimal points and small fractions. Each dollar spent had been cut up into pieces and paid out in this fashion:

Miscellaneous expense	$.0523
Rehearsal expense	.0735
Publicity, administration, etc.	.0928
Repairs to scenery, costumes, etc.	.1568
Theatre, warehousing, etc.	.2025
Musical staff, orchestra, chorus, ballet, stage hands	.2025
Artists	.2196

Add them up and they make an exact dollar. The item for artists is the largest, but it is not as large as had been supposed.

Interesting visitors always come to the opera. One of them was Mme. Eleanora Duse, the famous Italian actress. She was playing some matinée performances at the Auditorium that season, and occasionally came to the opera in the evening. Depressed and in bad health, she saw few callers, but she became fast friends with Galli-Curci.

"I gave away all my money during the war," she told her, "and I must act. I have to fight to do it. Each time I go on the stage I say, 'God, help me through this and I'll never ask anything else.'"

But the effort was too much for even that brave spirit. She died later in the season.

The operatic deficit was $325,000, so Mr. Insull told the guarantors, and each was assessed 65 per cent instead of the 70 per cent of the year before. He added some figures.

Costs were greater and operas more numerous, but attendance had improved. The season had been extended from ten to eleven and one-half weeks. Ninety-one performances of thirty-five operas had been given as against seventy-two of twenty-five operas the year before, and attendance had averaged 84 per cent of the total capacity of the theater. In figures, the receipts had been $910,123, which was 74 per cent of the financial capacity of the house, as against $757,000 the year before. Even the losses of the season before had been cut. His first estimate of 80 per cent on the guarantors had been reduced to 70 per cent.

It began to look rather cheerful. The public was learning to come to the opera.

CHAPTER XXIX

Vers libre advertising in flights of high-powered imagination is the first thing one notices in the season of 1924-25. Here are a few specimens, taken at random from newspaper columns of the period. No comment can be more eloquent than the poems themselves.

> If You Wish to See Fired
> Opals Lit With the
> Erubescence of Rubies in
> Jeweled Sounds of Song
> Come Tonight and Hear
>   LUCIA.

> Your Last Chance to See
> And Hear This Cingalese
> Love Affair Under Alluring
> Oriental Skies—Tonight—
> The Pearl Fishers.

> "The Little Mother"
> on Life's Highway
> 'Twixt Duty and Love
> Is the Lyric Drama
> of Werther—Tonight.

In the presence of something so closely approaching perfection, a Mona Lisa, a Venus de Milo, a Lake Louise of advertising copy, one makes no comments. One stands in speechless awe—and turns to the actual proceedings of the season.

There were quite a number of débuts that year: two conductors, Roberto Moranzoni and Henry G. Weber; two sopranos, Olga Forrai and Toti Dal Monte; two mezzo-sopranos, Flora Perini and Augusta Lenska; a tenor, Antonio Cortis; a baritone, Mario Stabile. Only two of these newcomers, Moranzoni and Cortis, are still members of the organization at the end of the period covered by this volume.

There were also a number of revivals and exhumations from ancient operatic literature. The season began Wednesday, November 5, with the time-honored "La Gioconda," rated second only to "Aïda" as a meritorious opening bill in the United States. It was sung by Raisa, Perini, Meisle, Cortis, Formichi and Kipnis, with Polacco conducting, a notable cast capable of extracting all the juice from the score. The next night came "Tosca," with Muzio and Hackett, Stabile as Scarpia and Moranzoni at the baton making their first appearances in Chicago. So far there was enough success to justify the anticipations of those who had the interests of the company most at heart.

But then came "The Prophet," "Le Prophête," if you belong among those who insist upon opera in a foreign tongue, and as must so frequently be recorded in these pages, it died with great suddenness and great thoroughness. Even the superb performance of Mme. Louise Homer, back again for some guest appearances, was not enough to delay its demise.

One of the least explicable items in the business of opera giving is that of success one time and failure another. It is something that lies close to the hearts of operatic givers, because a failure is expensive and not

to be regarded with joy. Campanini a few years before
had put on "Le Prophête" with a good deal of manner
and made a success out of it. This time the former spirit
was lacking and people refused to come. Or perhaps
the order of the last sentence should be reversed. People refused to come and the former spirit was lacking.

"The Pearl Fishers" was kept alive for a time, more
by the fine singing of Graziella Pareto and Charles
Hackett than by its own merits. For Bizet when he composed this score was only a mild, not to say feeble fore-
runner of what he was when he wrote "Carmen." Mme.
Pareto, a good looking, mannerly artist, was possessed
of a slender but lovely soprano voice, and excelled in
works calling for a voice of this nature.

First place in florid singing, however, was speedily
captured by Toti Dal Monte. Here was a case where
expert execution compensated for everything else. Dal
Monte was a strange little figure, with head set squarely
between two broad shoulders, and with altogether too
much displacement for her very moderate height. She
never attempted or pretended to be anything of an actress.
But when she set her heels together and rippled through
the cascades of the Mad Scene in "Lucia di Lammermoor," the house rose to her and called her a great
woman.

Olga Forrai was announced to début as Elisabeth
in "Tannhäuser," but she was not ready in the part, and
Rosa Raisa got up in it after having left it alone for
three years. She always disliked and distrusted German opera for her own use, and did as little of it as
possible, and the world is the loser, for there are parts
in the German repertoire which, had she chosen, she

could have made her own with few to contest her place.

Forrai was in many ways the reverse of Dal Monte, a good looking, stage-wise woman who was far from being a perfect singer. Her good looks and her stage wisdom stood her in great part when she finally got around to singing Octavian in "Der Rosenkavalier," but this was later. If memory is correct, she made her début as Nedda in "Pagliacci." At any rate it was as Nedda that one vivid recollection of the season remains. Following the "Ballatella" and the use of the whip upon Tonio, Silvio entered crying "Nedda" in accordance with normal procedure, and she in her best middle-European accent answered "Z-z-zilvio," to the enormous disgust of the Italians in the audience and the enormous joy of every one else.

Massenet's "Werther," a piece of excruciating sentimentality, was revived for the use of Miss Garden, and she put it across. Ansseau was the Werther to her Charlotte, lacking to some extent the overwhelming manner of Muratore, who, in Mrs. Malaprop's phrase, used to be the very pineapple of politeness in the part, but the opera was better liked by the public in this combination than before.

On December 31, 1924, it is noted that the Civic Opera sought an injunction in the Circuit Court against Chaliapin asking that he be enjoined from appearing in Washington in "Faust" on January 26, 1925. According to the petition, he was due to appear in that city with the Civic Opera Company in "Boris Godunoff" on February 10 of the same year, and that his earlier appearance with another company would greatly reduce the ticket sale for that occasion. Also that it was a breach of his contract with the Civic Opera company.

A temporary injunction was granted. Before the final hearing there was a chance for much conversation from the interested parties. Chaliapin proclaimed that he had an open date on January 26, and that was why he had agreed to go to Washington. The Washington people said that they were opening a new opera house on January 26, and that they did not wish to postpone their opening date, in fact they did not intend to postpone it. The opera company said nothing, but asked that the injunction be made permanent.

The final hearing was held on January 8, 1925, and it opened the eyes of everybody as to the possibilities of legal processes. Apparently there was nothing in Chaliapin's contract forbidding him from appearing anywhere he pleased at such times as he was not wanted by the Civic Opera. He was therefore permitted to fill the "Faust" engagement, but he and his agents were forbidden from advertising the fact, otherwise they were to be held in contempt of court. Naturally the Washington people were doing all the advertising and Chaliapin and his agents did not need to do any announcing at all. So he filled both dates, with the Washington and Chicago companies, and had large audiences on both occasions.

"This," said Edward Albion, general director of the Washington company, "is the greatest triumph for the cause of Art and American music in the history of our country. Chaliapin's appearance with the Washington opera in 'Faust' ushers in a new era of music for the capital, the culmination of which will mean the development of a genuine national opera."

It was also something else. It was probably one of the most comic decisions in the history of American jurisprudence, and its culmination was the loss of Chaliapin to the Chicago company.

For Chaliapin began to think that what was legal sauce for the opera company could be served as well for its most eminent basso. The injunction hearing had brought out the fact that he was being paid at the rate of $3,500 a performance, and that he was engaged for a tour of ten weeks after the Chicago season. Altogether the season meant about $84,000 to him.

For one reason and another it was decided that the tour should be eight instead of ten weeks long. At its end Chaliapin brought suit for the four, or possible six cachets he would have earned in the extra two weeks. The opera company resisted the claim, saying that arrangements for the shorter time had been made with his manager. Chaliapin's response was in effect that this might be true, but that no arrangements had been made with him, and that his manager had no power to enter into such an agreement. However, he sang six concerts during the two disputed weeks, thereby earning his full fee, or better, and he was never on hand when the case came up for hearing. Also, he did not return to the company.

Tito Schipa, too, or rather Mrs. Schipa, came in for a share of the headlines. There was an account in the *Tribune* on January 15, not very far from the review of "Martha" of the night before. This is it:

"It was after the opera hour when the Home Drug Company store at Wabash avenue and Congress street was crowded to capacity.

"Tito Schipa, the tenor himself, and his wife wandered in. Mrs. Schipa was negligently regarding the perfume counter. Mr. Schipa was as unconcernedly standing in the offing. Suddenly a feminine figure rushed upon the scene.

"Two feminine arms enlaced themselves about Schipa's neck. And a pair of very feminine lips gave Schipa a pair of very fervent kisses.

"Mrs. Schipa forgot to look further at the perfumes.

"Mrs. Schipa forgot to muse over the comparative merits of violet or hyacinth. In excited French she demanded of Mr. Schipa, presumably, whether he knew this person. In French as excited Mr. Schipa declared he did not.

"It was then that Mrs. Schipa proved her right to marry an opera star.

"One hundred and two pounds of opera star wife's fury went into a right and left. And the right and left were accompanied by French still more excited.

"But 'I love him. I love him. I have heard his voice.' Mr. Schipa's admirer would not be denied.

"As she was hustled out of the drug store and put into a cab, she gave her name as Evelyn Johnstone, and claimed she was a student at the University of Chicago.

" 'I have heard him sing. I love him,' she declared as she nursed her bruises and was driven away.

"And clad in a flaming red negligée, Mrs. Schipa in her suite at the Congress Hotel after the battle was over had the same phrase to repeat.

" 'I love him,' she said, 'but sometimes it's hard to be the wife of an opera star.' "

Of course it was all very impromptu and unexpected,

Tito Schipa as Edgardo in "Lucia di Lammermoor"

Edith Mason as Juliet in "Romeo and Juliet"

the tribute that flaming youth pays to glowing art. Wasn't it strange, though, that it should have happened in a public place before so many witnesses? Wasn't it stranger yet that a reporter should have been anonymously tipped off to be in the drug store about 11 o'clock that night and keep his eyes open?

The season closed with a deficit of $400,000, as Mr. Insull told the guarantors on the final Friday night. At that he found some elements of cheer in the situation. Attendance was growing faster than expense; the deficit for the three years of the Civic Opera Company's administration had been $1,075,000, or $600,000 less than the three years before the Civic Company took hold. Already he was at work for a plan to cut some of the costs. One of them was to be a new storage warehouse and workshop. It would cost $500,000; it would be paid for by a bond issue which would be retired in eight or nine years; when the bond issue was cleared, it would save the company between $80,000 and $90,000 a year.

Having given ninety-eight performances in Chicago, the company went away to give fifty-two more in Boston, Washington, Baltimore, Pittsburgh, Cleveland, Chattanooga, Memphis, Dallas, Tulsa, St. Louis, and Milwaukee.

The storage warehouse and workshop turned out to be one of the important achievements of the company. Never seen by the public at large, it solved many of the organization's operating problems. Located on Dearborn and 26th streets, it holds all the stage equipment and in addition gives all needed opportunity to build new productions. Scenes are designed, built and painted there, costumes are made, armor is constructed, properties of all kinds are made there. At the end of a season all the used equipment is gone over, repaired, repainted, and stored away in such a fashion that it will be in good shape to use the next season. Even the washing of costumes takes place there. Not only that, but the plant is equipped to do and frequently does work for other theaters in need of new productions.

Harry W. Beatty, technical director of the company, designed it. He has been known to say since that if he had it to do over again, there is nothing that he would need to change.

Mr. Insull's proposal to finance the undertaking was equally interesting. The company pays a certain amount of rent for the use of the building, that amount being at once diverted to an amortization of the bond issue. At the time this is being written about half the bonds have been paid off and retired. The plan worked so successfully that it became the basis of the vastly greater enterprise that came into being a few years later, something that was to be not only high finance but positive romance in building.

CHAPTER XXX

In these more or less rambling reminiscences only a little has been said about the activities of that ever present and highly industrious operatic official, the press agent. This is partly because your true press agent does so many of his good works by stealth, though there is little evidence that one was ever caught blushing to find them known.

Press agentry in its present complex and highly organized state is little more than a generation old. It developed through the discovery that newspapers are always on the lookout for something interesting to publish in their columns, "a good story," in their own vernacular, and that sometimes they could be assisted in the discovery thereof.

Good stories are of many kinds. Some classify as straight news, some as colorful or dramatic incidents, some merely as humorous items. Whatever they are, newspapers are likely to accept them gladly if they are good enough and infrequently repeated. Also a most abiding article of faith in the American mentality is the importance of being mentioned in newspaper columns. At that, some of the faith is justified. Justified or not, almost every concern you can mention has its own press agent and a good many private individuals as well. Every theater and every theatrical company has one or more press agents on its pay roll, so have banks, hotels, department stores, politicians, financial organizations, what not? And when you read of a large dinner or party in the society columns of the newspapers with a long list of the important guests, do you suppose that all this has come about through the far-reaching ability of the newspaper staff to know everything that is going on all the time? It is naturally the business of a newspaper to print news, and the more news it prints, the better newspaper it is. But frequently, more often than not, the society editor is assisted by a neatly typed list of guests, given her by the press agent of the hostess.

Hardly an activity in American life exists that does not have its own press agent, engaged for the purpose of letting the world know what it is doing. No one cares to be private any more. The theatrical press agents have come to the point where they have a national association and annual conventions where they listen to solemn addresses about minimum wage, betterment of the press agents' status, and the ethics of the profession. Some of them do not call themselves press agents: with the growth of the profession many have become influenced by grandeur and polysyllables. Counselors in public relations is one of the favored titles at present, but it translates simply into press agent.

One can see that in the business of giving opera where there is always a deficit, where the constant thought by day and night of every one concerned is to make the opera company better known in the community and hence to induce more persons to buy tickets, the expert press agent is a person of high importance. Consequently every opera company has a press agent with running instructions not to work more than twenty-four hours a day, and a good many artists employ personal publicity seekers on their own behalf besides. This latter is partly a business investment, the enlargement of the artist's sphere of influence, and thereby the possible enlargement of his or her future earnings. The other part is probably just personal satisfaction, one might even call it vanity, though this angle of psychology need not be gone into deeply just now.

It is to be believed that the early school of press agents leaned a little too heavily on Charles A. Dana's famous definition of news when he was editor of the New York *Sun*. He said that if a dog bit a man, it was not news, but if a man bit a dog, it was. This was only a picturesque way of saying that the unexpected is an important element in a news item, but in the world of opera and their press agents, it has been given a totally unwarranted importance. Certainly in the nineteen years of the Chicago company, the men and women of the company have been incited to bite nearly every kind of a dog of publicity that the ingenious imaginations of their press agents could devise.

They have christened infant arrivals in the animal pens of the Lincoln Park zoo; they have ridden in airplanes when airplanes were newer and more dangerous than they are now; they have sung in hospitals, insane asylums, jails, and penitentiaries; they have driven automobiles through the stop lights on street corners hoping to be arrested; they have been pursued by mythical lovers carrying daggers and love letters and no less fabulous enemies carrying revolvers and demands for money; they have posed for photographers over kitchen stoves, supposedly preparing their own favorite viands, though the

record of their or any one's else having partaken thereof
is not entirely complete, except in a few cases; for photographic purposes again they have had their pet dogs,
their pet cats, their pet monkeys, their pet fads of various
sorts and descriptions.

Once when Muratore was singing in "Romeo and
Juliet" at the Auditorium, a young man called upon the
newspapers bearing a typewritten account to the effect
that the summer before Mr. Muratore, an ardent archæ-
ologist, had gone to Verona, had dug into the real tomb
of the historical Romeo, and that the cloak he wore in
the second act of the opera was the actual cloak that once
hung from the shoulders of the living Romeo when he
went a-courting by nights to Juliet's window. What is
more, one of the newspapers in a weak moment yielded
and printed the story.

The trouble with such campaigns is that the number
of stunts that can be thought up by press agents and
executed by artists is limited, and once done, they and all
their kind are worn out. Once a private press agent carried to the papers the news of his artist's loss of some
jewelry taken by a pickpocket out of her handbag. As a
matter of fact the incident happened to be absolutely
and unassailably true, but the subject of prima donnas'
jewels was by that time a permanently dead issue with
Chicago newspapers, and the press agent was advised by
a hard-hearted city editor to go and take a Turkish bath
and then sign the temperance pledge.

Barnum was the first of the press agents. Read his
biography and you will learn how he put Jumbo on the
map, not to mention his circus, and before that his
museum, and, for once in music, Jenny Lind. But the field

was new and unworked then, and Barnum had a fertile imagination. He knew, moreover, what many of the later generations of press agents never learned, that the best way to evolve his marvels was to set the stage and let the newspapers discover the stories for themselves, of course with a guiding hint when such a move seemed advisable.

Has any one ever forgotten Anna Held and her milk baths? That episode was promoted according to the finest Barnum ideals. Once upon a time an actual suit was brought in an actual New York court to recover the price of some 720 gallons or so—I have forgotten the exact number—of milk. The newspapers were not even notified, but the large quantity of milk sold to a private individual, and the other curious features of the case excited attention and drifted out of the court room, as such things have a habit of doing. It was calmly alleged during the trial that the milk had been bought for the bathing purposes of a then unknown young French actress, and that she was indulging in this procedure in order to preserve the marvelous texture of her skin.

It was enough for the papers. They played it up for weeks. They even demanded proof, and one day a select committee was permitted to enter the room where Miss Held reclined in a tub, with just her head showing and the rest of her modestly undisclosed beneath a concealing flood of opaque white fluid. How many American women fell for the plan and adopted it for their own, history does not tell, but it made Miss Held famous.

The most notable Barnum method as applied to opera in America did not happen to the Chicago company, but to the one in Boston. Henry Russell was getting

ready to put on "Monna Vanna," the opera which had
been made out of Maurice Maeterlinck's play of the same
name, and he had engaged Georgette LeBlanc, Maeterlinck's former wife, to take the leading part. She and
Maeterlinck were separated at that time, but this fact did
not annoy the press agent. Perhaps it made his efforts
the more potent. At any rate, this, as briefly as possible,
was the procedure employed.

A man was hired to go to one of the less well known
Boston hotels, engage a room and sign the name of
Maurice Maeterlinck on the hotel register. That was his
sole function in the plot. Having done so much, he
promptly disappeared and was seen no more.

For the next scene—you see these things have to be
played up with some dramatic flash—another man appeared in the same hotel and fell into casual conversation
with another room clerk on the next watch, this episode
carefully timed so that there could be no personal descrip-
tion of the guest from the first one, in case some one
happened to be personally acquainted with Maeterlinck.
As the newcomer talked, he idly turned the leaves of the
register and read some of the names. Suddenly he started
back with intense interest depicted on his countenance.

"Great muses of literature and the stage!" he ex-
claimed, or words to that general effect. "Do you see
this? Do you realize what it means?"

The clerk naturally did not, but was willing to learn.

"Why, here is the name of Maurice Maeterlinck,
the Belgian dramatist, the most famous playwright in the
world to-day. I just happened to see that his 'Monna
Vanna' is going on at the Boston Opera House, and his
wife is going to take the leading part. Now nobody has

heard from him lately, and the chances are that he has come to Boston without announcing himself, registered at this hotel where he can be alone, and is going to gumshoe into the performance to see how she does it. Oh, this is rich!"

And he, too, permanently disappeared from the scene, with his work also done. Without doubt there is not a hotel clerk in all the forty-eight states who would not rejoice at the chance of seeing his hotel get into the newspaper columns on a story of such a nature, and this clerk was no exception. He did the rest. Apparently a stream of reporters poured into that hotel for the rest of the day, and for days and weeks the headlines of Boston newspapers asked of the world whether Maeterlinck was in Boston. It is not reported that the business of "Monna Vanna" fell off in consequence.

But these are rare instances, and deserving of mention because of their ingenuity. Most of the others are by no means as ingenious, and they have been sadly overworked. It began to get to the point that when a city editor received a message saying that Mme. So-and-So had been adopted as a full member of the tribe of Osage Indians, or that some one else was known as the successor of Patti, or that a third person proposed to run for mayor on the operatic ticket, he would throw the item on the floor with a few eloquent but forceful words.

Finally a new light fell on the publicity office of the Chicago Opera. A wise and experienced man of publicity, one who had worked on newspapers as well as in press departments and consequently knew both sides of the business, observed that things were not going as well as they should, and straightway conceived an idea. It was that if the public and the newspapers were getting tired of freak publicity, it would be a good plan to tell the public in detail and without exaggeration just what sort of entertainment was going on at the Auditorium. As he expressed it, the company had goods to sell, and the public might as well know what it was buying.

So he addressed himself to the public in plain statements of fact, and almost from the first day the business of the company began to pick up and flourish. Plain statements of fact have continued ever since. It was another of the things that were so simple that no one had ever thought of them.

CHAPTER XXXI

With the opening of the 1925 season on Tuesday, November 3, a capacity audience of us were given an enjoyable surprise with the matter provided, and a few of us with its manner. It was Richard Strauss' comic opera, "Der Rosenkavalier," a gem of a piece and a best seller of the German repertoire.

In one respect it lived up to the most famous of stage traditions. This was that a bad dress rehearsal means a good performance. Some of us had attended the dress rehearsal the Saturday before, and it was so far from ready then that I, for one, could not possibly see how it could struggle through without calamity. By Tuesday, however, all the rough spots had been ironed out, and the performance moved swiftly and with the very perfection of manner. Rosa Raisa had the part of the Princess, Edith Mason that of Sophie, Olga Forrai that of the boy, Octavian, Alexander Kipnis the baron, a long list of clever people filled the lesser parts, and Giorgio Polacco conducted.

A good part of its success as a performance can be laid to the presence of a highly competent stage director. It is a complex and tricky piece in performance, and so Charles Moor was brought over from Europe to stage it. For several seasons the company had been struggling along with little or no stage management, in fact from the beginning stage management had always been the weak point of the company's operations. There had been a whole series of stage directors, at least calling themselves by that title, but as they were almost invariably foreigners speaking no English, and as the unseen staff behind the scenes usually spoke nothing else, the struggle was frequently not a success. One of the electricians once complained that when the director came to him and haltingly said, "Sun—moon—snow," he had to be a mindreader to know what lighting effect was wanted.

And for some time there had not been even that degree of direction. Operas were pretty well permitted to stage themselves. At that, sometimes the plan, or lack of plan, worked. A good many of the artists were experienced and conscientious, and could be depended upon to do the right thing and help the others of less experience. Mr. Polacco, too, always had a well defined idea of what he wanted to take place in a performance, and used to stage his operas while rehearsing them. In other cases, however, it frequently did not work, and many performances were lamentably ragged. At the best and with the most competent of conductors, it puts an extra burden upon the conductor, who always has plenty to do without it.

Mr. Moor was and is a Scotchman who had widespread operatic experience both as conductor and stage director in various theaters of Germany. When the war broke out, he came back to England and served in the army; when peace was declared he returned to his profession in Germany, varying his life there with engagements during the spring season at Covent Garden, London. His name is really Moore, but being desirous of

Photo by Moffett

ALEXANDER KIPNIS AS BARON OCHS IN "ROSENKAVALIER"

keeping it in its proper single-syllabled form on German tongues, he dropped the final letter.

European engagements made it impossible for him to be in Chicago for more than a few weeks, so he merely made order out of what might have been semichaos in "Der Rosenkavalier" and then went back. The next season, however, he was a permanent member of the organization, and has remained there ever since.

There is a vast difference between Europe and America in giving opera. One is sometimes inclined to think that most of the fine singers are in America and most of the fine performances in Europe. In the most famous European opera houses, La Scala in Milan, Baireuth, Munich, various others, they develop performances with a wealth of detail and a care in preparation undreamed of on this side of the Atlantic. It is not enough that a performance shall be safe. It must be polished to the final button. Toscanini, artistic overlord of La Scala, has been known to cancel a performance on the day it was to be given because he was dissatisfied with something that no American company would think twice about. It is curious to see the docility of the Milan audiences at such times. They come to the theater, learn that it is dark, go home again, and nobody thinks of protesting. They have learned that Toscanini has a good reason for doing such things, and that he will make it up to them before the season is over.

There is a different point of view both on the stage and in the audience. No European director would dream of putting on operas at the high pressure accepted as normal in this country. They know that they cannot do it to the satisfaction of their patrons, and the patrons would be very quick to register disapproval if they tried. Only those who have been in a European opera house know what a vicious, spine-chilling sound a hiss can be when it comes from between some two thousand sets of the teeth of a displeased audience.

In Chicago it is by no means uncommon to present thirty-five different operas in a period of ten or twelve weeks. In Europe they would not give that many in forty weeks. For one thing, costs of operatic operations have been mounting of late years like the mercury of a thermometer on a summer day. One of the items of the 1925 season was an agreement between the opera company and the musicians' union that the orchestra men were to have their minimum scale raised from $111 to $119 a player a week, plus $5 extra for rehearsal periods, plus something more when any of them were required to play back of the scenes, and more yet if they were required to appear on the stage. Multiply that minimum by seventy or eighty or whatever number may happen to be in the orchestra, and you will have one of the items that put opera into high finance. And the orchestral scale has gone up since then, too.

The next night came "Manon Lescaut," the Puccini, not the Massenet version, with Claudia Muzio and Antonio Cortis as the two lovers. It was the first time it had been revived in fourteen years, but at that it was a success only by courtesy. "Manon Lescaut" is a tricky piece, requiring specialized casting and a specialized manner of performance, and this performance lacked the touch of an expert stage director.

"Manon Lescaut" was followed by "Carmen," in which Marguerite D'Alvarez made another guest ap-

pearance in the name part to the Don José of Fernand
Ansseau. If "Manon Lescaut" is so difficult to present
that Lucrezia Bori comes near to being the ideal artist
for it, "Carmen" seldom misses fire, and Mme. D'Alvarez, in spite of her unusually large physical proportions
for the name part, was greatly applauded. Ansseau was
always applauded, and rightfully, for everything that
he did. Though lacking just the final touch of elegance,
he was one of the most honest singers that ever put on
grease paint and costumes.

A greatly photographed young person begins to
appear in the public prints about this time. The Polacco
family had on the June before received its most cherished
addition in the person of Miss Graziella, to become forthwith by far the most important member of the house-
hold. Born in Milan, christened in Chicago, she belongs
to two lands and is a much traveled young lady, with
the habit of visiting both her homes every year.

Then came an explosion of Verdi so long drawn out
that it became almost a continuous bombardment: "A
Masked Ball" with Rosa Raisa, Cyrena Van Gordon,
Charles Marshall, and Robert Steel (début) on Saturday afternoon; "Rigoletto" with Edith Mason, Charles
Hackett, and Cesare Formichi Saturday night; "Traviata" with Claudia Muzio, Antonio Cortis, and Richard
Bonelli (début) Sunday afternoon; an unexplained side
excursion to "Martha" with Miss Mason, Irene Pavloska, Tito Schipa, and Virgilio Lazzari Monday night,
but back to "Aïda" Tuesday night with Raisa, Van
Gordon, Marshall, Formichi, Lazzari, and Kipnis.

A news item somewhat out of the ordinary as far
as opera is concerned became visible at that point. One

night during the first week of the season "Samoots" Amatuma, one of the most eminent and pecunious of the tribe of bootleggers, all of whom had been made highly prosperous since the passage of the Volstead act, was shot in a barber shop just after having been given a shave, a manicure, and a shoeshine. When picked up, four tickets for that night's opera performance were found in his pocket.

The claque made another demonstration, and each member of the company was served with a notice from the business office stating that purchased applause could affect his status in only one way—prejudicially. "Ignore cajolery, but if direct threats are made to you, please inform the management." Whereupon the *Tribune* came forth with a jesting editorial commending the practice of the claque for war, for opera, for every public activity, concluding with this: "What would football, what would baseball be without their claques? What would they be? Why, cricket, of course. 'I say, well played, old thing! Right-o.'"

Of other items of the period, the first anniversary of the death of Puccini was celebrated by a performance of "Madame Butterfly" in which Rosa Raisa made one of her few appearances in the name part; the centenary of "The Barber of Seville" with Toti Dal Monte; William Beck was found dead in his hotel room while the curtain was held for him to take his place in the cast of "Hérodiade."

Presumably Mr. Beck died of a sudden stroke of some kind. There was a report that he had become ill after receiving a present of some wine, and the bottle was held for analysis, but the contents disappeared before the chemist could do his work, and that part of it was never known.

One of the most interesting characters in the whole force of the Civic Opera Company is a man whom hardly one of the patrons ever sees. His name is Thomas Connolly. By trade he is a plasterer, and a good one. If you are around the Auditorium by day, you may perhaps notice him as he passes by from one job to the next, a gray-haired, bespectacled, overalled workman, apparently intent on nothing but the preservation of the Auditorium walls. But after hours he is a collector of matters pertaining to the stage, and what he has acquired during a period of years is something to make other collectors lick their lips enviously.

He has one of the greatest collections of theatrical and operatic playbills in existence, and he knows or has known more than casually all of the great operatic and dramatic stars for a third of a century. Some of his bills date back to the 1700's. In several cases he has complete files giving the records of every performance at some of the famous European playhouses for many years. Hundreds of his bills refer to Covent Garden and Drury Lane in London before 1800. His collection relating to Chicago performances covers more than half a century.

He also has a collection of rare books and documents, several thousand volumes now out of print, papers containing the authentic signatures of popes, cardinals, emperors, kings, and queens. Henry VIII, both Charles I and II of England are on his list, not to mention most of the monarchs since, and statesmen, poets, playwrights, authors almost without number.

He is in constant correspondence with celebrities,

and his collection has been the occasion of clearing up more than one moot point in historical research. Julia Marlowe counts him as one of her friends, and Ellen Terry used to send him letters regularly up to the time of her death.

And yet most Chicagoans do not know he is there.

Three American operas were planned for this season; two were actually staged. They were "Namiko San" by Aldo Franchetti and "A Light from St. Agnes" by W. Franke Harling. Charles Wakefield Cadman's "The Witch of Salem" could not be got ready in time and was deferred until the next season.

"Namiko San" was founded upon a classical Japanese play whose translated title is "The Daimyo." The composer, a nephew of another Franchetti who had written several Italian operas, put it into being for the benefit of Tamaki Miura, the little Japanese soprano, who because of her race seemed doomed to a perpetual succession of performance of "Madame Butterfly." She had done Mascagni's "Iris" on the road and a few performances of "Madame Chrysantheme," in Chicago, but it was as Cho-Cho-San that she was best known.

Mr. Franchetti wrote a melodious, consistent score to a consistent libretto that had been toned down a bit from the excessive goriness of the original. In the Japanese version, there was a call for Namiko San's head to be severed by a wielder of the snickersnee so dextrous that it was to remain on her shoulders. At a touch a few minutes later it was to fall off and roll across the stage. This was considered a bit thick even for grand opera, which shrinks at few horrors, and the ending was modified.

It went across to a definite if not overwhelming success, and the next season Miura took it on the road and sang in it across the country with the composer conducting. Before then a journalistic tempest broke out as to whether Franchetti should be classified as an American or Italian composer. As nearly as can be remembered, it was settled by the Italian papers calling him Italian and the American papers, such as were interested, pointing to his American naturalization proceedings.

"A Light from St. Agnes" was the musical version of a one-act play written and acted by Mrs. Minnie Maddern Fiske. Mr. Harling explained that in the score he was making some slight use of jazz, not dragged in by the heels for the sake of an operatic holiday, but intended for musical characterization, and that a few saxophones would be necessary to play it. This created some extra pains in rehearsals, for most of the saxophonists able to play good jazz found trouble in reading the score, and those who could read the score were not jazz experts.

In time all was straightened out. Rosa Raisa, Georges Baklanoff, Forrest Lamont and a male chorus sang the piece and Mr. Harling conducted. One reads of the first performance that when he was called before the curtain Miss Raisa gave him a public and hearty kiss, and that this apparently seemed a good example to all the opera in English adherents who attended. By the time he was able to draw the lapels of his coat over his blushing cheeks and beat a retreat from the theater lobby to his hotel rooms, Mrs. Harling acting as bodyguard, he had been kissed some 200 times according to the most accurate estimate.

Disregarding osculatory demonstrations, it was an

interesting piece, quite the most American in atmosphere that the Chicago, company had ever produced, but it was never revived. Then the decks were cleared for the final novelty of the season, Italian, this time.

This was "Resurrection," founded on Tolstoi's novel of the same name, libretto by Cesar Hanau, translation into French by Paul Ferrier, music by Franco Alfano.

In a conversation in Milan the summer before, Alfano, then deep in the work of completing Puccini's sketches for the last part of "Turandot," told me that to some extent he regretted the choice of "Resurrection." He said that while he would always maintain a profound affection for it as an earlier work, he felt that he had learned something about the art of composition since, and that he would like to see some of his later music accepted for performance.

Miss Garden, however, cast a farseeing eye on the dramatic possibilities of the piece, and recognized elements quite as marked as the musical ones. She was entirely right. Her performance of Caterina became the most stirring and popular part that she had had in years. The opera, somewhat episodic in character, consisted of four scenes, or perhaps more accurately, tableaux, and each one had a marked dramatic drive, the four running through most of the human emotions. It promptly took an important part in her standard repertoire.

Without doubt the most important date of that season was December 9. For on that day, Mr. Insull, speaking at a luncheon before 500 business men of the Association of Commerce, bared for the first time a

RICHARD BONELLI AS RENATO IN "A MASKED BALL"

CESARE FORMICHI AS ATHANAEL IN "THAIS"

stupendous dream that had been occupying him for some time. It was no less than a new opera house.

The time was near, he explained, when the citizens of Chicago must show their appreciation of opera and their willingness to support it. A new guaranty of $500,000 a year must soon be raised, for the old one would expire in another year. While the opera company was doing everything possible to increase income and lower expenses, unsubsidized opera seemed impossible. A new opera house would be both a civic center and a sound financial undertaking. It would be a magnificent memorial for the future; it would be a producer of income for the opera company.

"Assuming that we will have the support of the citizens," he concluded, "I know that my associates will not be willing to hand this proposition over to others until we have solved the problem of a home for grand opera of such a monumental character that it would be a credit to this great city of which we are so proud."

This was the beginning of what was to loom large.

CHAPTER XXXII

Mr. Insull was always of the firm opinion that opera, its enjoyments and advantages, should by no means be confined to one particular class or group of classes. He greatly preferred to think of its effect on the community as a whole, realizing the while that in order to have a general effect, it must be given a general patronage. He therefore established an innovation, about as interesting in theory and results as any that had been undertaken up to that time.

Lecturers, salesmen, pep advocates had at one time and another been incited to go before groups of wage earners and address them earnestly on the advantage of buying tickets for the opera. In such cases intentions were excellent but results not so satisfactory. It was difficult to induce a workman during his noon hour that he ought to tie himself up to the obligation of paying out a considerable sum for the privilege of going into an opera house among strangers to witness an entertainment that he might or might not enjoy, and this was true whether the wage earner was of the overalled or white-collared variety. Mr. Insull accordingly changed the angle of approach. Instead of urging these prospective patrons to buy tickets to the opera, why not invite them to come to the opera?

This was a theory going hand in hand with one that had been put into practice with great success by the

Chicago Symphony Orchestra. As far back as 1914, the orchestra, with precisely the same desire, that of extending the influence of music, had established a series of popular concerts, and, with the aid of the Civic Music Association of Chicago, had made them available for residents of such quarters of Chicago as ordinarily would never think of coming to the loop district to hear music. Blocks of tickets were distributed to civic centers of all kinds, settlement houses, welfare agencies of large commercial institutions, what not, with instructions to return all unsold tickets to Orchestra Hall on the Monday before the Thursday "pop" for the benefit of the public at large.

In the beginning, concerts were few—only four the first year—and programs were constructed with the most extreme care not to frighten off any one apprehensive of supposedly "high-brow" music. Much emphasis was laid upon Handel's Largo and Mendelssohn's Spring Song, to name only two well known established favorites.

In an astonishingly short time there began to be a growth. Popular concerts increased in number and the character of the programs began to change. Tentatively at first, Mr. Stock began to introduce single movements from symphonies. Finding they were as well liked as the briefer, lighter numbers, he put in more of them, then occasional complete symphonies of the lighter order. After a time—and this means that the concerts continued throughout the trying period of the war—a referendum was taken for a request program, and some fifteen standard symphonies led all other compositions on the vote.

Of recent years there has had to be a change in the manner of conducting these concerts, but the changes all tend to show that popular concerts have become popular. The general public has had to be excluded. Sixteen concerts are given each season, and in each case the audiences come entirely through the agencies just mentioned. More than that, there are so many agencies by now that they can not all be accommodated. Each agency must go without tickets for one out of every three concerts. And if you examine the programs for the year you will frequently be puzzled to distinguish between the "pops" and the standard Tuesday, Friday, and Saturday programs. Finally, only a few seasons went by before all the available Saturday night subscription tickets in the upper part of the house were absorbed by graduates of the popular series.

This is an orchestral, not an operatic experience, but it is cited because the opera company had an almost parallel experience. Some Sunday nights were set aside for the experiment. For each night a commercial institution was addressed. One Sunday was reserved, let us say, for the elevated railway company, another for the telephone company, a third for the gas company, a fourth for a steam railway company, and so on. But here the public was excluded in advance. No left-overs were put on sale at all. Even the critics were politely but firmly invited to stay away. Only the employes of one individual firm were present.

No concessions of performance were permitted. A popular opera was selected, but it was not cheapened in performance. It was sung and played exactly as it had been done for the $6 audience that had been present a few nights before, with the same leading artists, full orchestra, and complete chorus. The only concessions were in matters of prices for tickets. These audiences came in at reduced rates, the difference in cost being met by an agreement between the opera company and the different firms affected.

At first, says Mr. Insull, there was some difficulty in filling the house. Prospective patrons were a bit shy, perhaps distrustful. The experiment continued, however, and with the result often noted in other classifications of performances, that one of the most potent advertisements in the whole advertising world is what the person who has gone says to his friends who have not. At any rate, during the 1928-29 season eight Sunday night performances were given to capacity audiences, often with a history of over-subscription and a disappointed waiting list.

These two cases illustrate more plainly than volumes of exhortation what is really meant by the educational influence of music. The chief difference between these audiences and others is that they are likely to be considerably more appreciative and warmer in their demonstrations of appreciation. It is an interesting psychological fact, and it is a heartwarming one to those who have the good fortune to be present at such times.

There is another interesting fact as well, reacting entirely to the benefit of such audiences as are being discussed here. The warmth of appreciation so frequently observed, instantly floats to the other side of the footlights and returns in the form of a better performance. Artists feel it at once and are lifted out of themselves. There is not a professional musician in the world immune to the influence. I often wonder what must be the difference in the minds of the artists between an operatic performance in Germany, where continuity is the rule and all demonstrations of approval are sternly hissed down until the end of the act, and one in Italy, where a brilliant incident may stop the performance for whole minutes on end.

Getting back to opera on a subscription basis, the 1926-27 season started conventionally but brilliantly with "Aïda" on Monday, November 8, sung by Muzio, Van Gordon, Formichi, Lazzari, Kipnis, and a new tenor named Aroldo Lindi. Back in his home in Sweden, his name had been Harold Lindau, but for some reason or other, some said because of European contractual obligations, he was maintaining the Italianized form of his name.

He had had a sort of male Cinderella career, having run away from home as a boy, with a life that included incidents as a breaker boy in a mine, a foremast hand on shipboard, a piano mover in Boston, the whole mixed with aspirations for the prize ring. In order to make the story completely satisfactory he should have established himself as the world's foremost tenor that night in Chicago. Perhaps that brilliant chapter is still in his future. As it was, he did a competent though not wholly brilliant season with the Civic Opera and then went away to other opera houses.

Raisa, Lamont, and Rimini followed with "The Jewels of the Madonna," a flashing work that had for some seasons been allowed to get dim through inaccurate staging but was here restored to its former glow as a performance and popularity as a box office attraction. The same papers that carried this enlivening news also bore a sadder item to the effect that Joseph Schwarz, a great if somewhat eccentric baritone, was dead in Berlin following a surgical operation. He was only forty-six years old, and under happier circumstances, would have had years of brilliant career before him. No one has ever surpassed the performances he gave in Chicago in "Tannhäuser" and "Otello."

Mason, Pavloska, Cortis and a newcoming baritone, Luigi Montesanto, appeared on Wednesday in "La Bohême," another restudied and consequently improved performance. Garden, Ansseau, and the many others of the long cast took up "Resurrection" to ever increasing applause. Elsa Alsen, who had visited Chicago some years before with the German Opera company, made her first appearance at the Auditorium as Isolde in the Wagner work, to the Tristan of Marshall, the Kurwenal of Bonelli, the Brangæne of Van Gordon, and the Mark of Kipnis, with Polacco conducting. For once here was an opera almost too carefully prepared. It moved cautiously. It had everything except supple freedom. The week ended with more débuts, Eide Norena as Gilda in "Rigoletto" on Saturday afternoon, Louise Loring as Leonora in "Il Trovatore" in the evening. But by that time the presence of a distinguished visitor was attracting the attention of headlines.

Police whistles all over the city were blowing to clear the way for the automobiles of Queen Marie of Roumania, her son and daughter and attendant suite, and Chicago was rapidly dividing into three parts, those invited to meet the queen, those not invited to meet her, and those who had no hopes of anything but a passing view of her.

She came to the opera on Tuesday night, November 16, sat in lonely state in a box, incidentally demonstrating that one of the chief functions of royalty is to be an exhibition in itself, and made one silent but effective comment on Raisa's Aïda. It consisted in staying considerably longer during the performance than the royal schedule for the evening had contemplated, thereby causing considerable damage to the nervous systems of the attendant suite.

On November 16 it was told that about $520,000 had been pledged for another five years' continuance of the company. By this time some 2,000 names of guarantors appeared on the list, their subscriptions varying over a wide range.

With Queen Marie on her way, attention could once again revert to the opera and its novelties. The first was "La Cena delle Beffe," on November 27, a collection of thrills from the pen of Sem Benelli, with Umberto Giordano making his most laudable effort to underline each shiver with music. It had been played as a drama in Europe and America, in this country under the name of "The Jest" with Lionel and John Barrymore in the leading parts, and its success undoubtedly incited Giordano to set it to music and various opera companies to present it. For a theory exists that the book bears a large part in the success of an opera. Perhaps it is because composers have turned their attention to writing other things than tunes.

"La Cena delle Beffe" was a pleasant little idyl of torture and betrayal, murder and madness, all dressed up in the colorful era of Lorenzo the Magnificent of Florence. Musically it is little or nothing to go wild over in spite of the fact that the tenor after a few performances of it is usually ready to take a rest cure. In this case the tenor was Cortis, who did the best performance of his Chicago career up to that time. The baritone was Montesanto, and the lady of careless habits who could not make her eyes behave was Muzio. Because of a colorful setting and a performance put on with extraordinary care, the thrills of the piece got across to the audience and it was played several times that season, but not since.

The next was the English novelty deferred from the season before, "A Witch of Salem," book by Nelle Richmond Eberhart, music by Charles Wakefield Cadman, first presented on December 8. Mrs. Eberhart had been Mr. Cadman's collaborator for something like twenty years in a large number of songs and the previous opera, "Shanewis." This time, however, they turned away from the romance and dance rhythms of the Indians to a drab tale of puritan Massachusetts in 1692.

This was an error in the beginning. Only Verdi was ever able to be operatically gay with ancient Massachusetts, in "A Masked Ball," and even he did it unintentionally, having started with royal Sweden. Opera presupposes color, though it may be unpleasant color, and colonial New England had no great tendency toward anything but grayness. With that handicap Mrs. Eberhart wrote a fairly interesting story which in the form it was cast and the way it was presented never got quite up to full dramatic tension, and Mr. Cadman wrote some music of rather excellent entertaining values. Curiously enough the tune which seemed to go the best was a mere scrap of a pirate chanty that he had collected at one time and used here briefly to bring on the male chorus. Norena, Hackett, Pavloska, Lorna Doone Jackson, Augusta Lenska, and several others were concerned

in the performance, and tongues were set wagging again
about the value of the English language in opera. In this
case intelligibility ranged from bright clearness from the
lips of Mr. Hackett down through various ranges of
murk to total eclipse from some of the others.

Another effort at popularizing English, the most
industrious of all, came to pass with "Tiefland." This
was another case of a play turned into opera, the play
known in this country as "Marta of the Lowlands" when
Bertha Kalich acted in it, set to music by Eugen d'Albert
and sung with considerable success in Germany.

Here, distrusting a made-to-order translation, the
composer, Conductor Weber, and Stage Director Moor
had worked all the summer before trying to evolve a
translation that would stand up on its own merits and
be singable. It came to performance two nights before
Christmas with a cast composed of Alsen, Pavloska,
Jackson, Lamont, Rimini, Kipnis, and a number of others,
and did not take long to write itself on the list of ought-
never-to-have-beens. There was one good song in it, the
story of a fight with a wolf, sung by Lamont. For the
rest, the piece consisted of two acts, a prologue melting
into the first and each running for hours and hours and
hours, with musical phrases repeated and repeated and
repeated. Even at this comparatively recent interval I
should dislike very much to be given an examination on
what the story was about. There was something about a
seduction, but all the characters bore such forbidding
exteriors that seduction seemed to rank not as a sporting
enterprise but an act of positive heroism.

New Year's eve was one of the pleasantest events
of the season. It was celebrated by a performance of

Mozart's "Don Giovanni," all dressed up in new scenery, with a cast that came close to approaching perfection. It was a grand occasion, and some $20,000 worth of us—publicity department's figures—assembled to see it.

At first view the scenery seemed more important than the cast. It had been executed by Julian Dové of Chicago, the scenic artist of the company, from sketches by Schenck von Trapp of Germany. As the opera is in two acts with several changes of scene for each, it was necessary to avoid waits, consequently an inner proscenium had been built affording the use of colored curtains and changes behind them. It was a picture in reds and oranges, greens and purples, blues and yellows, lines curving off into semi-dementia and buildings that looked like a pastry cook's dream of paradise. But it was fascinating. It almost deserved the name of the Mozart Follies. And then there was the cast!

Vanni-Marcoux came back after a long absence to re-début as the Don. The three women of his affections were Raisa, Mason, and Loring. Schipa had the tenor part and one of the loveliest songs of all, "Il mio tesoro." Lazzari was the Leporello. Trevisan, the sole link with the performance of ten years before, was the Masetto. Kipnis was the Commendatore. Polacco conducted. There, I submit, was a performance, high comedy, suave, unsentimentalized, flashing, stimulating.

One reads of a somewhat astonishing performance of "Tosca" during this period, astonishing, that is, in its linguistic manifestations. Mr. Ansseau, as Mario, sang in Italian until the entrance of Miss Garden. Then he switched to French. At her exit he switched back again. She sang in French until the time for "Vissi d'arte" in the second act, which was her single Italian demonstration. Mr. Vanni-Marcoux confined himself to Italian throughout. And when in the second act Miss Garden swept down upon him, demanding "Combien?" and he, supposedly echoing her word, said "Quanto?" genuine emotion prevailed. It was the first time that this scene had been supposed to contain comic values.

For, as the proponents of opera in the original tongues always tell you, there is a subtle something in the original language much too precious to be lost, and so evanescent that it always evaporates in translation. Also, it is too much to expect an artist to learn a rôle in one language and then turn his tongue to another in the same melody.

"Judith" was the last novelty of the season. It is a brief work by Arthur Honegger, based upon the story in the Apocrypha of how Judith goes to Holofernes' tent and returns with his head. Miss Garden had selected it for her own use the summer before and had given frequent assurance by letter and word of mouth that it was a work of great genius.

Honegger's music is better known in the United States now than it was then. For that reason the trill on major sevenths with which the piece begins is less startling now, as are his other amiable demonstrations of writing in two keys simultaneously and calling it polytonality. There was some genuinely affecting music for the chorus, such as the incident of the wailing Bethulians in the first act. For the rest, it was mostly dramatic declamation with a lightly scored accompaniment, and with its effectiveness depending a good deal on the person who delivered it. Miss Garden made it greatly effective, in fact, it was a fine dramatic part throughout for her. But the super-thrills she promised, the incidents that were going to make "Salome" look like a sewing circle, completely failed to come off.

Mr. Insull's annual speech at the gala performance for guarantors on January 28 confirmed the promise of the new opera house. It was to be on the block bounded by Madison, Market, and Washington streets and the Chicago river, it was to have a greater seating capacity than the Auditorium but fewer boxes—there was a gasp from the boxholders at this—it was to be surmounted by a huge office building, and it was to cost between $15,-000,000 and $16,000,000.

Like a skilled dramatist, Mr. Insull led up to this as a climax. He first told how attendance had picked up, and how the guarantors were to pay 80 per cent that year, an average of 75 per cent for the first five years under the new plan. Then he passed to the coming building, explaining that the company's lease on the venerated Auditorium would be up in six months, that it could be renewed for a brief period, but that in course of time the Auditorium building must be torn down and the company must move. Of the new site, he added:

"It has the only thoroughfare in the city wide enough for a plaza, or square, near the center of business and transportation and comparable with European plazas.

"It cannot be purely monumental. It must be commercial, not only self-supporting, but profitable." Hence the opera house must be surrounded by a skyscraper office building, "suitable," he said, "to serve its part in the enlargement of the business center of the city which we contemplate it is likely to bring about."

Not only this, but he had detailed plans of how it was all going to be paid for. About half of the cost would be met by a mortgage loan, arrangements for which had already been made with the Metropolitan Life Insurance Company of New York. The balance was to be raised by the sale of preferred stock, and these securities would begin to be paid off within a few years after the opening of the building.

"Ultimately, probably within the lifetime of many of you present," he concluded, "the enterprise will provide us with a home for opera not only free of all charge, but with funds enough to pay any deficit on our season's operations as well as for other forms of musical entertainment and musical education for the public.

"If the plan goes through, we shall have created a great civic foundation with income enough to educate artists, musicians, choristers, dancers, and technicians, and to add prestige to this community as an artistic and financial center."

That night the audience went home with something to think about.

THE GRAND FOYER OF CHICAGO'S NEW CIVIC OPERA HOUSE

CHAPTER XXXIII

One hour every week during the season you are able, if you wish, to stay home and tune in on the performances of the Chicago opera. It has been an interesting and complex development. The first year that the Civic Opera was in existence it was tried out, with none too encouraging results. Radio was in its infancy then, a none too lusty infancy. Broadcasts were not very accurate, static filled the air, and those who owned machines were for a considerable period more interested in seeing how many stations could be located than in listening to any one attraction.

Because of this last fact, radio had become a considerable source of alarm to music makers of all sorts and descriptions. There were anticipations that the device would kill all profitable audiences, to say nothing of destroying public taste for good music, and consternation prevailed. It was freely told around the lobbies of the Auditorium that the company would have to stop broadcasting or else have no audiences at all. So it stopped for a time.

But no device in the world was ever improved more swiftly than radio. Before long machines began to appear on the market that gave some semblance of the tone qualities that they were trying to reproduce, and some degree of intelligibility to the words they were trying to transmit. It was also discovered that there were some cases, not all, but some, where broadcasting worked to the improvement of the operatic and concert business. The point of psychology seemed to be that hearing a voice or an instrument through the medium of a soulless machine provoked a curiosity to see and hear the artist at close range. Incidentally, there had been the same sort of panic and the same result years before when that other mechanical plaything, the talking machine and its records, began to come on the market. But as the world soon knew, records definitely aided concerts and artists alike.

Finally the National Broadcasting Company moved on the Civic Opera with a proposition that seemed feasible to accept. It was an elaborate job and it gave the broadcasting engineers a good bit of a problem. The task was to install no less than eighteen microphones on and about the stage in such a way that they would pick up the complete atmosphere of the theater. Four Chicago stations and the combined Red and Blue networks of the National Broadcasting Company took part in the transmitting.

You are seldom able to see more than one or two of the microphones from your seat in the audience. One, the visible one, is suspended from the ceiling over the heads of the patrons. Others are on the stage, down in the footlights, behind pieces of scenery, at the back of the stage and down in the orchestra pit. Those immediately behind the scenes had to have a special guard over each one, for it was found that in spite of all care and repeated warnings, artists, choristers or stage hands would gather about for a private chat of their own, and sometimes their conversation went on the air to the detriment of the music.

All microphones lead to a "mixing panel" at the

back of the stage where an operator whose function is something like that of an organist cuts out certain wires, cuts in others, combines them with reference to the action on the stage so that the most efficient blend of tone is produced. From the mixing panel the pick-up goes to the Chicago broadcasters and from there by wire to New York. It is then sent out over the regular network of stations, and thus you turn it on in your own library or drawing room and get what is happening on the Auditorium stage.

The amount of territory covered by the broadcast is so large as to be almost unbelievable. It runs east to the Atlantic, north well into Canada, west as far as the Rocky Mountains, south to Houston and El Paso, Texas, and there are reports every week to prove the statement. Estimates of how many persons listen in each week must of necessity be only estimates, but an audience of 2,000,000 is probably a small one.

So the 1927 season came into being to be both seen and unseen. The opening night, Thursday, November 3, was a tough one on the critics. For as it happened, another important attraction, the Boston Symphony Orchestra, was booked for a concert at Orchestra Hall on the same night. Wherefore, who could tell how much time to give to Muzio and Schipa and Conductor Polacco in "La Traviata" at the Auditorium, and when would be the right time to dash over to Orchestra Hall to hear the Boston Orchestra which had not visited Chicago for sixteen years, and Conductor Serge Koussevitzky, who was in Chicago for the first time in his life? One finds quite a desire on the part of the critics to be twins at least for that evening, but they filled both assignments ably.

One of the periodic attempts to make "Tannhäuser" popular followed, with about as much success as had been customary. It was an important event, however, because it introduced a superb young German baritone, Heinrich Schlusnus, in the part of Wolfram. Schlusnus did not become as well known as he should have, or as he undoubtedly will in seasons to come, because he was so unusual in voice, looks, manner, all the things that go to make up an impressive artist, that he was in great demand all over the civilized world, and it was only with the greatest difficulty that he could ever be engaged for more than one or two appointments in any one city. All of which is lucky for him, but less so for those who would like to know him better.

"Sniegurotchka," translated into English and called "Snow Maiden," came up on Saturday afternoon of the first week with a cast consisting of Mason, Jackson, Van Gordon, Lenska, Hackett, Rimini, Chase Baromeo (début), a host of others, and with a new ballet headed by Vechslav Swoboda and Maria Yurieva, and with Henry Weber conducting. It was a list of notables, but again it happened that the sparkle of the first season was lacking. The piece did not interest and did not draw, and in due time it became touched with frost and its bloom faded away.

Next came "Loreley," a queer compound of Rhine legend and score in an Italianized Wagnerian manner, the whole making something that might have been good for the movies some years before. Polacco had attempted it during the lifetime of Campanini, at which time it died with great promptness. Its life was not much longer on this occasion in spite of the fact that Muzio had studied it for presentation in South America and made considerable of a hit with it. She repeated her personal hit here, but the opera simply would not do. Perhaps it might have gone even then if the composer, Alfredo Catalini, had had the idea of putting in a smashing aria or two, but it was something that he neglected to do.

The season went on with pleasant items, revivals of "La Gioconda," "Martha," "Falstaff," "The Jewels of the Madonna," "Madame Butterfly," "Faust," others of the kind. Now that the new opera house was an assured fact in the none too distant future, it seemed wiser not to look for too many novelties nor to make too much scenery in elaborate revivals, since the new stage with its own different dimensions would enforce scenery built to its own size if new, and cutting down, patching, or even destruction, if old. But Miss Garden was in the offing, also the prospects of "Sapho."

She arrived, announcing that she was in love with Lindbergh, having sung "The Star-Spangled Banner" at his reception in Paris—and having been obliged to go in advance to a library to look up the words. She was also in love with Chicago policemen and had a few kind words for that "dear fellow," Gene Tunney. Having made the headlines, she was now ready for the opera season.

Her first appearance was in "Monna Vanna," with its good libretto and bad score. The two Maeterlinck plays with which she has had so much to do in their operatic form make a curious contrast. "Monna Vanna" projects itself so perfectly that music, even good music can be of no help. With "Pelléas et Mélisande" the case is quite different. In the several times that it was tried as a play, it was found that no amount of skill on the part of the actors was ever able to evoke the expected "spiritual overtones." This was a case where music had to be called upon for assistance, and music did what was expected. Of course there is some difference between the musical talents of Debussy and Fevrier.

Miss Garden added "Carmen," "Louise" and "Le Jongleur de Nôtre Dame" to her list of performances, meanwhile working on the preparation of "Sapho." It finally came into being on January 11, and a good many people wondered why. It was a most elaborate production, with a scene of a studio party in the first act that would have been labeled an orgy in the movies. Miss Garden was a flame of vitality, and the music promptly began to contest the place of "Monna Vanna" in the list of unimportant operatic scores. Dramatically most of its value had died out years before. Musically it was a poverty-stricken step-sister of "Werther," with a few fleeting resemblances to some of the non-essentials of "Thaïs" and an occasional disturbing caricature of "Le Jongleur." And that was about all that was left of Massenet when he composed "Sapho," wild and wicked as it had seemed when it was new.

A few nights before, New Year's eve, to be exact, the company for the first time in its history had gone in for actual operetta. This was Johann Strauss' perennial favorite, "The Bat," translated into English, songs, spoken dialogue and all, and cast for many notables of the company, among them Rosa Raisa, Irene Pavloska, Charles Hackett, Forrest Lamont, Jose Mojica, Chase Baromeo, and Virgilio Lazzari. Henry Weber conducted.

It was wonderfully tuneful, it was genuinely amusing, and it also showed the limitations of opera companies and opera houses when dealing with operettas. In the first performance there was more than had ever been in "The Bat," for the ballet danced to the music of the "Blue Danube," and Toti Dal Monte interpolated Benedict's variations on "The Carnival of Venice," the only non-Straussian music in the performance.

But if the audience went into a gale of laughter over Miss Raisa's "unfortunate passion for tenors" and Mr. Lazzari's abysmal absurdities as the drunken jailer, and if it applauded the fine Viennese tunes as tunes had seldom been applauded in the Auditorium, the performance as a whole was too slow. In so large a theater it was completely impossible to take up the true, sparkling operetta tempo, and this showed more plainly in the dialogue than in the music. Also the orchestra, expert in every detail of an immense repertoire of grand opera, was completely innocent of the rhythmic accent of Viennese dance music.

At about the same time it was told that transfer of the proposed site for the new opera house on Wacker drive had been completed, that wrecking the old buildings would start at once, and the new building would be started early in the spring. In concluding his speech to operatic guarantors at the gala performance January 27, Mr. Insull said:

"This work we are engaged in will, I feel, establish a monument to the efforts of the Chicago Civic Opera Company, and present to this community a heritage that means the upbuilding of musical education in this great city and the Mississippi valley of which it is the metropolis."

Details, descriptive and financial, and architect's drawings flooded the press. The company went on its annual tour, soon to confront what began to look like the worst luck in its history. When the company reached Detroit, Claudia Muzio's mother was stricken with a desperate illness, so serious that Miss Muzio was obliged to abandon the tour. In fact she was obliged to stay away all the next season, the final year of the company in the Auditorium.

Later in the year, after the tour was over, Toti Dal Monte took an engagement in Australia, and in course of time cabled back that she had decided to get married, and therefore would not be back at the Auditorium.

And to fill up the tale, Rosa Raisa, having finished the tour, was stricken by a desperate illness of her own while on board the steamship carrying her to Italy. For a time it was said that she would be unable to return, but she recovered in time to get back to Chicago after the season started. Incidentally she never sang better in her life than on this, the last year in the Auditorium.

The deficit for the semi-final year was $450,000.

CHAPTER XXXIV

The final season at the Auditorium created a curious feeling of unrest, compounded out of many elements. There was regret at leaving the venerated home of opera where so many famous incidents had taken place, where the rare phenomenon of perfect acoustics existed, just as Louis H. Sullivan had predicted many years before that they would exist, where through many seasons a lot of us had come to feel that we were at home. There was also the sense of impermanence, of getting ready to move out of an old home though into a new and more adequate one.

A considerable step in building for the future as well as the present of personnel appeared in the new engagements. No less than fourteen singers were added to the company, and exactly one-half were Americans. It might have been considered a move to quiet those who still continue to maintain the foreign domination of American artists, were it not that of late years the Civic Opera Company has seldom wasted time in such matters. Artists continue to be engaged on merit regardless of nationality, and foreign languages are kept in the repertoire because the public has so emphatically proved that foreign languages are preferred. It may be illogical, but the public expresses its feeling by the way it buys tickets.

The seven new Americans were Hilda Burke, Marion Claire, Antonietta Consoli, Alice Mock, and

Patricia O'Connell, all sopranos, Coe Glade, mezzo-soprano, and Barre Hill, baritone. From other parts of the world came Frida Leider, German soprano, Maria Olszewska, Austrian mezzo-soprano, Margherita Salvi, Spanish soprano, Eva Turner, English soprano, Ada Paggi, Italian mezzo-soprano, Giuseppe Cavadore, Italian tenor, and Ulysses Lappas, Greek tenor, the last named having been engaged for a few performances in the year of Miss Garden's consulship. The list gives a fair idea of how cosmopolitan an opera company of the major class may be.

It should be added that an assistant conductor, Mario Giuranna, arrived in the autumn. His labors, like those of all assistant conductors, were inaudible to the operatic audiences, being confined to rehearsals, but his wife turned out to be a composer of considerable merit. Among other works, three of her orchestral compositions were accepted by Frederick Stock and played several times during the season by the Chicago Symphony Orchestra to unusual success.

Another artist of whom considerable had been hoped, and who, in spite of his name, was American, Michele de Caro, baritone, died in Seattle, his home, during the summer of 1928, shortly before he had planned to come to Chicago and join the company.

The season started on Wednesday, October 31, amid the customary boom of photographers' flashlight powder outside the theater and the glitter of jewels inside, presenting Olszewska in the name part of "Carmen." If it had been intended as a ruse to attract attention, it could not have been more successful, for during the greater part of the season there were heated arguments as to whether she was a great Carmen or not.

The consensus of opinion settled down into an agreement that her Carmen was spanische and not quite espagnole. But opinion became unanimous on the Sunday afternoon following, when she appeared as Ortrud in "Lohengrin." Here she was generally and rightly acclaimed as a sensation, an Ortrud such as had not been seen on the Auditorium stage since the days when Schumann-Heink used to do it years before. Marion Claire appeared as Elsa, and with Réné Maison as Lohengrin, Robert Ringling as Telramund, Kipnis as King Henry, and Howard Preston as the herald, the performance became a good deal of a standard for other German operas, the sort of performance which if persisted in would have a tendency to make German opera popular. It was curious to note that in the dramatic incident in "Carmen" in which Mme. Olszewska had been most notable, the card scene, which she made to stand out brilliantly, she made use of the same manner which in "Lohengrin" was spread all through the performance.

Miss Claire's début, however, was not in "Lohengrin," but in "La Bohême" on the second night of the season. It was a very good performance, but the part of Mimi is almost, as they say on the dramatic stage, actor-proof, and there had been dozens, not to say hundreds of good Mimis before her. As Elsa she became considerably more distinctive.

Débuts continued. Miss Turner of England came on as Aïda in the like named work on Saturday afternoon, to be followed by Miss Mock of California as Gilda in "Rigoletto" in the evening, both scoring decisive hits, particularly Miss Turner, who disclosed a voice of unusual power and beauty. Two incidents took the "Aïda" performance out of the ordinary. One was that the unseen and in this case unnamed priestess who sang the temple music behind the scenes turned out to be Hilda Burke, who was to make her own technical début in the name part of the same opera a week later. The other, a less happy one, was that Ulysses Lappas, in his first start after his return, began the part of Radames in an able fashion, but lost his voice in the course of the performance, and ended, one might say, speechless, and unheard.

When Miss Burke made her actual Aïda appearance, she was joined by Coe Glade in the part of Amneris, and the two young artists made as agreeable and at times brilliant impressions as had ever been recorded in the company. Miss Glade was to demonstrate a Carmen of her own later in the season, and to prove that she had realized many of the possibilities of a very fine Carmen indeed. It was to have rather astonishing repercussions. One single performance it was, yet in the course of a few months she was to receive inquiries about it from as far away as Brazil.

Radio was continuing to show effects. Miss Burke the season before had divided the first prize in a nationwide radio contest for young artists with Kathryn Witwer of Gary, Indiana, and Miss Witwer had been a member of the Civic Opera forces the year before, but at the end had decided to go to Europe. Miss Burke's radio introduction would seem to have been the means of introducing her into an audition for opera, where she made a place for herself.

"The Tales of Hoffman" was announced for No-

Photo by Daguerre

MARIE OLSZEWSKA AS FRICKA IN "DIE WALKUERE"

Photo by Daguerre

FRIDA LEIDER AS BRUENNHILDE IN "DIE WALKUERE"

vember 24 with Vanni-Marcoux singing four distinct rôles—count 'em—four. But Miss Claire, who was due to sing two more, Giulietta and Antonia, woke up with a bad throat that morning, "Hoffman" was postponed, and Vanni-Marcoux introduced himself in "Boris Godunoff."

But other operatic joys impended. One of them was Frida Leider, a soprano of fame in Germany, whose American début made "Die Walküre" possible. With Lamont as Siegmund, Turner as Sieglinde, Kipnis as Wotan, Olszewska as Fricka, Leider herself as Brünnhilde, and Polacco conducting, it was a noble performance, marred only by such stage incidents as stuttering clouds and hissing steam in the last act. But with a new opera house in prospect, the deficiencies of the old were passed over lightly.

Another joy was Margherita Salvi, who promptly stepped into the affections of the public. Her voice was brilliant and flexible with that slightly acidulated tang which seems to be the heritage of Spanish sopranos, she was pretty, graceful, humorous and stage wise to a degree that few operatic artists ever attain. With another stage-wise cast, Schipa, Bonelli, Trevisan, Lazzari, and others, "The Barber of Seville" was another gorgeous rollic of song and mirth.

"Don Giovanni" went on again, with Leider, Burke, and Baromeo as newcomers as welcome as Vanni-Marcoux, Mason, Schipa, Trevisan, and the rest of the delectable cast that had done it before. Garden returned and Raisa got in about the same time. Christmas week was a time for operatic jubilee, for on the night before the holiday Miss Glade sang her Carmen—what a voice

that Carmen had and what a blithe young hussy she was!
—two nights after it "Der Rosenkavalier" again proved
that it was one of the company's finest exploits—Leider,
Mason, Olszewska, Kipnis and Polacco furnished the
proof—and on New Year's eve Raisa discovered again
that she had a host of friends when she reappeared in
the revival of "Norma."

"Norma" makes terrific demands on the part of the
artist who sings the name part. That is the reason it is
so seldom given. It has all that was ever known about
writing for the coloratura soprano magnified into terms
of the dramatic soprano, it has melodies of the purest
bel canto, broad declamation, a range extending from
middle C to high D, and all spread over four acts of
opera. It also calls for a singer of dignified, command-
ing figure.

Wherefore Miss Raisa stepped into an ovation.
With such associate artists as Miss Glade, Mr. Marshall,
and Mr. Lazzari, and with Mr. Polacco intent upon
pressing the last drop of ecstasy out of Bellini's score, the
audience saw its duty and did it. Palm beat upon enthusiastic palm, voices rose in high excitement, and roses were
carried out from behind the scenes until the star was lost
in them. And Miss Raisa responded by singing her part
in a voice all velvet and fire.

It was without a doubt the high spot of the season.
A novelty was to come, or rather an elaborately staged
revival of "The Marriage of Figaro," Miss Garden was
to appear in "Sapho," "The Love of Three Kings,"
"Pelléas et Mélisande" and "Judith," Miss Claire and
Conductor Weber were to be married; this event took
place on January 21. In fact there were many thrills of

varying degrees of intensity for opera goers still due before the season closed. But those who were present on New Year's eve will not forget the "Norma" performance.

One event was neither announced nor anticipated. It had to do with a performance of "The Barber of Seville" in which Desiré Defrere was the Dr. Bartolo and Rimini the Figaro. Defrere is one of the veterans of the company, able to take any one of dozens of baritone parts at short notice, a competent stage manager and an inveterate practical joker. It was he who on one occasion poured water into Colline's top hat in a performance of "La Bohême," and thereby caused Edouard Cotreuil, who was playing the part, to drench himself when he donned it.

After several such exploits, revenge was plotted and executed. Those who go to opera will remember the incident near the end of the second act of "The Barber" where Dr. Bartolo is stricken speechless and immovable by the thump of the soldiers' guns on the floor. He is awakened later, usually by tickling him on the nose with a feather, which provokes a vigorous stage sneeze. This night Rimini, instead of using the feather, gave Defrere a pinch of pepper in the nostrils, and the unprecedented fit of real sneezes and coughs that followed is said to have made the footlights flicker in sympathy.

"The Marriage of Figaro," produced on January 3, was another effort, like that of "Don Giovanni," to stage a classical opera in modernistic garb. It was fantastic to a degree, with a built-in proscenium, color clashing upon color, lines that led everywhere and nowhere, in fact stylized rococo carried to the point of madness.

There is a suspicion that they did protest too much.

The courtly, aristocratic comedy of Mozart began to turn into a good bit of a farce; the clashes of color in scenery and costumes simply did not fit Mozart's elegant simplicity of music. Subtlety was entirely lost. This manner of performance may be accepted in the future and may not. But in its first season it scored only a half-success. Turner, Mason, Claire, Claessens, Bonelli, Lazzari, Trevisan, Mojica and several others were in the cast, and Weber conducted.

At length the time came to give the last performance in the old theater. It was "Romeo and Juliet," the same work with which the Auditorium had been opened nearly forty years before. You will find the final cast, in fact both casts, on the first page of this volume. It was a combination of business and sentiment in performance. The last cast must catch the train and join the rest of the company in Boston. Yet there was a sigh as well as a smile over leaving the scene of many historic events. Miss Mason and Mr. Hackett sang their loveliest, and in one of the entr'actes Mr. Polacco signaled the orchestra, which played "Home, Sweet Home," and "Auld Lang Syne," the nearest approach to the recall of Patti. The house rose to its feet, and some of the spectators, including Miss Garden, sang as many words as they could remember.

Then outside, to see trucks hastily hauling scenery to the railroad station.

A View of the Interior of the New Civic Opera House Taken
from the First Row of Seats on the Main Floor and Showing the Seating Arrangement of the Main Floor, Box
Floor, and Two Balconies

Photos by Chicago Architectural Photographing Co.

The Steel Curtain, Proscenium Arch and Orchestra Pit of the
New Civic Opera House

CHAPTER XXXV

What's to come? The future is on the lap of the gods, but every prospect is of the most favorable sort.

The new opera house is a dream of Mr. Insull's, a dream realized in terms of steel and stonework. In entering it the opera company sloughs off a chrysalis and steps into new and gorgeous trappings. It has taken time, immense amounts of money, prolonged and intense concentration, but Mr. Insull is the kind of a dreamer whose dreams come true, a poet who does not write verse but accomplishes enormous and beautiful things for the betterment of his community and nation.

Work on Twenty Wacker Drive, the official name of the new structure, began on a drawing board as far back as 1925, when it was realized that the Auditorium sooner or later must be abandoned.

At the time these words are being written, the new building is still in process of construction. On this account some of the statements made here must be based upon earlier, though authoritative statements sent out by the proponents of the plan.

The new theater will seat 3,472, or 112 less than the Auditorium. At the same time there will be fewer boxes, thirty-one instead of fifty-six. The main floor will seat 1,682 as against the 959 of the Auditorium.

The main body of the structure, which combines the "monumental" character associated with the great opera houses of the world with the practical necessities of the Chicago situation, is of twenty-one stories, rising 270 feet from the street level. It has a frontage of 400 feet on Wacker Drive, 180 feet on Madison street, 150 feet on Washington street. In addition there is a tower of twenty-one floors more, forty-two in all, its top looking down 550 feet to the street.

The building is U-shaped, with front and sides occupied by shops and stores. The side portions, or wings, embrace the opera house. A small theater, seating 878 and intended for concert, theatrical production, ballet, and intimate performances generally, is also included.

Both the opera house and the theater embody the results of intensive study and research on a scale probably never before applied to similar undertakings. It is the hope of all concerned that in completeness, in perfection of detail, in adjustment to the purposes to be served, both will prove to be far ahead of any other now in existence.

As it was Mr. Insull's idea that in course of time the building will take the burden of paying for opera from the shoulders of the guarantors, provision is made for 739,600 square feet of rentable space, something like fifteen acres, in addition to that required by the two theaters. 577,600 square feet are in the main building, 162,000 more in the tower, with light and air on all sides and served by twenty-six high-speed elevators.

It is not to be expected that completion and occupancy of the building will at once dispense with the necessity of a guaranty fund for maintaining the opera company. But the financing of opera should be made somewhat easier when the building is finished and fully tenanted. Eventually Mr. Insull believes that the revenue from the building will serve in effect as an endowment, providing a home for the opera and paying its inevitable deficits.

Study of details which should be and could be incorporated into the building was begun soon after the end of the 1926-27 season. A committee went abroad to study the latest developments in opera house and theater design and equipment there as well as in the United States. Its members were Ernest Graham and Alfred Shaw of the firm of Graham, Anderson, Probst and White, architects of the new building; Herbert M. Johnson, business manager of the opera company; Harry W. Beatty, technical director; Charles Moor, stage director; and Edward H. Moore, chief electrician.

An impressive colonnade runs along practically the entire Wacker Drive frontage of the building. Here thirty-five to forty automobiles can be discharged at a time. Whatever the means of approach, by motor, by street car, or on foot, patrons will arrive first under this great colonnade which will be a protection from inclement weather, and from it enter the various lobbies and foyers connected with all floors of the opera house. The opera entrance is at the south end of the colonnade, the entrance to the smaller theater at the north.

From the grand foyer at the level of the parquet a grand staircase leads to the mezzanine lounge at the rear of the boxes. Separate stairs rise from the main lounge to the balconies, and there are additional stairs for convenient and ample access from all parts of the auditorium. Special elevator service to the balconies is also at hand.

The thirty-one boxes are in a double tier at the rear,

side boxes having been abolished. Above the box floor there is a dress circle and balcony and above that an upper balcony, each with approximately 800 seats.

It is the belief of all concerned that this auditorium is the first in the world in which the combined problems of proper vision and perfect acoustics have been worked out as one and then carried out on a large scale. The two problems were worked out together and each made to fit the other. In the operation, the architects drew upon the experience and knowledge of the foremost dozen or fifteen men in all the world who have made a study of acoustics.

The opera auditorium, the smaller theater, and the foyers of both are supplied with cool washed air from a combined cooling and ventilating system, so that at all times of the year a comfortable temperature can always be maintained. Similar completeness and perfection of detail have been in mind in planning the back stage features. The best features and the latest developments found in all the theaters and opera houses examined during the committee's investigating tour have been combined in the plans for Chicago.

The height of the stage and its mechanical equipment permit the establishment of a fixed cyclorama. Drops can be changed and scenes shifted more quickly than it has ever been done anywhere else. The stage lighting equipment marks a similar advance.

In fact the whole idea has been to preserve the fine features of the old Auditorium, while adding to them every idea that will add to the quality of the new achievement both before and behind the footlights.

One feature of special interest is the synchronization of light control with the work of the prompter during a performance. The prompter's box, that hooded structure that rises a bit from the stage floor down near the footlights, has been made large enough to house not only the prompter but the man in control of the lights. During a performance the two work side by side and together, the light control man making instant change on exact cues by means of a system of switches.

The opera house is able to provide storage space for scenery, properties, and all the equipment necessary for an entire season of opera. This provision, in conjunction with the shops and warehouses of the company, gives to the organization facilities far beyond those of any similar organization in the world.

Ample rehearsal facilities have also been provided, and on a similarly farsighted scale, for individuals, groups, chorus, orchestra, ballet, and complete ensembles. It is possible, for instance, to put on a complete rehearsal for a new performance, a complete production with every individual in his place just as it will be presented on the stage, without actually using the stage which may be occupied at the time by other activities.

The officers and directors of the Twenty Wacker Drive Corporation, which has built and now directs, operates, and owns the enterprise, are thus named:

President, Samuel Insull; vice-president, Stanley Field; treasurer, Herbert M. Johnson; secretary, John W. Evers; directors, Samuel Insull, Stanley Field, Samuel Insull, Jr., John F. Gilchrist, George F. Mitchell, and Herman Waldeck.

It is one thing to conceive such an undertaking, another to pay for it. The financing of the huge undertaking is another bit of farseeing imagination, fit, as Ko-Ko says in "The Mikado," to rank with most romances.

Twenty million dollars was required, and $20,000,000 was obtained at a cost told by Mr. Insull, after figuring interest, commissions, and all charges, of 5.84 per cent. When it is added that various large building operations in Chicago have cost over 7 per cent, one can see how carefully everything has been estimated.

Half of the sum, $10,000,000, was borrowed from the Metropolitan Life Insurance Company at 5 per cent, the company taking a mortgage on the property and holding the bond issue. For the rest 100,000 shares of 6 per cent preferred stock was issued by the corporation and underwritten by eight banking and investment houses. These were subsequently passed on to the public and absorbed by it.

"These financial arrangements," explained Mr. Insull, "contemplate the employment of 'customer-ownership' principles and practice—the first time, so far as I know, that customer-ownership has been applied to a commercial and office-building enterprise."

Finally, the common stock of the building, in which final control and ownership of the enterprise is vested, is deposited in a perpetual trust, and the administering trustees are the officers and directors of the corporation to whom reference has just been made.

The next task will be to pay off the building's indebtedness, and that, too, has been estimated with a care that makes its reading a delight. The Civic Opera Company will pay a rental of $180,000 a year, the smaller theater $70,000 more. The rental of office space, shops, lobby concessions, and the like, will bring the estimated revenue to a total of $2,476,700 a year. Operating expenses and taxes are estimated at $1,013,700 a year, leaving a net income of $1,463,000 to meet fixed charges.

Of this $500,000 goes as interest on the $10,000,000 loan, and $600,000 more as dividends on the preferred stock. There is still some money left to begin the retirement of the mortgage, and under the terms of the loan, $300,000 a year must be applied to that purpose beginning two years after the completion of the building. The preferred stock will also be called and retired by degrees. The announcement states that it is callable in part or in whole on thirty days' notice on or before January 15, 1933, at $107.50 a share, from then until January 15, 1940, at $105 a share, and thereafter at $102 a share.

Practically nothing has been left to chance. While, as Mr. Insull explains, there must be a guarantors' list for a number of years to come, the call upon them will grow gradually less. Sooner or later this great debt will pay itself off, sooner or later a large income from an immense building will become available to the trust fund common stock, and from there to the opera company.

Opera from the beginning has cost more than it earned. In the beginning its costs were met by kings, emperors, grand dukes, rulers of cities, and cities and countries themselves. Later they were met by citizens of more than common wealth; the experience of Mr. and Mrs. McCormick during the last years of the Chicago Opera Association was an example of this procedure. The Civic Opera Company began its operations with a list of guarantors to meet its expenses, it will end with a building whose income will take care of everything.

It is a prospect to make one pause and wonder. What Mr. Insull and his associates have accomplished has been more than the construction of a mighty building and the security of one of the world's great opera companies. In reality they have written an enormous civic poem, conceived, developed, made manifest in terms of beauty and imagination, going to the mental, emotional, spiritual well-being of their own generation and generations to come. No greater work of art was ever imagined, and they were the artists.

And so, as the Civic Opera of Chicago goes into its new home, this account bids it a cordial and optimistic farewell.

POSTSCRIPT

"AÏDA"

Opera in four acts and seven scenes. Libretto by
Antonio Ghislanzoni. Music by Giuseppe Verdi.
Presented in dedication of the new Civic Opera
House, 20 Wacker Drive, by the Civic Opera
Company, Monday evening, November 4, 1929.

THE CAST

THE KING OF EGYPT............Chase Baromeo
AMNERIS, *his daughter*......Cyrena Van Gordon
RADAMES, *captain of the guard*..Charles Marshall
AÏDA, *an Ethiopian slave*............Rosa Raisa
RAMFIS, *high priest*............Virgilio Lazzari
AMONASRO, *King of Ethiopia*....Cesare Formichi
PRIESTESS......................Hilda Burke
A MESSENGER.............Giuseppe Cavadore

Incidental dances in Act II:

SCENE 1—By Misses Arrowsmith, Coffey, Dee,
Haller, Laundy, Napier, Park, Perrot, Salisky,
Shott.

SCENE 2—By Laurent Novikoff, Ruth Pryor,
Julia Barashkova, and Edward Caton, assisted
by the Misses Harriet Lundgren, Bradshaw,
Crofton, Smith and the Ballet.

CONDUCTOR...................Giorgio Polacco
STAGE DIRECTOR................Charles Moor

Since the last words of the preceding chapter were written, it has been permitted to reopen the forms and record the fact that Mr. Insull's dream of opera came true with a degree of magnificence hardly anticipated even by those who had been most hopeful over the enterprise.

As is seen above, the first performance in the new house was "Aïda." Just as the Chicago Grand Opera Company had opened nineteen years ago, just as the Civic Opera Company had given its first performance seven years ago, just as an infinite number of opera seasons during the past half-century had opened, the performance was "Aïda." This time, however, Aïda," with all its opulence of music and lavishness of display, was not the important feature of the evening. The opera took second place to the opera house.

In fact during all the first week, as the first seven audiences took their places considerably more attention was paid to the new home of opera, its structure, its scheme of decoration, in certain cases its acoustics, than to the actual proceedings on the stage. It was not until patrons came to make their second or third visit to the opera house that they began to come to a realizing sense of the actual opera season. In all conscience, there was plenty to observe besides the performances.

The building stands on historic ground. Only a few feet to the north, and hardly one hundred years before had stood the Sauganash Hotel, the first place of accommodation for man and beast in all Chicago. By 1860 the Sauganash had disappeared, and on its site was erected the old Wigwam, wherein the Republican party nominated Abraham Lincoln as its candidate for the

Chicago Civic Opera Photo

THE TRIUMPH SCENE FROM "AÏDA" AT THE OPENING PERFORMANCE OF THE NEW
CIVIC OPERA HOUSE

presidency of the United States. One reads in the earlier records of how the wolves used to howl around the spot, of how easy it used to be to go out in the swamp land thereabouts with a shotgun and come back laden with ducks, geese, snipe, woodcock, not to mention the multitude of game that existed in the higher and drier prairie land.

From a hunter's paradise to an operatic center in less than ten decades! It is a concrete symbol of the marvel that is Chicago, the greater marvel that is America. And so on the day before the opening, November 3, the Huntington (West·Virginia) *Herald Dispatch* was disagreeable enough to announce the event under the heading, "Chicago Abandons Bombs and Turns Opera-Minded."

When the first audience came, it found a rose-colored grotto at the base of a forty-five story, twenty million dollar structure, whose rentals are to sustain opera in perpetuity. It was splendid. It was dignified. It contained the most scientifically constructed stage in the world, not even forgetting Baireuth. Within the house were miracles of color and line. Back on the stage were other miracles of mechanism.

What actually happens on the stage is necessarily a secret to the audience, but a few days before the opening a chosen few of us were invited to inspect the house thoroughly, front and back, Mr. Insull taking special pride in acting as guide. Then and there we learned about some of the triumphs of machinery, the elevator, seventy-five feet long, that silently deposited back drops in storage racks thirty-five feet below the stage, the devices that raised the stage in whole or in part, the gridiron for the changing of scenery that ran 140 feet above the stage—up to the level of the fourteenth floor of the building. Everything was beautiful, everything was spacious, everything was ingenious beyond all telling.

Out in the front of the house one was greeted by a lofty foyer of travertine aglow with rose and gold. One stepped into the house, again rose and gold, old rose and gold leaf, with every angle and every line leading the spectator's eye to the stage opening, its steel firecurtain marching across the vision with a pageant of some forty heroes and heroines of opera. One sank into his seat and found comfort, safety, good acoustics, good vision, gracious surroundings.

Perhaps a line or two of statistics may not be amiss here. At 6.30 o'clock on November 4, lights flamed from the fifty-five great bronze lanterns and lamps that hung above the 365 feet of colonnade of the opera house. People came early that night, and long before the curtain was ready to go up nearly every one was there. When they were all seated there were 3,471 persons in the house, representing an intake of $16,500, and a company of 580 artists and mechanicians was engaged in presenting "Aïda." Of these 3,471, 1,682 were on the main floor in thirty-nine rows. Here twenty-six rows cost $6 a seat and the remaining thirteen $5 a seat. The rest of the audience were in the boxes, thirty-one boxes, the dress circle, and the balcony.

Climbing aloft to the upper part of the house— those who preferred could take elevators—it was found that the same care for the comfort of patrons had been taken as on the main floor. The seats were just as commodious, just as deeply upholstered, just the same color

—though not quite of the same rich materials—as those below. The pitch of the floors was humane. There was none of the feeling that if one were unfortunate enough to stumble he would fly through the air and land on the stage hundreds of feet below. And while there a test of the acoustics was made which tended to prove that acoustics was no longer an accident but a science.

A voice speaking in the tone of an ordinary telephone conversation carried from the stage to the top row of the gallery. During the later opera performances it was found that this was no isolated instance. The Civic Opera House is kind to the voices of its singers, and particularly kind to the orchestra.

Here there was something else to be considered, for the orchestra pit is considerably wider than most pits. If necessary, it can accommodate a band of 120 players, and they are all concealed from the sight of the audience. The floor of the pit can likewise be raised or lowered on demand and according to the exigencies of the occasion. Being floored and backed with hard wood, it was found that the orchestra sits in the midst of a marvelous sounding board, or resonator, and the orchestral tones come through to the audience with a richness that surpassed even that of the wonderful old Auditorium.

In fact it was an uncommonly interesting, one might almost say astonishing, experience. In feet and inches the dimensions of the house, its length particularly, are huge. Yet by its every line leading stageward, its incessant, serene blending of old rose and gold, it had an extraordinary effect of intimacy. For its lines one was willing to give three cheers for the firm of Graham, Anderson, Probst & White, architects. For its colorings, other cheers went to Jules Guerin. He, by the way, worked all summer on the decorations, pronounced himself satisfied with the effect, and left Chicago before the opening of the house, saying that being satisfied, he had not the slightest interest in what other people might say about it.

So on the first night there were two pageants, one on each side of the footlights. Only once in a great while is an audience privileged to be present at such an event. As a matter of fact the actual performance was one in which to take pride under any circumstances. It just happened that its glories were a bit obscured by the opening of the opera house.

For the sake of the record, what each successive audience of the first week after "Aïda" saw is here summarized.

Tuesday, November 5—"Iris," with book by Luigi Illica and music by Pietro Mascagni.

CIECO, *a blind man*............Virgilio Lazzari
IRIS, *his daughter*.................Edith Mason
OSAKA, *a rich young man*........Antonio Cortis
KYOTO, *keeper of a resort*........Giacomo Rimini
A geisha........................Hilda Burke
A peddler..................Lodovico Oliviero
Two rag pickers............{Giuseppe Cavadore
                             {Eugenio Sandrini

Incidental dances by Edward Caton, Misses Smith and Zarin.

CONDUCTOR...............Roberto Moranzoni

Wednesday, November 6—"La Traviata," by Verdi.

VIOLETTA VALERY.............Claudia Muzio
FLORA BERVOIX.............Alice d'Hermanoy

ALFREDO GERMONT............Charles Hackett
GIORGIO GERMONT, *his father*....Richard Bonelli
GASTON, *Viscount of Letorieres*..Lodovico Oliviero
BARON DOUPHAL...............Desiré Defrere
MARQUIS D'OBIGNY..........Eugenio Sandrini
DOCTOR GRENVIL.............Antonio Nicolich
ANNINA, *servant to Violetta*.......Anna Correnti
Servant to Flora...............Gildo Morelato

Incidental dances by Edward Caton, Julia Barashkova and Ballet.

CONDUCTOR...............Roberto Moranzoni

Thursday, November 7—"Romeo and Juliet," by Gounod.

CAPULET, *a Veronese noble*......Cesare Formichi
JULIET, *his daughter*...........Mary McCormic
TYBALT, *his nephew*............Theodore Ritch
ROMEO, *a Montague*..............Rene Maison
MERCUTIO, *friend of Romeo*......Desiré Defrere
STEPHANO, *page of Romeo*........Irene Pavloska
DUKE OF VERONA...........Antonio Nicolich
FRIAR LAWRENCE...........Edouard Cotreuil
GERTRUDE, *Juliet's nurse*........Maria Claessens
GREGORIO, *servant to Capulet*....Eugenio Sandrini

CONDUCTOR.............Emil Cooper (début)

Saturday afternoon, November 9—"Tristan und Isolde," by Wagner.

TRISTAN..............Theodore Strack (début)
KING MARK.................Alexander Kipnis
ISOLDE........................Frida Leider
KURVENAL...................Richard Bonelli
MELOT ....Desiré Defrere
BRANGAENE.................Maria Olszewska
A shepherd................Giuseppe Cavadore

The helmsman................Antonio Nicolich
A sailor's voice..............Giuseppe Cavadore

CONDUCTOR......................Egon Pollak

Saturday night, November 9—"Il Trovatore," by Verdi.

LEONORA.....................Claudia Muzio
INEZ, her attendant..........Alice d'Hermanoy
COUNT OF LUNA..............Giacomo Rimini
MANRICO.....................Antonio Cortis
AZUCENA................Cyrena Van Gordon
FERRANDO....................Virgilio Lazzari
RUIZ.......................Lodovico Oliviero
An old gipsy.................Eugenio Sandrini

CONDUCTOR...............Roberto Moranzoni

Sunday afternoon, November 10—"Norma," by Bellini.

POLLIONE, Roman Proconsul....Charles Marshall
OROVESO, chief of druids.........Chase Baromeo
NORMA, his daughter...............Rosa Raisa
ADALGISA, a priestess................Coe Glade
CLOTILDE, confidante of Norma.Alice d'Hermanoy
FLAVIUS, friend of Pollione....Lodovico Oliviero

CONDUCTOR.....................Emil Cooper

Some of the artists of this season were not assigned to the first week and a few had not reached Chicago at that time. Some, like Hallie Stiles and Giovanni Inghilleri, were ill, though they both made successful débuts later. But in general the first week's list showed a cross section of the company, even to the extent that a few had passed the turn of the wheel and were beginning to repeat.

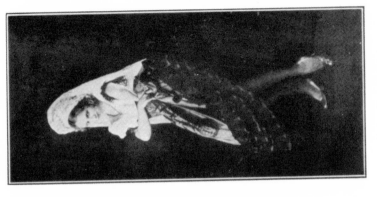

JULIA BARASHKOVA,
CHICAGO CIVIC OPERA BALLET

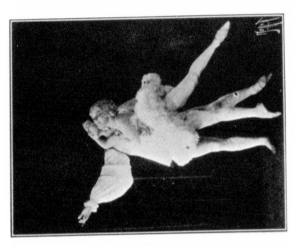

EDWARD CATON AND RUTH PRYOR,
CHICAGO CIVIC OPERA BALLET

Photographs by Moffett

HARRIET LUNDGREN,
CHICAGO CIVIC OPERA BALLET

Emil Cooper, of Russian birth, was new among the conductors. Egon Pollak, German, returned to Chicago after an absence of nearly thirteen years. They, together with Frank St. Leger, also returning after several seasons' absence, added to Director Polacco and Mr. Moranzoni, of continuing service, made up what was universally acknowledged to be the strongest staff of conductors that the Chicago Opera had ever possessed.

"Iris" was the first novelty of the season. It had not been heard in Chicago since the time that the city took its operatic service from visits by the Metropolitan Opera Company. With its Japanese locale, some unusually pictorial settings, and some unusually effective music for Miss Mason's voice, it became an interesting addition to the repertoire.

Incidentally, one of the greatest reasons for rejoicing over the new opera house was its stage lighting system. With this, marvels began to be worked. Lights could be directed to any spot from any angle, and at once, with the result that old scenery became transformed, new scenery appeared lovely beyond all telling. and light changes were made directly on the cue instead of waiting an appreciable time thereafter. They used to do the best that they could in the Auditorium, but in the Civic Opera House their best became enormously better.

There was no speech making at the dedication of the house. This in itself was an astonishing innovation. For decades past it had always been the custom to inaugurate a new undertaking with a flow of language, and seldom was to be found the person who did not feel delighted at the chance to talk, less often yet the audience that was not profoundly bored.

Mr. Insull was more humane. He forbade any one to talk. Instead, he wrote a few words which he described as the speech he might have made, but which he gave to the newspapers and the opera programs. This is its keynote:

"Merely to build a beautiful house and give it the best equipment possible was not the fundamental idea of this undertaking. That idea was, and still is, to give opera an abiding place in Chicago, and, through the Chicago Music Foundation, the organization of which has already been announced, to train and educate men and women for the production of opera and thereby make Chicago a music center worthy of its place in the world's affairs.

"As has also been announced, the new opera house is now the property of the foundation as a gift, and already the absorption of the debt upon the property has begun. Already a group consisting of Messrs. Stanley Field, Ernest R. Graham, Edward F. Swift, Donald R. McLennan, Bernard A. Eckhart, C. Ward Seabury, Mrs. Insull, my son, and myself have placed 3,750 shares of preferred stock ($375,000) at the disposal of the trustees of the foundation, and 2,000 other shares have also been placed at the disposal of the corporation, a total of more than half a million dollars, to be used in wiping out the obligations of the building."

Once again there is reason to look at the future with hope.

APPENDIX

A statistical résumé of The Chicago Grand Opera Company, The Chicago Opera Association and The Chicago Civic Opera Company's performances, Nov. 3, 1910, to March 26, 1929:

THE CHICAGO COMPANIES AT HOME

(Works presented in Chicago and total performances to March 26, 1929)

60 Italian

Africana, L'	3	Huguenots, The	3
Aïda	65	Isabeau	6
Amore dei Tre Re, L'	19	Jacquerie	3
Andrea Chenier	11	Jewels of the Madonna, The	41
Barber of Seville, The	37	Jewess, The	16
Bohême, La	43	Linda di Chamounix	8
Boris Godunoff	13	Loreley	6
Cavalleria Rusticana	46	Lovers' Quarrel, A	4
Cene della Beffe, La	3	Lucia di Lammermoor	39
Conchita	1	Madame Butterfly	46
Crispino e la Comare *	2	Maestro di Capella, Il	1
Cristoforo Colombo	2	Manon Lescaut	6
Daughter of the Regiment, The	3	Marriage of Figaro, The	5
Dinorah	8	Martha	22
Edipo Re	3	Masked Ball, A	13
Elisir d'Amore, L'	9	Mefistofele	12
Ernani	2	Mignon	1
Falstaff	7	Namiko San	3
Fedora	6	Nave, La	2
Forza del Destino, La	4	Norma	4
Fra Diavolo	2	Otello	21
Francesca da Rimini	4	Pagliacci, I	54
Gianni Schicchi	10	Pasquale, Don	3
Gioconda, La	15	Rigoletto	55
Giovanni, Don	8	Secret of Suzanne, The	8
Girl of the Golden West, The	8	Sonnambula, La	9
Hamlet	2	Suor Angelica	3

* One special performance in Chicago at the close of the 1913 tour—April 21.

60 Italian (Cont'd)

Tabarro, Il	3	Zaza	1
Tosca, La	52	Zingari, I	2
Traviata, La	45		
Trovatore, Il	40		873

41 French

Aphrodite	1	Noël	2
Carmen	67	Pearl Fishers, The	4
Cendrillon	10	Pelléas and Mélisande	13
Chemineau, Le	5	Prophête, Le	4
Cléopatre	7	Quichotte, Don	4
Dejanire	2	Quo Vadis	4
Faust	38	Ranz des Vaches, Le	2
Gismonda	2	Resurrection	9
Griselidis	2	Romeo and Juliet	25
Hérodiade	10	Salome	4
Heure Espagnol, L'	1	Samson and Delilah	28
Jongleur de Nôtre Dame, Le..	23	Sapho	7
Judith	4	Sauteriot, Le	1
Lakmé	16	Snowmaiden, The	9
Louise	27	Tales of Hoffman	22
Love for Three Oranges	2	Tell, William	2
Madame Chrysantheme	2	Thaïs	33
Manon	16	Traviata, La	1
Mignon	8	Vieil Aigle, Le	2
Monna Vanna	19	Werther	9
Navarraise, La	2		449

10 German

Götterdämmerung	2	Siegfried	4
Königskinder	7	Tannhäuser	19
Lohengrin	17	Tristan and Isolde	11
Parsifal	8	Walküre, Die	25
Rheingold, Das	2		
Rosenkavalier, Der	9		104

17 English

Azora	3	Madeleine	2
Cricket on the Hearth	5	Martha	1
Daughter of the Forest	1	Natoma	6
Fledermaus, Die	3	Rip Van Winkle	3
Hansel and Gretel	22	Snowbird, The	2
Light from St. Agnes, A	1	Snowmaiden, The	3
Lohengrin	3	Tiefland	3
Lovers' Knot, A	1		
Lovers' Quarrel, A	4		63

SEASON 1910–1911—CHICAGO GRAND OPERA COMPANY

BOARD OF DIRECTORS

Frederick W. Bode
R. T. Crane, Jr.
Charles G. Dawes
Robert Goelet
George J. Gould
Frank Gray Griswold
Frederick T. Haskell
Charles L. Hutchinson
Otto H. Kahn
Philip M. Lydig
Clarence H. Mackay

Harold F. McCormick
John J. Mitchell
Ira N. Morris
La Verne W. Noyes
Max Pam
Julius Rosenwald
John C. Shaffer
John G. Shedd
Charles A. Stevens
Harry Payne Whitney
H. Rogers Winthrop

EXECUTIVE COMMITTEE

Clarence H. Mackay, Chairman
Otto H. Kahn
Philip M. Lydig
Charles G. Dawes

John C. Shaffer, Vice-Chairman
Julius Rosenwald
Harry Payne Whitney
H. Rogers Winthrop

John G. Shedd

OFFICERS

Harold F. McCormick .... President
Charles G. Dawes .... Vice-President
Otto H. Kahn .... Vice-President
Charles L. Hutchinson .... Treasurer
Philip M. Lydig .... Secretary
Andreas Dippel .... General Manager
Cleofonte Campanini .... General Musical Director
Bernhard Ulrich.................................Business Manager

Conductors
  Campanini, Cleofonte
  Charlier, Marcel
  Parelli, Attilio
  Perosio, Ettore

Stage Director
  Almanz, Fernand

Stage Manager
  Engel, Joseph C.
  Muzio, Carlo, Assistant
  Katzman, Sam, Assistant

Chorus Master
  Nepoti, Pietro

Ballet Master
  Albertieri, Luigi

Première Danseuse
  Zanini, Ester

Assistant Conductor
  Rosenstein, Arthur

Technical Director
  Bairstow, William H.

Scenic Artist
  Meisener, Karl

Orchestra Manager
  Raffaelli, Joseph

Season
  Thursday, November 3rd, to
  Wednesday, January 18th, 1911.
  63 performances

1 Gala performance
8 Campanini Sunday concerts
1 Sunday Song Recital
21 Operas

Sopranos
Cavan, Marie
Dumesnil, Suzanne
Egener, Minnie
Farrar, Geraldine
Gadski, Johanna
Garden, Mary
Grenville, Lillian
Korolewicz, Jeanne
La Salle Rabinoff, Marie
Lipkowska, Lydia
Melba, Nellie
Melis, Carmen
Osborn-Hannah, Jane
Riegelman, Mabel
Scalfaro, Serafina
Sylva, Marguerite
White, Carolina
Zeppilli, Alice

Contraltos
Bressler-Gianoli, Clotilde
De Angelo, Tina
De Cisneros, Eleanora
Giaconia, Giuseppina
Olitzka, Rosa
Pattini, Ferrari
Walker, Marion

Tenors
Bassi, Amadeo
Caruso, Enrico
Constantino, Florencio
Dalmores, Charles
Delparte, Jean
Daddi, Francesco
Guardabassi, Mario
McCormack, John
Venturini, Emilio
Warnery, Edmond
Zerola, Nicolo
Zucchi, Dante

Baritones
Beck, William
Costa, Alfredo
Crabbe, Armand
Defrere, Desiré
Dufranne, Hector
Fossetta, Nicolo
Renaud, Maurice
Sammarco, Mario
Scotti, Antonio

Bassos
Angelis, Nazzareno De
Arimondi, Vittorio
Berardi, Berardo
Huberdeau, Gustave
Malatesta, Pompilio
Nicolay, Constantin
Sampieri, Michele

14 Italian

Aïda	5	Otello	1
La Bohême	3	I Pagliacci	5
Cavalleria Rusticana	4	Rigoletto	4
The Girl of the Golden West	5	La Tosca	4
Lucia di Lammermoor	1	La Traviata	2
Madame Butterfly	3	Il Trovatore	3
A Masked Ball	1	Gli Ugonotti	1

7 French

Carmen	3	Salome	2
Faust	3	The Tales of Hoffman	4
Louise	4	Thaïs	6
Pelléas and Mélisande	4		

SEASON 1911–1912—CHICAGO GRAND OPERA COMPANY

BOARD OF DIRECTORS

Frederick Bode	Harold F. McCormick
H. M. Byllesby	John J. Mitchell
R. T. Crane, Jr.	Ira N. Morris
Charles G. Dawes	La Verne W. Noyes
Robert Goelet	Max Pam
George J. Gould	George F. Porter
Frank Gray Griswold	Julius Rosenwald
Frederick T. Haskell	John C. Shaffer
Charles L. Hutchinson	John G. Shedd
Otto H. Kahn	Charles A. Stevens
Philip M. Lydig	F. D. Stout
Clarence H. Mackay	Harry Payne Whitney

H. Rogers Winthrop

EXECUTIVE COMMITTEE

Philip M. Lydig, Chairman	Clarence H. Mackay
John C. Shaffer, Vice-Chairman	Harold F. McCormick
R. T. Crane, Jr.	La Verne W. Noyes
Charles G. Dawes	Max Pam
Robert Goelet	John G. Shedd
Frank Gray Griswold	Harry Payne Whitney
Otto H. Kahn	H. Rogers Winthrop

OFFICERS

Harold F. McCormick .... President
Charles G. Dawes .... Vice-President
Otto H. Kahn .... Vice-President
Charles L. Hutchinson .... Treasurer
George F. Porter .... Secretary
Andreas Dippel .... General Manager
Cleofonte Campanini .... General Musical Director
Bernhard Ulrich .... Business Manager

Conductors
  Campanini, Cleofonte
  Charlier, Marcel
  Parelli, Attilio
  Perosio, Ettore

Stage Director
  Almanz, Fernand

Stage Manager
  Engel, Joseph C.
  Muzio, Carlo, Assistant
  Katzman, Sam, Assistant

Chorus Master
  Nepoti, Pietro

Ballet Master
  Albertieri, Luigi

Première Danseuse
  Galli, Rosina

Technical Director
  Bairstow, William H.

Scenic Artist
  MacDonald, Julian L.

Orchestra Manager
  Raffaelli, Joseph

Season

Wednesday, November 22nd, 1911, to Thursday, February 1st, 1912.

72 Performances
1 Gala Performance
1 Ballet Divertissement
6 Campanini Sunday Concerts
1 Song Recital
24 Operas

Sopranos
Cavan, Marie
Dufau, Jennie
Egener, Minnie
Eversman, Alice
Frease-Green, Rachel
Fish, Eleanore
Fremstad, Olive
Garden, Mary
Osborn-Hannah, Jane
Riegelman, Mabel
Tetrazzini, Luisa
Teyte, Maggie
Saltzmann-Stevens, Minnie
Starrell, Marguerite
White, Carolina
Zeppili, Alice

Contraltos
Berat, Louise
Cisneros, Eleanora De
Gerville-Reache, Jeanne
Giaconia, Giuseppina
Guernsey, Charlotte

Contraltos (Cont'd)
Ingram, Frances
Schumann-Heink, Ernestine
Spiesberger, Minna
Wittkowska, Martha

Tenors
Bassi, Amadeo
Daddi, Francesco
Dalmores, Charles
Guardabassi, Mario
Hamlin, George
Hensel, Heinrich
Hoose, Ellison Van
Remella, Luigi
Venturini, Emilio
Warnery, Edmond

Baritones
Crabbe, Armand
Costa, Alfredo
Defrere, Desiré
Dufranne, Hector
Fossetta, Nicolo
Sammarco, Mario
Whitehill, Clarence

Bassos
Berardi, Berardo
Huberdeau, Gustave
Malatesta, Pompilio
Nicolay, Constantin
Preisch, Frank
Sampieri, Michele
Schorr, Friedrich
Scott, Henri

10 Italian

The Barber of Seville	1	I Pagliacci	2
Cavalleria Rusticana	2	Rigoletto	2
The Jewels of the Madonna	6	The Secret of Suzanne	5
Lucia di Lammermoor	3	La Traviata	2
The Marriage of Figaro	2	Il Trovatore	1

2 English

Hansel and Gretel	5	Natoma	5

9 French

Carmen	5	Quo Vadis	4
Cendrillon	6	Samson and Delilah	3
Faust	1	The Tales of Hoffman	3
Le Jongleur de Nôtre Dame	4	Thaïs	4
Lakmé	2		

3 *German*

Lohengrin 4   Die Walküre 4
Tristan and Isolde 2

SEASON 1912-1913—CHICAGO GRAND OPERA COMPANY

BOARD OF DIRECTORS

Frederick Bode	Harold F. McCormick
H. M. Byllesby	John J. Mitchell
R. T. Crane, Jr.	Ira N. Morris
Paul D. Cravath	La Verne W. Noyes
Charles G. Dawes	Max Pam
George J. Gould	George F. Porter
Frederick T. Haskell	Julius Rosenwald
Charles L. Hutchinson	John C. Shaffer
Otto H. Kahn	John G. Shedd
Alvin W. Krech	Charles A. Stevens
Philip M. Lydig	F. D. Stout
Clarence H. Mackay	Harry Payne Whitney

EXECUTIVE COMMITTEE

Philip M. Lydig, Chairman	Clarence H. Mackay
John C. Shaffer, Vice-Chairman	Harold F. McCormick
R. T. Crane, Jr.	La Verne W. Noyes
Paul D. Cravath	Max Pam
Charles G. Dawes	John G. Shedd
Otto H. Kahn	Harry Payne Whitney

OFFICERS

Harold F. McCormick .... President
Otto H. Kahn .... Vice-President
Charles G. Dawes .... Vice-President
Charles L. Hutchinson .... Treasurer
F. H. Chandler .... Secretary

ADMINISTRATION

Andreas Dippel .... General Manager
Cleofonte Campanini .... General Musical Director
Bernhard Ulrich .... Business Manager

Conductors
  Campanini, Cleofonte
  Charlier, Marcel
  Parelli, Attilio
  Perosio, Ettore
  Winternitz, Arnold

Stage Director
  Almanz, Fernand

Stage Manager
  Engel, Joseph C.

Chorus Master
  Nepoti, Pietro

Ballet Master
  Albertieri, Luigi

Première Danseuse
  Galli, Rosina

Technical Director
Bairstow, William H.

Scenic Artist
MacDonald, Julien L.

Orchestra Manager
Raffaelli, Joseph

Season
Tuesday, November 26th, 1912,
to Saturday, February 1st, 1913.
  71 Performances
   1 Gala Performance
   1 Concert
   2 Ballet Divertissements
  30 Operas

Sopranos
Berry, Agnes
Cavan, Marie
Clay, Enrica
Darch, Edna
Dufau, Jenny
Egener, Minnie
Eversman, Alice
Garden, Mary
Garrette, Elsa
Gugliardi, Cecelia
Nordica, Lillian
Osborn-Hannah, Jane
Riegelman, Mabel
Saltzmann-Stevens, Minnie
Stanley, Helen
Tarquini, Tarquinia
Tetrazzini, Luisa
Teyte, Maggie
Warram, Helen
White, Carolina
Zeppilli, Alice

Contraltos
Berat, Louise
Cisneros, Eleanora De

Contraltos (Cont'd)
Claussen, Julia
Gay, Maria
Gray, Hope
Heyl, Ruby
Keyes, Margaret
Logard, Adele
Schumann-Heink, Ernestine

Tenors
Daddi, Francesco
Dalmores, Charles
Calleja, Icilio
Campagnola, Leon
Gaudenzi, Giuseppe
Giorgini, Aristodemo
Hamlin, George
Harrold, Orville
Hoose, Ellison Van
Orsati, Pietro
Schoenert, Kurt
Venturini, Emilio
Warnery, Edmond
Zenatello, Giovanni

Baritones
Crabbe, Armand
Costa, Alfredo
Defrere, Desiré
Dufranne, Hector
Fossetta, Nicolo
Mascal, Georges
Polese, Giovanni
Rossi, Anafesto
Ruffo, Titta
Sammarco, Mario
Whitehill, Clarence

Bassos
Huberdeau, Gustave
Nicolay, Constantin
Scott, Henri
Preisch, Frank
Trevisan, Vittorio

15 Italian

Aïda	4	I Pagliacci	5
La Bohême	2	Rigoletto	3
Cavalleria Rusticana	5	The Secret of Suzanne	3
Hamlet	1	La Tosca	3
The Jewels of the Madonna	5	La Traviata	2
A Lovers' Quarrel	2	Il Trovatore	1
Lucia di Lammermoor	2	Conchita	1
Manon Lescaut	3		

2 English

The Cricket on the Hearth 4   Hansel and Gretel 3

10 French

Carmen 3   Louise 2
Cendrillon 4   Mignon 5
Faust 1   Noël 2
Hérodiade 3   The Tales of Hoffman 2
Le Jongleur de Nôtre Dame.... 2   Thaïs 2

3 German

Lohengrin 2   Die Walküre 3
Tristan and Isolde 1

SEASON 1913–1914—CHICAGO GRAND OPERA COMPANY

BOARD OF DIRECTORS

Frederick Bode
H. M. Byllesby
R. T. Crane, Jr.
Charles G. Dawes
Frederick T. Haskell
Charles L. Hutchinson
Otto H. Kahn
Harold F. McCormick
John J. Mitchell

Ira N. Morris
La Verne W. Noyes
Max Pam
George F. Porter
Julius Rosenwald
John C. Shaffer
John G. Shedd
Charles A. Stevens
F. D. Stout

EXECUTIVE COMMITTEE

John C. Shaffer, Chairman
R. T. Crane, Jr.
Charles G. Dawes
Harold F. McCormick

La Verne W. Noyes
Max Pam
George F. Porter
John G. Shedd

OFFICERS

Harold F. McCormick .... President
Charles G. Dawes .... Vice-President
Otto H. Kahn .... Vice-President
Charles L. Hutchinson.................................... Treasurer

ADMINISTRATION

Cleofonte Campanini .... General Director
Bernhard Ulrich .... Business Manager

Conductors
Campanini, Cleofonte
Charlier, Marcel
Herbert, Victor
Leoncavallo, Ruggiero

Parelli, Attilio
Perosio, Ettore
Sturani, Giuseppe
Winternitz, Arnold

Chorus Master
Nepoti, Pietro

Stage Director
Almanz, Fernand

Stage Manager
Engel, Joseph C.
Moore, H. E., Assistant
Katzman, Sam, Assistant

Ballet Master
Romeo, V.

Première Danseuse
Galli, Rosina

Technical Director
Bairstow, William H.

Scenic Artist
Donigan, P. T.

Orchestra Manager
Raffaelli, Joseph

Season
Monday, November 24th, 1913,
to Saturday, January 31, 1914.
70 Performances
  1 Gala Performance
  1 Ballet Divertissement
  1 Sunday Concert
  37 Operas

Sopranos
Alda, Frances
Cavalieri, Lina
Dorda, Martha
Dufau, Jenny
Egener, Minnie
Evans, Amy
Hempel, Frieda
Garden, Mary
Macbeth, Florence
Melba, Nellie
Osborn-Hannah, Jane
Raisa, Rosa
Riegelman, Mabel

Sopranos (Cont'd)
Saltzman-Stevens, Minnie
Teyte, Maggie
Warram, Helen
Wheeler, Beatrice
White, Carolina
Zeppilli, Alice

Contraltos
Berat, Louise
Claussen, Julia
Heyl, Ruby
Keyes, Margaret
Van Gordon, Cyrena
Schumann-Heink, Ernestine

Tenors
Bassi, Amadeo
Bergmann, Gustav
Daddi, Francesco
Dalmores, Charles
Errolle, Ralph
Giorgini, Aristodemo
Hamlin, George
Marak, Otto
Muratore, Lucien
Venturini, Emilio
Warnery, Edmond

Baritones
Crabbe, Armand
Defrere, Desiré
Dufranne, Hector
Federici, Francesco
Fossetta, Nicolo
Polese, Giovanni
Ruffo, Titta
Turner, Alan
Vanni-Marcoux
Whitehill, Clarence

Bassos
Hinckley, Allen
Huberdeau, Gustave
Nicolay, Constantin
Preisch, Frank
Scott, Henri
Trevisan, Vittorio

19 Italian

Aïda	2	Don Giovanni	1
The Barber of Seville	2	Fedora	3
La Bohême	3	La Gioconda	1
Cristoforo Colombo	2	The Girl of the Golden West	1

19 Italian (Cont'd)

The Jewels of the Madonna...	4	La Sonnambula	1
A Lovers' Quarrel	1	La Tosca	2
Lucia di Lammermoor	1	La Traviata	1
Madame Butterfly	3	Il Trovatore	1
I Pagliacci	3	I Zingari	2
Rigoletto	2		

4 English

The Cricket on the Hearth.....	1	Martha	1
Hansel and Gretel	2	Natoma	1

12 French

Carmen	3	Manon	2
Don Quichotte	4	Monna Vanna	2
Faust	2	Le Ranz Des Vaches	2
Hérodiade	1	Samson and Delilah	3
La Jongleur de Nôtre Dame....	2	The Tales of Hoffman	2
Louise	1	Thaïs	3

2 German

Parsifal	2	Die Walküre	3

SEASON 1915–1916—CHICAGO OPERA ASSOCIATION

GUARANTORS

Robert Allerton
J. Ogden Armour
Carson, Pirie, Scott & Co.
Congress Hotel Company
R. T. Crane, Jr.
Charles G. Dawes
The Drake Hotel Company
Marshall Field & Co.
Frederick T. Haskell
Charles L. Hutchinson
Samuel Insull
William V. Kelley
L. B. Kuppenheimer

Adolph J. Lichtstern
William A. Lydon
Cyrus Hall McCormick
Harold F. McCormick
John J. Mitchell
Max Pam
George F. Porter
Julius Rosenwald
Martin A. Ryerson
John G. Shedd
Charles A. Stevens & Bros.
F. D. Stout
Edward F. Swift

ADMINISTRATION

Cleofonte Campanini .... General Director
Bernhard Ulrich .... Business Manager
Herbert M. Johnson .... Auditor

Conductors
Campanini, Cleofonte
Charlier, Marcel

Ferrari, Rodolfo
Parelli, Attilio
Pollak, Egon

Stage Directors
Chalmin, Victor
Capotini, Napoleone
Taylor, Loomis

Stage Manager
Engel, Joseph C.
Katzman, Sam, Assistant

Chorus Master
Nepoti, Pietro

Ballet Master
Ambrosini, François

Première Danseuse
Rosina Tiovella

Assistant Conductor
Spadoni, Giacomo

Technical Director
Bairstow, William H.

Scenic Artist
Donigan, P. T.

Orchestra Manager
Raffaelli, Joseph

Season
Monday, November 15th, to Saturday, January 22, 1916.
73 Performances
1 Gala Performance
35 Operas

Sopranos
Alda, Frances
Beriza, Marguerite
Darch, Edna
Destinn, Emmy
Dresser, Maria Van
Easton, Florence
Eden, Hazel
Edvina, Louise
Farrar, Geraldine
Frease-Green, Rachel
Gresham, Lillian
Fremstad, Olive
Hall, Mabel
Kousenezoff, Maria

Sopranos (Cont'd)
Jovelli, Minnie
Lindgren, Lydia
Lynbrook, Katarina
Macbeth, Florence
Melba, Nellie
Melis, Carmen
Peterson, Alma
Phillippe, Dora De
Rose, Frances
Sharlow, Myrna
Stanley, Helen
Supervia, Conchita
Verlet, Alice

Contraltos
Cisneros, Eleanora De
Claussen, Julia
Ingram, Frances
Lenska, Augusta
Maubourg, Jeanne
Mosco, Myrtle
Pavloska, Irene
Schaffer, Virginia
Schumann-Heink, Ernestine
Van Gordon, Cyrena
Wait, Barbara

Tenors
Bassi, Amadeo
Corallo, Giuseppe
Daddi, Francesco
Dalmores, Charles
Dua, Octave
Ferrari-Fontana, Edgardo
Ferraresi, Federico
Hamlin, George
MacLennan, Francis
McCormack, John
Moreas, Costas
Muratore, Lucien
Procter, Warren
Reiss, Albert
Stiles, Vernon
Vogliotti, Giuseppe
Zerola, Nicolo

Baritones
Ancona, Mario
Beck, William
Defrere, Desiré
Dufranne, Hector
Federici, Francesco
Maguenat, Charles

Baritones (Cont'd)
Marr, Graham
Scotti, Antonio
Whitehill, Clarence

Bassos
Arimondi, Vittorio

Bassos (Cont'd)
Cochems, Carl Von
Goddard, James
Hinckley, Allen
Journet, Marcel
Nicolay, Constantin
Trevisan, Vittorio

15 Italian

Aïda	2	Lucia di Lammermoor	1
L'Amore dei Tre Re	3	Madame Butterfly	5
La Bohême	3	I Pagliacci	3
Cavalleria Rusticana	1	Rigoletto	1
Don Giovanni	1	Il Trovatore	1
La Gioconda	3	La Tosca	4
The Jewels of the Madonna	4	Zaza	1
A Lovers' Quarrel	1		

1 English

The Lovers' Knot 1

12 French

Carmen	6	Monna Vanna	4
Cléopatre	3	La Navarraise	2
Déjanire	2	Romeo and Juliet	2
Faust	2	Thaïs	2
Louise	3	La Traviata	1
Mignon	3	Werther	2

7 German

Götterdämmerung	1	Tannhäuser	3
Parsifal	2	Tristan and Isolde	1
Das Rheingold	1	Die Walküre	2
Siegfried	1		

SEASON 1916–1917—CHICAGO OPERA ASSOCIATION

GUARANTORS

Robert Allerton
J. Ogden Armour
Carson, Pirie, Scott & Co.
Congress Hotel Company
R. T. Crane, Jr.
Charles G. Dawes
The Drake Hotel Company
Marshall Field & Co.
Frederick T. Haskell
Charles L. Hutchinson
Samuel Insull
William V. Kelley
L. B. Kuppenheimer

Adolph J. Lichtstern
William A. Lydon
Cyrus Hall McCormick
Harold F. McCormick
John J. Mitchell
Max Pam
George F. Porter
Julius Rosenwald
Martin A. Ryerson
John G. Shedd
Charles A. Stevens & Bros.
F. D. Stout
Edward F. Swift

EXECUTIVE STAFF

Cleofonte Campanini .... General Director
Herbert M. Johnson .... Business Comptroller

Conductors
Campanini, Cleofonte
Charlier, Marcel
Pollak, Egon
Sturani, Giuseppe

Stage Directors
Engel, Joseph C.
Verande, Louis F.

Assistant Stage Managers
Defrere, Desiré
Katzman, Sam

Chorus Master
Nepoti, Pietro

Ballet Master
Ambrosini, François

Première Danseuse and Danseurs
Tamara Swirskaia
Andreas Pavley
Serge Oukrainsky

Assistant Conductor
Spadoni, Giacomo

Technical Director
Bairstow, William H.

Scenic Artist
Donigan, P. T.

Orchestra Manager
Raffaelli, Joseph

Season
Monday, November 13th, 1916, to
Sunday, January 21st, 1917.
81 Performances
1 Gala Performance
1 Italian-French Benefit
38 Operas

Sopranos
Amsden, Elizabeth
Buckler, Marguerite

Sopranos (Cont'd)
Dresser, Marcia Van
Easton, Florence
Eden, Hazel
Edvina, Louise
Farrar, Geraldine
Forsaith, Leta Mae
Galli-Curci, Amelita
Goodman, Melba
Hall, Mabel Preston
Libberton, Cora
Matzenauer, Margaret
Mooney, Miriam
Peterson, Alma
Prindiville, Ethel
Phillippe, Dora De
Raisa, Rosa
Sharlow, Myrna

Contraltos
Berat, Louise
Claessens, Maria
Claussen, Julia
Moses, Myrtle
Olitzka, Rosa
Pavloska, Irene
Reynolds, Sarame
Schaffer, Virginia
Van Gordon, Cyrena

Tenors
Crimi, Giulio
Daddi, Francesco
Dalmores, Charles
Dua, Octave
Dore, Georges
Errolle, Ralph
Hamlin, George
Kingston, Morgan
MacLennan, Francis
Muratore, Lucien
Nadal, Juan
Proctor, Warren
Venturini, Emilio

Baritones
Beck, William
Defrere, Desiré

Baritones (Cont'd)
Dufranne, Hector
Franzini, Rocco
Kreidler, Louis
Polese, Giovanni
Rimini, Giacomo
Whitehill, Clarence

Bassos
Arimondi, Vittorio
Goddard, James
Hinckley, Allen
Journet, Marcel
Nicolay, Constantin
Sargeant, Gaston
Trevisan, Vittorio

15 Italian

Aïda	4	Madame Butterfly	2
Andrea Chenier	3	I Pagliacci	3
The Barber of Seville	3	Rigoletto	4
La Bohême	2	La Tosca	2
Cavalleria Rusticana	3	La Traviata	2
Falstaff	2	Il Trovatore	1
Francesca da Rimini	3	Gli Ugonotti	1
Lucia di Lammermoor	4		

12 French

Carmen	5	Manon	3
Faust	3	Le Prophête	2
Griselidis	2	Romeo and Juliet	4
Hérodiade	1	The Tales of Hoffman	2
Le Jôngleur de Nôtre Dame	2	Thaïs	3
Louise	3	Le Vieil Aigle	1

2 English

Hansel and Gretel	1	Madeleine	2

9 German

Götterdämmerung	1	Parsifal	1
Königskinder	5	Tannhäuser	1
Lohengrin	1	Tristan and Isolde	1
Das Rheingold	1	Die Walküre	1
Siegfried	1		

SEASON 1917–1918—CHICAGO OPERA ASSOCIATION

GUARANTORS

Robert Allerton
J. Ogden Armour
Giulio Bolognesi
Congress Hotel Company
R. T. Crane, Jr.
Charles G. Dawes
Charles L. Hutchinson
Samuel Insull
L. B. Kuppenheimer
A. J. Lichtstern
Cyrus Hall McCormick

Harold F. McCormick
Edith Rockefeller McCormick
John J. Mitchell
Max Pam
George F. Porter
Julius Rosenwald
Martin A. Ryerson
John G. Shedd
Mrs. H. H. Spaulding, Jr.
Frank D. Stout
Edward F. Swift

EXECUTIVE STAFF

Cleofonte Campanini .... General Director
Herbert M. Johnson .*........................ Business Comptroller

Conductors
Campanini, Cleofonte
Sturani, Giuseppe
Conti, Arnoldo
Charlier, Marcel

Stage Director
Merle-Forest, Emile

Stage Managers
Engel, Joseph C.
Verande, Louis P.
Katzman, Samuel (Assistant)

Chorus Master
Nepoti, Pietro

Ballet Master
Ambrosini, François

Première Danseuse
Pelucchi, Annetta

Assistant Conductor
Bigalli, Dino (Librarian)

Technical Director
Beatty, Harry W.

Scenic Artist
Donigan, Peter J.

Orchestra Manager
Raffaelli, Joseph

Season
Monday, November 12th, 1917,
to Saturday, January 19th, 1918.
73 Performances
1 Gala Performance
3 Concerts
30 Operas

Sopranos
Bonnar, Diana
Buckler, Marguerite
Christian, Jessie

Sopranos (Cont'd)
Evans, Ruby
Fitziu, Anna
Galli-Curci, Amelita
Garden, Mary
Hall, Mabel Preston
Maxwell, Margery
Melba, Nellie
Parnell, Evelyn
Peterson, Alma
de Phillippe, Dora
Pruette, Juanita
Peralta, Francesca
Pruzan, Marie
Raisa, Rosa
Sharlow, Myrna
Vix, Genevieve

Contraltos
Berat, Louise
Claessens, Maria
Lazzari, Carolina
Swartz, Jeska
Van Gordon, Cyrena

Tenors
Crimi, Giulio
Daddi, Francesco
Dalmores, Charles
Dua, Octave
Lamont, Forrest
McCormack, John
Muratore, Lucien
Nadal, Juan
Paltrinieri, Giordano
Zinovieff, Leone

Baritones
Baklanoff, Georges
Defrere, Desiré
Dufranne, Hector
Fornari, Rodolfo
Van Hulst, Carl
Kreidler, Louis
Landesman, Bernard
Maguenat, Alfred
Middleton, Arthur
Rimini, Giacomo
Stracciari, Ricardo

Bassos
Arimondi, Vittorio
Goddard, James
Huberdeau, Gustave
Nicolay, Constantin
Preisch, Frank
Trevisan, Vittorio

16 Italian

Aïda	4	Isabeau	4
The Barber of Seville	1	Lucia di Lammermoor	1
La Bohême	4	I Pagliacci	3
Cavalleria Rusticana	3	Rigoletto	3
Dinorah	5	La Tosca	4
Ernani	2	La Traviata	4
Francesca da Rimini	1	Il Trovatore	1
The Jewels of the Madonna	4	Gli Ugonotti	1

12 French

Carmen	2	Monna Vanna	1
Faust	4	Pelléas et Mélisande	2
Le Jôngleur de Nôtre Dame	3	Romeo and Juliet	5
Lakmé	2	Sapho	2
Louise	2	Le Sauteriot	1
Manon	2	Thaïs	1

2 English

Azora	3	A Daughter of the Forest	1

SEASON 1918–1919—CHICAGO OPERA ASSOCIATION

BOARD OF DIRECTORS

Robert Allerton
Giulio Bolognesi
R. T. Crane, Jr.
Charles G. Dawes
Stanley Field
E. R. Graham
Charles L. Hutchinson
Samuel Insull
S. R. Kaufman

L. B. Kuppenheimer
Cyrus Hall McCormick
Harold F. McCormick
John J. Mitchell
Max Pam
Martin A. Ryerson
John G. Shedd
Frank D. Stout
Edward F. Swift

EXECUTIVE COMMITTEE

Max Pam, Chairman
R. T. Crane, Jr.
Stanley Field
Samuel Insull

Harold F. McCormick
John J. Mitchell
Frank D. Stout
Edward F. Swift

OFFICERS

Harold F. McCormick .... President
Charles G. Dawes .... Vice-President
Max Pam .... Vice-President

Officers (Cont'd)

Stanley Field .... Secretary
Charles L. Hutchinson .... Treasurer

ADMINISTRATION

Cleofonte Campanini .... General Director
Herbert M. Johnson .... Business Comptroller

Conductors
Campanini, Cleofonte
Polacco, Giorgio
Sturani, Giuseppe
Hasselmans, Louis
Charlier, Marcel

Stage Director
Merle-Forrest, Emile

Stage Manager
Engel, Joseph C.
Katzman, Samuel (Assistant)

Chorus Master
Nepoti, Pietro

Ballet Master
Ambrosini, François

Première Danseuse
Tell, Sylvia
Premiers Danseurs
Pavley, Andreas
Oukrainsky, Serge
Karalli

Assistant Conductors
Spadoni, Giacomo
Sturani, Cesare
Conti, Arnoldo
St. Leger, Frank
Ruffo, Ettore
Bigalli, Dino (Librarian)

Technical Director
Beatty, Harry W.

Scenic Artist
Donigan, Peter J.

Orchestra Manager
Raffaelli, Joseph

Season
Monday, November 18, 1918, to
Saturday, January 25, 1919.
63 Performances
6 Concerts
29 Operas

Sopranos
Brown, Beryl
Fitziu, Anna
Gall, Yvonne
Galli-Curci, Amelita
Garden, Mary
Gerhardt-Downing, Frederica
Gibson, Dora
Macbeth, Florence
Maxwell, Margery
Miura, Tamaki
Namara, Marguerite
Noe, Emma
Peterson, Alma
Pruzan, Marie
Raisa, Rosa
Sharlow, Myrna
Sylva, Marguerite

Contraltos
Berat, Louise
Claessens, Marie
Lazzari, Carolina
Pavloska, Irene
Van Gordon, Cyrena

Tenors
Carpi, Fernando
Ciccolini, Guido
Daddi, Francesco
Dolci, Alessandro
Dua, Octave
Fontaine, Charles
Lamont, Forrest
McCormack, John
Muratore, Lucien

Tenors (Cont'd)
  Oliviero, Lodovico
  O'Sullivan, John
  Proctor, Warren
  Rogerson, William

Baritones
  Baklanoff, Georges
  Bouilliez, Auguste
  Defrere, Desiré
  Landesman, Bernard
  Maguenat, Alfred

Baritones (Cont'd)
  Rimini, Giacomo
  Stracciari, Riccardo

Bassos
  Arimondi, Vittorio
  Huberdeau, Gustave
  Journet, Marcel
  Lazzari, Virgilio
  Nicolay, Constantin
  Trevisan, Vittorio

16 Italian

Aïda	2	Loreley	2
The Barber of Seville	3	Lucia di Lammermoor	2
La Bohême	2	Madame Butterfly	4
Cavalleria Rusticana	2	I Pagliacci	2
Crispino e la Comare	1	Rigoletto	2
La Gioconda	2	La Tosca	2
Isabeau	2	La Traviata	2
Linda di Chamounix	4	Il Trovatore	3

13 French

Carmen	4	Romeo and Juliet	2
Le Chemineau	1	Samson and Delilah	3
Cléopatre	1	The Tales of Hoffman	1
Faust	3	William Tell	2
Gismonda	2	Thaïs	2
Manon	2	Werther	2
Monna Vanna	1		

SEASON 1919–1920—CHICAGO OPERA ASSOCIATION

BOARD OF DIRECTORS

Robert Allerton
Giulio Bolognesi
R. T. Crane, Jr.
Charles G. Dawes
Stanley Field
E. R. Graham
Charles L. Hutchinson
Samuel Insull
S. R. Kaufman

L. B. Kuppenheimer
Cyrus H. McCormick
Harold F. McCormick
John J. Mitchell
Max Pam
Martin A. Ryerson
John G. Shedd
Frank D. Stout
Edward F. Swift

EXECUTIVE COMMITTEE

Max Pam, Chairman
R. T. Crane, Jr.
Stanley Field
Samuel Insull

Harold F. McCormick
John J. Mitchell
Frank D. Stout
Edward F. Swift

OFFICERS

Harold F. McCormick .... President
Charles G. Dawes .... Vice-President
Max Pam .... Vice-President
Stanley Field .... Secretary
Charles L. Hutchinson .... Treasurer

ADMINISTRATION

Cleofonte Campanini .... General Director
Herbert M. Johnson .... Business Comptroller

Conductors
  Campanini, Cleofonte
  De Angelis, Teofilo
  Marinuzzi, Gino
  Charlier, Marcel
  Hasselmans, Louis
  Smallens, Alexander

Stage Director
  Speck, Jules

Stage Manager
  Engel, Joseph C.
  Katzman, Samuel (Assistant)

Chorus Master
  Nepoti, Pietro

Ballet Masters
  Pavley, Andreas
  Oukrainsky, Serge
  Bolm, Adolph

Assistant Conductor
  Bigalli, Dino (Librarian)

Technical Director
  Beatty, Harry W.

Scenic Artist
  Donigan, Peter J.

Orchestra Manager
  Raffaelli, Joseph

Season
  Tuesday, November 16, 1919, to
  Saturday, January 24, 1920.
  66 Performances
  2 Concerts (John McCormack)
  35 Operas
  3 Ballets

Sopranos
  Brown, Beryl
  Darch, Edna
  Follis, Dorothy
  Gall, Yvonne
  Galli-Curci, Amelita
  Garden, Mary
  Herbert, Evelyn
  Jardon, Dorothy
  Langaard, Borghild
  Macbeth, Florence
  Miura, Tamaki
  Morgana, Nina
  Namara, Marguerite
  Noe, Emma
  de Phillippe, Dora
  Raisa, Rosa
  Sharlow, Myrna

Contraltos
  D'Alvarez, Marguerite
  Claessens, Maria
  Correnti, Anna
  Eubank, Lillian
  Hager, Mina
  Pavloska, Irene
  Slade, Louise Harrison
  Van Gordon, Cyrena

Tenors
  Bonci, Alessandro
  Boardman, Arthur
  Daddi, Francesco
  Dolci, Alessandro
  Fontaine, Charles
  Johnson, Edward
  Lamont, Forrest
  Mojica, Jose
  Oliviero, Lodovico
  Rogerson, William

Tenors (Cont'd)
Schipa, Tito
O'Sullivan, John
Warnery, Edmond

Baritones
Baklanoff, Georges
Defrere, Desiré
Dufranne, Hector
Galeffi, Carlo
Landesman, Bernard
Maguenat, Alfred

Baritones (Cont'd)
Rimini, Giacomo
Ruffo, Titta

Bassos
Arimondi, Vittorio
Blanchart, Ramon
Cotreuil, Edouard
Huberdeau, Gustave
Lazzari, Virgilio
Nicolay, Constantin
Trevisan, Vittorio

20 Italian

Aïda	2	Madame Butterfly	5
A Masked Ball	3	La Nave	2
The Barber of Seville	2	Norma	2
La Bohême	3	I Pagliacci	2
Don Pasquale	2	Rigoletto	3
L'Elisir d'Amore	2	Suor Angelica	3
Fedora	3	La Sonnambula	3
Gianni Schicchi	3	Il Tabarro	3
Hamlet	1	La Traviata	1
Lucia di Lammermoor	3	Tosca	2

14 French

Carmen	1	Louise	1
Le Chemineau	2	Mme. Chrysantheme	2
Cléopatre	1	Manon	1
Faust	1	Monna Vanna	1
Hérodiade	3	Pelléas and Mélisande	1
L'Heure Espagnol	1	Thaïs	1
Le Jongleur de Nôtre Dame	1	Le Vieil Aigle	1

1 English

Rip Van Winkle 3

SEASON 1920–1921—CHICAGO OPERA ASSOCIATION

BOARD OF DIRECTORS

Monday, January 17, 1921

Mary Garden .... General Director
Jacques Coini .... Stage Director
George M. Spangler .... Business Manager

Conductors
Marinuzzi, Gino
Cimini, Pietro
Morin, Henri
Santini, Gabriel
Smallens, Alexander

Stage Director
Francioli, Romeo

Stage Managers
Engel, Joseph C.
Raybaut, Luigi
Katzman, Samuel (Assistant)

Chorus Master
Bernabini, Attico
Bigalli, Dino (Assistant)

Ballet Masters
Pavley, Andreas
Oukrainsky, Serge
McRae, Elma (Assistant)

Assistant Conductors
Bellini, Renato
Lauwers, Charles
Ruffo, Ettore
St. Leger, Frank

Technical Director
Beatty, Harry W.

Scenic Artist
Dové, Julian

Orchestra Manager
Raffaelli, Joseph

Season
Wednesday, November 17, 1920,
to Saturday, January 22, 1921.
70 Performances
34 Operas
Sunday, December 19, 1920:
Campanini Memorial Concert.

Sopranos
Carrara, Olga
Craft, Marcella
Diemer, Elsa
Francis, Dorothy
Gall, Yvonne
Galli-Curci, Amelita
Garden, Mary
Goudard, Marcelle
Macbeth, Florence
Maxwell, Margery

Sopranos (Cont'd)
Raisa, Rosa
Storchio, Rosina

Contraltos
Besanzoni, Gabriella
Claessens, Maria
Falco, Philine
Gannon, Rose
Paperte, Frances
Pascova, Carmen
Van Gordon, Cyrena

Tenors
Bonci, Alessandro
Hislop, Joseph
Johnson, Edward
Lamont, Forrest
Marshall, Charles
Martin, Riccardo
Mojica, Jose
Muratore, Lucien
Oliviero, Lodovico

Tenors (Cont'd)
Paillaird, Albert
Schipa, Tito

Baritones
Baklanoff, Georges
Civai, Sallustio
Defrere, Desiré
Dufranne, Hector
Galeffi, Carlo
Kreidler, Louis
Landesman, Bernard
Rimini, Giacomo
Ruffo, Titta

Bassos
Bitterl, Carl
Cotreuil, Edouard
Dentale, Teofile
Lazzari, Virgilio
Nicolay, Constantin
Trevisan, Vittorio

23 Italian

Aïda	2	Linda di Chamounix	2
L'Amore dei Tre Re	2	Lucia di Lammermoor	2
Andrea Chenier	2	Madame Butterfly	3
The Barber of Seville	2	Mignon	1
La Bohême	2	Otello	2
Cavalleria Rusticana	3	I Pagliacci	4
Edipo Re	3	Rigoletto	2
L'Elisir d'Amore	2	La Tosca	4
Falstaff	1	La Traviata	3
Gianni Schicchi	3	Il Trovatore	2
Jacquerie	3	La Sonnambula	1
The Jewels of the Madonna	4		

9 French

Aphrodite	1	Manon	1
Carmen	2	Monna Vanna	2
Le Chemineau	2	Romeo and Juliet	2
Faust	1	The Tales of Hoffman	2
Lakmé	3		

1 English

Lohengrin ... 3

1 German

Die Walküre ... 2

SEASON 1921-1922—CHICAGO OPERA ASSOCIATION

BOARD OF DIRECTORS

Robert Allerton
Giulio Bolognesi
R. T. Crane, Jr.
Charles G. Dawes
Stanley Field
E. R. Graham
Charles L. Hutchinson
Samuel Insull
S. R. Kaufman

L. B. Kuppenheimer
Cyrus H. McCormick
Harold F. McCormick
John J. Mitchell
Max Pam
Martin A. Ryerson
John G. Shedd
Frank D. Stout
Edward F. Swift

EXECUTIVE COMMITTEE

Charles G. Dawes, Chairman
R. T. Crane, Jr.
Stanley Field
Samuel Insull

Harold F. McCormick
John J. Mitchell
Frank D. Stout
Edward F. Swift

OFFICERS

Harold F. McCormick .... President
Charles G. Dawes .... Vice-President
Max Pam .... Vice-President
Stanley Field .... Secretary
Charles L. Hutchinson .... Treasurer

ADMINISTRATION

Mary Garden .... General Director
George M. Spangler .... } Business Managers
Clark A. Shaw .... }

Conductors
Polacco, Giorgio
Cimini, Pietro
Ferrari, Angelo
Smallens, Alexander

Stage Director
Coini, Jacques

Stage Managers
Engel, Joseph C.
Raybaut, Luigi
Saks, Mischa (Assistant)

Chorus Master
Nepoti, Pietro

Ballet Masters
Pavley, Andreas
Oukrainsky, Serge

Assistant Conductors
Bigalli, Dino
Bianchi-Rosa, Gino
Lauwers, Charles
Spadoni, Giacomo
St. Leger, Frank
Van Grove, Isaac

Technical Director
Beatty, Harry W.

Scenic Artist
Dové, Julian F.

Orchestra Manager
Raffaelli, Joseph

Season
Monday, November 14, 1921, to
Saturday, January 21, 1922.

Season (Cont'd)
  67 Performances
  29 Operas
  1 Ballet
  5 Concerts

Sopranos
  Dusseau, Jeanne
  Dux, Claire
  Galli-Curci, Amelita
  Garden, Mary
  Goodman, Melba
  d'Hermanoy, Alice
  Ivogun, Maria
  Koshetz, Nina
  Kottlar, Beatrice
  McCormic, Mary
  Mason, Edith
  Namara, Marguerite
  Raisa, Rosa
  Schneider, Jeanne

Contraltos
  D'Alvarez, Marguerite
  Claessens, Maria
  Falco, Philine
  Paperte, Frances
  Pavloska, Irene
  Reynolds, Eleanor
  Van Gordon, Cyrena

Tenors
  Dua, Octave
  Johnson, Edward

Tenors (Cont'd)
  Lamont, Forrest
  Lappas, Ulysses
  Marshall, Charles
  Martin, Riccardo
  Mojica, Jose
  Muratore, Lucien
  Oliviero, Lodovico
  Pattiera, Tino
  Ritch, Theodore
  Rocca, Antonio
  Schipa, Tito
  Schubert, Richard

Baritones
  Baklanoff, Georges
  Ballester, Vicente
  Beck, William
  Civai, Sallustio
  Defrere, Desiré
  Dufranne, Hector
  Maguenat, Alfred
  Rimini, Giacomo
  Schwarz, Joseph

Bassos
  Cotreuil, Edouard
  Lankow, Edward
  Lazzari, Virgilio
  Nicolay, Constantin
  Payan, Paul
  Trevisan, Vittorio
  Uhl, Jerome
  Wolf, James

13 Italian

Aïda	3	Madame Butterfly	4
L'Amore dei Tre Re	3	Otello	2
The Barber of Seville	2	I Pagliacci	1
La Bohême	3	Rigoletto	4
The Girl of the Golden West	1	La Tosca	4
Lucia di Lammermoor	1	La Traviata	2
The Jewels of the Madonna	2		

13 French

Carmen	3	Monna Vanna	3
Faust	1	Pélleas and Mélisande	2
Le Jongleur de Nôtre Dame	3	Romeo and Juliet	3
Lakmé	1	Salome	2
Love for the Three Oranges	2	Samson and Delilah	2
Louise	1	Thaïs	2
Manon	1		

3 German

Lohengrin	1	Tristan and Isolde	2
Tannhäuser	5		

SEASON 1922–1923—CHICAGO CIVIC OPERA COMPANY

OFFICERS

Mr. Samuel Insull .... President
Mr. Charles G. Dawes .... Vice-President
Mr. Richard T. Crane, Jr. .... Vice-President
Mr. Charles L. Hutchinson .... Treasurer
Mr. Stanley Field .... Secretary

BOARD OF TRUSTEES

Mr. Robert Allerton	Mr. L. B. Kuppenheimer
Mrs. Jacob Baur	Mr. Cyrus Hall McCormick
Mr. R. T. Crane, Jr.	Mr. Harold F. McCormick
Mr. Charles G. Dawes	Mrs. Rockefeller McCormick
Mr. Stanley Field	Mr. John J. Mitchell
Mr. Edward E. Gore	Mr. Joseph R. Noel
Mr. E. R. Graham	Mr. Max Pam
Mr. Charles L. Hutchinson	Mr. Martin A. Ryerson
Mr. Samuel Insull	Mr. John G. Shedd
Mr. Robert E. Kenyon	Mr. Frank D. Stout

Mr. Edward F. Swift

EXECUTIVE COMMITTEE

Mr. Samuel Insull, Chairman	Mr. E. R. Graham
Mrs. Jacob Baur	Mr. Charles L. Hutchinson
Mr. R. T. Crane, Jr.	Mrs. Rockefeller McCormick
Mr. Charles G. Dawes	Mr. Joseph R. Noel
Mr. Edward E. Gore	Mr. Martin A. Ryerson

Mr. Frank D. Stout

FINANCE COMMITTEE

Mr. Samuel Insull, Chairman	Mr. L. B. Kuppenheimer
Mr. Stanley Field, Vice-Chairman	Mr. John J. Mitchell

Mr. John G. Shedd

COMMITTEE ON MANAGEMENT

Mr. Samuel Insull .... President
Mr. Stanley Field .... Secretary
Mr. Clark A. Shaw .... Business Manager
Mr. Giorgio Polacco .... Musical Director

Conductors	Cimini, Pietro
Polacco, Giorgio	Hageman, Richard
Panizza, Ettore	

Stage Director
Merle-Forest, Emile

Stage Manager
Engel, Joseph C.

Chorus Master
Bernabini, Attico

Ballet Master
Bolm, Adolph

Assistant Conductors
St. Leger, Frank
Van Grove, Isaac
Spadoni, Giacomo
Lauwers, Charles
Bigalli, Dino (Librarian)

Technical Director
Beatty, Harry W.

Scenic Artist
Dové, Julian F.

Orchestra Manager
Raffaelli, Joseph

Season
Monday, November 13, 1922, to
Saturday, January 20, 1923.
70 Performances
1 Gala Performance
1 Concert
25 Operas

Sopranos
Eden, Hazel
Fitziu, Anna
Galli-Curci, Amelita
Garden, Mary
d'Hermanoy, Alice
Holst, Grace
Macbeth, Florence
McCormic, Mary

Sopranos (Cont'd)
Mason, Edith
Muzio, Claudia
Passmore, Malvena
Raisa, Rosa

Contraltos
Bourskaya, Ina
Browne, Kathryn
Cannon, Dorothy
Claessens, Maria
Correnti, Anna
Homer, Louise
Pavloska, Irene
Van Gordon, Cyrena

Tenors
Crimi, Giulio
Lamont, Forrest
Marshall, Charles
Martin, Riccardo
Minghetti, Angelo
Mojica, Jose
Oliviero, Lodovico
Schipa, Tito

Baritones
Baklanoff, Georges
Beck, William
Civai, Sallustio
Defrere, Desiré
Formichi, Cesare
Luka, Milo
Oster, Mark
Rimini, Giacomo

Bassos
Chaliapin, Feodor
Cotreuil, Edouard
Gould, Herbert
Lazzari, Virgilio
Steschenko, Ivan
Trevisan, Vittorio

18 Italian

Aïda	4	Lucia di Lammermoor	2
L'Amore dei Tre Re	3	Madame Butterfly	3
The Barber of Seville	1	Martha	2
La Bohême	3	Mefistofele	5
Cavalleria Rusticana	2	I Pagliacci	2
La Forza del Destino	2	Rigoletto	4
The Girl of the Golden West.	1	La Tosca	4
The Jewels of the Madonna	3	La Traviata	3
The Jewess	3	Il Trovatore	5

4 French

Carmen 5   Samson and Delilah 2
Manon 2   Sniegurotchka 6

1 English

Snowbird 1

2 German

Parsifal 3   Die Walküre 3

SEASON 1923–1924—CHICAGO CIVIC OPERA COMPANY

OFFICERS

Mr. Samuel Insull .... President
Mr. Charles G. Dawes .... Vice-President
Mr. L. B. Kuppenheimer .... Vice-President
Mr. Charles L. Hutchinson .... Treasurer
Mr. Stanley Field .... Secretary

BOARD OF TRUSTEES

Mr. Robert Allerton   Mrs. Rockefeller McCormick
Mrs. Jacob Baur   Mr. Harold F. McCormick
Mr. R. T. Crane, Jr.   Mrs. Arthur Meeker
Mr. Charles G. Dawes   Mr. John J. Mitchell
Mr. Stanley Field   Mr. Joseph R. Noel
Mr. E. R. Graham   Mr. Max Pam
Mr. Charles L. Hutchinson   Mr. Martin A. Ryerson
Mr. Samuel Insull   Mr. John G. Shedd
Mr. Robert E. Kenyon   Mr. Judson F. Stone
Mr. L. B. Kuppenheimer   Mr. Frank D. Stout
              Mr. Edward F. Swift

EXECUTIVE COMMITTEE

Mr. Samuel Insull, Chairman   Mr. L. B. Kuppenheimer
Mrs. Jacob Baur   Mrs. Rockefeller McCormick
Mr. Charles G. Dawes   Mr. Joseph R. Noel
Mr. E. R. Graham   Mr. Martin A. Ryerson
Mr. Charles L. Hutchinson   Mr. Judson F. Stone
              Mr. Frank D. Stout

FINANCE COMMITTEE

Mr. Samuel Insull, Chairman   Mr. L. B. Kuppenheimer
Mr. Stanley Field, Vice-Chairman   Mr. John J. Mitchell
              Mr. John G. Shedd

COMMITTEE ON MANAGEMENT

Mr. Samuel Insull .... President
Mr. Stanley Field .... Secretary
Mr. Herbert M. Johnson .... Assistant to the President
Mr. Clark A. Shaw .... Business Manager
Mr. Giorgio Polacco .... Musical Director

Conductors
Polacco, Giorgio
Panizza, Ettore
Cimini, Pietro

Stage Director
Merle-Forest, Emile

Stage Managers
Engel, Joseph C.
Defrere, Desiré (Assistant)
Drumheller, Charles H. (Assist.)

Chorus Master
Bernabini, Attico

Ballet Master
Bolm, Adolph

Première Danseuse
Ludmila, Anna

Assistant Conductors
Bigalli, Dino (Librarian)
Lauwers, Charles
Spadoni, Giacomo
St. Leger, Frank
Van Grove, Isaac

Technical Director
Beatty, Harry W.

Scenic Artist
Dové, Julian

Orchestra Manager
Raffaelli, Joseph

Season
Tuesday, November 8, 1923, to
Saturday, January 26, 1924.
84 Performances
1 Gala Concert
35 Operas

Sopranos
Brown, Beryl
Dux, Claire
Fabian, Mary
Galli-Curci, Amelita
Garden, Mary
Kerr, Elizabeth
d'Hermanoy, Alice
Macbeth, Florence
Mason, Edith

Sopranos (Cont'd)
Maxwell, Margery
Muzio, Claudia
Paggi, Tina
Pareto, Graziella
Sharlow, Myrna
Sherwood, Mabel
Raisa, Rosa
Westen, Lucie

Contraltos
Browne, Kathryn
Claessens, Maria
Fernanda, Doria
Gentle, Alice
Homer, Louise
Meisle, Kathryn
Pavloska, Irene
Steckiewicz, Tamara
Van Gordon, Cyrena

Tenors
Ansseau, Fernand
Crimi, Giulio
Errolle, Ralph
Hackett, Charles
Hart, Charles
Karolik, Maxim
Lamont, Forrest
Marshall, Charles
Minghetti, Angelo
Mojica, Jose
Oliviero, Lodovico
Piccaver, Alfred
Schipa, Tito
Steier, Harry

Baritones
Baklanoff, Georges
Beck, William
Defrere, Desiré
Formichi, Cesare
Gandolfi, Alfredo
Luki, Milo
Morelato, Gildo
Rimini, Giacomo
Schwarz, Joseph

Bassos
Chaliapin, Feodor
Cotreuil, Edouard
Kipnis, Alexander
Lazzari, Virgilio
Trevisan, Vittorio

19 Italian

Aïda 4	Il Maestro di Capella 1
L'Africana 3	Martha 4
Andrea Chenier 2	Mefistofele 4
The Barber of Seville 2	Otello 3
Boris Godunoff 4	I Pagliacci 2
Cavalleria Rusticana 3	Rigoletto 3
Dinorah 3	La Sonnambula 2
La Forza del Destino 2	La Traviata 3
The Jewess 4	Il Trovatore 2
Lucia di Lammermoor 4	

12 French

Carmen 4	Manon 2
Cléopatre 2	Monna Vanna 2
Faust 1	Romeo and Juliet 2
Le Jongleur de Nôtre Dame.... 2	Samson and Delilah 3
Lakmé 3	Sniegurotchka 3
Louise 3	Thaïs 2

2 English

Hansel and Gretel 5	Snowbird 1

2 German

Königskinder 2	Siegfried 2

SEASON 1924-1925—CHICAGO CIVIC OPERA COMPANY

OFFICERS
Mr. Samuel Insull .... President
Mr. Charles G. Dawes .... Vice-President
Mr. L. B. Kuppenheimer .... Vice-President
Mr. Stanley Field .... Secretary

BOARD OF TRUSTEES

EXECUTIVE COMMITTEE *(Cont'd)*

Mr. E. R. Graham
Mr. L. B. Kuppenheimer
Mrs. Rockefeller McCormick

Mr. Joseph R. Noel
Mr. Martin A. Ryerson
Mr. Frank D. Stout

FINANCE COMMITTEE

Mr. Samuel Insull, Chairman
Mr. Stanley Field, Vice-Chairman
Mr. John G. Shedd

Mr. L. B. Kuppenheimer
Mr. John J. Mitchell

COMMITTEE ON MANAGEMENT

Mr. Samuel Insull .... President
Mr. Stanley Field .... Secretary
Mr. Herbert M. Johnson .... Business Manager
Mr. Giorgio Polacco .... Musical Director

Conductors
Polacco, Giorgio
Moranzoni, Roberto
Cimini, Pietro

Stage Managers
Engel, Joseph C.
Defrere, Desiré
Drumheller, Charles (Assistant)

Chorus Master
Bernabini, Attico

Ballet Master
Oukrainsky, Serge

Premières Danseuses
Milar, Edris
Elisius, Vera
Shermont, Viola
Nemeroff, Maria

Assistant Conductors
Bigalli, Dino (Librarian)
Lauwers, Charles
Spadoni, Giacomo
St. Leger, Frank
Van Grove, Isaac
Weber, Henry G.

Technical Director
Beatty, Harry W.

Scenic Artist
Dové, Julian F.

Orchestra Manager
Raffaelli, Joseph

Season
Wednesday, November 5, 1924,
to Saturday, January 24, 1925.
98 Performances
1 Gala Performance
35 Operas
1 Ballet Divertissement
3 Concerts

Sopranos
Barr, Leila
Dal Monte, Toti
Derzbach, Helen
Freund, Helen
Forrai, Olga
Garden, Mary
d'Hermanoy, Alice
Hidalgo, Elvira
Kerr, Elizabeth
Macbeth, Florence
McCormic, Mary
Mason, Edith
Muzio, Claudia
Pareto, Graziella
Raisa, Rosa
Taylor, Louise
Westen, Louise

Contraltos
Claessens, Maria
Correnti, Anna

Contraltos (Cont'd)
Homer, Louise
Lenska, Augusta
Meisle, Kathryn
Orens, Edith
Perini, Flora
Swarthout, Gladys
Van Gordon, Cyrena

Tenors
Ansseau, Fernand
Boscassi, Romeo
Cortis, Antonio
Dneproff, Ivan
Hackett, Charles
Lamont, Forrest
Marshall, Charles
Mojica, Jose
Oliviero, Lodovico
Piccaver, Alfred
Schipa, Tito

Baritones
Baklanoff, Georges
Beck, William
Defrere, Desiré
Formichi, Cesare
Morelato, Gildo
Rimini, Giacomo
Schwarz, Joseph
Stabile, Mario
Stanbury, Douglas

Bassos
Chaliapin, Feodor
Cotreuil, Edouard
Kipnis, Alexander
Lazzari, Virgilio
Nicolich, Antonio
Trevisan, Vittorio

20 Italian

Aïda	8	Lucia di Lammermoor	4
L'Amore dei Tre Re	3	Madame Butterfly	3
The Barber of Seville	3	Martha	2
La Bohême	3	Mefistofele	3
Boris Godunoff	2	Otello	2
Cavalleria Rusticana	3	I Pagliacci	3
Fra Diavolo	2	Rigoletto	4
La Gioconda	4	La Tosca	5
The Jewels of the Madonna	2	La Traviata	4
The Jewess	1	Il Trovatore	3

13 French

Carmen	2	Le Prophête	2
Faust	2	Romeo and Juliet	1
Le Jongleur de Nôtre Dame	2	Samson and Delilah	3
Lakmé	3	The Tales of Hoffman	2
Louise	2	Thaïs	3
Pelléas and Mélisande	1	Werther	3
The Pearl Fishers	4		

1 English

Hansel and Gretel 2

1 German

Tannhäuser 4

SEASON 1925-1926—CHICAGO CIVIC OPERA COMPANY

OFFICERS

Mr. Samuel Insull .... President
Mr. Charles G. Dawes .... Vice-President
Mr. L. B. Kuppenheimer .... Vice-President
Mr. Stanley Field .... Secretary and Treasurer

BOARD OF TRUSTEES

Mr. Robert Allerton
Mrs. Jacob Baur
Mr. John Alden Carpenter
Mr. R. T. Crane, Jr.
Mr. Charles G. Dawes
Mr. William R. Dawes
Mr. Stanley Field
Mr. E. R. Graham
Mr. Samuel Insull
Mr. Robert E. Kenyon

Mr. L. B. Kuppenheimer
Mrs. Rockefeller McCormick
Mr. Harold F. McCormick
Mrs. Arthur Meeker
Mr. John J. Mitchell
Mr. Joseph R. Noel
Mr. Martin A. Ryerson
Mr. John G. Shedd
Mr. Frank D. Stout
Mr. Edward F. Swift

EXECUTIVE COMMITTEE

Mr. Samuel Insull, Chairman
Mrs. Jacob Baur
Mr. John Alden Carpenter
Mr. Charles G. Dawes
Mr. William R. Dawes
Mr. E. R. Graham

Mr. L. B. Kuppenheimer
Mrs. Rockefeller McCormick
Mr. Joseph R. Noel
Mr. Martin A. Ryerson
Mr. Frank D. Stout

FINANCE COMMITTEE

Mr. Samuel Insull, Chairman
Mr. Stanley Field, Vice-Chairman
Mr. John G. Shedd

Mr. L. B. Kuppenheimer
Mr. John J. Mitchell

COMMITTEE ON MANAGEMENT

Mr. Samuel Insull .... President
Mr. Stanley Field .... Secretary and Treasurer
Mr. Herbert M. Johnson .... Business Manager
Mr. Giorgio Polacco .... Musical Director

Conductors
  Polacco, Giorgio
  Moranzoni, Roberto
  Grovlez, Gabriel
  Weber, Henry G.

Stage Director
  Moor, Charles

Stage Managers
  Engel, Joseph C.

Defrere, Desiré
Drumheller, Charles (Assistant)

Chorus Master
  Bernabini, Attico

Ballet Master
  Oukrainsky, Serge

Premières Danseuses
  Samuels, Helene
  Shermont, Viola

Premières Danseuses (Cont'd)
Dobbins, Christine
Nemeroff, Maria

Assistant Conductors
Bigalli, Dino (Librarian)
Lauwers, Charles
Rubeling, Robert
Sabino, Antonio
St. Leger, Frank
Spadoni, Giacomo

Technical Director
Beatty, Harry W.

Scenic Artist
Dové, Julian F.

Orchestra Manager
Raffaelli, Joseph

Season
Tuesday, November 3, 1925, to
Saturday, January 23, 1926.
91 Performances
  1 Gala Performance
  4 Concerts
 32 Operas
  1 Ballet
  4 Concerts

Sopranos
Dal Monte, Toti
Fitziu, Anna
Forrai, Olga
Freund, Helen
Garden, Mary
Garrison, Mabel
d'Hermanoy, Alice
Kerr, Elizabeth
Macbeth, Florence
Mason, Edith
Melius, Luella
Miura, Tamaki

Sopranos (Cont'd)
Muzio, Claudia
Norelli, Stella
Raisa, Rosa
Sawyer, Eleanor
Shear, Clara

Contraltos
d'Alvarez, Marguerite
Claessens, Maria
Homer, Louise
Lenska, Augusta
Nadworny, Devora
Pavloska, Irene
Van Gordon, Cyrena

Tenors
Ansseau, Fernand
Cortis, Antonio
Hackett, Charles
Lamont, Forrest
Marshall, Charles
Mojica, Jose
Oliviero, Lodovico
Ritch, Theodore
Schipa, Tito

Baritones
Baklanoff, Georges
Beck, William
Bonelli, Richard
Defrere, Desiré
Formichi, Cesare
Morelato, Gildo
Rimini, Giacomo
Ruffo, Titta
Steel, Robert
Torti, Ernesto

Bassos
Cotreuil, Edouard
Kipnis, Alexander
Lazzari, Virgilio
Nicolich, Antonio
Trevisan, Vittorio

19 Italian

Aïda	4	The Jewess	1
Andrea Chenier	4	Lucia di Lammermoor	2
The Barber of Seville	4	Madame Butterfly	4
Boris Godunoff	2	A Masked Ball	3
Cavalleria Rusticana	3	Manon Lescaut	3
Falstaff	2	Martha	5

19 Italian (Cont'd)

Namiko San	3	La Tosca	4
Otello	3	La Traviata	5
I Pagliacci	5	Il Trovatore	4
Rigoletto	3		

8 French

Carmen	5	Pelléas and Mélisande	1
Faust	4	Resurrection	5
Hérodiade	2	Samson and Delilah	2
Louise	1	Werther	2

2 English

Hansel and Gretel	2	A Light from St. Agnes	1

3 German

Lohengrin	2	Die Walküre	2
Der Rosenkavalier	4		

SEASON 1926–1927—CHICAGO CIVIC OPERA COMPANY

OFFICERS

Mr. Samuel Insull .... President
Mr. Charles G. Dawes .... Vice-President
Mr. Louis B. Kuppenheimer .... Vice-President
Mr. Stanley Field .... Secretary and Treasurer

Conductors
Polacco, Giorgio
Moranzoni, Roberto
Weber, Henry G.
St. Leger, Frank

Stage Director
Moor, Charles

Stage Managers
Engel, Joseph C.
Defrere, Desiré
Drumheller, Charles H. (Asst.)

Chorus Master
Bernabini, Attico

Ballet Master
Oukrainsky, Serge

Premières Danseuses
Samuels, Helene
Shermont, Viola
Chapman, Evelyn
Nemeroff, Maria

Assistant Conductors
Bigalli, Dino (Librarian)
Sabino, Antonio
Lauwers, Charles
Spadoni, Giacomo

Technical Director
Beatty, Harry W.

Scenic Artist
Dové, Julian

Orchestra Manager
Raffaelli, Joseph

Season
Monday, November 8, 1926, to
Saturday, January 29, 1927.
91 Performances
1 Gala Performance
34 Operas
3 Concerts

Sopranos
Alsen, Elsa
Dal Monte, Toti
d'Hermanoy, Alice
Freund, Helen
Garden, Mary
Hamlin, Anna
Kurenko, Maria
Loring, Louise
Macbeth, Florence
Mason, Edith
Misgen, Florence
Muzio, Claudia
Norena, Eide
Raisa, Rosa
Sawyer, Eleanor
Shear, Clara

Contraltos
Claessens, Maria
Correnti, Anna
Jackson, Lorna Doone
Lenska, Augusta
Pavloska, Irene
Van Gordon, Cyrena

Tenors
Ansseau, Fernand
Cortis, Antonio
Hackett, Charles
Lamont, Forrest
Lindi, Aroldo
Marshall, Charles

Tenors (Cont'd)
Mojica, Jose
Oliviero, Lodovico
Rappaport, Albert
Ritch, Theodore
Schipa, Tito

Baritones
Bonelli, Richard
Defrere, Desiré
Formichi, Cesare
Montesanto, Luigi
Vanni-Marcoux

Baritones (Cont'd)
Morelato, Gildo
Polese, Giovanni
Preston, Howard
Rimini, Giacomo
Torti, Ernesto

Bassos
Cotreuil, Edouard
Kipnis, Alexander
Lazzari, Virgilio
Nicolich, Antonio
Trevisan, Vittorio

24 Italian

Aïda	5	The Jewess	5
L'Amore dei Tre Re	3	Lucia di Lammermoor	3
The Barber of Seville	3	Madame Butterfly	1
La Bohême	5	Martha	4
Boris Godunoff	1	A Masked Ball	1
Cavalleria Rusticana	2	Otello	3
La Cena della Beffe	3	I Pagliacci	2
The Daughter of the Regiment	3	Rigoletto	3
Don Giovanni	3	La Sonnambula	2
L'Elisir d'Amore	2	La Tosca	2
Gianni Schicchi	2	La Traviata	4
The Jewels of the Madonna	4	Il Trovatore	5

5 French

Carmen	6	Resurrection	3
Faust	1	Samson and Delilah	2
Judith	2		

3 English

Hansel and Gretel	1	The Witch of Salem	2
Tiefland	3		

2 German

Der Rosenkavalier	2	Tristan and Isolde	4

SEASON 1927–1928—CHICAGO CIVIC OPERA COMPANY

OFFICERS

Mr. Samuel Insull .... President
Mr. Charles G. Dawes .... Vice-President
Mr. L. B. Kuppenheimer .... Vice-President
Mr. Stanley Field .... Secretary and Treasurer

Season
  Thursday, November 3, 1927, to
  Saturday, January 28, 1928.
  102 Performances
    1 Gala Performance
    4 Concerts
    5 Performances in Milwaukee
   34 Operas
    3 Ballets

Sopranos
  Alsen, Elsa
  Dal Monte, Toti
  d'Hermanoy, Alice
  Elderkin, Eleanor
  Freund, Helen
  Garden, Mary
  Hamlin, Anna
  Kargau, Olga
  Kruse, Leone
  Macbeth, Florence
  Mason, Edith
  Meusel, Lucille
  Muzio, Claudia
  Norena, Eide
  Raisa, Rosa
  Samoiloff, Della
  Witwer, Kathryn

Contraltos
  Claessens, Maria
  Correnti, Anna
  Eberhart, Constance
  Jackson, Lorna Doone
  Lenska, Augusta
  Marlo, Elinor
  Meisle, Kathryn
  Pavloska, Irene

Contraltos (Cont'd)
  Van Gordon, Cyrena
  Rappold, Marie
  Sharlow, Myrna

Tenors
  Ansseau, Fernand
  Cortis, Antonio
  Hackett, Charles
  Lamont, Forrest
  Maison, Rene
  Marshall, Charles
  Mojica, Jose
  Oliviero, Lodovico
  Rappaport, Albert
  Schipa, Tito
  Sample, John

Baritones
  Bonelli, Richard
  Defrere, Desiré
  Formichi, Cesare
  Montesanto, Luigi
  Polese, Giovanni
  Preston, Howard
  Rimini, Giacomo
  Ringling, Robert
  Sandrini, Eugenio
  Schlusnus, Heinrich
  Vanni-Marcoux
  Morelato, Gildo

Bassos
  Baromeo, Chase
  Cotreuil, Edouard
  Kipnis, Alexander
  Lazzari, Virgilio
  Nicolich, Antonio
  Trevisan, Vittorio

19 Italian

Aïda	4	Madame Butterfly	4
The Barber of Seville	3	Martha	5
Cavalleria Rusticana	4	A Masked Ball	2
Falstaff	2	Otello	2
Gianni Schicchi	2	I Pagliacci	3
The Jewels of the Madonna	3	Rigoletto	3
La Gioconda	5	La Tosca	5
Linda di Chamounix	2	La Traviata	5
Loreley	4	Il Trovatore	5
Lucia di Lammermoor	3		

9 French

Carmen	3	Resurrection	1
Faust	6	Romeo and Juliet	1
Le Jongleur de Nôtre Dame	2	Samson and Delilah	1
Louise	4	Sapho	3
Monna Vanna	3		

4 English

Die Fledermaus	3	Snow Maiden	3
Hansel and Gretel	1	Witch of Salem	1

2 German

Lohengrin	3	Tannhäuser	6

SEASON 1928–1929—CHICAGO CIVIC OPERA COMPANY

OFFICERS

Mr. Samuel Insull .... President
Mr. Charles G. Dawes .... Vice-President
Mr. L. B. Kuppenheimer .... Vice-President
Mr. Stanley Field .... Secretary and Treasurer
Mr. John W. Evers, Jr. .... Assistant Secretary and Treasurer

BOARD OF TRUSTEES

Mr. Robert Allerton	Mr. Robert E. Kenyon
Mrs. Jacob Baur	Mr. L. B. Kuppenheimer
Mr. John Alden Carpenter	Mrs. Rockefeller McCormick
Mr. R. T. Crane, Jr.	Mr. Harold F. McCormick
Mr. Charles G. Dawes	Mrs. Arthur Meeker
Mr. Samuel A. Ettelson	Mr. Joseph R. Noel
Mr. Stanley Field	Mr. Martin A. Ryerson
Mr. John F. Gilchrist	Mrs. Charles H. Schweppe
Mr. E. R. Graham	Mr. Edward F. Swift
Mr. Samuel Insull	Mr. Herman Waldeck

Mr. Frank F. Winans
(as President of the Chicago Association of Commerce)

FINANCE COMMITTEE

Mr. Samuel Insull, Chairman	Mr. E. R. Graham
Mr. Stanley Field, Vice-Chairman	Mr. L. B. Kuppenheimer
Mr. John F. Gilchrist	

EXECUTIVE COMMITTEE

Mrs. Jacob Baur	Mr. E. R. Graham
Mr. John Alden Carpenter	Mr. L. B. Kuppenheimer
Mr. Charles G. Dawes	Mrs. Rockefeller McCormick
Mr. Stanley Field	Mr. Joseph R. Noel

EXECUTIVE COMMITTEE (*Cont'd*)

Mr. Martin A. Ryerson
Mr. Frank F. Winans (ex-officio)
Mr. Samuel Insull, Chairman (ex-officio)

COMMITTEE ON MANAGEMENT

Mr. Samuel Insull .... President
Mr. Stanley Field .... Secretary and Treasurer
Mr. Herbert M. Johnson .... Business Manager
Mr. Giorgio Polacco .... Musical Director

Conductors
Polacco, Giorgio
Moranzoni, Roberto
Weber, Henry G.
Lauwers, Charles

Stage Director
Moor, Charles

Chorus Master
Bernabini, Attico

Premières Danseuses
Stewart, Muriel
Yurieva, Maria

Soloists
Barashkova, Julia
Lundgren, Harriet
Pryor, Ruth
Swoboda, Vechslav
Caton, Edward

Assistant Conductors
Bigalli, Dino (Librarian)
Giuranna, Mario
Somma, Guglielmo
Spadoni, Giacomo
Tyroler, William

Stage Manager
Defrere, Desiré
Drumheller, Charles H.
(Assistant)

Technical Director
Beatty, Harry W.

Scenic Artist
Dové, Julian

Orchestra Manager
Raffaelli, Joseph

Season
Wednesday, October 31, 1928, to
Saturday, January 26, 1929.
97 Performances
4 Performances in Milwaukee
32 Operas
1 Ballet Divertissement

Sopranos
Burke, Hilda
Claire, Marion
Consoli, Antonietta
d'Hermanoy, Alice
Freund, Helen
Garden, Mary
Kerr, Elizabeth
Leider, Frida
Mason, Edith
Meusel, Lucille
Mock, Alice
Muzio, Claudia (on leave)
Platt, Clara
Raisa, Rosa
Salvi, Margherita
Turner, Eva

Contraltos
Claessens, Maria
Eberhart, Constance
Glade, Coe
Olszewska, Maria
Paggi, Ada
Pavloska, Irene
Van Gordon, Cyrena

Tenors
   Cavadore, Giuseppe
   Cortis, Antonio
   Hackett, Charles
   Lamont, Forrest
   Maison, Rene
   Marshall, Charles
   Mojica, Jose
   Oliviero, Lodovico
   Schipa, Tito

Baritones
   Bonelli, Richard
   Defrere, Desiré
   Formichi, Cesare
   Hill, Barre

Baritones (Cont'd)
   Montesanto, Luigi
   Preston, Howard
   Rimini, Giacomo
   Ringling, Robert
   Sandrini, Eugenio
   Schipper, Emil
   Vanni-Marcoux

Bassos
   Baromeo, Chase
   Cotreuil, Edouard
   Kipnis, Alexander
   Lazzari, Virgilio
   Nicolich, Antonio
   Trevisan, Vittorio

19 Italian

Aïda	6	Madame Butterfly	2
L'Amore dei Tre Re	2	A Masked Ball	3
La Bohême	5	The Marriage of Figaro	3
The Barber of Seville	5	Norma	2
Boris Godunoff	4	Otello	3
Cavalleria Rusticana	6	I Pagliacci	4
Don Giovanni	3	Rigoletto	5
Don Pasquale	1	La Tosca	1
L'Elisir d'Amore	3	Il Trovatore	2
The Jewess	2		

10 French

Carmen	5	Romeo and Juliet	3
Faust	2	Samson and Delilah	4
Judith	2	Sapho	2
Lakmé	2	Thaïs	2
Pelléas and Mélisande	2	The Tales of Hoffman	4

3 German

Lohengrin	4	Die Walküre	5
Der Rosenkavalier	3		

THE CHICAGO COMPANIES ON TOUR

TOTAL TOUR PERFORMANCES BY CITIES

Akron, Ohio	5	Chattanooga, Tennessee	14
Amarillo, Texas	1	Cincinnati, Ohio	26
Baltimore, Maryland	47	Cleveland, Ohio	32
Birmingham, Alabama	9	Columbus, Ohio	8
Boston, Massachusetts	143	Dallas, Texas	26
Brooklyn, New York	1	Denver, Colorado	21
Buffalo, New York	8	Des Moines, Iowa	5
Butte, Montana	1	Detroit, Michigan	26

TOTAL TOUR PERFORMANCES BY CITIES (*Cont'd*)

El Paso, Texas	4	Phoenix, Arizona	2
Fort Wayne, Indiana	1	Pittsburgh, Pennsylvania	32
Fort Worth, Texas	5	Portland, Oregon	21
Fresno, California	2	Rochester, New York	1
Helena, Montana	1	Sacramento, California	3
Houston, Texas	10	St. Joseph, Missouri	1
Indianapolis, Indiana	1	St. Louis, Missouri	24
Jackson, Mississippi	4	St. Paul, Minnesota	22
Joplin, Missouri	1	Salt Lake City, Utah	1
Kansas City, Missouri	13	San Antonio, Texas	11
Lincoln, Nebraska	2	San Diego, California	1
Little Rock, Arkansas	2	San Francisco, California	73
Los Angeles, California	45	Shreveport, Louisiana	2
Memphis, Tennessee	10	Seattle, Washington	17
Miami, Florida	9	Sioux City, Iowa	2
Milwaukee, Wisconsin	44	Sioux Falls, South Dakota	2
Minneapolis, Minnesota	13	Spokane, Washington	1
Nashville, Tennessee	1	Springfield, Illinois	2
New Orleans, Louisiana	2	Tulsa, Oklahoma	12
New York City, New York	216	Washington, D. C.	20
Oakland, California	8	Wichita, Kansas	7
Oklahoma City, Oklahoma	5	Wichita Falls, Texas	2
Omaha, Nebraska	3		
Peoria, Illinois	2	Total Tour Performances	1225
Philadelphia, Pennsylvania	189		

AKRON, OHIO
Season 1926–1927

March 22 (matinée) .... Rigoletto
March 22 (night) .... Il Trovatore

Season 1927–1928

February 14 .... Aïda
February 15 (matinée) ....Hansel and Gretel
February 15 (night) .... La Traviata

AMARILLO, TEXAS
Season 1928–1929

March 18 .... Thaïs

BALTIMORE, MARYLAND
Season 1910-1911

January 27 .... Aïda
February 2 .... The Tales of Hoffman
February 9 .... The Girl of the Golden West
February 16 .... Carmen
February 23 .... Les Huguenots
March 2 .... Thaïs
March 9 .... Natoma
March 16 .... La Bohème
March 23 ....·.................... Lucia di Lammermoor
March 30 ......The Secret of Susanne, and Le Jongleur de Nôtre Dame

Season 1911-1912

November 7 .... Thaïs
November 9 .... The Marriage of Figaro
November 16 .... Samson and Delilah
February 15 .... Die Walküre
February 22 .... The Jewels of the Madonna
February 29 .... Lohengrin
March 7 .... The Secret of Susanne and I Pagliacci and Ballet
March 21 .... Aïda
March 22 .... Tristan and Isolde

Season 1912–1913

November 1 .... Carmen
November 8 .... Aïda
November 15 .... Manon Lescaut
November 22 .... Mignon
February 7 .... Lucia di Lammermoor
February 14 .... La Tosca
May 1 .... Hansel and Gretel

Season 1913–1914

November 7 .... Rigoletto
November 14 .... La Bohême
November 21 .... La Tosca
February 6 .... Madame Butterfly
February 13 .... Die Walküre
February 20 .... The Tales of Hoffman
February 27 .... The Jewels of the Madonna

Season 1920-1921

March 7 .... Monna Vanna
March 8 .... La Traviata
March 9 .... Otello

Season 1921-1922

March 6 ....L'Amore dei Tre Re
March 7 .... Tannhäuser
March 8 .... La Bohême

Season 1924–1925

February 11 .... Thaïs
February 12 .... Mefistofele
February 14 .... La Gioconda

Season 1925–1926

February 8 .... La Tosca
February 11 .... A Masked Ball

Season 1926–1927
February 14 .... Aïda
February 15 .... Resurrection
February 17 .... Tristan and Isolde

BIRMINGHAM, ALABAMA
Season 1925–1926
March 1 .... Aïda
March 2 .... La Traviata
March 3 .... Thaïs

Season 1926–1927
February 28 .... Il Trovatore
March 1 (matinée) .... Resurrection
March 1 (night) .... La Tosca

Season 1928–1929
February 22 .... Norma
February 23 (matinée) .... Carmen
February 23 (night) .... Faust

BOSTON, MASS.
Season 1917-1918
February 18 .... Aïda
February 20 (matinée) .... Carmen
February 20 (night) .... Lucia di Lammermoor
February 21 .... Isabeau
February 22 (matinée) .... Rigoletto
February 22 (night) .... Thaïs
February 23 (matinée) .... Faust
February 23 (night) .... Cavalleria Rusticana and I Pagliacci
February 25 (matinée) .... Dinorah
February 25 (night) .... Manon
February 27 (matinée) .... La Bohême
February 27 (night) .... The Jewels of the Madonna
February 28 .... The Barber of Seville
March 1 .... Romeo and Juliet
March 2 (matinée) .... La Traviata
March 2 (night) .... Aïda

Season 1919–1920
March 1 .... La Gioconda
March 2 .... La Traviata
March 3 .... Aphrodite
March 4 .... Aïda
March 5 ".................................Pelléas and Mélisande
March 6 (matinée) .... L'Elisir d'Amore
March 6 (night) ....L'Heure Espagnole and I Pagliacci
March 7 .... Concert at Symphony Hall
March 8 .... Louise
March 9 .... Il Tabarro, Suor Angelica and Gianni Schicchi

Season 1919-1920 *(Cont'd)*

March 10 .... Rigoletto
March 11 .... Thaïs
March 12 ....Don Pasquale and Boudour (ballet)
March 13 (matinée) .... Carmen
March 13 (night) .... A Masked Ball

Season 1922-1923

January 22 .... Aïda
January 23 .... La Tosca
January 24 (matinée) .... Rigoletto
January 24 (night) .... Cavalleria Rusticana and I Pagliacci
January 25 ....L'Amore dei Tre Re
January 26 .... Die Walküre
January 27 (matinée) .... La Bohême
January 27 (night) .... Il Trovatore
January 29 ....L'Amore dei Tre Re
January 30 .... Parsifal
January 31 (matinée) .... Snow Maiden
January 31 (night .... La Tosca
February 1 .... Die Walküre
February 2 .... Madame Butterfly
February 3 (matinée) .... Carmen
February 3 (night) .... The Jewels of the Madonna

Season 1923-1924

January 28 .... L'Africana
January 29 .... Louise
January 30 (matinée) .... Snow Maiden
January 30 (night) .... The Barber of Seville
January 31 .... Siegfried
February 1 .... Carmen
February 2 (matinée) ....Boris Godunoff
February 2 (night) .... Faust
February 4 .... Mefistofele
February 5 .... Louise
February 6 (matinée) ....La Traviata
February 6 (night) .... Carmen
February 7 .... Boris Godunoff
February 8 .... Manon
February 9 (matinée)..Jongleur de Nôtre Dame and Maestro di Capella
February 9 (night) .... Otello

Season 1924-1925

January 26 .... Aïda
January 27 .... Louise
January 28 (matinée) .... Boris Godunoff
January 28 (night) .... La Bohême
January 29 .... Tannhäuser
January 30 .... Carmen
January 31 (matinée) ....Romeo and Juliet

Season 1924–1925 (*Cont'd*)

January 31 (night) .... La Tosca
February 2 .... Faust
February 3 .... Thaïs
February 4 (matinée) .... Madame Butterfly
February 4 (night) .... Rigoletto
February 5 ....L'Amore dei Tre Re
February 6 .... The Barber of Seville
February 7 (matinée) ....Pelléas and Mélisande
February 7 (night) .... The Jewels of the Madonna

Season 1925–1926

January 25 .... Andrea Chenier
January 26 .... Die Walküre
January 27 (matinée) .... Carmen
January 27 (night) .... La Traviata
January 28 .... Der Rosenkavalier
January 29 .... Thaïs
January 30 (matinée) .... Faust
January 30 (night) .... A Masked Ball
February 1 .... Falstaff
February 2 ....Pelléas and Mélisande
February 3 (matinée) .... Lohengrin
February 3 (night) .... Hérodiade
February 4 .... Manon Lescaut
February 5 .... Resurrection
February 6 (matinée) ....Samson and Delilah
February 6 (night) .... Il Trovatore

Season 1926–1927

January 31 .... Aïda
February 1 .... Resurrection
February 2 (matinée) .... Faust
February 2 (night) .... The Jewels of the Madonna
February 3 ....La Cena della Beffe
February 4 ·······························Tristan and Isolde
February 5 (matinée) ....Pelléas and Mélisande
February 5 (night) .... Lucia di Lammermoor
February 7 .... Boris Godunoff
February 8 .... The Daughter of the Regiment and I Pagliacci
February 9 (matinée) .... Carmen
February 9 (night) .... Rigoletto
February 10 .... Don Giovanni
February 11 .... Judith and Gianni Schicchi
February 12 (matinée) .... La Bohême
February 12 (night) .... Il Trovatore

Season 1927–1928

January 30 .... La Gioconda
January 31 .... Sapho
February 1 (matinée) .... Lohengrin
February 1 (night) ....La Tosca and Les Sylphides (ballet)

Season 1927–1928 (*Cont'd*)

February 2 .... The Witch of Salem and I Pagliacci
February 3 Le Jongleur de Nôtre Dame and Caprice Espagnole (ballet)
February 4 (matinée).............................Romeo and Juliet
February 4 (night) .... Aïda
February 6 .... Louise
February 7 .... The Jewels of the Madonna
February 8 (matinée) .... Carmen
February 8 (night) .... Tannhäuser
February 9 .... Martha
February 10 .... La Traviata
February 11 (matinée)..........................Samson and Delilah
February 11 (night) .... Rigoletto

Season 1928–1929

January 28 .... Lohengrin
January 29 .... Don Pasquale and Judith
January 30 (matinée) ....La Bohême
January 30 (night) .... Aïda
January 31 .... Die Walküre
February 1 .... Lakmé
February 2 (matinée) ....Boris Godunoff
February 2 (night) .... Thaïs
February 4 .... The Marriage of Figaro
February 5 .... Carmen
February 6 (matinée) ....Pelléas and Mélisande
February 6 (night) .... Otello
February 7 .... Der Rosenkavalier
February 8 .... L'Amore dei Tre Re
February 9 (matinée) ....Madame Butterfly
February 9 (night) .... Lucia di Lammermoor

BROOKLYN, NEW YORK
Season 1910–1911

November 14 .... Thaïs

BUFFALO, NEW YORK
Season 1925–1926

February 22 .... Aïda
February 23 .... Thaïs

Season 1926–1927

February 21 .... Il Trovatore
February 22 .... Resurrection
February 23 .... La Traviata

Season 1928–1929

February 11 .... Faust
February 12 .... Lohengrin
February 14 .... Sapho—Ballet

BUTTE, MONTANA
Season 1912-1913
April 8 .... Thaïs

CHATTANOOGA, TENNESSEE
Season 1923-1924
February 22 .... The Jewess
February 23 (matinée) .... Cléopatre
February 23 (night) .... Mefistofele

Season 1924-1925
February 23 .... Thaïs
February 24 (matinée) .... Boris Godunoff
February 24 (night) .... Tannhäuser

Season 1925-1926
February 26 .... Aïda
February 27 (matinée) .... Carmen
February 27 (night) .... La Traviata

Season 1926-1927
February 25 .... Il Trovatore
February 26 (matinée) .... Madame Butterfly
February 26 (night) ....A Masked Ball

Season 1927-1928
February 23 .... Resurrection
February 24 .... Cavalleria Rusticana and I Pagliacci

CINCINNATI, OHIO
Season 1911-1912
February 6 .... Natoma
February 7 (matinée).....The Secret of Susanne and Hansel and Gretel
February 7 (night) ....Tristan and Isolde

Season 1912-1913
November 25 .... Aïda
April 26 (matinée) ....Le Jongleur de Nôtre Dame
April 26 (night) .... Die Walküre
April 27 .... Concert
April 28 .... Rigoletto
April 29 .... The Jewels of the Madonna

Season 1919-1920
March 19 .... Lucia di Lammermoor
March 20 (matinée) ....Cavalleria Rusticana and I Pagliacci
March 20 (night) .... La Tosca

Season 1920–1921

March 18 .... Lohengrin
March 19 (matinée) .... Rigoletto
March 19 (night) .... Monna Vanna

Season 1923–1924

February 21 (matinée) .... Salome
February 21 (night) .... Boris Godunoff

Season 1924–1925

March 9 .... Mefistofele
March 10 .... Thaïs
March 11 .... Romeo and Juliet
March 12 .... La Gioconda

Season 1925–1926

February 24 .... Aïda
February 25 (matinée) .... Louise
February 25 (night) .... Der Rosenkavalier

Season 1926–1927

February 24 (matinée) ....La Bohême
February 24 (night) .... Resurrection

CLEVELAND, OHIO
Season 1910–1911

January 19 ....Cavalleria Rusticana and I Pagliacci

Season 1911–1912

November 20 .... Thaïs
November 21 (matinée) .... Hansel and Gretel
November 21 (night) .... Lucia di Lammermoor
February 8 (matinée) .... The Tales of Hoffman
February 8 (night) .... Gala Performance

Season 1913–1914

March 2 (matinée) ....The Jewels of the Madonna
March 2 (night) .... La Tosca

Season 1919–1920

March 25 ....L'Amore dei Tre Re
March 26 .... Lucia di Lammermoor
March 27 (matinée).............. Cavalleria Rusticana and I Pagliacci
March 27 (night) .... La Tosca

Season 1920–1921

March 14 .... Monna Vanna
March 15 .... Lohengrin
March 16 .... La Traviata
March 17 .... Rigoletto

Season 1923–1924
February 11 .... The Jewess
February 12 .... Mefistofele
February 13 .... Salome
February 14 .... Cavalleria Rusticana and I Pagliacci

Season 1924–1925
February 19 .... La Gioconda
February 20 .... The Barber of Seville
February 21 (matinée) .... Thaïs
February 21 (night) .... Tannhäuser

Season 1925–1926
February 15 .... La Tosca
February 16 .....:.............................. Madame Butterfly
February 17 .... Martha
February 18 ....:. Die Walküre
February 19 (matinée) .... Hansel and Gretel
February 19 (night) .... Otello
February 20 (matinée) .... Carmen
February 20 (night) .... Lucia di Lammermoor

COLUMBUS, OHIO
Season 1912–1913
April 30 (matinée) .... Hansel and Gretel
April 30 (night) .... Lucia di Lammermoor

Season 1927–1928
February 20 .... Aïda
February 21 .... Resurrection
February 22 .... Rigoletto

Season 1928–1929
February 18 .... Faust
February 19 .... Thaïs
February 20 .... Carmen

DALLAS, TEXAS
Season 1912–1913
February 28 (matinée) .... Hansel and Gretel and I Pagliacci
February 28 (night) .... Thaïs
March 1 (matinée) .... Die Walküre
March 1 (night) .... Lucia di Lammermoor

Season 1913–1914
March 4 .... Rigoletto
March 5 .... La Bohême
March 6 .... La Tosca
March 7 (matinée) ....Cavalleria Rusticana and I Pagliacci
March 7 (night) .... Aïda

Season 1920–1921

March 23 .... Carmen
March 24 .... Lohengrin
March 26 (matinée) .... La Traviata
March 26 (night) .... Cavalleria Rusticana and I Pagliacci

Season 1923–1924

February 29 .... The Jewess
March 1 (matinée) .... Mefistofele
March 1 (night) .... Salome

Season 1924–1925

March 2 .... La Gioconda
March 3 (matinée) ....Boris Godunoff
March 3 (night) .... Tannhäuser

Season 1926–1927

March 10 .... La Traviata
March 11 (matinée) .... Hansel and Gretel
March 11 (night) .... The Jewels of the Madonna
March 12 (matinée) .... Resurrection
March 12 (night) .... Rigoletto

Season 1928–1929

February 27 .... Faust
February 28 .... Lohengrin

DENVER, COLORADO
Season 1912–1913

April 10 .... The Jewels of the Madonna
April 11 .... Thaïs
April 12 (matinée)—Second Act of The Tales of Hoffman, followed by
Hansel and Gretel.
April 12 (night) .... Lucia di Lammermoor
April 13 .... Concert

Season 1913–1914

April 7 .... La Tosca
April 8 (matinée) .... Aïda
April 8 (night) .... Cavalleria Rusticana and I Pagliacci

Season 1920–1921

April 26 .... Otello
April 27 (matinée) ....La Traviata
April 27 (night) .... Monna Vanna
April 28 .... Lohengrin
April 30 (matinée) ....L'Elisir d'Amore
April 30 (night) .... Carmen

Season 1921-1922

April 17 .... Thaïs
April 18 ....L'Amore dei Tre Re
April 20 .... Tannhäuser

Season 1923-1924

March 18 .... The Jewess
March 19 .... Cléopatre

Season 1927-1928

March 27 .... Aïda
March 28 .... Resurrection

DES MOINES, IOWA
Season 1913-1914

April 13 .... Thaïs

Season 1917-1918 (preliminary tour)

October 17 .... Faust
October 18 .... Lucia di Lammermoor

Season 1920-1921 (preliminary tour)

October 22 .... Cavalleria Rusticana and I Pagliacci
October 23 .... La Traviata

DETROIT, MICHIGAN
Season 1918-1919

March 14 .... The Barber of Seville
March 15 (matinée) .... Madame Butterfly
March 15 (night) .... Cavalleria Rusticana and I Pagliacci
March 17 .... Thaïs
March 18 .... Romeo and Juliet
March 19 .... Il Trovatore
March 20 .... Carmen

Season 1919-1920

March 22 .... La Tosca
March 23 .... Lucia di Lammermoor
March 24 (matinée) .... Rigoletto
March 24 (night) .... A Masked Ball

Season 1923-1924

February 18 .... Mefistofele
February 19 .... Salome
February 20 .... The Jewess

Season 1926–1927

March 19 (matinée) .... La Tosca
March 19 (night) .... The Jewels of the Madonna
March 20 .... Aïda
March 21 .... Resurrection

Season 1927–1928

February 16 .... La Gioconda
February 17 .... Madame Butterfly
February 18 (matinée) .... Carmen
February 18 (night) .... Il Trovatore

Season 1928–1929

February 15 .... Faust
February 16 (matinée) .... Lohengrin
February 16 (night) .... Thaïs
February 17 .... Norma

EL PASO, TEXAS
Season 1920–1921

April 1 .... La Tosca
April 2 .... Carmen

Season 1928–1929

March 4 .... Thaïs
March 5 .... Lohengrin

FORT WAYNE, INDIANA
Season 1924–1925

November 20 .... Aïda

FORT WORTH, TEXAS
Season 1917–1918 (preliminary tour)

October 24 .... Faust
October 25 .... Lucia di Lammermoor

Season 1919–1920 (preliminary tour)

October 27 .... Aïda
October 28 (matinée) .... Madame Butterfly
October 28 (night) .... A Masked Ball

FRESNO, CALIFORNIA
Season 1927–1928

March 12 .... Sapho

Season 1928–1929

March 12 .... Norma

HELENA, MONTANA
Season 1921–1922

March 20 .... Thaïs

HOUSTON, TEXAS
Season 1917–1918 (preliminary tour)
October 26 .... Faust
October 27 .... Lucia di Lammermoor

Season 1919–1920 (preliminary tour)
October 30 .... Aïda
October 31 .... A Masked Ball

Season 1920–1921
March 28 (matinée) .... La Traviata
March 28 (night) .... Carmen

Season 1923–1924
February 27 .... The Jewess
February 28 .... Boris Godunoff

Season 1926–1927
March 5 .... Resurrection
March 6 .... Aïda

INDIANAPOLIS, INDIANA
Season 1913–1914
December 5 .... Die Walküre

JACKSON, MISSISSIPPI
Season 1926–1927
March 3 .... Resurrection
March 4 .... Cavalleria Rusticana and I Pagliacci

Season 1928–1929
February 25 .... Norma
February 26 .... Thaïs

JOPLIN, MISSOURI
Season 1926–1927
March 16 .... Aïda

KANSAS CITY, MISSOURI
Season 1912–1913
April 15 .... The Jewels of the Madonna
April 16 (matinée) .... Thaïs
April 16 (night) .... Lucia di Lammermoor

Season 1913–1914
April 11 .... Le Jongleur de Nôtre Dame
April 12 (matinée) .... Rigoletto
April 12 (night) .... Parsifal

Season 1917–1918 (preliminary tour)

October 19 .... Faust
October 20 .... Lucia di Lammermoor

Season 1919–1920 (preliminary tour)

October 22 .... Aïda
October 23 (matinée) ....Madame Butterfly
October 23 (night) .... La Tosca

Season 1923–1924

March 22 (matinée) .... Salome
March 22 (night) .... Boris Godunoff

LINCOLN, NEBRASKA
Season 1927–1928

March 29 .... Il Trovatore

Season 1928–1929

March 21 .... Faust

LITTLE ROCK, ARKANSAS
Season 1919–1920 (preliminary tour)

November 1 .... Aïda
November 3 .... Madame Butterfly

LOS ANGELES, CALIFORNIA
Season 1912–1913

March 4 .... Thaïs
March 5 (matinée)—Second Act of The Tales of Hoffman, followed by
  Hansel and Gretel.
March 5 (night) .... Rigoletto
March 7 .... Die Walküre
March 8 (matinée) .... Natoma
March 8 (night) .... Lucia di Lammermoor
March 9 .... Campanini Concert
March 10 ....Tristan and Isolde
March 11 .... Natoma

Season 1913–1914

March 10 .... Rigoletto
March 11 (matinée) ....The Jewels of the Madonna
March 11 (night) ....Le Jongleur de Nôtre Dame
March 12 (matinée and night)............................. Parsifal
March 13 .... Louise
March 14 (matinée) .... Hamlet
March 14 (night) .... Lohengrin

Season 1920–1921
April 4 .... Otello
April 5 .... Carmen
April 6 .... La Traviata
April 7 .... L'Amore dei Tre Re
April 8 .... Lohengrin
April 9 (matinée) .... Monna Vanna
April 9 (night) .... L'Elisir d'Amore

Season 1921–1922
April 10 .... L'Amore dei Tre Re
April 11 .... The Jewels of the Madonna
April 12 (matinée) .... Thaïs
April 12 (night) .... Romeo and Juliet
April 13 .... Louise
April 14 .... Tannhäuser
April 15 .... Salome

Season 1923–1924
March 3 .... Cléopatre
March 4 (matinée) .... Salome
March 4 (night) .... Mefistofele
March 5 .... The Jewess

Season 1927–1928
March 5 .... Tannhäuser
March 6 .... Resurrection
March 7 .... La Gioconda
March 8 .... Il Trovatore
March 9 .... The Witch of Salem and Cavalleria Rusticana
March 10 (matinée) .... Sapho
March 10 (night) .... Aïda

Season 1928–1929
March 8 .... Norma
March 9 (matinée) .... Thaïs
March 9 (night) .... Faust
March 11 .... Lohengrin

MEMPHIS, TENNESSEE
Season 1924–1925
February 26 .... Mefistofele
February 27 .... La Gioconda
March 28 (matinée) .... Thaïs
February 28 (night) .... Tannhäuser

Season 1925–1926
March 4 .... Aïda
March 5 .... La Traviata
March 6 (matinée) .... Carmen
March 6 (night) .... Rigoletto

Season 1927–1928

February 25 (matinée) .... Resurrection
February 25 (night) .... The Jewels of the Madonna

MIAMI, FLORIDA
Season 1925–1926

March 8 .... Aïda
March 9 .... Thaïs
March 10 .... La Traviata
March 11 .... Madame Butterfly
March 12 .... Otello
March 13 (matinée) .... Carmen
March 13 (night) .... Il Trovatore
March 14 .... Rigoletto
March 15 .... Cavalleria Rusticana and I Pagliacci

MILWAUKEE, WISCONSIN
Season 1910–1911

December 9 .... Salome
December 23 .... Thaïs

Season 1911–1912

December 8 .... Samson and Delilah
December 29 .... Carmen
January 5 .... Die Walküre

Season 1912–1913

December 6 .... Aïda
December 13 .... The Jewels of the Madonna
December 27 .... Mignon
January 10 .....The Secret of Susanne and Le Jongleur de Nôtre Dame
January 31 .... Lucia di Lammermoor
April 25 .... Hansel and Gretel

Season 1913–1914

November 28 .... La Gioconda
January 2 (matinée) .... Madame Butterfly
January 2 (night) .... La Tosca
April 23 .... Parsifal
April 24 .... Louise
April 25 (matinée) .... La Bohême
April 25 (night) .... Lohengrin

Season 1917–1918 (preliminary tour)

October 15 .... Faust
October 16 .... Lucia di Lammermoor

Season 1918–1919

December 5 .... The Barber of Seville
December 12 .... La Tosca

Season 1919–1920 (preliminary tour)
October 13 .... Aïda
October 14 .... A Masked Ball

Season 1920–1921 (preliminary tour)
October 18 .... Cavalleria Rusticana and I Pagliacci
October 19 .... La Traviata

Season 1921–1922
March 13 ....L'Amore dei Tre Re
March 14 .... Tannhäuser
March 15 .... Salome

Season 1924–1925
March 13 .... Mefistofele
March 14 .... La Gioconda
March 15 .... Rigoletto

Season 1926–1927
November 26 .... Aïda
December 10 ....Tristan and Isolde
January 7 .... Resurrection

Season 1927–1928
November 18 .... La Traviata
December 2 .... The Jewels of the Madonna
December 16 (matinée) ....Hansel and Gretel
December 16 (night) .... Louise
January 6 .... Lohengrin

Season 1928–1929
November 16 .... Faust
November 30 .... Carmen
December 14 .... Lakmé
January 4 .... Cavalleria Rusticana and I Pagliacci

MINNEAPOLIS, MINN.
Season 1912–1913
April 22 .... Thaïs
April 23 (matinée) .... Die Walküre
April 23 (night) .... The Jewels of the Madonna
April 24 (matinée) ....Le Jongleur de Nôtre Dame
April 24 (night) .... Lucia di Lammermoor

Season 1927–1928
March 30 .... Aïda
March 31 (matinée) .... Resurrection
March 31 (night) .... Tannhäuser
April 2 .... Snow Maiden

Season 1928–1929
March 22 .... Carmen
March 23 (matinée) .... Faust
March 23 (night) .... Thaïs
March 25 .... Lohengrin

NASHVILLE, TENNESSEE
Season 1928–1929
February 21 .... Thaïs

NEW ORLEANS, LA.
Season 1917–1918 (preliminary tour)
October 29 .... Faust
October 30 .... Lucia di Lammermoor

NEW YORK CITY
Season 1910–1911
January 24 .... Thaïs
January 31 .... Louise
February 7 ....Pelléas and Mélisande
February 14 .... The Tales of Hoffman
February 21 .... Carmen
February 28 .... Natoma
March 7 .... Natoma
March 14 ....Secret of Susanne and Jongleur de Nôtre Dame
March 18 .... Thaïs
March 21 .... Louise
April 4 .... Quo Vadis

Season 1911–1912
February 13 .... Carmen
February 20 .... Cendrillon
February 27 ....Secret of Susanne and Jongleur de Nôtre Dame
March 5 .... The Jewels of the Madonna

Season 1912–1913
November 19 .... Hamlet
February 4 .... Louise
February 11 .... Conchita
February 18 .... Thaïs
February 25 .... Le Ranz des Vaches
May 3 .... Lucia di Lammermoor

Season 1913–1914
February 3 .... Don Quichotte
February 10 .... Louise
February 17 .... Monna Vanna
February 24 .... The Jewels of The Madonna

Season 1917–1918

January 23 .... Monna Vanna
January 24 .... The Jewels of the Madonna
January 25 .... Thaïs
January 26 (matinée) ....Romeo and Juliet
January 26 (night) .... Azora
January 27 .... Concert at Hippodrome
January 28 .... Dinorah
January 30 .... Manon
January 31 (matinée) ....Pelléas and Mélisande
January 31 (night) .... Lucia di Lammermoor
February 1 .... Aïda
February 2 (matinée) .... Monna Vanna
February 2 (night) .... Cavalleria Rusticana and I Pagliacci
February 3 .... Concert at Hippodrome
February 4 (matinée) .... Louise
February 4 (night) .... Faust
February 6 .... Dinorah
February 7 ....Le Jongleur de Nôtre Dame and Cavalleria Rusticana
February 8 .... Carmen
February 9 (matinée) .... Rigoletto
February 9 (night) .... Aïda
February 10 .... Concert at Hippodrome
February 11 .... Le Sauteriot
February 13 (matinée) ....The Barber of Seville
February 13 (night) .... Isabeau
February 14 .... Faust
February 15 .... La Traviata
February 16 (matinée) .... Thaïs
February 16 (night) .... Carmen
February 17 .... Concert at Hippodrome
March 3 .... Concert at Hippodrome

Season 1918–1919

January 27 .... Gismonda
January 28 .... Romeo and Juliet
January 29 .... Madame Butterfly
January 30 .... Monna Vanna
January 31 .... Le Chemineau
February 1 (matinée) .... Thaïs
February 1 (night) .... The Tales of Hoffman
February 2 .... Concert at Hippodrome
February 3 .... Isabeau
February 4 .... Linda di Chamounix
February 5 ....Pelléas and Mélisande
February 6 .... Manon
February 7 .... Lucia di Lammermoor
February 8 (matinée) .... Gismonda
February 8 (night) .... Madame Butterfly
February 9 .... Concert at Hippodrome
February 10 .... Le Chemineau

414   FORTY YEARS OF OPERA IN CHICAGO

Season 1918-1919 (*Cont'd*)

February 11 .... Cléopatre
February 12 .... The Barber of Seville
February 13 .... Loreley
February 14 ....Le Jongleur de Nôtre Dame and Ballet
February 15 (matinée) .... La Traviata
February 15 (night) .... Faust
February 16 .... Concert at Hippodrome
February 17 .... Crispino e la Comare
February 18 .... Werther
February 19 .... Thaïs
February 20 .... Dinorah
February 21 .... Carmen
February 22 (matinée) .... Madame Butterfly
February 22 (night) .... Il Trovatore
February 23 .... Concert at Hippodrome
February 24 .... Cléopatre
February 25 .... Fedora
February 26 .... La Traviata
February 27 .... Pélleas and Mélisande
February 28 ....Cavalleria Rusticana, Le Vieil Aigle and Ballet
March 1 (matinée) ....Lucia di Lammermoor
March 1 (night) .... Rigoletto

Season 1919-1920

January 26 ....L'Amore dei Tre Re
January 27 ....Pelléas and Mélisande
January 28 (matinée) ....L'Heure Espagnole and I Pagliacci
January 28 (night) ....Madame Chrysantheme
January 29 ....L'Amore dei Tre Re
January 30 .... Rip Van Winkle
January 31 (matinée) .... A Masked Ball
January 31 (night) .... Madame Butterfly
February 1 .... Concert at Hippodrome
February 2 .... La Traviata
February 3 .... Norma
February 4 ....Le Jongleur de Nôtre Dame
February 5 .... La Sonnambula
February 6 .... Falstaff
February 7 (matinée) .... Louise
February 7 (night) .... La Bohême
February 8 .... Concert at Hippodrome
February 9 .... Thaïs
February 10 .... Lucia di Lammermoor
February 11 ....Il Tabarro, Suor Angelica and Gianni Schicchi
February 12 (matinée) .... L'Elisir d'Amore
February 12 (night) .... Hérodiade
February 13 .... Hamlet
February 14 (matinée) .... Don Pasquale
February 14 (night) .... A Masked Ball
February 15 .... Concert

Season 1919–1920 (*Cont'd*)

February 16 ....I Pagliacci and Boudour (ballet)
February 17 ....L'Amore dei Tre Re
February 18 .... Dinorah
February 19 .... Norma
February 20 .... Rigoletto
February 21 (matinée)......Cavalleria Rusticana and Boudour (ballet)
February 21 (night) .... Carmen
February 22 .... Concert
February 23 (matinée)—L'Heure Espagnole and The Birthday of the
       Infanta (ballet)
February 23 (night) .... Hamlet
February 24 .... The Barber of Seville
February 25 .... Gismonda
February 26 .... La Traviata
February 27 .... Aphrodite
February 28 (matinée) .... Rigoletto
February 28 (night) .... Aïda
February 29 .... Concert at Hippodrome

Season 1920–1921

January 24 .... Norma
January 25 .... Monna Vanna
January 26 .... La Tosca
January 27 .... The Jewels of the Madonna
January 28 .... Carmen
January 29 (matinée) ....Le Chemineau
January 29 (night) .... Rigoletto
January 31 .... Lucia di Lammermoor
February 1 .... Otello
February 2 .... Manon
February 3 .... Thaïs
February 4 .... Jacquerie
February 5 (matinée) ....La Sonnambula
February 5 (night) .... Faust
February 7 .... Madame Butterfly
February 8 .... The Jewels of the Madonna
February 9 .... Romeo and Juliet
February 10 ....L'Amore dei Tre Re
February 11 .... The Barber of Seville
February 12 (matinée) ....Monna Vanna
February 12 (night) .... Otello
February 14 .... Carmen
February 15 .... Lakmé
February 16 ....Le Jongleur de Nôtre Dame
February 17 .... Otello
February 18 .... Manon
February 19 (matinée) ....La Traviata
February 19 (night) .... Cavalleria Rusticana and I Pagliacci
February 20 .... Concert at Hippodrome
February 21 .... Edipo Re

Season 1920–1921 (*Cont'd*)

February 22 (matinée) .... La Tosca
February 22 (night) .: .... Romeo and Juliet
February 23 ....L'Amore dei Tre Re
February 24 .... La Bohême
February 25 .... Cavalleria Rusticana and I Pagliacci
February 26 (matinée) .... Faust
February 26 (night) .... Rigoletto
February 28 .... Monna Vanna
March 1 .... The Barber of Seville
March 2 .... La Traviata
March 3 ....Le Jongleur de Nôtre Dame
March 4 .... Otello
March 5 (matinée) .... Hamlet
March 5 (night) .... Carmen

Season 1921–1922

January 23 .... Monna Vanna
January 24 .... La Traviata
January 25 ....Pelléas and Mélisande
January 26 .... The Girl of the Golden West
January 27 ....Madame Butterfly
January 28 .... The Barber of Seville
January 30 ....L'Amore dei Tre Re
January 31 .... Tristan and Isolde
February 1 ....La Bohême and La Fête à Robinson (ballet)
February 2 ....I Pagliacci and The Birthday of the Infanta (ballet)
February 3 .... The Jewels of The Madonna
February 4 (matinée) .... Madame Butterfly
February 4 (night) .... Salome
February 6 .... La Traviata
February 7 .... Louise
February 8 .... Tannhäuser
February 9 .... Rigoletto
February 10 .... Salome
February 11 (matinée) ....The Girl of the Golden West
February 11 (night) .... Lucia di Lammermoor
February 13 .... Tannhäuser
February 14 ....L'Amore dei Tre Re
February 15................... The Jewels of the Madonna
February 16 .... Thaïs
February 17 ......I Pagliacci and The Birthday of the Infanta (ballet)
February 18 (matinée) .... Aïda
February 18 (night) .... Salome
February 20 .... Manon
February 21 ..Le Jongleur de Nôtre Dame and Fête à Robinson (ballet)
February 22 .... Otello
February 23 .... Samson and Delilah
February 24 .... Thaïs
February 25 (matinée) .... Rigoletto
February 25 (night)................................L'Amore dei Tre Re

OAKLAND, CAL.
Season 1927–1928

March 13 .... Aïda
March 14 .... Resurrection
March 15 .... La Gioconda
March 16 .... Snow Maiden

Season 1928–1929

March 14 .... Lohengrin
March 15 .... Thaïs
March 16 (matinée) .... Faust
March 16 (night) .... Norma

OKLAHOMA CITY, OKLA.
Season 1917–1918 (preliminary tour)

October 22 .... Faust
October 23 .... Lucia di Lammermoor

Season 1919–1920 (preliminary tour)

October 24 .... Aïda
October 25 (matinée) ....Madame Butterfly
October 25 (night) .... La Tosca

OMAHA, NEB.
Season 1913–1914

April 14 .... Thaïs

Season 1919–1920 (preliminary tour)

October 20 .... Aïda
October 21 .... A Masked Ball

PEORIA, ILL.
Season 1919–1920 (preliminary tour)

October 15 .... Aïda
October 16 .... A Masked Ball

PHILADELPHIA, PA.
Season 1910–1911

January 20 .... Aïda
January 21 (matinée) .... Thaïs
January 21 (night) .... Rigoletto
January 23 .... The Girl of the Golden West
January 25 .... Carmen
January 27 .... La Bohême
January 28 (matinée) .... Louise
January 28 (night) .... Il Trovatore
January 30 .... Cavalleria Rusticana and I Pagliacci
February 1 .... Thaïs
February 3 .... The Girl of the Golden West
February 4 (matinée) ....The Tales of Hoffman

Season 1910-1911 (*Cont'd*)

February 4 (night) .... Lucia di Lammermoor
February 6 .... Otello
February 8 .... Faust
February 10 ....Pelléas and Mélisande
February 11 (matinée) .... Madame Butterfly
February 11 (night) .... Les Huguenots
February 13 .... Carmen
February 15 .... Aïda
February 17 .... Thaïs
February 18 (matinée) ....Cavalleria Rusticana and I Pagliacci
February 18 (night) .... La Traviata
February 20 ....,........................ The Tales of Hoffman
February 22 .... Madame Butterfly
February 24 .... Rigoletto
February 25 (matinée) .... La Bohême
February 25 (night) .... Natoma
February 27 .... Il Trovatore
March 1 .... The Tales of Hoffman
March 3 .... Natoma
March 4 (matinée) .... Aïda
March 4 (night) .... Cavalleria Rusticana and I Pagliacci
March 6 ....Le Jongleur de Nôtre Dame
March 8 .... La Tosca
March 10 .... The Tales of Hoffman
March 11 (matinée) .... Natoma
March 11 (night) .... Madame Butterfly
March 13 .... La Bohême
March 15 .... Natoma
March 17 ....Secret of Susanne and Le Jongleur de Nôtre Dame
March 18 .... La Tosca
March 20 .... Aïda
March 22 .... Rigoletto
March 24 .... Carmen
March 25 (matinée)—Secret of Susanne, 2nd act, The Tales of Hoff-
man, and Russian Ballet
March 25 (night) .... Quo Vadis
March 27 .... Quo Vadis
March 28 .... Natoma and Secret of Susanne
March 29 .... Cavalleria Rusticana and I Pagliacci
March 31 .... Quo Vadis
April 1 (matinée) .... Quo Vadis
April 1 (night)—3rd act La Bohême, 2nd act The Tales of Hoffman,
The Secret of Susanne, 2nd act Thaïs, 4th act Faust.
April 3 .... Natoma
April 5 .... Quo Vadis

Season 1911–1912

November 3 .... Carmen
November 4 (matinée) ....The Marriage of Figaro
November 4 (night) .... Il Trovatore
November 6 .... Cendrillon

Season 1911–1912 *(Cont'd)*

November 8 .... Samson and Delilah
November 10 .... Die Walküre
November 11 (matinée) .... Thaïs
November 11 (night) .... Cavalleria Rusticana and I Pagliacci
November 13 .... Carmen
November 15 .... Lucia di Lammermoor
November 17 .... Cendrillon
November 18 (matinée) .... La Traviata
November 18 (night) .... Hansel and Gretel
February 12 .... Quo Vadis
February 14 .... The Jewels of the Madonna
February 16 .... The Tales of Hoffman
February 17 (matinée) .... Cendrillon
February 17 (night) .... La Traviata
February 19 .... Cavalleria Rusticana and I Pagliacci
February 21 .... Thaïs
February 23 ....Tristan and Isolde
February 24 (matinée) .... Natoma
February 24 (night) .... Rigoletto
February 26 .... Samson and Delilah
February 28 ....Le Jongleur de Nôtre Dame
March 1 .... The Jewels of The Madonna
March 2 (matinée) .... Faust
March 2 (night) ....The Secret of Susanne, I Pagliacci and Ballet
March 4 ....Pelléas and Mélisande
March 6 ....A Lovers' Quarrel and The Tales of Hoffman
March 8 .... Aïda
March 9 (matinée) .... Die Walküre
March 9 (night) .... Carmen
March 11 .... The Jewels of the Madonna
Marsh 13 .... The Jewels of the Madonna
March 14 .... Carmen
March 15 .... Lohengrin
March 16 (matinée) ....A Lovers' Quarrel, and Hansel and
Gretel and Ballet
March 16 (night) .... The Tales of Hoffman
March 18 .... Aïda
March 19 .... The Jewels of the Madonna
March 20 (matinée) .... The Jewels of the Madonna
March 20 (night) .... Louise

Season 1912–1913

October 31 .... Aïda
November 2 (matinée) .... Manon Lescaut
November 2 (night) .... The Tales of Hoffman
November 4 .... Rigoletto
November 6 .... A Masked Ball
November 7 ....The Cricket on the Hearth
November 8 .... Aïda
November 9 (matinée) .... Rigoletto

Season 1912-1913 (*Cont'd*)

November 9 (night) .... Carmen
November 11 .... Aïda
November 13 (matinée) ....The Cricket on the Hearth
November 13 (night) .... Hamlet
November 14 .... Manon
November 16 (matinée) ....Cavalleria Rusticana and I Pagliacci
November 16 (night) .... La Traviata
November 18 .... Mignon
November 20 ....Tristan and Isolde
November 21 .... Il Trovatore
November 23 (matinée)...................The Jewels of the Madonna
November 23 (night) .... Cavalleria Rusticana and I Pagliacci
February 3 .... Lucia di Lammermoor
February 5 .... Mignon
February 6 .... Conchita
February 8 (matinée)—The Secret of Susanne and Le Jongleur de
        Nôtre Dame
February 8 (night) .... Lohengrin
February 10 ....Noël and I Pagliacci
February 12 (matinée) .... La Traviata
February 12 (night) .... La Tosca
February 13 .... Die Walküre
February 15 (matinée) .... Thaïs
February 15 (night) .... Faust
February 17 .... La Bohême
February 19 .... Conchita
February 20 ....A Lovers' Quarrel and Crispino e la Comare
February 21 .... Ranz des Vaches
Fberuary 22 (matinée) ....Lucia di Lammermoor
February 22 (night) .... The Jewels of the Madonna
February 24 .... Ranz des Vaches
February 25 .... The Barber of Seville
May 3 .... Hansel and Gretel

Season 1913-1914

November 3 .... La Tosca
November 5 .... The Barber of Seville
November 6 .... Aïda
November 8 (matinée) ....The Girl of the Golden West
November 8 (night) .... Lucia di Lammermoor
November 10 .... Rigoletto
November 12 (matinée) ....The Jewels of the Madonna
November 12 (night) .... La Tosca
November 13 .... Cavalleria Rusticana and I Pagliacci
November 15 (matinée) ....Don Quichotte
November 15 (night) .... Natoma
November 17 .... La Gioconda
November 19 .... Don Quichotte
November 20 .... Cristoforo Colombo
November 21 .... La Tosca

Season 1913–1914 (Cont'd)
November 22 (matinée) ....Cristoforo Colombo
November 22 (night) .... The Jewels of the Madonna
February 2 .... La Sonnambula and I Pagliacci
February 4 .... Carmen
February 5 .... La Traviata
February 7 (matinée) .... Manon
February 7 (night) .... Aïda
February 9 .... Faust
February 11 .... Hérodiade
February 12 .... Thaïs
February 14 (matinée) ....Monna Vanna
February 14 (night) .... Madame Butterfly
February 16 ....I Zingari and The Tales of Hoffman
February 18 .... Rigoletto
February 19 .... Louise
February 21 (matinée) ....Don Giovanni
February 21 (night) .... La Tosca
February 23 .... Cristoforo Colombo
February 25 .... Mignon
February 26 ....Cassandra and A Lovers' Quarrel
February 28 (matinée) .... Hamlet
February 28 (night) .... Rigoletto

Season 1918–1919
March 3 .... Cléopatre
March 4 .... Lucia di Lammermoor
March 5 .... Gismonda
March 6 (matinée) ....Madame Butterfly
March 6 (night) .... The Barber of Seville
March 7 .... Thaïs
March 8 .... Romeo and Juliet

Season 1921–1922
February 27 .... Tannhäuser
February 28 .... Salome
March 1 ....Le Jongleur de Nôtre Dame
March 2 .... Romeo and Juliet
March 3 ....Pelléas and Mélisande
March 4 (matinée) ....The Jewels of the Madonna
March 4 (night) .... Monna Vanna

PHOENIX, ARIZ.
Season 1928–1929
March 6 .... Thaïs
March 7 .... Carmen

PITTSBURGH, PA.
Season 1911–1912
February 9 .... Natoma
February 10 (matinée)....The Secret of Susanne and Hansel and Gretel
February 10 (night) ....Tristan and Isolde

Season 1918–1919
March 10 .... Thaïs
March 11 .... Madame Butterfly
March 12 .... The Barber of Seville
March 13 .... Il Trovatore

Season 1919–1920
March 15 (matinée) ....Lucia di Lammermoor
March 15 (night) .... La Tosca
March 16 .... A Masked Ball
March 18 .... Cavalleria Rusticana and I Pagliacci

Season 1920–1921
March 10 .... La Traviata
March 11 .... Lohengrin
March 12 (matinée) .... Rigoletto
March 12 (night) .... Carmen

Season 1921–1922
March 9 ....L'Amore dei Tre Re
March 10 .... Faust
March 11 (matinée) .... Salome
March 11 (night) .... Aïda

Season 1922–1923
February 8 .... The Jewels of the Madonna
February 9 .... Aïda
February 10 (matinée) .... Carmen
February 10 (night) .... Cavalleria Rusticana and I Pagliacci

Season 1923–1924
February 15 .... Mefistofele
February 16 (matinée) .... Cléopatre
February 16 (night) .... The Jewess

Season 1924–1925
February 16 .... Boris Godunoff
February 17 .... Tannhäuser
February 18 .... Thaïs

Season 1926–1927
February 18 .... La Traviata
February 19 (matinée) .... Resurrection
February 19 (night) .. .. Aïda

PORTLAND, ORE.
Season 1912–1913
March 31 .... The Jewels of the Madonna
April 1 .... Thaïs
April 2 (matinée).....2nd act Tales of Hoffman and Hansel and Gretel
April 2 (night) .... Lucia di Lammermoor

Season 1913–1914
April 2 .... Cavalleria Rusticana and I Pagliacci
April 3 .... Parsifal
April 4 (matinée) .... Aïda
April 4 (night) .... La Tosca

Season 1921–1922
March 22 .... Monna Vanna
March 23 .... Lohengrin
March 24 .... Romeo and Juliet
March 25 (matinée) .... Thaïs
March 25 (night) .... Aïda

Season 1923–1924
March 10 .... Cléopatre
March 11 .... Boris Godunoff
March 12 (matinée) .... Salome
March 12 (night) .... The Jewess

Season 1927–1928
March 22 .... Aïda
March 23 .... Snow Maiden
March 24 (matinée) .... Resurrection
March 24 (night) .... Il Trovatore

ROCHESTER, N. Y.
Season 1927–1928
February 13 .... Resurrection

SACRAMENTO, CAL.
Season 1927–1928
March 17 (matinée) .... Resurrection
March 17 (night) .... Cavalleria Rusticana and I Pagliacci

Season 1928–1929
March 13 .... Thaïs

ST. JOSEPH, MO.
Season 1913–1914
April 15 .... Thaïs

ST. LOUIS, MISSOURI
Season 1910–1911
January 13 (matinée) .... The Tales of Hoffman
January 13 (night) .... Carmen
January 14 (matinee) .... The Girl of the Golden West
January 14 (night) .... Louise
January 15 .... Concert

424   FORTY YEARS OF OPERA IN CHICAGO

Season 1911–1912
February 2 .... Thaïs
February 3 (matinée)....The Secret of Susanne and Hansel and Gretel
February 3 (night) ....Tristan and Isolde
February 5 .... Carmen

Season 1912–1913
April 17 .... The Jewels of the Madonna
April 18 ....Le Jongleur de Nôtre Dame
April 19 (matinée) ....Lucia di Lammermoor
April 19 (night) .... Die Walküre
April 20 .... Concert

Season 1913–1914
April 16 .... Parsifal
April 17 .... Cavalleria Rusticana and I Pagliacci
April 18 (matinée) .... La Tosca
April 18 (night) .... Aïda

Season 1917–1918 (preliminary tour)
November 2 .... Faust
November 3 .... Lucia di Lammermoor

Season 1924–1925
March 6 .... La Gioconda
March 7 (matinée) .... Mefistofele
March 7 (night) .... Tannhäuser

Season 1926–1927
March 18 .... Resurrection

St. Paul, Minnesota
Season 1911–1912
January 28 .... Concert
January 29 ....Tristan and Isolde
January 30 (matinée)...........Le Jongleur de Nôtre Dame and Ballet
January 30 (night) .... The Jewels of the Madonna
January 31 (matinée) ....Die Walküre
January 31 (night) .... Natoma

Season 1913–1914
April 20 .... Rigoletto
April 21 (matinée) .... Manon
April 21 (night) .... La Bohême
April 22 ....Cavalleria Rusticana and I Pagliacci

Season 1918–1919 (preliminary tour)
October 16 .... La Tosca
October 17 .... The Barber of Seville

Season 1919–1920 (preliminary tour)
October 17 .... Aïda
October 18 (matinée) ....Madame Butterfly
October 18 (night) .... A Masked Ball

Season 1920–1921 (preliminary tour)
October 29 .... Rigoletto
October 30 (matinée) .... La Traviata
October 30 (night) .... Cavalleria Rusticana and I Pagliacci

Season 1921–1922
March 16 .... Romeo and Juliet
March 17 .... Thaïs
March 18 (matinée) .... Salome
March 18 (night) .... Tannhäuser

SALT LAKE CITY, UTAH
Season 1923–1924
March 17 .... Gala performance

SAN ANTONIO, TEXAS
Season 1920–1921
March 30 (matinée) .... La Tosca
March 30 (night) .... Thaïs

Season 1926–1927
March 7 .... Aïda
March 8 .... Resurrection
March 9 .... La Traviata

Season 1927–1928
March 2 .... La Gioconda
March 3 (matinée) .... La Tosca
March 3 (night) .... Il Trovatore

Season 1928–1929
March 1 .... Faust
March 2 (matinée) .... Lohengrin
March 2 (night) .... Norma

SAN DIEGO, CALIFORNIA
Season 1912–1913
March 6 .... Thaïs

SAN FRANCISCO, CALIFORNIA
Season 1912–1913
March 12 .... Rigoletto
March 13 (matinée)......Hansel and Gretel and The Secret of Susanne
March 13 (night) .... Thaïs
March 14 .... Die Walküre
March 15 (matinée) .... La Traviata
March 15 (night) .... Natoma
March 16 .... Concert

Season 1912–1913 *(Cont'd)*

March 17 .... Louise
March 18 .... Lucia di Lammermoor
March 19 (matinée) .... Carmen
March 19 (night) .... Noël and I Pagliacci
March 20 ....'.... Crispino e la Comare
March 21 .... Concert
March 22 (matinée).A Lovers' Quarrel and Le Jongleur de Nôtre Dame
March 22 (night) .... Tristan and Isolde
March 23 .... Concert
March 24 .... Rigoletto
March 25 .... Salome
March 26 (matinée) .... Lucia di Lammermoor
March 26 (night) .... The Jewels of the Madonna
March 27 .... Salome
March 28 (matinée) ....The Jewels of the Madonna
March 28 (night) .... Hansel and Gretel
March 29 (matinée) .... Thaïs
March 29 (night) .... Gala performance

Season 1913–1914

March 16 .... Rigoletto
March 17 .... Aïda
March 18 (matinée) .... La Bohême
March 18 (night) .... Louise
March 19 .... Hérodiade
March 20 .... Thaïs
March 21 (matinée) ....Cavalleria Rusticana and I Pagliacci
March 21 (night) .... The Jewels of the Madonna
March 22 .... Parsifal
March 23 .... La Tosca
March 24 .... Lohengrin
March 25 .... La Traviata
March 26 .... Parsifal
March 27 .... Louise
March 28 .... Thaïs
March 29 .... Madame Butterfly

Season 1920–1921

April 11 .... Otello
April 12 .... Carmen
April 13 .... La Traviata
April 14 ....L'Amore dei Tre Re
April 15 .... Il Trovatore
April 16 (matinée) .... Lucia di Lammermoor
April 16 (night) .... Faust
April 18 .... Rigoletto
April 19 .... Cavalleria Rusticana and I Pagliacci
April 20 .... Thaïs
April 21 .... Lohengrin
April 22 .... Rigoletto
April 23 (matinée) .... Monna Vanna
April 23 (night) .... La Tosca

Season 1921–1922
March 27 .... Aïda
March 28 ....L'Amore dei Tre Re
March 29 .... Rigoletto
March 30 .... Tannhäuser
March 31 .... Lohengrin
April 1 (matinée) ....Romeo and Juliet
April 1 (night) .... The Jewels of the Madonna
April 3 .... Madame Butterfly
April 4 .... Tannhäuser
April 5 .... Louise
April 6 .... Salome
April 7 .... La Bohême
April 8 (matinée) .... Monna Vanna
April 8 (night) .... The Girl of the Golden West

Season 1923–1924
March 6 .... Mefistofele
March 7 .... Cléopatre
March 8 (matinée) ....Boris Godunoff
March 8 (night) .... The Jewess

SHREVEPORT, LOUISIANA
Season 1917–1918 (preliminary tour)
October 31 .... Faust
November 1 .... Lucia di Lammermoor

SEATTLE, WASHINGTON
Season 1912–1913
April 3 .... The Jewels of the Madonna
April 4 .... Thaïs
April 5 (matinée)—Second Act of Tales of Hoffman and Hansel and
    Gretel.
April 5 (night) .... Lucia di Lammermoor
April 6 .... Concert

Season 1913–1914
March 30 .... Cavalleria Rusticana and I Pagliacci
March 31 .... Lohengrin
April 1 (matinée) .... Aïda
April 1 (night) .... La Tosca

Season 1923–1924
March 13 .... Mefistofele
March 14 .... The Jewess
March 15 (matinée) .... Salome
March 15 (night) .... Boris Godunoff

Season 1927–1928

March 19 .... La Gioconda
March 20 .... Aïda
March 21 (matinée) .... Snow Maiden
March 21 (night) .... Resurrection

SIOUX CITY, IOWA
Season 1920–1921 (preliminary tour)

October 25 .... Cavalleria Rusticana and I Pagliacci
October 26 .... La Traviata

SIOUX FALLS, SOUTH DAKOTA
Season 1920–1921 (preliminary tour)

October 27 .... Cavalleria Rusticana and I Pagliacci
October 28 .... La Traviata

SPOKANE, WASHINGTON
Season 1912–1913

April 7 .... Thaïs

SPRINGFIELD, ILLINOIS
Season 1920–1921 (preliminary tour)

October 20 .... Cavalleria Rusticana and I Pagliacci
October 21 .... La Traviata

TULSA, OKLAHOMA
Season 1920–1921

March 21 .... Thaïs
March 22 .... La Traviata

Season 1923–1924

February 25 .... Cléopatre
February 26 .... Mefistofele

Season 1924–1925

March 4 .... La Gioconda
March 5 .... Boris Godunoff

Season 1926–1927

March 14 .... Aïda
March 15 .... La Traviata

Season 1927–1928

February 27 .... Il Trovatore
February 28 .... Rigoletto

Season 1928–1929

March 19 .... Lohengrin
March 20 .... Thaïs

WASHINGTON, DISTRICT OF COLUMBIA
Season 1911–1912
March 25 (matinée) .... Aïda
March 25 (night) .... Natoma

Season 1912–1913
February 7 .... La Tosca
February 14 .... Lucia di Lammermoor
May 2 .... Hansel and Gretel

Season 1913–1914
February 13 .... Madame Butterfly

Season 1922–1923
February 5 .... Aïda
February 6 .... La Tosca
February 7 .... Snowmaiden

Season 1924–1925
February 9 .... Tannhäuser
February 10 .... Boris Godunoff
February 13 .... Lucia di Lammermoor
February 14 .... Thaïs

Season 1925–1926
February 9 .... La Tosca
February 10 .... Louise
February 12 .... Martha
February 13 (matinée) .... Carmen
February 13 (night) .... Rigoletto

Season 1926–1927
February 16 .... A Masked Ball
February 17 .... Resurrection

WICHITA, KANSAS
Season 1912–1913
April 14 .... Lucia di Lammermoor

Season 1913–1914
April 9 .... Thaïs

Season 1921–1922
April 21 .... Carmen
April 22 .... Aïda

Season 1923–1924
March 20 .... Mefistofele
March 21 .... Cléopatre

Season 1926–1927

March 17 .... Cavalleria Rusticana and I Pagliacci

WICHITA FALLS, TEXAS
Season 1927–1928

February 29 .... Aïda
March 1 .... Resurrection

THE END

Opera Biographies

An Arno Press Collection

Albani, Emma. **Forty Years of Song.** With a Discography by
W. R. Moran. [1911]

Biancolli, Louis. **The Flagstad Manuscript.** 1952

Bispham, David. **A Quaker Singer's Recollections.** 1921

Callas, Evangelia and Lawrence Blochman. **My Daughter
Maria Callas.** 1960

Calvé, Emma. **My Life.** With a Discography by W. R. Moran. 1922

Corsi, Mario. **Tamagno, Il Più Grande Fenomeno Canoro
Dell'Ottocento.** With a Discography by W. R. Moran. 1937

Cushing, Mary Watkins. **The Rainbow Bridge.** With a Discography
by W. R. Moran. 1954

Eames, Emma. **Some Memories and Reflections.** With a
Discography by W. R. Moran. 1927

Gaisberg, F[rederick] W[illiam]. **The Music Goes Round.** 1942

Gigli, Beniamino. **The Memoirs of Beniamino Gigli.** 1957

Hauk, Minnie. **Memories of a Singer.** 1925

Henschel, Horst and Ehrhard Friedrich. **Elisabeth Rethberg:**
Ihr Leben und Künstlertum. 1928

Hernandez Girbal, F. **Julian Gayarre:** El Tenor de la Voz
de Angel. 1955

Heylbut, Rose and Aimé Gerber. **Backstage at the Metropolitan
Opera** (Originally published as **Backstage at the Opera**). 1937

Jeritza, Maria. **Sunlight and Song:** A Singer's Life. 1929

Klein, Herman. **The Reign of Patti.** With a Discography by
W. R. Moran. 1920

Lawton, Mary. **Schumann-Heink:** The Last of the Titans. With a
Discography by W. R. Moran. 1928

Lehmann, Lilli. **My Path Through Life.** 1914

Litvinne, Félia. **Ma Vie et Mon Art:** Souvenirs. 1933

Marchesi, Blanche. **Singer's Pilgrimage.** With a Discography by
W. R. Moran. 1923

Martens, Frederick H. **The Art of the Prima Donna and Concert Singer.** 1923

Maude, [Jenny Maria Catherine Goldschmidt]. **The Life of Jenny Lind.** 1926

Maurel, Victor. **Dix Ans de Carrière, 1887-1897.** 1897

Mingotti, Antonio. **Maria Cebotari,** Das Leben Einer Sangerin. [1950]

Moore, Edward C. **Forty Years of Opera in Chicago.** 1930

Moore, Grace. **You're Only Human Once.** 1944

Moses, Montrose J. **The Life of Heinrich Conried.** 1916

Palmegiani, Francesco. **Mattia Battistini:** Il Re Dei Baritoni. With a Discography by W. R. Moran. [1949]

Pearse, [Cecilia Maria de Candia] and Frank Hird. **The Romance of a Great Singer.** A Memoir of Mario. 1910

Pinza, Ezio and Robert Magidoff. **Ezio Pinza:** An Autobiography. 1946

Rogers, Francis. **Some Famous Singers of the 19th Century.** 1914

Rosenthal, Harold [D.] **Great Singers of Today.** 1966

Ruffo, Titta. **La Mia Parabola:** Memorie. With a Discography by W. R. Moran. 1937

Santley, Charles. **Reminiscences of My Life.** With a Discography by W. R. Moran. 1909

Slezak, Leo. **Song of Motley:** Being the Reminiscences of a Hungry Tenor. 1938

Stagno Bellincioni, Bianca. **Roberto Stagno e Gemma Bellincioni Intimi** and Bellincioni, Gemma, **Io e il Palcoscenico:** Trenta e un anno di vita artistica. With a Discography by W. R. Moran. 1943/1920. Two vols. in one.

Tetrazzini, [Luisa]. **My Life of Song.** 1921

Teyte, Maggie. **Star on the Door.** 1958

Tibbett, Lawrence. **The Glory Road.** With a Discography by W. R. Moran. 1933

Traubel, Helen and Richard G. Hubler. **St. Louis Woman.** 1959

Van Vechten, Carl. **Interpreters.** 1920

Wagner, Charles L. **Seeing Stars.** 1940